걸프 사태

유엔안전보장이사회 동향 4

걸프 사태

유엔안전보장이사회 동향 4

한국학술정보

| 머리말

걸프 전쟁은 미국의 주도하에 34개국 연합군 병력이 수행한 전쟁으로, 1990년 8월 이라크의 쿠웨이트 침공 및 합병에 반대하며 발발했다. 미국은 초기부터 파병 외교에 나섰고, 1990년 9월 서울 등에 고위 관리를 파견하며 한국의 동참을 요청했다. 88올림픽 이후 동구권 국교 수립과 유엔 가입 추진 등 적극적인 외교 활동을 펼치는 당시 한국에 있어 이는 미국과 국제 사회의 지지를 얻기 위해서라도 피할 수 없는 일이었다. 결국 정부는 91년 1월부터 약 3개월에 걸쳐 국군의료지원단과 공군수송단을 사우디아라비아 및 아랍 에미리트 연합 등에 파병하였고, 군 · 민간 의료 활동, 병력 수송 임무를 수행했다. 동시에 당시 걸프 지역 8개국에 살던 5천여 명의 교민에게 방독면 등 물자를 제공하고, 특별기 파견 등으로 비상시 대피할 수 있도록 지원했다. 비록 전쟁 부담금과 유가 상승 등 어려움도 있었지만, 걸프전 파병과 군사 외교를 통해 한국은 유엔 가입에 박차를 가할 수 있었고 미국 등 선진 우방국, 아랍권 국가 등과 밀접한 외교 관계를 유지하며 여러 국익을 창출할 수 있었다.

본 총서는 외교부에서 작성하여 30여 년간 유지한 걸프 사태 관련 자료를 담고 있다. 미국을 비롯한 여러 국가와의 군사 외교 과정, 일일 보고 자료와 기타 정부의 대응 및 조치, 재외동포 철수와 보호, 의료지원단과 수송단 파견 및 지원 과정, 유엔을 포함해 세계 각국에서 수집한 관련 동향 자료, 주변국 지원과 전후복구사업 참여 등 총 48권으로 구성되었다. 전체 분량은 약 2만 4천여 쪽에 이른다.

2024년 3월

한국학술정보(주)

| 일러두기

· 본 총서에 실린 자료는 2022년 4월과 2023년 4월에 각각 공개한 외교문서 4,827권, 76만 여 쪽 가운데 일부를 발췌한 것이다.

· 각 권의 제목과 순서는 공개된 원본을 최대한 반영하였으나, 주제에 따라 일부는 적절히 변경하였다.

· 원본 자료는 A4 판형에 맞게 축소하거나 원본 비율을 유지한 채 A4 페이지 안에 삽입하였다. 또한 현재 시점에선 공개되지 않아 '공란'이란 표기만 있는 페이지 역시 그대로 실었다.

· 외교부가 공개한 문서 각 권의 첫 페이지에는 '정리 보존 문서 목록'이란 이름으로 기록물 종류, 일자, 명칭, 간단한 내용 등의 정보가 수록되어 있으며, 이를 기준으로 0001번부터 번호가 매겨져 있다. 이는 삭제하지 않고 총서에 그대로 수록하였다.

· 보고서 내용에 관한 더 자세한 정보가 필요하다면, 외교부가 온라인상에 제공하는 『대한민국 외교사료요약집』 1991년과 1992년 자료를 참조할 수 있다.

| 차례

정리보존문서목록

기록물종류	일반공문서철	등록번호	2019070038	등록일자	2019-07-18
분류번호	731.33	국가코드	XF	보존기간	30년
명 칭	걸프사태 후 유엔안전보장이사회 동향, 1991. 전3권				
생 산 과	국제연합1과/중동1과	생산년도	1991~1991	담당그룹	
권 차 명	V.1 4-5월				
내용목차	* 4.9 사무총장의 유엔 옵서버단(UNIKOM) 배치 계획 승인 결의안(689호) 채택 5.2 유엔 사무총장, 이라크.쿠웨이트 국경획정안(S/22558) 제출(5.21 국경획정위원회 설치) 5.8 유엔 옵서버단 배치완료(5.6)에 따른 다국적군 철군 완료				

0001

원 본

외 무 부

종 별 :

번 호 : UNW-0828 일 시 : 91 0408 1700

수 신 : 장 관(국연,중동일,기정)

발 신 : 주 유엔 대사

제 목 : 걸프사태(안보리)

연: UNW-0823,0824

1. 안보리 휴전결의 (687호) 수락에 관한 이락 A.HUSSEIN 외상의 4.6.자 유엔사무총장, 안보리의장앞 서한이 금 4.8. 안보리문서로 배포된바 (S/22456) 동 상세는 별첨 참조 바람.

2.사무총장은 상기 안보리결의 본문 5항에 의거 유엔군사 옵서버단 (UNIKOM) 배치 계획서를 4.5.자로 안보리에 제출한바 (S/22454), 동계획에 의하면, 초기단계에서 동 옵서버단 규모는 기간요원 (300 명) 에 지원요원 (보평,공벼,보급)을 합쳐 총1,440 이하로 하되, 동규모는 추후 조정가능하게 되어있음.처음 6개월간 옵서버단 경비는 8,300 만불, 다음 6개월은 4,000 만불 수준으로 추정하고있음. (S/22454/ADD.1)

3. 상기 UNIKOM 배치계획관련 M.GOULDING사무차장은 4.6. 쿠웨이트, 이락측과 협의한 것으로 알려졌으며, 양국 반응은 추후 공개될 예정이라고함.본건 옵서버단 단장 (CHIEF MILITARYOBSERVER) 으로는 G.GREINDL 전 UNFICYP사령관 (오스트리아 소장)이 거론되고있음. 동옵서버단에는 안보리 상임이사국 5개국이 모두참여할 예정이며, 총 20-30 개국정도가 참여할 전망이라고함.

4.한편 사무총장은 이락 쿠르드족 난민문제와 관련 유엔조사단 파견을 검토중인 것으로 알려짐.(안보리결의 688 호참조)

5.금 4.8. 오후 안보리는 비공식협의를 갖고 상기 사무총장 UNIKOM 배치계획서를 검토할예정임.

첨부:상기 안보리문서: UNW(F)-158

끝

(대사 노창희-국장)

국기국 1차보 중아국 정문국 안기부

PAGE 1

91.04.09 09:48 WG

외신 1과 통제관

0002

원 본

외 무 부

종 별 :

번 호 : UNW-0839 일 시 : 91 0408 2300

수 신 : 장 관(국연,중동일,기정)

발 신 : 주 유엔 대사

제 목 : 걸프사태(안보리)

연: UNW-0828

안보리는 금 4.8.(월) 오후 표제사태 관련 비공식회의를 가진바, 주요결과를 아래보고함.

1. 이락의 안보리휴전결의(687호) 수락

이락측의 수락통보 (S/22456) 에 대해 별첨 안보리 의장 회신을 4.9. 보내기로함.

2. 유엔옵서버단(UNIKOM) 배치계획

연호 사무총장 계획서를 재가하고 동 배치 계속여부 및 방식을 6개월마다 심사키로 한다는 요지의 결의안 채택문제를 명 4.9. 협의키로함.

3. 이락내 난민 보호지역 설정문제

금일 비공식 협의시 영국은 난민, 특히 쿠르드족에 대한 효과적인 구호를 위해 보호지역을 설정하는 문제를 제기한바, 미,불이 지지입장을 표명함.본건은 사무총장이 추진중인 유엔의 난민조사단 파견과도 연계, 명일 재협의가 있을예정임.

첨부:상기 안보리 의장 회신(안) 및 결의안 초안:UNW(F)-161

끝

(대사 노창희-국장)

국기국 1차보 중아국 정문국 안기부 장관실 차관실 2차보 청와대

PAGE 1

91.04.09 12:38 WG

외신 1과 통제관

0003

원 본

외 무 부

종 별 : 지 급

번 호 : UNW-0852 일 시 : 91 0409 2000

수 신 : 장 관(국연,중동일,기정)

발 신 : 주 유엔대사

제 목 : 걸프사태(안보리)

연: UNW-0839

1. 안보리는 금 4.9 (화) 17:50-18:05 공식회의를 개최하여 연호 사무총장의 유엔 옵서버단(UNIKOM)배치계획을 승인하는 결의(689호)를 만장일치로 채택한바, 동 회의 주요경과는 다음과 같음.

가.프랑스 신임대표(J.B.MERIME 대사)환영

나.쿠웨이트,이락 토의 참가 초청

다.의제채택(S/AGENDA/2983)

라.결의안 초안(S/22470) 표결

1)상기 초안(연호문안 일부수정) 표결 결과 만장일치로 채택됨.

2)표결전, 표결후 발언 없었음.

3)동 결의안 본문 1항에 언급된 S/22454/ADD.2는 배치지역도이며, ADD.3 은 이락(4.8),쿠웨이트(4.9) 의 배치계획(S/22454) 수락 및 협조용의를 확인하는 내용임.

2.상기 UNIKOM 배치관련 사무총장이 참여를 요청중인 국가는 안보리 상임이사국 5개국, 비상임이사국 3개국(인도, 오스트리아, 에쿠아돌), 여타국 24개국(싱가폴, 방글라데쉬, 피지, 인니, 말련, 파키스탄, 스웨덴, 카나다, 터키, 덴마크, 핀란드, 그리스 노르웨이,애란, 이태리 헝가리 폴랜드,루마니아, 우루과이, 베네주엘라, 가나케냐, 나이제리아, 세네갈) 총32개국으로 알려짐.

3.한편 안보리는 상기 공식회의에 앞서 금일 개별 , 그룹, 비공식협의를 가진바, 주요결과는 다음과 같음.

가.이락측의 휴전결의 687호 수락통보(S/22456) 에 대한 연호 안보리 의장회신(휴전 발효확인) 은 이락 국회의 수락결정사실이 확인될때까지 발송을 일단

국기국 장관 차관 1차보 2차보 중아국 정문국 청와대 안기부

미주국

PAGE 1

91.04.10 09:33 WH

외신 1과 통제관

0004

보류키로됨.(미,영 의견반영)

나.연호 이락내 난민보호지역 설정문제는 유엔난민조사단 파견결과를 보아 추후재협의키로 함.금 4.9. 사무총장은 동 난민 조사단장으로 E.SUY 전 사무차장(벨지움국적)을 임명하였음.

4.상기 조사단장 임명과 별도로 사무총장은 이락.쿠웨이트,이락-터어키 접경지역, 이락-이란 접경지역에서의 유엔의 인도적 활동을 총괄할 대표(S.KHAN) 를 임명한바, 별첨 보도자료 참조바람.

첨부:1.안보리 결의안,2.유엔보도자료: UNW(F)-162

끝

(대사 노창희-국장)

APR 09 '91 18:42 KOREAN ≡ION

P.1

UNW(FI)-162 10409 2000
(국연.중동일.기타)

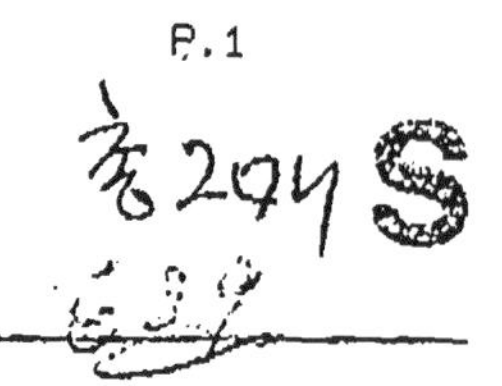

UNITED
NATIONS

Security Council

PROVISIONAL

S/22470
9 April 1991

ORIGINAL: ENGLISH

Draft resolution

The Security Council,

Recalling its resolution 687 (1991),

Acting under Chapter VII of the Charter,

1. Approves the report of the Secretary-General on the implementation of paragraph 5 of Security Council resolution 687 (1991) contained in document S/22454 and Add. 1-3 of 5 April 1991;

2. Notes that the decision to set up the observer unit was taken in paragraph 5 of resolution 687 (1991) and can only be terminated by a decision of the Council. The Council shall therefore review the question of termination or continuation every six months;

3. Decides that the modalities for the initial six-month period of the United Nations Iraq-Kuwait Observation Mission shall be as set out in accordance with the above-mentioned report and shall also be reviewed every six months.

3095E

#UNW-0852 의
첨부물

2-1

0006

United Nations

Press Release

Department of Public Information • News Coverage Service • New York

SG/A/455
IK/15
9 April 1991

SECRETARY-GENERAL APPOINTS SADRUDDIN AGA KHAN TO COORDINATE HUMANITARIAN PROGRAMME FOR IRAQ, KUWAIT, BORDER AREAS

The following is attributable to the Spokesman for the Secretary-General:

In view of the exceptional dimensions of the human tragedy unfolding in the region and the need for urgent measures by the United Nations system, the Secretary-General has today appointed Sadruddin Aga Khan as his Executive Delegate in the context of a United Nations Inter-Agency Humanitarian Programme for Iraq, Kuwait and the Iraq/Turkey and Iraq/Iran border areas. The Secretary-General feels that a collective effort of the United Nations system is required to ensure a prompt and effective response to these needs. To this end, the Executive Delegate will:

-- Facilitate the identification of needs, future problems and operational gaps in the United Nations system at work in the Persian Gulf, and suggest appropriate measures;

-- Prepare, together with relevant components of the United Nations system, timely consolidated appeals and ensure their regular updating.

-- Act as a catalyst to highlight humanitarian needs and stimulate a generous response from the international community, as required;

-- Keep the Secretary-General informed about humanitarian issues relating to the Gulf crisis by constant monitoring and reporting;

-- Provide a means of bringing urgent matters to the attention of the Secretary-General, donors, appropriate government authorities and United Nations agencies at the request either of affected countries or other United Nations agencies;

-- Represent the Secretary-General at Inter-Agency and other meetings, and ensure that his overall policy guidelines are adhered to; and

-- Maintain contacts, at high level, with all Governments, particularly those directly concerned, both in Geneva and in the field.

The Executive Delegate will be based in Geneva and will be assisted by a small group of staff drawn from the organizations and agencies involved.

* *** *

2-2

2639P

주 국 련 대 표 부

주국련 20313- 248 1991. 4. 11.

수신 장 관

참조 국제기구조약국장, 중동아프리카국장

제목 걸프사태 (안보리)

표제사태 관련 안보리 문서를 별첨과 같이 송부합니다.

첨 부 : 상기 문서. 끝.

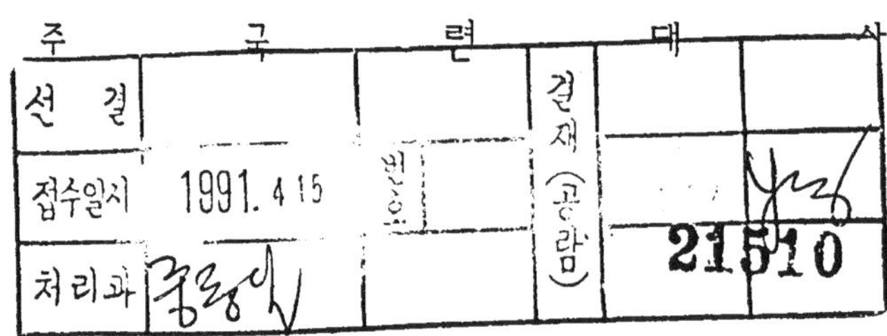

0008

UNITED
NATIONS

S

Security Council

Distr.
GENERAL

S/22476
10 April 1991
ENGLISH
ORIGINAL: ARABIC

LETTER DATED 10 APRIL 1991 FROM THE PERMANENT REPRESENTATIVE OF IRAQ TO THE UNITED NATIONS ADDRESSED TO THE SECRETARY-GENERAL

On instructions from my Government, I have the honour to provide you with the following information:

1. American air activity on 8/9 April amounted to 98 sorties flown by 49 formations.

2. The aircraft, which were identified as F-16s, F-15s and F-14s, flew at altitudes ranging from 1 to 9 kilometres, at speeds ranging from 600 to 1,200 kilometres per hour.

3. The flights took place chiefly, with regard to 15 formations, over Baghdad, and, with regard to 34 formations, over Kut, Aziziyah, eastern Baghdad, Habbaniyah, Ramadi and Hashimiyah.

4. The flights were carried out for the purposes of observation and reconnaissance operations, provocation and the creation of a disturbance, which they achieved by passing over the capital, Baghdad, breaking the sound barrier at 0040 hours on 9 April 1991.

I should be grateful if you would have this letter circulated as a document of the Security Council.

(*Signed*) Abdul Amir AL-ANBARI
Ambassador
Permanent Representative

91-11664 2282e (E)

0009

UNITED NATIONS

S

Security Council

Distr.
GENERAL

S/22477
10 April 1991
ENGLISH
ORIGINAL: ARABIC AND ENGLISH

LETTER DATED 10 APRIL 1991 FROM THE CHARGE D'AFFAIRES A.I. OF THE PERMANENT MISSION OF KUWAIT TO THE UNITED NATIONS ADDRESSED TO THE SECRETARY-GENERAL

Upon instructions from my Government, I should like to inform you that the State of Kuwait will fully cooperate with the United Nations towards successfully accomplishing the tasks that the United Nations Iraq-Kuwait Observation Mission shall undertake in accordance with Your Excellency's report (S/22454 and Add.1-3) dated 5 and 9 April 1991 on the implementation of paragraph (5) of Security Council resolution 687 (1991), which was endorsed by the Council in resolution 689 (1991) of 9 April 1991.

I should appreciate it if you would arrange for this letter to be circulated as a document of the Security Council.

(Signed) Mohammad AL SALLAL
Chargé d'affaires a.i.

91-11670 2890a (E)

0010

UNITED
NATIONS

S

Security Council

Distr.
GENERAL

S/22478
10 April 1991

ORIGINAL: ENGLISH

LETTER DATED 9 APRIL 1991 FROM THE SECRETARY-GENERAL
ADDRESSED TO THE PRESIDENT OF THE SECURITY COUNCIL

I have the honour to refer to my report dated 5 April 1991 concerning proposed arrangements for the establishment of the United Nations Iraq/Kuwait Observation Mission (UNIKOM) (S/22454 and Add.1-3), which was approved by the Security Council in its resolution 689 (1991) of 9 April 1991. In paragraph 4 (a) of my report (S/22454), I stated that the command of UNIKOM would be exercised by a Chief Military Observer appointed by the Secretary-General with the consent of the Security Council.

I now wish to inform you that it is my intention, with the consent of the Council, to appoint Major-General Günther Greindl of Austria as Chief Military Observer of UNIKOM.

I should be grateful if you could bring this matter to the attention of the members of the Security Council.

(*Signed*) Javier PEREZ de CUELLAR

91-11677 2265h (E)

0011

UNITED
NATIONS

Security Council

Distr.
GENERAL

S/22479
10 April 1991
ENGLISH
ORIGINAL: FRENCH

LETTER DATED 10 APRIL 1991 FROM THE PRESIDENT OF THE SECURITY COUNCIL ADDRESSED TO THE SECRETARY-GENERAL

I have the honour to inform you that your letter dated 9 April 1991 (S/22478) concerning your proposal to appoint Major-General Günther Greindl of Austria as Chief Military Observer of the United Nations Iraq/Kuwait Observation Mission (UNIKOM) has been brought to the attention of the members of the Security Council. They considered the matter on 10 April 1991 and agreed with the proposal contained in your letter.

(Signed) Paul NOTERDAEME
President of the Security Council

91-11683 2407d (E)

0012

주 국 련 대 표 부

주국련 20313- 244 1991. 4. 11.

수신 장 관

참조 국제기구조약국장, 중동아프리카국장

제목 걸프사태 (경제제재 조치 관련 경제난 문제)

표제 관련 유엔사무총장의 91.4.11 안보리 비공식 협의시 보고내용을 별첨과 같이 송부합니다.

첨 부 : 상기 자료. 끝.

주 국 련 대

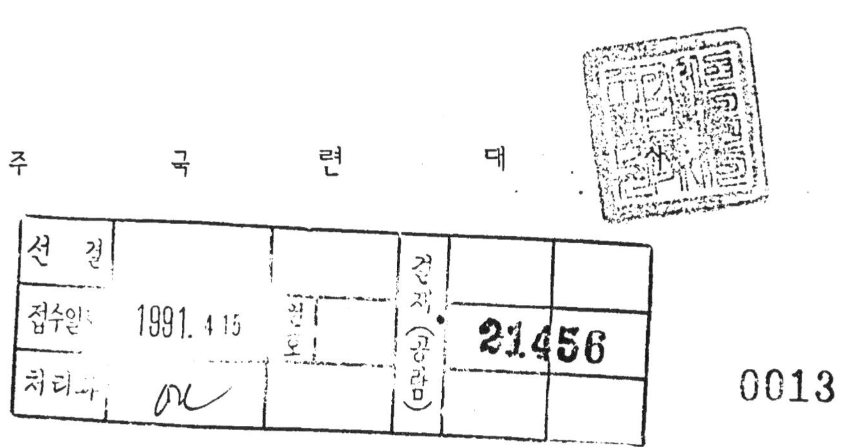

선 결			결재 (공람)		
접수일시	1991. 4 15	번호		21456	
처리과					

0013

Remarks of the Secretary-General
at informal consultations
of the Security-Council - April 1991

Iraq-Kuwait/Article 50 of the Charter

A. Introduction

Mr. President,

Members of the Council will recall that at their informal consultations held on 27 March 1991, concern was expressed about the international response to the situation of Member States confronted with special economic problems arising from the application of sanctions against Iraq, and the then occupied-Kuwait, pursuant to Council resolution 661 (1990). Particular reference was made at that time to a memorandum (S/22382) of 22 March, by which those 21 Member States that had earlier addressed themselves to the Security Council under Article 50 of the Charter, now made a further appeal for an urgent and effective international response to their situation.

0014

In informing me of the discussion which took place
in those informal consultations on 27 March, Mr. President,
your distinguished predecessor indicated to me the wish of Council members
to be briefed on this subject.
It is in response to that desire on the part of Council Members
and in accordance with the recommendations of the Committee
that I now take the floor.

Mr. President,

Since the adoption on 6 August 1990
of resolution 661, 21 Member States requested consultations
with the Council under Article 50 of the Charter.
In addressing the Council,
those States described the special economic problems
arising from the implementation of resolution 661
and sought its assistance in solving these problems.
The Council adopted, on 24 September 1990, resolution 669,
by which it entrusted
to the Committee Established by Resolution 661,
the tasks of examining requests for assistance under Article 50 and of making recommendations
to the President of the Security Council for appropriate action.

The Committee established by Resolution 661,
through its Working Group,
considered the individual situations
of the Member States in question
and made a series of recommendations to the Security Council
concerning each one of them.
Past Presidents of the Council have informed me
of those recommendations
and have indeed referred them to me for appropriate action.

B. The Case of Jordan

Mr. President,

Even from the outset of the crisis in the Persian Gulf,
it was clear that the vulnerability of Jordan
placed that State in a unique situation.
Indeed, Jordan was among the first Member States
to approach the Security Council under Article 50 of the Charter.
It did so by a letter dated 20 August 1990 (S/21620).
On 24 September 1990, the then Council President
conveyed to me a Special Report of the "661 Committee"
concerning Jordan (S/21786), and requested me
to implement the actions envisaged in that report.

In response to that request,
I sent to the Council on 22 October 1990, a report (S/21938), drawn up by former Director-General, Mr. Jean Ripert,
whom I had asked to travel to Jordan for that purpose.
Mr. Ripert's report underscored the gravity
of Jordan's situation, and the urgent need for action to alleviate it.

On 30 October 1990,
I also addressed letters to the Foreign Ministers of all States,
strongly supporting the "661 Committee's" appeal
for the immediate provision of assistance to Jordan
in order to mitigate the difficulties faced by that State
as a result of its application of economic sanctions against Iraq.
By separate letters dated 22 November and 30 December 1990,
respectively, I called on the relevant agencies,
organs, organizations and bodies of the United Nations system
to intensify their programmes of assistance
in response to the pressing needs of Jordan.
In those communications,
which were accompanied by copies
of the "661 Committee's" recommendations
and the report of Mr. Ripert's mission, I requested the recipients
to provide me with all relevant information
on their assistance to Jordan.

C. Paris meeting of eminent persons

In the meantime, it was essential
to explore all possible ways to respond effectively
to the needs of the adversely affected countries.
With this objective in mind,
I convened a meeting in Paris on 17 November 1990
of a group of 20 eminent persons to discuss informally
the consequences of the Persian Gulf crisis on the world economy.
That informal exchange of views was extremely useful
and helped generate various ideas
on the role that the United Nations could play
to help the innocent victims of the crisis.
Subsequently, I formed a group of five participants
on a regional basis, as well as IMF, the World Bank and EEC -
to advise me on the further course of action.

D. Action on Requests for Assistance from 18 Member States

Later on, by a letter of 21 December 1990 (S/22033),
the President of the Security Council requested me to implement
the actions envisaged in further recommendations
adopted by the "661 Committee"
in connection with requests for assistance under Article 50
of the Charter, received from the following 18 States:

Bulgaria, Tunisia, Romania, India, Yugoslavia, Lebanon, Philippines, Sri Lanka, Yemen, Czechoslovakia, Poland, Mauritania, Pakistan, Sudan, Uruguay, Viet Nam, Bangladesh and Seychelles (S/22021 and Add. 1).

Accordingly on 23 January 1991,
I addressed another letter to the Foreign Ministers of all States
expressing my strongest possible support
for the urgent appeal of the "661 Committee"
for technical, financial and material assistance
to be provided immediately to those States
in order to mitigate the adverse impact on their economies of the application of the sanctions.
On the same date,
I also addressed separate communications to the Heads of the competent organs
and Specialized Agencies of the United Nations system
including the International Financial Institutions,
and the Regional Development Banks, requesting them
to review their programmes of assistance to those countries
with a view to alleviating their special economic problems.

Pursuant to the recommendations of the "661 Committee",
I requested States and the concerned organs and agencies
of the United Nations system, to provide me with information
on action taken by them to alleviate the special economic problems

0019

of the States concerned. I further proposed
that such information be made available to me on a quarterly basis,
with first reports to reach me by the end of February 1991.

I can now report to you, Mr. President, on the responses which I have received.

E. Main features of the replies

Unfortunately, the number of responses that I have received - especially from states - is limited. Moreover,
many of the responses from organs
and agencies of the United Nations system
contained general or preliminary information
and reached my Office only recently.
For these reasons, it has not been feasible before now,
to present to Council members
anything like a comprehensive report on the matter.
Let me, at this point, nonetheless list the replies
which I had received as of 5 April 1991,
and briefly outline their main features.
The texts of the individual replies
could be made available to the members of the Council,
should they so wish.

With regard to Jordan,
I received replies only from the Governments of
Denmark, Liechtenstein, Norway and Switzerland.
Communications were also received
from the following Specialized Agencies: FAO, GATT,
ILO, IMO, ITU, UNESCO and UNIDO, as well as of IAEA.
Among relevant United Nations bodies,
WFP, UNRWA and UNEP responded.

As regards the 18 other affected countries,
I have received eight replies from the Governments
of Czechoslovakia, France, Haiti, Germany,
Japan, Norway, Oman and the USSR.
Responses were received from the Heads
of the following Specialized Agencies: FAO, GATT,
IFAD, ILO, IMO, ITU and the World Bank;
as well as from the Asian Development Bank
and the European Bank for Reconstruction and Development.
From among the relevant United Nations entities,
eleven replies have been received:
these came from WFP, HABITAT, UNOV, UNCTC, ESCAP,
UNDRO, UNDP, UNFPA, UNRWA, ECA and DTCD.

I should now like to outline the main substantive features
of these replies -

0021

As regards replies received from States,
five countries, France, Germany, Japan, Norway and the USSR,
provided specific information on their assistance
to several affected countries,
in particular to those which had invoked Article 50.
Denmark, Liechtenstein, and Switzerland and once again Norway,
reported on their assistance to Jordan.
Three countries, Czechoslovakia, Haiti and Oman,
indicated that they were not in a position to provide assistance.

As regards Specialized Agencies,
their replies indicate that all of them share the concern about
the pressing needs of the countries affected by the Gulf crisis -
and have taken due note of
the recommendations of the "661 Committee".
Accordingly, most agencies contemplate
intensifying their assistance activities
in the countries that have invoked Article 50 of the Charter -
within their respective mandates and, importantly,
according to the availability of financial resources.
In addition to their existing technical co-operation programmes
with the countries concerned,
some of the Agencies undertook emergency measures
and launched special assistance projects.

0022

For example, ILO has taken several steps to assist Bangladesh, India, Jordan, Pakistan, the Philippines, Sri Lanka and Yemen, in particular in regard to repatriation - and rehabilitation of returning migrants; FAO provided emergency assistance to Jordan and established a special Task Force for monitoring the food situation in the Gulf region, as well as for identifying and monitoring field projects under way and in the pipeline which contribute to the food and agricultural development of the countries most affected; ITU provided assistance to Romania and offered advisory services to Jordan; UNESCO approved emergency assistance to Jordan and undertook finance mobilization efforts; UNIDO intends to dispatch a mission to Jordan.

Turning to the International Financial Institutions, I have recently received a letter from Mr. Barber B. Conable, President of the World Bank, transmitting a summary of the latest review of the Bank's assistance programme relating to the Gulf crisis. Copies of this document will be circulated presently to Council Members.

0023

The Bank indicates
that the basic elements of its assistance programme,
set out last November, remain valid.
For IBRD borrowers,
planned additional lending in excess of $1.1 billion
remains on schedule, in particular to Eastern Europe and to
the most immediately impacted countries in the Middle East,
including Jordan.
At the same time, some SDR 550 million,
or 85 percent of the overall IDA programme
envisaged so far in response to the Gulf crisis,
will assist most immediately-impacted developing countries
such as Bangladesh, India, Pakistan and Sri Lanka,
and will include emergency operations in Egypt and Yemen.
Finally, the Bank expects to commit about $2 billion
in additional IBRD/IDA lending,
although not all of this will fall in financial year 1991.

I might mention here in parenthesis
that the First regular session
of the Administrative Committee on Coordination for 1991,
to be held in Paris from 17 to 19 April,
will discuss the economic and social impact of the Gulf conflict
and its implications for international co-operation.

For my part, I intend to ensure that these deliberations of ACC should serve the objective of enhancing a co-ordinated response of the United Nations system to the grave economic consequences of the conflict.

Among the regional development banks, the Asian Development Bank submitted a document on its proposed assistance to the affected countries prepared for its Board of Directors. The European Bank is not yet operational, but expects to become so on 15 April 1991.

As for United Nations bodies and organs, their reports, in many instances, referred to their current activities - and existing technical co-operation programmes, within their respective mandates and budgets. In terms of special and emergency operations undertaken or proposed by them to assist affected countries, the following examples are of relevance. UNDP has recently decided to allot up to $4 million from the Special Programme Resources, as seed money, to help address the most immediate humanitarian needs of the developing countries affected by the Gulf crisis.

0025

These resources will also be used to help the affected countries in impact-assessment, and in the launching of plans of action in critical areas - such as integration of returnees and human development, rehabilitation of institutions and infrastructure, economic management and environmental recovery.

WFP is already undertaking or has recently approved projects and emergency operations for 15 of the most affected countries, with particular focus on food aid to the poorest strata of the population.

It also widened its special assistance to such affected countries as Bangladesh, India, Lebanon, Mauritania, Pakistan and Bulgaria.

UNDRO, as a UN lead agency, co-ordinated international assistance for the emergency operation carried out in Jordan in August-November 1990 for the repatriation of over 700,000 third country nationals from at least 10 developing countries.

UNRWA undertook emergency relief measures for Palestine refugees in Jordan, Syria and Lebanon.

F. Recent requests for assistance from Syria and Djibouti

Recently, by a letter dated 21 March 1991 (S/22398), the President of the Security Council informed me of the further recommendations - with regard to Syria and Djibouti

0026

(S/22021/Add.2), adopted by the "661 Committee"
in response to requests by those states
for assistance under the provisions of Article 50 of the Charter.
In this context, too
I am addressing as in the past communications to all concerned.
In doing so, I shall recall my earlier communications
and reiterate my request for relevant information on a quarterly basis.

G. Memorandum of 21 States

Mr. President,

Finally, I should like to revert to the Memorandum
conveyed by 21 Member States on 22 March 1991
to the President of the Security Council (S/22382).
As stated in that Memorandum,
"the problems affecting these countries persist,
and in certain respects have been aggravated,
while the appeals launched pursuant to the recommendations
of the Security Council Committee
and addressed to all concerned by the Secretary-General,
have not evoked responses
commensurate with the urgent needs of the affected countries."

In light of this factual situation,
the 21 States have now launched a collective appeal,
particularly to all donor States,
to respond urgently and effectively
in providing assistance to the affected countries,
by allocating additional financial resources -
both through bilateral channels
and by supporting the actions of the competent organs
and specialized agencies of the United Nations system.
The 21 States believe that,
given the magnitude of the difficulties they face,
the Security Council
should devote renewed attention to these problems
with a view to finding quick and effective solutions.
I would like to express strong support for their appeal.
Insufficient attention to their difficulties
will not only complicate their immediate situations
with unpredictable consequences;
it may also have ramifications
for the way in which vulnerable nations frame their response
to any future developments
like those that followed 2 August 1990.

Thank you Mr. President.

0028

Attachment

Gulf Crisis: Review of World Bank Assistance Program

Following the onset of the Gulf crisis, the Bank took prompt action to assist affected countries recognizing that without urgent additional external assistance, development programs in many of these countries could otherwise be derailed and further deterioration of economic conditions would follow from delayed or inadequate policy responses. From its initial country assessments, the Bank agreed on a number of measures encompassing the following main areas:

- Assistance in designing appropriate policy responses.
- Accelerated disbursements from existing loans and credits.
- Expanded IBRD or IDA lending.
- Aid coordination, and assistance in mobilizing appropriate financial packages, including debt and debt-service relief.

The assistance program set out in November called for an increase in IBRD lending of about $1.1 billion and in IDA lending of SDR 800 million in FY91. It envisaged that half of the additional IDA lending of SDR 800 million could be covered by the use of existing resources such as the carry-over of funds from IDA-8, reprogramming of IDA-9 and accelerated use of IBRD funds due to IDA. As for the rest of the required concessional financing, it was agreed that management would seek additional resources from donors on a voluntary basis.

With the cessation of hostilities, it became necessary to re-examine the financial needs of affected countries. While it is still too early to estimate precisely the effects on individual countries, it is clear that many countries, particularly the front-line states of Egypt, Jordan, and Turkey have been seriously impacted by the crisis. Significant losses have also been incurred by several Eastern European countries with close trade links to Iraq, a number of countries in Sub-Saharan Africa, and those countries heavily dependent on workers' remittances (in particular, Bangladesh, India, Philippines, and Yemen) as well as tourism.

An improved economic scenario, influenced in part by lower oil prices and oil import expenditures, is now in prospect. But many countries still face serious difficulties and uncertainties regarding the pace of recovery, including the need for migrant workers to be re-absorbed in the domestic economy, social safety nets to be established, and loss of foreign exchange earnings from remittances to be recovered. Such difficulties, likely to be severe as countries struggle to adjust, call for a substantial international response.

0029

Since the basic elements of its assistance are still valid, the Bank intends to implement the bulk of the crisis-lending operations originally envisaged in the Fall. For IBRD borrowers, planned additional lending in excess of $1.1 billion remains on schedule. A substantial part of this program will supplement adjustment operations in Eastern Europe which faces in 1991 the largest relative costs from the Gulf crisis. Another major element consists of investment operations in other most immediately impacted countries in the Middle East, including a small emergency operation in Jordan. Overall, the IBRD/IDA current Gulf Program includes special emergency operations, increased investments, and additional adjustment lending in several affected countries.

An expanded IDA program of about SDR 640 million for FY91 is expected to be virtually completely financed through SDR 400 million from IDA's existing resources, SDR 200 million through a proposed allocation of IBRD FY90 net income to IDA, and a supplementary contribution to IDA-9 of SDR 27 million from the Government of Kuwait (of which about SDR 10 million has already been committed). Some SDR 550 million or 85 percent of the overall IDA program envisaged so far in response to the Gulf crisis will assist most immediately impacted countries such as Bangladesh, India, Pakistan, and Sri Lanka. It also includes emergency operations in Egypt and Yemen aimed at setting up infrastructure, social services and employment-creation programs for repatriated workers. The rest of the IDA-type funds (about SDR 100 million) will go to several African and a few Central American low-income countries most seriously affected by the crisis. In addition, the Bank is prepared to accelerate disbursements from both IBRD and IDA through the temporary raising of cost-sharing limits for affected countries on new as well as existing loans and credits. Increased disbursements from such changes in cost-sharing limits are estimated at $500 million in FY91. About 40 percent of this amount will go to most immediately impacted countries in Asia.

The program laid out last November remains appropriate despite the change in circumstances. The Bank will continue to process that part of its Bank's operational response that is already in the pipeline and expect to commit about $2 billion in additional IBRD/IDA lending, although not all of this will fall in FY91. While implementation of the work program has been disrupted by the security situation in the Gulf and in a number of other countries, the Bank still expects to substantially meet the objectives originally approved by the Board.

0030

주 국 련 대 표 부

주국련 20313- 1991. 4. 11.

수신 장 관 245

참조 국제기구조약국장, 중동아프리카국장

제목 걸프사태 관련 유엔 난민구호활동

표제 관련 유엔측으로 부터 입수한 자료를 별첨과 같이 송부합니다.

첨 부 : 상기 자료. 끝.

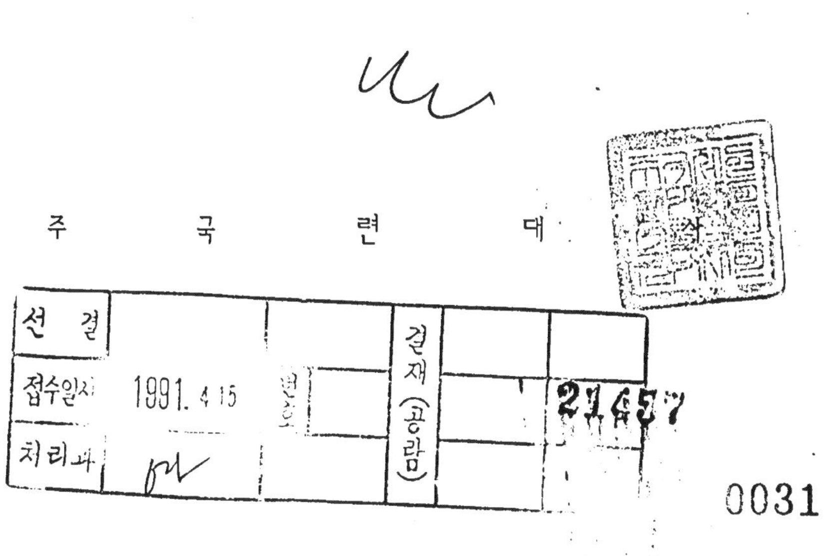

주 국 련 대

선 결			결재(공람)		
접수일시	1991. 4. 15	번호			21457
처리과					

0031

UNDRO XXXX

TO : LISTS 1, 2, 3 PLUS MISSIONS OF BANGLADESH, EGYPT, IRAN, JORDAN, LEBANON, OMAN, PAKISTAN, PHILIPPINES, SRI LANKA, SYRIA, TURKEY, SAUDI ARABIA, YEMEN, PLUS UNDP/JORDAN, SYRIA, IRAN, SAUDI ARABIA, LEBANON, OMAN, EGYPT, YEMEN, BANGLADESH, INDIA, PAKISTAN, PHILIPPINES AND SRI LANKA

MIDDLE EAST/PERSIAN GULF - EMERGENCY SITUATION
UNDRO SITUATION REPORT NO. 30 - 11 APRIL 1991

1. ON 5 APRIL 1991, UNDRO, ON BEHALF OF THE ORGANIZATIONS PARTICIPATING IN THE UN INTER-AGENCY WORKING GROUP AND IOM IN GENEVA (IAWG), LAUNCHED AN APPEAL FOR USD 137 MILLION, WHICH TOGETHER WITH THE START-UP COSTS, REPRESENTED THE FULL FUNDING OF THE REGIONAL HUMANITARIAN PLAN OF ACTION (RHPA) FOR 400,000 REFUGEES/DISPLACED. TODAY THE NUMBER OF PEOPLE IN NEED OF IMMEDIATE ASSISTANCE IN IRAN AND TURKEY HAS ALMOST TRIPLED.

2. TO COPE WITH THE DRAMATIC SITUATION, THE IAWG MET ON 8 APRIL TO EVALUATE REPORTS AND PREPARE A COMMON STRATEGY. AS A RESULT, IN ADDITION TO THE FULL ACTIVATION OF THE ORIGINAL RHPA AND MOBILIZATION OF ALL AVAILABLE RESOURCES, A SECOND UPDATE OF THE RHPA HAS BEEN PREPARED.

3. THIS DOCUMENT, WHICH REVISES THE INDIVIDUAL RESPONSIBILITIES OF U.N. AGENCIES AND IOM, CALLS FOR THE INTERNATIONAL COMMUNITY, MEMBER STATES AND OTHER HUMANITARIAN ORGANIZATIONS TO JOIN EFFORTS AND AVOID A MAJOR HUMAN TRAGEDY. THE ESTIMATED COST OF SUCH AN OPERATION IS USD 400 MILLION, TO ASSIST 1.5 MILLION PEOPLE FOR 90 DAYS.

4. CONTRIBUTIONS CHANNELED THROUGH THE UNDRO/IAWG MECHANISM, WILL BE ALLOCATED ACCORDING TO THE FOLLOWING SHARES: UNHCR 59.6 PERCENT, WFP 11.7 PERCENT, WHO 7.7 PERCENT, UNICEF 5.8 PERCENT, IOM 14.2 PERCENT, UNDRO 1 PERCENT.

5. THIS DOCUMENT DESCRIBES ALSO THE CO-ORDINATION MECHANISM IN GENEVA AND IN THE FIELD. IN THIS REGARD FULL COOPERATION WILL ALSO BE EXTENDED TO PRINCE SADRUDDIN AGA KHAN AS THE SECRETARY-GENERAL'S EXECUTIVE DELEGATE OF THE UN PROGRAMME FOR IRAQ, KUWAIT AND THE IRAQ/TURKEY AND IRAQ/IRAN BORDER AREAS, WHOSE APPOINTMENT COINCIDED WITH THE FINALIZATION OF THE UPDATED RHPA.

6. TO MAXIMIZE THE IMPACT OF INTERNATIONAL ASSISTANCE, ALL DONORS ARE REQUESTED, AS A MATTER OF URGENCY, TO CO-ORDINATE WITH UNHCR HQS THE DELIVERY OF RELIEF SUPPLIES. THIS WILL FACILITATE THE SELECTION OF DISTRIBUTION SITES AND CONSEQUENTLY, AVOID DUPLICATION OF EFFORTS OR POCKETS OF UNASSISTED PEOPLE.

7. ALL DONORS ARE ALSO REQUESTED TO REPORT TO UNDRO/UNHCR DETAILED INFORMATION ON ITEMS CONTRIBUTED FOR THIS EMERGENCY, GIVING EXACT DESCRIPTION OF ITEMS, QUANTITIES, DESTINATIONS, ETA, CHANNELS AND VALUES IN USD.

8. BILATERAL CONTRIBUTIONS PROVIDED DIRECTLY TO THE GOVERNMENTS OF IRAN AND TURKEY, OR CHANNELED THROUGH OTHER HUMANITARIAN AGENCIES, TO EXTENT THEY ADDRESS THE REQUIREMENTS OF THE SECOND UPDATE OF THE RHPA, WILL BE CONSIDERED AS PART OF THE INTERNATIONAL RESPONSE.

0032

9. AN ADVANCE COPY OF THE SECOND UPDATE OF THE RHPA HAD BEEN PLACED THIS MORNING IN THE LETTER BOX OF UN MISSIONS OF MEMBER STATES AT THE PALAIS DES NATIONS IN GENEVA (DOOR E 154 - GATE 49). IT WILL BE PRESENTED AT THE UNDRO INFORMATION MEETING ON THE PERSIAN GULF CRISIS IN GENEVA ON FRIDAY 12 APRIL 1991.

10. FOLLOWING ARE LATEST REPORTS RECEIVED FROM THE FIELD AND SOME PRELIMINARY INFORMATION ON U.N. RESPONSE.

SITUATION IN TURKEY
----

11. REPORTS AS OF 10 APRIL INDICATE THAT BETWEEN 300,000 AND 400,000 IRAQI ASYLUM-SEEKERS ARE PRESENTLY ALONG THE TURKEY- IRAQ BORDER, WITH THOUSANDS MORE IN ROUTE. THIS POPULATION, OF KURDISH ORIGIN, IS CONCENTRATED IN TWO MAIN AREAS, AROUND THE TOWNS OF ULUDERE AND CUKURCA, IN THE MOUNTAIN REGION. IN ULUDERE NEARLY 100,000 IRAQI KURDS ARE REPORTED TO BE LOCATED ON THE SIDE OF A VERY STEEP MOUNTAIN. ACCESS IS DIFFICULT SINCE MOST ROADS IN THE AREA ARE DIRT TRACKS, MANY OF WHICH WASHED AWAY IN HEAVY RAINS.

12. THE IRAQI ASYLUM-SEEKERS ARE IN DESPERATE CONDITIONS. A UNHCR MISSION THAT HAS JUST RETURNED FROM THE BORDER REPORTS MOST OF THE POPULATION, WHICH INCLUDES A LARGE PERCENTAGE OF WOMEN AND CHILDREN, HAVE BEEN WALKING FOR SEVERAL DAYS AND HAVE ARRIVED WITHOUT ANY BELONGINGS AND INSUFFICIENT CLOTHING. THEIR PHYSICAL CONDITIONS ARE GENERALLY MARKED BY EXTREME EXHAUSTION. WHILE THEY HAVE BEEN PROVIDED WITH QUANTITIES OF FOOD, BLANKETS, SHOES AND PLASTIC TARPAULINS, THEY HAVE LITTLE WATER AND NO SHELTER, ESPECIALLY IN ULEDERE.

13. THE CAPACITY OF THE TRANSIT CENTRES AND REFERRAL CAMPS IN TURKEY, ESTABLISHED UNDER THE FIRST UPDATE OF THE REGIONAL HUMANITARIAN PLAN OF ACTION, BEARS NO RELATION TO THE EXTRAORDINARY NUMBERS OF PERSONS NOW ON THE BORDER. UNHCR HAS NOW REVISED ITS PLANNING FIGURE IN ORDER TO PROVIDE ASSISTANCE TO 500,000 PERSONS IN TURKEY AND THE BORDER.

14. ASSISTANCE MUST BE, FOR THE TIME BEING, DISTRIBUTED TO THE REFUGEES AT THEIR IMMEDIATE ARRIVAL POINTS, A TASK MADE EXTREMELY DIFFICULT BY ADVERSE WEATHER CONDITIONS AND ROUGH TERRAIN. THE URGENCY OF THIS TASK CANNOT BE EXAGGERATED IN VIEW OF THE VERY CRITICAL CONDITIONS DESCRIBED ABOVE IN WHICH THE POPULATION FINDS ITSELF. ACCORDINGLY, A SERIES OF STOCKPILES AND DISTRIBUTION POINTS NEEDS TO BE SET UP ALONG THE BORDER, FED BY SUPPLIES THAT, IT IS EXPECTED, CAN BE FLOWN DIRECTLY TO AIR BASES IN SOUTHEASTERN TURKEY.

15. UNHCR IS SEEKING TO ESTABLISH A PRESENCE IN THE AFFECTED PROVINCES AND IN THE BORDER AREA. THE UNHCR BRANCH OFFICE IN ANKARA HAS ALREADY DEPLOYED FIVE STAFF TO THE REGION WHO WILL USE DIYARBAKIR AS THEIR BASE IN THE COMING DAYS. THE STAFFING LEVEL OF THE UNHCR OFFICE IS INCREASING THIS WEEK WITH THE ARRIVAL OF AN EMERGENCY CO-ORDINATOR AND OTHER EXPERIENCED SENIOR OFFICERS. A DETAILED NEEDS ASSESSMENT MISSION IS DUE TO BE UNDERTAKEN, IN CO-OPERATION WITH THE TURKISH AUTHORITIES. IN ANKARA THE UN-IOM INTER-AGENCY EMERGENCY TEAM, LED BY THE UN RESIDENT CO-ORDINATOR, CONTINUES TO FOLLOW THE SITUATION AND FACILITATES NECESSARY

0033

ACTIONS

PRIORITY NEEDS IN TURKEY

16. FOOD

WFP HAS NOT YET RECEIVED A FORMAL REQUEST FROM THE GOVERNMENT OF TURKEY. HOWEVER, AN EMERGENCY OPERATION (EMOP) IS BEING PREPARED TO COVER THE FOOD NEEDS FOR 500,000 BENEFICIARIES FOR 90 DAYS INITIALLY.

THE ESTIMATED QUANTITIES, SUBJECT TO FURTHER DISCUSSION WITH THE TURKISH AUTHORITIES, WOULD BE:

COMMODITY	TOTAL REQUIREMENTS (MT)
WHEAT FLOUR	25,200
RICE	4,500
VEGETABLE OIL	1,350
PULSES	900
CANNED MEAT/FISH	900
SUGAR	450

THE ABOVE BEING STILL UNDER NEGOTIATIONS, CANNOT BE CONSIDERED YET AS WFP'S COMMITMENT.

UNDER A SUPPLEMENTARY FEEDING PROGRAMME (SFP), UNHCR WILL PROVIDE THE REFUGEES WITH HIGH PROTEIN BISCUITS FOR 20 DAYS.

17. NON FOOD

AS OF 31 MARCH, ALL CONCERNED UN AGENCIES HAD STOCK PILED FOR THE NEEDS OF 20,000 PERSONS AND HAD PROVIDED CASH CONTRIBUTIONS TO ENABLE THE GOVERNMENT OF TURKEY TO ESTABLISH INFRASTRUCTURE FOR FOUR TRANSIT CENTRES. EQUIPMENT ALREADY PROVIDED BY THE UN TO THE TURKISH RED CRESCENT SOCIETY INCLUDE SHELTER MATERIAL, SURVIVAL ITEMS AND OTHER RELIEF GOODS WORTH OVER USD 4,000,000. IN ADDITION, CERTAIN UNHCR STOCKS IN SYRIA, ARE ALSO BEING REDEPLOYED TO TURKEY.

THE ITEMS LISTED BELOW ARE URGENTLY REQUIRED IN TURKEY. THE PROVISION OF SHELTER, WATER, FOOD AND MEDICAL ASSISTANCE ARE IMMEDIATELY NEEDED LIFE-SAVING PRIORITIES. THESE QUANTITIES ARE BASED ON THE PRESENT POPULATION OF 300,000 PERSONS UNLESS OTHERWISE INDICATED. THEY DO NOT REPRESENT THE TOTAL REQUIREMENTS FOR THE OPERATION, WHICH WILL BE DETERMINED IN THE UPCOMING DETAILED NEEDS ASSESSMENT MISSION TO THE BORDER PROVINCES. CO-ORDINATION AND OPERATIONAL RESPONSIBILITIES ARE DEFINED IN THE SECOND UPDATE OF THE RHPA.

QUANTITY	DESCRIPTION
100,000	HEAVY DUTY TENTS (5 PERSON FOR 500,000 PEOPLE
100,000	TARPAULINS (FOR 500,000 PEOPLE)

0034

▬00	ROLLS OF PLASTIC SHEETING
25,000	GROUND MATTRESSES OR THERMAL GROUND SHEETS
900,000	WOOL BLANKETS
150	RUBBER WATER TANKS (5,000 LITRES)
60,000	JERRY CANS (10 LITRES)
FOR 300,000 PERSONS	WARM CLOTHING AND SHOES
FOR 300,000 PERSONS	FIELD KITCHENS
4	FIELD HOSPITALS
50	TRUCKS (10 TON)
10	AMBULANCES

ADDITIONAL SECTORIAL REQUIREMENTS WILL BE DIRECTLY DISSEMINATED BY CONCERNED UN SPECIALIZED AGENCIES.

SITUATION IN IRAN
--------- -- ----

18. INFLUX

AS OF THE EVENING OF 7 APRIL 1991 THE INFLUX OF IRAQI REFUGEES INTO THE ISLAMIC REPUBLIC OF IRAN STOOD AT 771,850. THERE WAS A DRAMATIC INCREASE OF 220,000 PERSONS REPORTED ON 7 APRIL. UNHCR HAS BEEN INFORMED OF CONTINUED INCREASED IN THE THREE NORTHERN PROVINCES, BUT THESE HAVE NOT YET BEEN OFFICIALLY CONFIRMED BY INDIVIDUAL PROVINCES, THE CENTRAL AUTHORITIES IN TEHRAN OR UNHCR MISSIONS IN THE BORDER AREA AS OF 10 APRIL 1991.

TWO ROVING UNHCR MISSIONS, ONE MONITORING KHUZISTAN AND ILAM PROVINCES AND THE SECOND WEST AZERBAIJAN, KURDISTAN AND BAKHTARAN PROVINCES, HAVE REPORTED EYEWITNESS ACCOUNTS OF SUBSTANTIAL BACKLOGS OF PEOPLE AND VEHICLES AT OFFICIAL BORDER ENTRY POINTS.

IT IS UNDERSTOOD THAT THE ABOVE INFLUX FIGURES ARE EXPECTED TO INCREASE AS SOON AS ACCURATE DATA IS MADE AVAILABLE TO THE CENTRAL AUTHORITIES FROM THE BORDER PROVINCES. THIS INFORMATION IS EXPECTED TODAY.

19. BREAKDOWN BY PROVINCE

AS OF 7 APRIL 1991 THE BREAKDOWN OF THE INFLUX BY PROVINCE IS AS FOLLOWS:

- KHUZISTAN	68,150
- ILAM	2,500
- BAKHTARAN	426,500
- KURDISTAN	31,500
- WEST AZERBAIJAN	243,200
TOTAL	771,650

20. CASELOAD CHARACTERISTICS

THE CASELOAD IN KHUZISTAN AND ILAM PROVINCES OF 70,650 IS COMPOSED PRIMARILY OF IRAQIS FROM SOUTH IRAQ AND THE BASRAH REGION. AN ESTIMATED 4,000 IN KHUZISTAN ARE KNOWN TO BE OF

0035

YRANI__—RIGIN.

THE REST OF THE CASELOAD OF 701,200 IS BELIEVED TO BE COMPOSED OF ALMOST EXCLUSIVELY IRAQIS FROM THE NORTH. UNHCR MISSION TO WEST AZERBAIJAN HAS REPORTED THAT THE ESTIMATED COMPOSITION OF THE CASELOAD IS 20 PER CENT MEN, 30 PER CENT WOMEN AND 50 PER CENT CHILDREN.

ENTRY OF THE CASELOAD IS BEING HAMPERED BY THE PRESENCE IN LARGE NUMBERS OF MINES ALONG THE BORDER. FOR SAFETY REASONS THEREFORE ENTRY IS BEING CONDUCTED ONLY THROUGH OFFICIAL BORDER ENTRY POINTS. THE FACTOR OF MINES IS PARTICULARLY ACUTE IN ILAM PROVINCE, ESPECIALLY ALONG THE BORDER AS A RESULT OF THE EIGHT YEAR WAR.

OPERATIONS/COORDINATION
----

21. THE FULL COMPLEMENT OF UN ASSISTANCE UNDER THE HUMANITARIAN PLAN OF ACTION FOR 35,000 HAS ALREADY ARRIVED IN IRAN OR HAS BEEN COMMITTED IN THE FORM OF INTERNATIONAL PROCUREMENT.

STATUS IMPLEMENTATION FIRST UPDATE RHPA
------ -------------- ----- ------ ----

22. FUNDS FOR THE CONSTRUCTION AND PREPARATION REFUGEE CAMPS, TRANSIT CENTRES AS WELL AS ENTRY POINTS HAVE BEEN OBLIGATED AT USD 840,500.

RELIEF MATERIAL FOR 35,000 INCLUDING TENTS, TARPAULINS, BLANKETS, DOMESTIC ITEMS AS WELL AS 10 GENERATORS HAVE ALREADY BEEN RECEIVED. ITEMS SUCH AS SOAP AND DETERGENT HAVE BEEN RELEASED FROM NATIONAL STOCKS AND REPLACEMENTS FOR REPLENISHMENT HAVE BEEN PROCURED AND ARE EXPECTED TO ARRIVE IN IRAN WITHIN THE NEXT FEW WEEKS.

UNDER THE SECTOR INTERNAL TRANSPORT OF NON-FOOD GOODS, CRITICAL ITEMS SUCH AS TRUCKS, VEHICLES AS WELL AS RUB HALL TENTS HAVE BEEN PROCURED AND HAVE ALREADY ARRIVED OR ARE IN TRANSIT.

23. A PLANNING FIGURE OF 100,000 WAS BEING CONSIDERED BY THE END OF MARCH FOLLOWING AN INCREASE IN THE CASELOAD MAINLY IN KHUZISTAN PROVINCE WITH THE COLLAPSE OF THE POPULAR UPRISING IN SOUTH IRAQ. BY 5 APRIL WITH THE COLLAPSE OF THE POPULAR UPRISING IN THE NORTH, THE INFLUX OF REFUGEES BEGAN TO INCREASE DRAMATICALLY AND BY 7 APRIL 1991 THE INFLUX FIGURE IS NEARLY 800,000. THE INFLUX HAS NOT STABILIZED AND IS EXPECTED TO INCREASE.

24. A NUMBER OF CONSIDERATIONS IN DEALING WITH THIS MASS EXODUS IS NOW ESSENTIAL. THE UNHCR OFFICE IN TEHRAN FOLLOWING URGENT CONSULTATIONS WITH THE AUTHORITIES HAVE DIVIDED THE ASSISTANCE PHASES INTO PRIORITY PHASES.

CURRENT EMERGENCY PHASE
----

25. MASSES OF PEOPLE OF WHICH THE MAJORITY ARE WOMEN AND CHILDREN HAVE BEEN IN TRANSIT IN THE OPEN UNDER HARSH WINTER CONDITIONS

0036

FOR [illegible]MBER OF DAYS BEFORE REACHING TH[illegible]RANIAN BORDER. AT THE BORDER IN BAKHTARAN, WEST AZERBAIJAN, KHUZISTAN AND ESPECIALLY ILAM PROVINCES DUE TO THE PRESENCE OF MINES, THEY CAN ONLY SAFELY ENTER THROUGH OFFICIAL BORDER RECEPTION ENTRY POINTS. IN KURDISTAN, ON THE OTHER HAND, WHICH APPEARS TO BE RELATIVELY FREE OF THIS PROBLEM, THERE ARE SIX IDENTIFIED ENTRY POINTS. THIS RESULTS IN FURTHER SUFFERING DUE TO THE ELEMENTS AND HARSH WINTER CONDITIONS. HYPOTHERMIA, MALNUTRITION, AS WELL AS OTHER SYMPTOMS INCLUDING SHOCK ARE COMMON AMONG CHILDREN AND WOMEN. THE CASELOAD WITHOUT EXCEPTION HAS VERY LITTLE IF ANY PROPER WINTER CLOTHING. THE WATER AND SANITATION REQUIREMENTS AT THE THREE NORTHERN PROVINCIAL LEVELS HAVE BEEN OVERWHELMED BY THE SHEER NUMBERS INVOLVED.

PRIORITY NEEDS IN IRAN
----

26. FOOD

WFP IS PROPOSING AN EMERGENCY OPERATION (EMOP) BASED ON 1,000,000 BENEFICIARIES FOR 90 DAYS INITIALLY. THE ESTIMATED QUANTITIES, ONCE THE EMOP WILL BE APPROVED, WILL BE:

COMMODITY	QUANTITY (MT)
WHEAT	31,500
RICE	13,500
VEGETABLE OIL	2,700
PUSLES	2,700
WHEAT	31,500
RICE	13,500
VEGETABLE OIL	2,700

UNHCR WILL PROVIDE HIGH PROTEIN BISCUITS FOR A SUPPLEMENTARY FEEDING PROGRAMME, QUANTITY REQUIRED IS 1,200MT.

27. NON FOOD

THE PROVISION OF TEMPORARY SHELTER BOTH BY THE UN AS WELL AS THE RED CROSS/CRESCENT MOVEMENT WAS FOR 35,000 AND SOME 50,000 RESPECTIVELY. THE ISLAMIC REPUBLIC OF IRAN HAD AN ESTIMATED CAPACITY OF ABOUT 50,000 WITH THE IRANIAN RED CRESCENT SOCIETY, AS WELL AS AN UNKNOWN AMOUNT LEFT OVER FROM PREVIOUS RELIEF STOCKS AIRLIFTED AFTER THE RECENT EARTHQUAKE. FURTHER FLOODS IN SISTEM BALUCHISTAN LAST MARCH HAVE DEPLETED THE NATIONAL STOCKS.

28. THE UNHCR MISSION IN WEST AZERBAIJAN REPORTS THAT SCHOOLS AND OTHER PUBLIC BUILDINGS ARE BEING MOBILIZED FOR THE PURPOSE. THERE ALSO EXISTS SOME EXTRA CAPACITY FOR A FEW THOUSAND IN WEST AZERBAIJAN AND KURDISTAN FROM AN ONGOING UNHCR ASSISTANCE PROGRAMME FOR IRAQI KURDS FROM THE 1988 HALABJA CASELOAD.

29. PROVISION OF TENTS AND IN THE ABSENCE OF TEMPORARY SHELTER OR OTHER FORMS OF SHELTER SUCH AS THE REHABILITATION OF EXISTING STRUCTURES/PUBLIC BUILDINGS DAMAGED IN THE EIGHT YEAR WAR, BUT SUITABLE FOR IMMEDIATE SHELTER REQUIREMENTS, IS A PRIORITY.

0037

30. UNHCR MISSIONS IN NORTHERN PROVINCES REPORT THAT PROVINCIAL STOCKS, AS WELL AS TRANSPORT CAPACITY, ARE NOT ABLE TO ADDRESS THE NEEDS.

31. PRELIMINARY REPORTS INDICATED THE FOLLOWING IMMEDIATE REQUIREMENTS:

DESCRIPTION	QUANTITY
HEAVY DUTY TENTS (FOR 5 PERSONS)	144,455
WOOL BLANKETS	1,490,000
GROUND SHEETS	144,455

A MORE DETAILED LIST OF SPECIFIC SECTORIAL REQUIREMENTS WILL FOLLOW SOONEST, AS REPORTS ON NEEDS AND CONTRIBUTIONS RECEIVED.

32.. FOR CO-ORDINATION PURPOSES, ADDRESSES ARE REQUESTED TO INFORM UNDRO RAPIDLY BY TELEX 414242 DRO CH, FAX 41-22-7335623, OR UNIENET UNDPROREG UNX008 OR THEIR CONTRIBUTIONS.

= ESSAAFI UNDRO GENEVA 414242 DRO CH +

UNDRO EMERGENCY TELEPHONE NUMBER: X-41-22-733 20 10

UNDRO TELEX: 414242 DRO CH

UNDRO FAX: X-41-22-733 56 23

UNDRO ELECTRONIC MAIL: UNIENET ID UNX008

0038

FOR INFORMATION OF UNITED NATIONS SECRETARIAT ONLY
[illegible]t for Distribution or Dissemi[illegible]on

11 April 1991

PRESS CONFERENCE BY EXECUTIVE DELEGATE TO CO-ORDINATE

UNITED NATIONS INTER-AGENCY HUMANITARIAN PROGRAMME

Prince Sadruddin Aga Khan, newly-appointed Executive Delegate of the Secretary-General to co-ordinate a United Nations inter-agency humanitarian programme for Iraq, Kuwait and the Turkish and Iranian border areas, briefed journalists at the Palais des Nations in Geneva Thursday afternoon 11 April on the appeal being launched today. Mrs. Sadako OGATA, United Nations High Commissioner for Refugees also participated.

Stating that he was very pleased to be back after a brief interruption in his work for the United Nations, the Prince said he would not make a long introductory statement on his new assignment but would, instead, respond to their questions. The speaker recalled the history of the establishment of the humanitarian emergency appeal in Iraq by the Secretary-General and said he was happy that it was being launched at Geneva. It was logical that Geneva played a key role in this endeavour, as it was the centre for United Nations humanitarian activities.

As UNHCR and UNDRO had already set up a regional emergency plan, they could not delay in trying to deal with the massive flow of hundreds of thousands of Kurds fleeing the conflict, he said. They had also evaluated the emergency needs of Kuwait, in particular as it involved UNEP in dealing with the oil-well fire disaster, as well as medical needs as evaluated by the World Health Organization. There would also be plans to cope with the uprooted peoples in the entire region. He also referred to the mission of Eric Suy, who had been appointed to lead the United Nations mission to estimate the needs of refugees in northern Iraq.

With regard to these various missions to try to aid all the affected populations, they would have to be able to be "objective, impartial and above all, not politicize developments". It was very important for them to ensure that heretofore, the United Nations system had a unified approach to address all the various problems.

Mrs. Ogata stated that all the agencies, particularly her own, were ready to co-operate with the Prince in his role as Co-ordinator of the United Nations humanitarian programme.

Asked whether he supported the British prposal for a sanctuary in Iraq, the Prince said he in no way supported or opposed proposals by Member States - he was instead seeking lasting solutions which would enable the uprooted people to return to their places of habitual residence. "One could not have another Gaza Strip in the province of Kurdistan - it was much easier to open refugee camps then to close them", he added. Regarding immediate humanitarian solutions as far as the Kurds were concerned, a safe haven might also be seen as being "apolitical", but the problem was where to put the people and how to deal with their needs. They had to get aid to the people. The UNDRO/UNHCR appeal spoke of needs which seemed to be huge, but they represented a small

.../... 0039

amount per refugee. They had to reach the people where they were or else bring them to where the help was. On the other side, they had to monitor the distribution of aid within Iraq.

The genesis of the UNDRO/UNHCR plan being launched was based on an updating of developments and needs, the Prince noted, aimed at displaced persons who had crossed the borders. The appeal the Prince was launching for needs within Iraq was for $117 million. Thus there were two distinct appeals which should not be confused with each other. The $423 million under the UNDRO/UNHCR plan worked out to under $3.00 per person per day.

Unless things changed somehow, it was very difficult for people to go home. One should not compare this situation to the problem at Afghanistan, for example, as every case was specific unto itself. What was fundamental here was the role the United Nations would play. He hoped that Member Governments would give the United Nations the wherewithal to help the uprooted populations go home. He also hoped that conditions in northern Iraq would not be threatened by continued hostilities.

In response to a question, the Prince said he most certainly planned to visit the region in the near future, once the appeal's framework was set up and working. In the meantime, the High Commissioner for Refugees, Mr. Suy and other high-level staff would be visiting the region.

Asked what kind of political reassurances the Kurdish people needed to return to Iraq, he said that the people had to decide such a question for themselves. In his view, prerequisites were a strong United Nations presence and the question of the distribution of aid. They had to be both speedy and pragmatic. UNDP, UNHCR, UNICEF and WHO were currently in Baghdad. It was a small presence, which they hoped to increase and substantially strengthen in coming weeks.

Asked for further details on the Iraq plan as well as what he would say to donors who were sceptical over the presence of Saddam Hussein, the Prince replied that the report addressed the basic needs of the affected populations, as well as the problem of co-ordination and monitoring. It did not cover the needs of Iraq beyond the emergency stage. The success of the plan's implementation hinged on the United Nations presence. Furthermore, if they were going to try to encourage voluntary repatriation, something had to be done about basic living conditions within Iraq, particularly as summer approached.

It was obvious that in some areas it would be difficult to maintain a strong UN presence. However, they should be able to do so in the main distribution areas. The signs at present were that they would be able to establish a "productive dialogue with the Iraqi authorities ... the indications were encouraging", despite the fact that they had not received "iron-clad assurances" from the authorities concerning the actual implementation of tbe plan.

Asked if he believed that the Iranians would have serious logistical difficulties to deal with the hundreds of thousands of displaced persons on their territory, he replied that, to date Iran's attitude in this regard had been "exemplary". Like the Turkish authorities, he said, the Iranians also hoped that the underlying problems could be resolved so that the uprooted populations could soon return to their homes.

0040

* *** *

FOR INFORMATION OF UNITED NATIONS SECRETARIAT ONLY
Not for Distribution or Dissemination

11 April 1991

PRESS CONFERENCE BY HIGH COMMISSIONER FOR REFUGEES

The United Nations High Commissioner for Refugees, Sadako OGATA, told a press conference at the United Nations Office at Geneva this morning that the exodus of Iraqi nationals after the cessation of hostilities had pushed the number of persons seeking asylum in Turkey from 4,700 on 27 February to 300,000 at present. In Iran, the number had grown from 20,000 to 800,000 in the same period. Relief supplies had been pre-positioned in Jordan, Syria, Iran and Turkey for 100,000 persons, in accordance with the plan of action of the International Organization of Migration and the United Nations. As the situation became more acute contacts with the different Governments had intensified. On 1 April she had made a special appeal to the Turkish Government to keep its borders open.

Mrs. Ogata said that she was satisfied with the appointment of Saddrudin Aga Khan as Executive Delegate of the Secretary-General for humanitarian assistance. This was specially significant in this time when the different components of the United Nations must work together to address the problems faced.

It had been estimated, she continued, that the plan of action would require US$ 400 million to cover the needs of 1 million refugees in Iran and 500,000 in Turkey. Until further notice, the contingency targets announced for Syria and Jordan would remain the same. However, the efforts undertaken so far were almost insignificant compared with the magnitude of the problem.

The High Commissioner announced that she would leave tomorrow on a visit of Iran and Turkey to get a first-hand impression of the situation. The trip had been made possible, she said, by a relief flight organized by Norway. This flight would deliver 50 tonnes of supplies. At the request of the Secretary-General, and subject to the views of the authorities concerned, she would also attempt to visit the south of Iraq to assess the situation there.

Mrs. Ogata added that in this time of crisis, the other 15 million refugees around the world should not be forgotten. There were 1.3 million refugees in Ethiopia at present, as opposed to 8 million in January. She would visit that country in the near future. The situation in Sierra Leone and Liberia should also be kept in mind. She was happy to announce, she said, that contacts were on-going between UNHCR and the South African Government on the return of exiles to South Africa. The UNHCR was also following the situation in Southeast Asia and in Central America, from where the Deputy High Commisisoner had just returned.

Asked how the perception of the problem had changed in view of the offer of sanctuary for the Kurds being discussed, Mrs. Ogata said that persons in need of international protection should receive it and that neighbouring countrie should provide assistance.

.../...

0041

Responding to a question on the source of funding for the Plan of Action, Mrs. Ogata said that funding for the regular programmes had been assured from the regular contributions. To fund the special programme the UNHCR was making a special appeal. Three weeks ago, she recalled, she had launched an appeal in connection with the situation in Ethiopia.

Mrs. Ogata had told an interviewer in Berne, said a correspondent, that she favoured the establishment of protection zones for the Kurds. Mrs. Ogata replied that she favoured any arrangement that would assure the protection of refugees. She was not committed to any particular form of safe haven. This was a consideration of a political nature for governments to explore.

Would she discuss with the Iranian authorities the situation of the refugees in that country prior to the current events? asked a correspondent. She replied that they had not gone into the question of which refugees would be discussed with the Iranian Government.

Should the refugees stay in Turkey or should they go back once the situation is settled? she was asked. A solution of a durable nature would involve people going back where they came from, she said.

Representatives of the ICRC and the Red Crescent Society of Iran had said that UNHCR was not present in Northern Iran, said a correspondent. Kamel MORJANE, Director of the UNHCR's Regional Bureau for Southwest Asia, North Africa and the Middle East, said that the UNHCR was indeed present in Northern Iran but not in operation. The organization was not an operational body and as such it needed an implementation partner -- in this case, the Interior Ministry of Iran. The UNHCR had delivered assistance for Iran for 50,000 refugees through the Plan of Action.

Was the UNHCR playing any role to convince other countries to take in Kurds? a correspondent asked. Mrs. Ogata said no other countries were being asked to take in the Kurds. The organization was asking for protection of the Kurds where they were.

How many of the Kurds in Iran had asked for political asylum? Mr. Morjane replied that all the Kurds in Iran were asylum seekers and this was a matter for the Iranian Government to handle. Mrs. Ogata clarified that what the correspondent had probably meant was how many had asked for re-settlement. That was also a matter for individual Governments.

Asked whether there were Shiites among the refugees in Iran, Mr. Morjane said most of them were Shiites.

Were the 300,000 Kurdish refugees all inside Turkey? Mrs. Ogata responded that that was hard to say since they were in a border area.

Some NGOs had affirmed that the supplies being air-dropped to the Kurds were insufficient, said a correspondent. The High Commissionr said, "the only thing we can do is to accelerate the relief effort to assure better delivery ...".

0042

.../...

Responding to another question she said the UNHCR's representative had gone back to Baghdad but that there had been no contacts regarding the refugee situation.

Were there any figures on the number of Kurds crossing daily into Turkey? It was very hard to say how many had crossed the border. Asked whether she planned to visit the affected areas, she replied that she would like to. This would be discussed during her upcoming trip.

Had she any figures on the aid sent so far? She said 800 tonnes had been positioned. There was no breakdown on what had reached the border.

How many UNHCR staffers were in Iran? There were six expatriates and 30 locally-recruited staffers, she said. Some were in the camps, while others were in Teheran.

Did the US$ 400 million figure include efforts from individual countries? She replied that countries did not inform the UNCHR of their efforts so they could not be taken into account. The UNCHR itself would need US$ 238 million.

Asked whether the refugees in the coalition-held area of Iraq would receive UNHCR assistance, Mrs. Ogata answered yes. However, the modalities concerning this zone were still under discussion.

Finally, when asked what she thought of her functions as High Commissioner, Mrs. Ogata said they were enormous. The best way to learn a new job was to be put in a crisis situation.

* *** *

0043

OFFICE DES NATIONS UNIES A GENÈVE

UNITED NATIONS OFFICE AT GE

REGIONAL HUMANITARIAN
PLAN OF ACTION
RELATING TO THE CRISIS
BETWEEN IRAQ AND KUWAIT

SECOND UPDATE

9 April 199

-0044

Introduction and Background

1. This is the second update of the Regional Humanitarian Plan of Action relating to the crisis between Iraq and Kuwait.

2. Iraq's invasion of Kuwait on 2 August 1990, precipitated an exodus of more than one million people into neighboring countries, mainly Jordan. The great majority of evacuees were "third country nationals" from various Arab and Asian countries who were forced by events to return to their home countries.

3. To deliver assistance to these people and facilitate their repatriation a Regional Humanitarian Plan of Action was first issued by UNDRO on 19 October 1990 and then updated on 11 January 1991, few days prior to the dead line set by the Security Council and outbreak of hostilities. The plan and its first update assumed that 400,000 people would need assistance for 3 months in each transit country, and Iran, Jordan, Syria and Turkey, were indicated as the main routes of escape. At that time an appeal was made for funding of start up costs in the order of one fourth of the plan, i.e. USD 38 million.

4. When hostilities began on 17 January, the Humanitarian Plan of Action became operational. However, due to the military operations and logistic constraints the outflow of evacuees, mainly third country nationals, of whom 36,368 were repatriated by IOM.

5. After the cessation of hostilities between the Coalition and Iraqi forces a wave of unrest and turmoil struck Iraq with widespread fighting in the country.

6. As a result, hundreds of thousands of Iraqi nationals, mainly of Kurdish origin, crossed the borders into Turkey and Iran. In a few days some 800,000 Iraqis sought refuge and protection in the Islamic Republic of Iran, while about 300,000 crossed into Turkey.

7. On 5 April 1991, UNDRO on behalf of the participating agencies appealed for USD 137 million together with the start-up costs representing the full funding of the Regional Humanitarian Plan of Action. Today, only a few days later, the number of refugees in the region has almost tripled. Due to the fluidity of the present situation, the indication of more people heading for the borders and, at the same time, taking into consideration the diplomatic efforts to ease conditions in Iraq, the number of 1.5 million refugees in the region has been fixed as a planning figure. In particular, the target refugee population have been estimated at 1 million for Iran and 500,000 for Turkey. Nevertheless, until further notice, the contingency measures for Syria and Jordan remain in force due to the unpredictability of further movements into these countries, altough number of beneficiaries will be adapted to the number of arrivals of refugees and evacuees.

8. In order to assist 1.5 million refugees in Turkey and Iran, the financial inputs required, for a period of 90 days, are estimated at USD 400.2 million, which includes the USD 137 million in the appeal of 5 April. In view of the presence of 1.1 million Iraqi nationals in Iran and on the Turkish border region, donors are requested to give urgent priority to immediate contributions for at least 75 per cent of the total appeal.

0045

Co-ordination Mechanism

At this stage of the crisis, to guarantee the prompt and adequate assistance to the affected population, it is essential to ensure the cohesion and co-ordination of the joint efforts of the International community, the U.N. system, other international organizations and NGO's.

Due to the change in the nature of the ongoing emergency, the U.N. Inter-Agency Working Group and IOM met in Geneva on 8 April 1991 to revise the division of responsibilities among the concerned technical agencies according to specific mandates and fields of expertise.

The situation has become a "refugee" emergency. Therefore, UNHCR is to undertake full operational responsibility, with the other organizations of the U.N. system and IOM playing a supportive role.

The needs are extremely urgent and demand immediate action.

Full co-ordination among the U.N. agencies and IOM will continue to take place at Headquarters and field levels.

In addition, the U.N.-IOM Inter-Agency Working Group in Geneva will also co-ordinate with the newly appointed Secretary-General's Executive Delegate for the U.N. Humanitarian Programme for Iraq, Kuwait and border areas with Turkey and Iran, to facilitate activities in fields of common interest.

In this context, at the Headquarters level UNDRO will continue to provide the framework for overall co-ordination, in full co-operation with UNHCR and the other participants in the Inter-Agency Working Group.

At field level, in close association with the U.N. Resident Co-ordinator, UNHCR is responsible for all relevant negotiations with host governments, implementing partners and donor countries.

In particular, the responsibilty of each agency can be summerized as follows:

- UNICEF: Emergency assistance to vulnerable groups (children under 15 and mothers), particularly responsible for immunization, control of diarrhoeal diseases, safe motherhood, supply of high energy food and clothes for children. In addition, UNICEF will provide technical assistance and procure appropriate equipment to support UNHCR in water supply and sanitation in the camps.

- UNDP: The UNDP Resident Representatives in the field, who act also as U.N. Resident Co-ordinators and UNDRO Representatives, will continue to place a major role in the co-ordination effort by facilitating, when required, contacts at all levels with governments, donors and NGOs. The U.N. Resident Co-ordinator will also continue to lead the local inter-agency emergency groups.

- UNHCR: overall operational co-ordination and direct responsibility for protection and assistance, camp management, provision of camp infrastructure, including water and sanitation, transport of non-food and complimentary and supplementary food items.

0046

- WFP: Technical and operational assistance for mobilization, procurement and transportation of food requirements. In addition, WFP will assist in updating records of food pledges/contributions for this crisis.

- WHO: Technical assistance for design and implementation of public health services for refugees with emphasis on norms and standards, epidemiological surveillance, staff training and supply of drugs and medical equipment.

- IOM: Will continue to be responsible for operational assistance in all programmes concerning internal transportation of refugees and displaced persons, and for the repatriation of third country nationals as required.

Further UNESCO stands ready to provide its contribution to UNHCR- assistance programmes for activities of its concern in the refugees camps.

0047

Proposed Plan for the Islamic Republic of Iran

1. At the time of drafting this update, over 700,000 Iraqi refugees have already arrived in Iran. They are presently located in five western provinces, namely: Khuzistan (68,150), Ilam (2,500), Bakletaran (426,500), Kurdistan (31,500) and West Azerbaijan (243,200).

2. The Iranian authorities are providing emergency assistance to this population, mainly from local resources, with the support of the International Community which has already provided, through the implementation of the U.N. Regional Humanitarian Plan of Action, relief items and camp equipment and material for 35,000 people. Since the beginning of the present influx, the United Nations is delivering additional assistance to Iran, particularly through either the redeployment of stocks held by UNICEF, WHO, WFP and UNHCR in places such as Denmark, Holland, Bulgaria, Germany, Cyprus, Pakistan, etc. or the provision of financial support.

3. However, this effort is almost insignificant compared to the magnitude of the human tragedy which is unfolding in western Iran. Therefore, the burden of the humanitarian response, at present lies with the government and people of Iran.

4. In this connection, the Iranian spiritual leader, Ayathollah Khamenei has appealed to the government and nation to extend whatever assistance necessary to the Iraqi refugees. A special bank account has been established to receive cash contributions from the public, while the Iranian Red Crescent Society and the Imam Relief Committees are utilizing and channelling public donations to the affected areas. Similarly, a presidential decree, issued on 7 April, is requesting all government organizations and companies to put at the disposal of the Ministry of Interior financial and in kind resources.

5. Therefore, in order to provide meaningful support to existing relief efforts in Iran, the United Nations is endeavouring to urgently channel substantial additional relief to Iran in order to assist up to 800,000 people, bearing in mind that there are clear indications that the pace of increase would be maintained or even enhanced. To meet this target, financial and in kind support of an exceptional magnitude is urgently required from the International Community.

6. As mentioned in the update of 11 January, the Iranian authorities are providing the focal point for emergency relief operations, while the United Nations and IOM focus on supporting the government action and assist in mobilizing requested financial support, monitoring the activities, procuring relief supplies and co-ordinating the international response.

0048

Proposed Plan of Action for Jordan

1. As mentioned in the up-date of the Humanitarian Regional Plan of Action of 11 january 1991 Jordan had already a reliable basic infrastructure for about 60,000 to 70,000 persons through a network which included camps managed by ICRC and the Jordanian Red Crescent Society. This capacity was further strengthened through the United Nations input during the first quarter of 1991, which brough the potential reception capacity of the country to almost 100,000 persons.

2. During this period, contrary to several expectations, less than 50,000 third country nationals came to Jordan (only a handful of Iraqi nationals arrived) and most of them were rapidly transferred to their home countries. Presently, there are less than 1,000 persons in the country, and daily arrivals have come down to less than one hundred, while IOM endeavours to transfer them to either their countries of origin or to countries where they are granted residency.

3. In this connection, third country nationals, especially Egyptians, constitute the majority of the current new inflow. While in Jordan, they are assisted by UNHCR and then receive repatriation assistance from IOM through now well established mechanisms. Most of them are repatriated within a matter of days.

4. Since 17 January, and as of 8 April, 28,257 persons had been repatriated. Others returned to their home countries by their own means or through arrangements made by their own governments.

5. Some five hundred persons of concern to UNHCR (mainly Somalis) have not been able to leave the country yet. At their request, IOM and UNHCR are endeavouring to organize the voluntary repatriation of the vast majority; in spite of numerous difficulties to find reliable routes and transportation facilities.

6. Therefore, considering the fact that part of the objectives of the Plan of Action are already met, but also that arrivals are still taking place and that the evolving situation in Iraq may still originate further departures to or via Jordan, a certain level of preparedness should be maintained and the situation closely monitored.

0049

Proposed Plan of Action for Syria

1. During the first months of 1991, only several hundred of Iraqi and third country nationals arrived in Syria, where over 1,000 Iraqis had already arrived during the second semester of 1990.

2. Through the United Nations Regional Humanitarian Plan of Action, camps and stockpiling for 25,000 people were set up and stored. This has been achieved with the full co-operation of the Syrian authorities who, noting the reduced number of arrivals but still concerned by the possibility of large influxes, should the situation in Iraq prevail, have agreed to release part of the relief items provided by the United Nations for redeployment to more severely affected countries. This has been agreed in the understanding that part of the stockpiling will remain in the country, until the situation returns to normal in Iraq. Besides, should large movements to Syria take place, the United Nations will, again, strengthen the reception and assistance capacity of the government of Syria.

3. In Syria, as in Iran and Turkey, those now entering the country are mainly Iraqis, with approximately 1,500 persons having arrived in the last few weeks, bringing the total to some 4,500 people. An additional 330 evacuees have been repatriated by IOM.

4. Considering the relatively small number of arrivals, and the adequacy of resources previously established in the country, UNHCR will maintain stockpiles for some 15,000 persons in Syria and transfer remaining items (for a total of 10,000 people) to Turkey.

5. Moreover, in order to keep an adequate level of preparedness, and considering that the majority of the caseload is made up of refugees, the UNHCR Emergency team will remain in the country until further notice, while the camps established in El Hol (capacity: 10,000 people) and Tartous (capacity: 2,500) will remain operational. Other camp sites are kept on hold, but can be completed at any given time, should new and massive arrivals take place.

6. Therefore, although no additional financial or in kind support is required for the time being, except for ongoing transportation requirements of IOM, preparedness levels for at least 10,000 remain in force.

0050

Proposed Plan of Action for the Republic of Turkey

1. Events have confirmed the pattern of movements of displaced persons from Iraq that was described in the update of the Regional Humanitarian Plan of Action of 11 January 1991. At the beginning of March about 5,000 people had reached the Turkish territory.

2. However, during March, dispite of the still hard weather conditions, far over a hundred thousand Iraqi nationals have left their home areas and headed towards the border between Iraq and Turkey. At the time of the drafting of the present document, according to the Turkish authorities, over 250,000 Iraqi nationals have reached the border area after a dramatic exodus.

3. The number of Iraqi nationals presently within the Turkish boundaries is still unknown, as large numbers are stranded at the border in the Iraqi territory. The government of Turkey has expressed its willingness to assist them, in particular numerous children, women and elderly, who urgently need shelter, medical care, food and other basic assistance. In spite of the deployment of relief items to the border by the Turkish authorities, the needs are such that national resources are insufficient to cope with the emergency.

4. To help a population whose health and living conditions have reached an almost unbearable dimension and hoping to prevent further suffering which might lead to the death of the weakest among the most vulnerable groups (mainly children, women and elderly), the governments of several countries, as well as some non-governmental organizations, are air dropping, or sending through Ankara, into the border area planeloads of relief goods.

5. All United Nations Agencies present in the country and IOM have offered their assistance to the government. Stocks of relief goods available in Turkey or abroad have been released and sent to the reception areas. Several interagency missions have proceeded to the border in order to assess the situation. Their preliminary reports confirm the urgent need for humanitarian assistance.

6. Nevertheless, inspite of the fact that the border has not been officially opened, it seems that a large proportion of the reported 250,000 people who have reached it, has managed to enter the Turkish territory.

7. In these circumstances, financial and in kind support should be put at the disposal of the United Nations for them to provide the Turkish authorities with sufficient relief equipment and material in order to reinforce the existing infrastructure set up during the last phase of the Regional Humanitarian Plan of Action.

8. According to several sources, further movements of thousands of Iraqi nationals towards the Turkish border are still taking place. Hence, the already dramatic situation prevailing in the border area, may still worsen to unprecedent levels of hardship.

9. Therefore, while requesting donors immediate support on behlaf of 300,000 people presently located in or heading toward the border area between Turkey and Iraq, preparedness measures for an eventual further arrival of at least 200,000 additional people should be taken into consideration.

Resource Mobilization

Financial contributions for which the United Nations and IOM are now appealing amount to USD $400.2 million and represents an urgent imperative requirement. This amount is to cover the needs of 1.5 million refugees for three months in Iran and Turkey (one million and 500,000 beneficiaries respectively). Due to the uncertainty of the present conditions in Iraq, will need to be revised as the situation requires.

However, considering the presence of 1.1 million Iraqi nationals in Iran (800,000) and along the Turkish border with Iraq (300,000), donors are requested to give urgent priority to immediate contributions for at least 75 per cent of the total appeal.

Agencies financial requirements for emergency programmes for refugees in Iran and Turkey can be summarized as follows:

Agency	USD
UNHCR	238,521,000
WFP	47,500,000
WHO	31,500,000
UNICEF	23,700,000
IOM	57,040,000
UNDRO	2,000,000
TOTAL	400,261,000

This budget has been established keeping in mind that numerous governments have, or will, offer direct assistance to both countries through bilateral action. Therefore, to prevent duplications and keep track of the overall international effort, donors providing bilateral support to the governments of Iran and Turkey, or through other humanitarian organizations, are requested to announce their contributions to UNDRO. These contributions, to the extent they address the requirements of the U.N. Plan of Action, will be considered as part of the international response.

Details on financial requirements can be obtained directly from concerned agencies, which will be available to provide donors with the elements of organization/country programmes.

As for the past, all agencies will continue to directly seek support from donors with specific fund-raising follow-up actions placed within the context of this Plan of Action.

The present appeal includes the USD $137 million requested on 5 April to activate the full original Plan of Action.

0052

원 본

외 무 부

종 별 :

번 호 : UNW-0894 일 시 : 91 0412 1830

수 신 : 장 관 (국연,중동일,기정)

발 신 : 주 유엔 대사

제 목 : 걸프사태

연: UNW-0852,0873,0888

1. 유엔 옵서버단 (UNIKOM) 참여국은 4.12 오후 현재 확정되지는 않았으나, 연호 32개국에서 에쿠아돌이 제외되고 알젠틴 칠레 태국이 추가되어 총 34개국과 협의중이며, 스위스도 참여의사를 밝히고 있는 것으로 알려짐.

2.사무총장 대변인에 의하면, 연호 UNIKOM선발대는 G.GREINDL 단장 포함 30여명수준이라고 하며 4.13 쿠웨이트 도착예정임.실제배치는 선발대가 쿠웨이트,이락 당국과 사전협의한 후에 이루어질 것이라고함.

3.한편 유엔 난민조사단 (E.SUY 단장 포함 6-7명) 은 4.13 이락도착 예정임.동 조사단과 별도로, 걸프사태 관련 인도적 활동을 총괄하는 연호 S.KHAN 대표도 금주말 이락에 도착한다고함.

4. A.VELAYATI 이란외상은 4.11 자 사무총장앞 서한을 통해 자국유입 이락난민 (90 만명)의 송환과 안전보장을 위한 유엔조치를 요청하였음. (S/22482) 끝

(대사 노창희-국장)

중아국 1차보 [illegible] 정문국 청와대 안기부

PAGE 1

91.04.13 10:41 WG

외신 1과 통제관

0053 

UN 장

원 본

외 무 부

종 별 :

번 호 : UNW-0922 일 시 : 91 0415 2400

수 신 : 장 관(국연,중동일,기정)

발 신 : 주 유엔 대사

제 목 : 걸프사태(안보리)

연: UNW-0894

1. 금 4.15 사무국 및 관련 대표부에 확인한바, 유엔옵서버단 (UNIKOM) 은 연호 34개 회원국에 네팔이 추가되었으며, 스위스를 합쳐 총 36개국으로 구성예정이며 안보리도 이미 동의하였다함. 스위스는 소형 수송기 (2대)제공예정이라함.

2. 영국 I.CLIFF 담당관에 의하면, 난민문제관련 현재 이락방문중인 S.KAHN 유엔대표와 이락 당국간의 난민보호 문제에관한 협의결과가 금명간 발표될 가능성이 있다고함. 한편 동담당관은 지난 4.12. 상임이사국들 (PERM-5) 간에 이락내 난민보호 지역관련 결의안문제를 필요시에 대비하여 협의하였으나 특기사항은 없었다고함. 끝

(대사 노창희-국장)

국기국 1차보 중아국 정문국② 안기부 미주국

PAGE 1

91.04.16 14:48 WG

외신 1과 통제관

0054

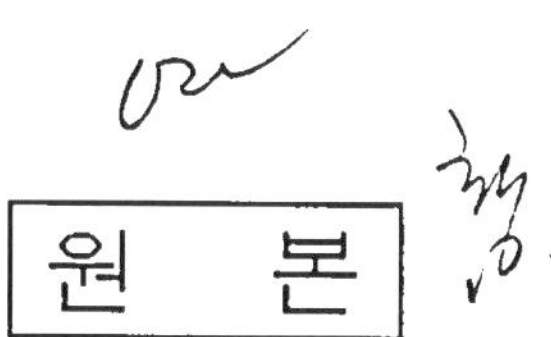

원 본

외 무 부

종 별 :

번 호 : UNW-0937 일 시 : 91 0416 1930

수 신 : 장 관(국연,중동일,기정)

발 신 : 주 유엔 대사

제 목 : 걸프사태(안보리)

연: UNW-0806

1. 휴전결의 후속조치

가. 안보리 휴전결의 (687 호) 이행관련 업무총괄을 위해 유엔사무국내에 설치된 연호 기획단은 그간 수차회의를 갖고 제반후속조치 문제들을 계속 협의하고 있는 것으로 알려짐.

나. 휴전결의 본문 9항에 의거 이락측은 4.18까지 생화학무기, 미사일관련 자료를 유엔사무총장에게 제출토록 되어있는바, 이에대비하여 앞으로 이락 무기파기 관련 업무를 관장할 특별위원회 (SPECIAL COMMISSION)설치를 위해 사무국 (Y.AKASHI 사무차장 주관)과 관련국간에 사전협의가 현재 진행중이라고함.

다. 일본대표부에 의하면 상기 특별위원회는 25명정도의 전문가로 이루어질 것으로 보인다고함. (일본도자국 전문가 추천을 요청받고있음.)안보리상임이사국들이 모두 동 위원회에 참여하게 되며, 의장에는 이집트, 부의장에는 미국이 유력하다고함. 라. 한편 유엔옵서버단 (UNIKOM) 경비문제에 대한 토의가 총회속개회의 (91.4.29-5.3)중있을 것으로 알려짐.

2. 이락 난민구호 활동

가. 4.15자 일본 안보리문서 (S/22499) 에 의하면, 동국은 천만불 공여에 추가하여 구호품, 인력지원예정임. 또한 동 문서를 통해 일본은 미, 영, 불등의 구호품 공수활동에 적극적인 지지를 표명함.

나. 스웨덴은 프레스릴리스를 통해 쿠르드족난민구호를 위한 1,630 만불 지원계획을 발표함. (동국의 걸프사태관련 인도적지원총액 : 6870 만불)희랍도 쿠르드족에 대한 구호품공여 계획을 발표하였음. (규모미상)

3. 이란-이락휴전 합의 위반주장

국기국 1차보 중아국 정문국 청와대 안기부

PAGE 1 91.04.17 10:06 WG

외신 1과 통제관

0055

최근 양국은 88.8월 휴전합의 위반 사례를 안보리 문서를 통해 상호 비난해 오고 있는바, 특히 이란은 4.14. 이락군이 자국 GHAR-E-SHIRIN북부지역 (국경에서 3 KM) 을 공격, 점령중이라고 주장함.끝

(대사 노창희-국장)

外務部 걸프戰 事後 對策班

題　目 : 유엔 이라크.쿠웨이트 監視團 (UNIKOM)構成

91. 4. 17.
中 東 1 課

1. 4.9字 유엔 安保理 決議(689號)에 따른 「유엔 이라크.쿠웨이트 監視團(UNIKOM)」은 아래 36個國,총 1,440명으로 構成될 것으로 알려짐.

- o 安保理 常任理事國(5) : 美, 英, 佛, 中, 蘇
- o 유엔 會員國 (30) : 印度, 싱가폴, 방글라데시, 휘지, 인니, 말레이지아, 파키스탄, 泰國, 네팔, 스웨덴, 카나다, 오스트리아, 티키, 덴마크, 핀랜드, 희랍, 노르웨이, 아일랜드, 이태리, 헝가리, 폴란드, 루마니아, 우루과이, 베네수엘라, 알젠틴, 칠레, 가나, 케냐, 나이제리아, 세네갈
- o 유엔 非會員國(1) : 스위스 (小型 輸送機 2臺 提供)

2. 한편, Greindl 團長(오스트리아軍 少將)을 비롯한 UNIKOM 先發隊 30여명은 4.13 이라크에 到着했으며, 實際 配置는 이라크, 쿠웨이트 當局과 協議한 후 이루어질 豫定임.

3. 지금까지 把握된 國別 派遣人員은 다음과 같음.(該當公館報告)

- o 카나다(300명), 덴마크(145명), 오스트리아(150명), 노르웨이(11명), 스웨덴(10명)　　끝.

0057

원 본

외 무 부

종 별 :

번 호 : UNW-0954 일 시 : 91 0417 2000

수 신 : 장 관(국연,중동일,기정)

발 신 : 주 유엔 대사

제 목 : 걸프사태(안보리)

연: UNW-0937

1.4.16 이락은 식량을 비롯한 필수품 긴급수입 (4개월분)을 위해 약 10억불 상당의 석유수출을 허가해 줄것을 안보리 제재위원회에 요청하여 온바, 동 위원회 의장 (오지리대사)은 이사국들과의 개별협의를 거쳐 4.19 경 위원회소집 예정인 것으로 알려짐.

2.유엔 S.KHAN 대표일행은 이락 당국과 쿠르드족, 쉬아교파 난민보호소 (RECEPTION CENTERS)설치문제를 협의해온바, 금명간 동협의결과가 발표될것으로 관측되고있음. 한편 이락 북부지역에 미, 영, 불 병력이 관할하는 난민수용소 (5-6 개소)를 설치하는 문제에 대한 유엔사무총장 반응은 별첨 총장대변인 발표내용 참조바람.

3.안보리 휴전결의 (687호) 후속조치 문제와 관련하여 다음사항 참고바람.

가.무기폐기 관련 특별위원회

동 위원회 (위원:20-25 명)는 5가지분야 (화학무기, 미사일, 핵무기, 검증, 지원업무)로 나누어 분임반 (UNITS)을 두며, 상당수지원인력 (수백명)을 갖게될 것으로알려짐.위원회 의장국으로 스칸디나비아 국가도 거론되고 있음.

나.배상기금

동 기금 적립을 위한 이락 석유수출수입 공제분은 10-15 프로 수준이 보도되고있음.(4.17자 NYT 지)

첨부:사무총장 대변인 발표내용: UNW(F)-172

끝

(대사 노창희-국장)

국기국 1차보 정문국 청와대 안기부 중아국

PAGE 1

91.04.18 10:39 WG

외신 1과 통제관

0058 

UNW(FI)-172 10417 2008
(국연. 중동일. 기정) 총1매

Asked if the intention of the United States, the United Kingdom and Franco to provido military protoction for tho Kurdc had been discuccod, the Secretary-General said that it was an aspect "on which we have to reflect; because we would first of all like to be in touch with the Iraqis to see what their reaction would be to this military presence on their territory." Did a military presence constitute a problem, he was asked? "It depends", the Secretary-General replied. "If it is a military presence under the UN flag, of course I must obtain the consent, so to speak, of the Security Council. If it is up to countries which do not request the UN flag, the situation is completely different."

Did this mean, the Secretary-General was asked further, that a resolution would be needed before action was taken? The Secretary-General replied "not necessarily. But in any case, we are studying the situation with a great deal of attention so that Iraq's sovereignty shall be respected, and we hope that the Iraqis will understand that the objective of the three countries is quite simply humanitarian, as also is that of the UN. The Iraqi government received my team, Sadruddin Aga Khan and Ambassador Suy, and I shall see them in Paris on Saturday when they will inform me of what they heard and then we shall take decisions."

Asked whether he was hostile to a military presence in Iraq, the Secretary-General said "the word 'military' is awkward. If the objective is humanitarian, I do not see a difficulty, I mean a difficulty from the moral point of view. But from the legal point of view, of course it is a problem."

The Secretary-General was then asked what he thought about the possibility of establishing enclaves in Iraqi territory. He replied "the word 'enclave' has never been used. The term that is used is 'reception centre'. The word 'enclave' has, of course, a connotation which affects the sovereignty of Iraq. I still have good hopes that the Iraqis will accept the reception centres. Whether these centres will have a kind of military observation or not, that is another story."

Asked whether the military presence could be established in Iraq before a reply from the Iraqi government, the Secretary-General replied "No, no, no. For me, we have in any case first of all to be in touch with the Iraqis - it is a question of sovereignty."

UNW-0954 첨부물

0059

주 국 련 대 표 부

군사국안

주국련 20313- 276　　　　　　　　　　1991. 4. 18.

수신 장 관

참조 국제기구조약국장, 중동아프리카국장

제목 걸프사태

표제 관련 안보리 문서를 별첨과 같이 송부합니다.

첨 부 : 상기 안보리 문서. 끝.

주 국 련 대 사

23314

0060

UNITED
NATIONS

S

Security Council

Distr.
GENERAL

S/22480
11 April 1991
ENGLISH
ORIGINAL: ARABIC

LETTER DATED 10 APRIL 1991 FROM THE PERMANENT REPRESENTATIVE OF IRAQ TO THE UNITED NATIONS ADDRESSED TO THE PRESIDENT OF THE SECURITY COUNCIL

In accordance with your request, we transmit herewith the National Assembly decision adopted on 6 April 1991 concerning acceptance of Security Council resolution 687 (1991).

(Signed) Abdul Amir A. AL-ANBARI
Ambassador
Permanent Representative

91-11809 2366j (E)

/...

0061

Annex

In the Name of God, the Merciful, the Compassionate

Republic of Iraq | No.:

National Assembly | Date:

Decision

The National Assembly has decided at its session held on 6 April 1991 to agree to United Nations Security Council resolution 687 (1991).

(*Signed*) Saadi Mehdi SALIH
President of the National Assembly

0062

UNITED
NATIONS

S

Security Council

Distr.
GENERAL

S/22482
11 April 1991

ORIGINAL: ENGLISH

LETTER DATED 11 APRIL 1991 FROM THE PERMANENT REPRESENTATIVE OF THE ISLAMIC REPUBLIC OF IRAN TO THE UNITED NATIONS ADDRESSED TO THE SECRETARY-GENERAL

Upon instructions from my Government, and pursuant to my letter of 4 April 1991 (S/22447), I have the honour to enclose herewith the text of a letter by His Excellency Dr. Ali-Akbar Velayati, Minister for Foreign Affairs of the Islamic Republic of Iran addressed to Your Excellency.

It would be highly appreciated, if this letter and its annex were circulated as a document of the Security Council.

(Signed) Kamal KHARRAZI
Ambassador
Permanent Representative

91-11825 2266f (E)

/...

0063

Annex

Letter dated 11 April 1991 from the Minister for Foreign Affairs of the Islamic Republic of Iran addressed to the Secretary-General

The influx of Iraqi refugees into the Islamic Republic of Iran and other neighbouring countries has surpassed all estimates and preparations, and has reached and indeed passed dangerous levels, jeopardizing the lives of tens of thousands of innocent human beings. In addition to the unprecedented human suffering, this massive influx directly or by consequence is threatening peace and security of the recipient countries and indeed of the whole region.

Even our own estimates transmitted to Your Excellency on 4 April have now been proven by far lower than the actual number of civilians who have up to now sought refuge in Iran. According to the latest information, about 900,000 Iraqis have crossed our borders in the south, centre and the north. Such massive flow of refugees - whose most common characteristic is not ethnicity but fear of repression, hunger, dehydration, and exhaustion of a tedious journey of several days of escaping bullets and freezing cold is bound to lead to nothing but disaster and human tragedy of unprecedented dimensions.

Even if the up-to-now negligible international assistance were to gain some badly needed momentum and substance, it is highly unlikely that any degree of local effort and international relief aid could meet the most primary requirements of the mass of wounded, sick, hungry and cold-stricken refugees and prevent the unfolding tragedy.

It is, therefore, the strong conviction of my Government, that, without prejudice to the sovereignty and territorial integrity of Iraq, the necessary arrangements should be made for the safe and dignified repatriation of these refugees to their homeland. In order to provide a credible alternative to exodus and create the necessary atmosphere of confidence for voluntary return of the refugees, the process should be carried out under active and effective United Nations supervision and with United Nations guarantees for the safety and honour of the affected population, with the necessary safeguards to preclude any hampering - however temporary - of Iraq's territorial integrity.

The magnitude of the disaster requires immediate action by the United Nations without further delay both in order to address the basic needs of the refugees and also to arrange for their repatriation. The Islamic Republic of Iran is prepared to extend its full cooperation to the United Nations and Your Excellency in these efforts.

(Signed) Ali Akbar VELAYATI
Minister for Foreign Affairs
of the Islamic Republic of Iran

0064

UNITED NATIONS

S

Security Council

Distr.
GENERAL

S/22483
11 April 1991
ENGLISH
ORIGINAL: ARABIC

LETTER DATED 10 APRIL 1991 FROM THE PERMANENT REPRESENTATIVE OF IRAQ TO THE UNITED NATIONS ADDRESSED TO THE SECRETARY-GENERAL

On instructions from my Government, I have the honour to inform you of the continued flights of aircraft of the United States Air Force over Iraqi territory, as follows:

1. American-Saudi air activity on 9/10 April 1991 totalled 128 sorties flown by 63 formations and 2 individual sorties, at altitudes ranging from 3 to 9 kilometres and speeds ranging from 700 to 850 kilometres per hour.

2. The aircraft were identified as F-15s and F-14s. The flights were concentrated chiefly over Baghdad, Hashimiyah and Tharthar, their purpose being observation and the creation of a disturbance.

I should be grateful if you would have this letter circulated as a document of the Security Council.

(*Signed*) Abdul Amir AL-ANBARI
Ambassador
Permanent Representative

91-11831 2448b (E)

0065

UNITED NATIONS

S

Security Council

Distr.
GENERAL

S/22484
11 April 1991
ENGLISH
ORIGINAL: ARABIC

LETTER DATED 11 APRIL 1991 FROM THE PERMANENT REPRESENTATIVE OF IRAQ TO THE UNITED NATIONS ADDRESSED TO THE SECRETARY-GENERAL

On instructions from my Government and further to our letters, the last of which was dated 8 April 1991, I have the honour to inform you of new incidents involving Iranian actions in violation of the cease-fire agreement between Iraq and Iran and the flagrant interference of Iran in Iraq's internal affairs, as follows:

1. At 0300 hours on 3 March 1991 four infiltrators attempted to enter Iraqi territory from Iranian territory in the district of Badrah, governorate of Diyala, riding a white pickup truck bearing number 51565 (Sulaymaniyah) and exchanged fire with Iraqi border guards. One of the infiltrators was killed and the rest fled. Ninety-six Kalashnikov rifles and 63 magazines were found, together with an Arabic typewriter.

2. At 0900 hours on 4 March 1991 a group of infiltrators encircled the second border guard headquarters in the region of Al-Shayb, governorate of Maysan, and managed to occupy a number of positions.

3. At 0800 hours on 6 March 1991 a group of infiltrators coming from the Iranian town of Khosrow carried out an attack on the Iraqi Mundhiriyah guardhouse in the governorate of Diyala, and also on the border commands, the border complex, the residence complex and the customs police. The clash resulted in the capture of three officers and 12 persons of other ranks belonging to the Mundhiriyah border complex. At the same time as above, the customs police station of Khanaqin and other official quarters in the town of Khanaqin sustained attacks by infiltrators from Iran, estimated at 150 in number, using military vehicles.

4. At 1930 hours on 6 March 1991 the headquarters of a border guard detachment in the governorate of Wasit was the object of an attack by infiltrators from Iran, who succeeded in taking prisoner 20 soldiers from the ranks of the detachment.

91-11837 2271h (E) /...

0066

5. At 1230 hours on 9 March 1991 a party of infiltrators from Iran estimated at 15 persons attacked the forces of the Iraqi border guard in the area of the Fakkah-Bazargan-Shayb crossroads in the governorate of Maysan. The Iraqi forces managed to kill 11 infiltrators and to destroy the vehicle in which they were riding, which was one of those bearing the words "Hakim Forces". At 1520 hours the infiltrators renewed the attack on the point mentioned above with a force estimated at 300 armed persons, and after fighting with our troops who were present at the site, they succeeded in gaining control of the crossroads. At the same time as above, a detachment of infiltrators estimated at 500 armed persons attacked the Shayb Iraqi border point and succeeded in gaining control of the point at 1650 hours.

6. At 1400 hours on 10 March 1991 the infiltrators succeeded in crossing to the east side of the Diyala River, and at 1500 hours they managed to gain control of the Dabbabah bridge.

7. On 11 March 1991, four Iranian soldiers who had infiltrated near the Ali guardhouse in the area of Naft Khaneh in the governorate of Diyala were arrested.

8. At 1220 hours on 11 March 1991 the infiltrators attacked the town of Khanaqin from the direction of Imam Baba Mahmud and Al-Nahr.

9. At 1315 hours on 12 March 1991 an Iranian helicopter performed a flight over the Chelat guardhouse within Iraq's international borders in the governorate of Maysan for a period of five minutes at a low altitude, then returned to Iranian territory. At 1400 hours on the same day the Iranians opened fire on Iraqi border guards in the vicinity of border marker 50. The incident resulted in miscellaneous damage to three vehicles.

10. On 15 March 1991 the infiltrators clashed with Iraqi troops at the following guardhouses: Sayhah, Arafat, Tariq Ibn Ziyad, Ziyada, Qutaybah and Karmashiyah.

11. At 2330 hours on 19 March 1991 Iranian troops fired on the forward positions of the Iraqi border points in the governorate of Diyala at different times, with various weapons: mortars, 107-mm rockets and machine-guns.

These Iranian acts of violation and others referred to in our previous notes, together with what is yet to be discovered, confirm the full responsibility of the Government of Iran for all the damage inflicted on Iraq as a result of these violations.

/...

0067

I should be grateful if you would have this letter circulated as a document of the Security Council.

(Signed) Abdul Amir AL-ANBARI
Ambassador
Permanent Representative

0068

UNITED
NATIONS

S

Security Council

Distr.
GENERAL

S/22485
11 April 1991
ENGLISH
ORIGINAL: FRENCH

LETTER DATED 11 APRIL 1991 FROM THE PRESIDENT OF THE SECURITY COUNCIL ADDRESSED TO THE PERMANENT REPRESENTATIVE OF IRAQ TO THE UNITED NATIONS

I have the honour to acknowledge receipt of your communication dated 6 April 1991 (S/22456).

You thereby transmit to me the letter addressed to me by the Minister for Foreign Affairs of Iraq, the penultimate paragraph of which contains official notification of the acceptance, irrevocable and without qualifying conditions, by Iraq of resolution 687 (1991), in accordance with paragraph 33 of that resolution.

You have subsequently confirmed to me on behalf of your Government, during our meeting on 8 April 1991, that the above-mentioned letter constitutes Iraq's irrevocable and unqualified acceptance of resolution 687 (1991) in accordance with paragraph 33 of that resolution. You have also transmitted to me the acceptance by Iraq's National Assembly on 6 April 1991 of the aforesaid resolution (S/22480), and confirmed to me, in the name of your Government, that the Revolution Command Council has used its constitutional powers to make this decision legally binding in the Republic of Iraq.

The members of the Security Council have, accordingly, asked me to note that the conditions established in paragraph 33 of resolution 687 (1991) have been met and that the formal cease-fire referred to in paragraph 33 of that resolution is therefore effective.

The members of the Council welcome this development as a positive step towards the full implementation of resolution 687 (1991).

(Signed) Paul NOTERDAEME
President of the Security Council

0069

91-11847 2269h (E)

UNITED
NATIONS

S

Security Council

Distr.
GENERAL

S/22486
11 April 1991
ENGLISH
ORIGINAL: FRENCH

LETTER DATED 11 APRIL 1991 FROM THE PERMANENT REPRESENTATIVE OF LUXEMBOURG TO THE UNITED NATIONS ADDRESSED TO THE SECRETARY-GENERAL

I have the honour to inform you that, following the extraordinary European Council held on 8 April 1991 in Luxembourg, the European Community and its 12 member States have decided to grant special assistance in the amount of 150 million ECUs - equivalent to 185 million dollars - for refugees and displaced Iraqis, particularly Kurds.

In view of the urgency and magnitude of the problem, this programme of assistance was launched on Tuesday, 9 April 1991 in close cooperation with the competent international humanitarian organizations, including UNHCR and ICRC.

This assistance is complemented by the assistance which member States are providing on a bilateral basis.

I should be grateful if you would have the text of this letter circulated as a document of the Security Council.

(*Signed*) Jean FEYDER
Ambassador
Permanent Representative

91-11866 2246g (E)

0070

UNITED
NATIONS

S

Security Council

Distr.
GENERAL

S/22487
12 April 1991
ENGLISH
ORIGINAL: ARABIC

LETTER DATED 12 APRIL 1991 FROM THE PERMANENT REPRESENTATIVE OF IRAQ TO THE UNITED NATIONS ADDRESSED TO THE SECRETARY-GENERAL

On instructions from my Government, I have the honour to inform you of the continued flights of the United States Air Force in Iraqi airspace, as follows:

1. American-Saudi Arabian air activity on 10/11 April 1991 totalled 120 sorties flown by 60 formations.

2. The aircraft, which were identified as F-15s and F-14s, flew at altitudes ranging from 5.5 to 8 kilometres and at a speed of 720 kilometres per hour.

3. The flights took place chiefly over Baghdad, the area south of Baghdad, the Tammuz air base, the area south of Suwayrah, and Diwaniyah, for the purpose of reconnaissance and observation and for creating a disturbance.

I request you to have this letter circulated as a document of the Security Council.

(_Signed_) Abdul Amir AL-ANBARI
Ambassador
Permanent Representative

91-11963 2415d (E)

0071

UNITED
NATIONS

S

Security Council

Distr.
GENERAL

S/22488*
12 April 1991

ORIGINAL: ENGLISH

LETTER DATED 11 APRIL 1991 FROM THE SECRETARY-GENERAL
ADDRESSED TO THE PRESIDENT OF THE SECURITY COUNCIL

I have the honour to refer to Security Council resolutions 687 (1991) of 3 April 1991 and 689 (1991) of 9 April 1991, in which the Council decided to set up the United Nations Iraq-Kuwait Observation Mission (UNIKOM).

I intend to proceed without delay with the deployment of UNIKOM.

Having consulted the parties, I propose that UNIKOM be composed of contingents from the following Member States, all of whom have expressed their readiness in principle to make the necessary personnel available: Argentina, Austria, Bangladesh, Canada, Chile, China, Denmark, Fiji, Finland, France, Ghana, Greece, Hungary, India, Indonesia, Ireland, Italy, Kenya, Malaysia, Nepal, Nigeria, Norway, Pakistan, Poland, Romania, Senegal, Singapore, Sweden, Thailand, Turkey, Union of Soviet Socialist Republics, United Kingdom of Great Britain and Northern Ireland, United States of America, Uruguay and Venezuela. The Government of Switzerland has also informed me of its readiness to contribute to UNIKOM.

I should be grateful if you would bring this matter to the attention of the members of the Security Council.

(Signed) Javier PEREZ de CUELLAR

-----

* Reissued for technical reasons.

91-12071 2456b (E)

0072

UNITED
NATIONS

S

Security Council

Distr.
GENERAL

S/22489
12 April 1991

ORIGINAL: ENGLISH

LETTER DATED 12 APRIL 1991 FROM THE PRESIDENT OF THE SECURITY COUNCIL ADDRESSED TO THE SECRETARY-GENERAL

I have the honour to inform you that your letter dated 11 April 1991 (S/22488) concerning the proposed composition of the United Nations Iraq-Kuwait Observation Mission (UNIKOM) has been brought to the attention of the members of the Security Council. They considered the matter on 12 April 1991 and agreed with the proposal contained in your letter.

(*Signed*) Paul NOTERDAEME
President of the Security Council

91-11994 2286e (E)

0073

UNITED NATIONS

S

Security Council

Distr.
GENERAL

S/22490
13 April 1991

ORIGINAL: ENGLISH

LETTER DATED 12 APRIL 1991 FROM THE PERMANENT REPRESENTATIVE OF THE ISLAMIC REPUBLIC OF IRAN TO THE UNITED NATIONS ADDRESSED TO THE SECRETARY-GENERAL

Upon instructions from my Government, and further to my letter of 3 April 1991 (S/22436), I have the honour to draw attention to the following serious violations by Iraq of the terms of cease-fire between Iran-Iraq.

On 25 March 1991, at 11.30 hrs., two Iraqi helicopters violated the air space of the Islamic Republic of Iran in the city of Manzarieh and Khosravi border area. The Iraqi helicopters left the area after conducting reconnaissance operations.

On 26 March 1991, between 0900 and 1400 hrs., Ghasr-e-Shirin became the target of 30 shells fired from Iraqi artillery and 120 mm mortars. Three shells compacted the Khosravi border post and two shells hit the Khosravi camp which resulted in injury of one border guard.

These violations of the terms of cease-fire have been officially protested to by the Ministry of Foreign Affairs of the Islamic Republic of Iran to the Embassy of the Republic of Iraq in Tehran. The text of the note verbale No. 598/4180 of 11 April 1991 to that effect is herewith annexed.

It will be highly appreciated, if this letter and its annex were circulated as a document of the Security Council.

(Signed) Kamal KHARRAZI
Ambassador
Permanent Representative

91-20006 2247g (E)

/...

0074

Annex

Note verbale dated 11 April 1991 from the Ministry of Foreign Affairs of the Islamic Republic of Iran addressed to the Embassy of the Republic of Iraq in Tehran

The Ministry of Foreign Affairs of the Islamic Republic of Iran presenting its compliments, hereby informs:

1- On 25 March 1991, at 11.30 hrs., two Iraqi military helicopters flew over the city of Manzarieh and its heights as well as the Khosravi border areas. They engaged in reconnaissance operations of the Iranian forces stationed in the region and subsequently left the area without any action.

2- On 26 March 1991, from 0900 hrs. to 1400 hrs., 30 artillery and 120 mm mortar shells of Iraqi military were fired to the territory of the Islamic Republic of Iran in general area of Ghasr-e-Shirin. Three of the shells compacted the border post station at Khosravi and two shells hit the tents of Khosravi camp. As a result of the compact against the wall of the border post station, one border guard was injured.

The Foreign Ministry of the Islamic Republic of Iran draws the attention of the Government of the Republic of Iraq to the repercussions of such hostile acts on the relations between the two countries and herewith calls for their halt.

The Foreign Ministry of the Islamic Republic of Iran avails itself of the opportunity to renew the assurances of its highest consideration.

Hoping for the victory of the oppressed over the oppressors,

Ministry of Foreign Affairs
of the Islamic Republic of Iran

UNITED
NATIONS

S

Security Council

Distr.
GENERAL

S/22491
13 April 1991
ENGLISH
ORIGINAL: ARABIC

LETTER DATED 13 APRIL 1991 FROM THE PERMANENT REPRESENTATIVE OF IRAQ TO THE UNITED NATIONS ADDRESSED TO THE SECRETARY-GENERAL

On instructions from my Government and further to our previous letters, the latest being letter No. 29 of 10 April 1991, I have the honour to inform you that, at 1400 hours on Tuesday, 9 April 1991, a detachment entered Iraqi territory from Iranian territory in the central-sector district of Badrah. It abducted nine Iraqi soldiers and opened fire on one other soldier, who was killed instantly. The detachment then went back into Iran.

This breach once again confirms the Iranian Government's determination to violate the provisions of the cease-fire between the two countries and deliberate policy of infringing Iraq's sovereignty and security. The Government of Iraq repeats its affirmation that the Iranian Government is responsible for all damage resulting from such violations and calls upon that Government to return the abducted soldiers.

I should be grateful if you would have this letter circulated as a document of the Security Council.

(Signed) Abdul Amir A. AL-ANBARI
Ambassador
Permanent Representative

91-20012 2175c (E)

0076

UNITED
NATIONS

S

Security Council

Distr.
GENERAL

S/22492
13 April 1991
ENGLISH
ORIGINAL: ARABIC

LETTER DATED 13 APRIL 1991 FROM THE PERMANENT REPRESENTATIVE OF IRAQ TO THE UNITED NATIONS ADDRESSED TO THE SECRETARY-GENERAL

On instructions from my Government, I have the honour to inform you that the American Air Force has continued to operate flights in Iraqi airspace. Details are as follows:

1. American/Saudi air activity on 11/12 April amounted to 128 sorties flown by 63 formations, at altitudes ranging from 4,000 to 8,000 metres and at an average speed of 750 kilometres per hour.

2. The aircraft, which were identified as F-14s, F-15s and F-16s, flew mostly over the areas of Baghdad, Ramadi, Kut, Diwaniyah and Mosul. Their mission was to carry out reconnaissance and cause disturbance.

I should be grateful if you would have this letter circulated as a document of the Security Council.

(Signed) Abdul Amir A. AL-ANBARI
Ambassador
Permanent Representative

91-20018 2201i (E)

0077

UNITED
NATIONS

S

Security Council

Distr.
GENERAL

S/22496
15 April 1991
ENGLISH
ORIGINAL: ARABIC

LETTER DATED 14 APRIL 1991 FROM THE PERMANENT REPRESENTATIVE OF IRAQ TO THE UNITED NATIONS ADDRESSED TO THE SECRETARY-GENERAL

On instructions from my Government, I have the honour to inform you of the continued flights of aircraft of the United States Air Force in Iraqi airspace, as follows:

1. American-Saudi air activity on 12/13 April 1991 totalled 119 sorties flown by 59 formations and 1 individual sortie, at altitudes ranging from 4,000 to 7,000 metres and at a speed of 720 kilometres per hour.

2. The aircraft, which were identified as F-14s and F-15s, flew mostly over the areas of Baghdad, Kut, Suwayrah and Ba'qubah. Their mission was to carry out reconnaissance and surveillance.

I should be grateful if you would have this letter circulated as a document of the Security Council.

(*Signed*) Abdul Amir A. AL-ANBARI
Ambassador
Permanent Representative

91-12084 2293e (E)

0078

UNITED
NATIONS

S

Security Council

Distr.
GENERAL

S/22497
15 April 1991
ENGLISH
ORIGINAL: ARABIC

LETTER DATED 14 APRIL 1991 FROM THE PERMANENT REPRESENTATIVE OF IRAQ TO THE UNITED NATIONS ADDRESSED TO THE SECRETARY-GENERAL

On instructions from my Government, I have the honour to inform you of the continued flights of aircraft of the United States Air Force in Iraqi airspace, as follows:

1. American-Saudi air activity on 13/14 April 1991 totalled 144 sorties flown by 72 formations, at altitudes ranging from 4,000 to 7,000 metres and at speeds of 800 to 1,000 kilometres per hour.

2. The aircraft, which were identified as F-14s and F-15s, flew mostly over the areas of Baghdad, Habbaniyah, Kut, Aziziyah and Suwayrah. Their mission was to carry out reconnaissance and surveillance and cause disturbance.

I should be grateful if you would have this letter circulated as a document of the Security Council.

(*Signed*) Abdul Amir A. AL-ANBARI
Ambassador
Permanent Representative

91-12090 2902a (E)

0079

UNITED
NATIONS

S

Security Council

Distr.
GENERAL

S/22498
15 April 1991
ENGLISH
ORIGINAL: ARABIC

LETTER DATED 14 APRIL 1991 FROM THE PERMANENT REPRESENTATIVE OF IRAQ TO THE UNITED NATIONS ADDRESSED TO THE SECRETARY-GENERAL

On instructions from my Government and further to our letters, the last of which was dated 13 April 1991, I have the honour to inform you of further incidents involving Iranian actions in violation of the cease-fire agreement between Iraq and Iran, as follows:

1. On 15 March 1991, Iranian forces, estimated at an infantry regiment supported by artillery, attacked the Iraqi Ziyada guard house in the central sector. The attack was preceded by preliminary shelling from Iranian territory by rocket launchers and various types of mortars. At the same time, the Iranian side attacked the Iraqi Sayhah guard house in the central sector, also after preliminary shelling by artillery and rocket launchers. At 2305 hours on the same day the Iranian side attacked the Sayhah border post a second time, and at the same time it attacked the Arafat guard house using machine-guns and rocket launchers.

2. On 19 March 1991, the Iranian side destroyed and blew up the following Iraqi border posts with TNT: Qutaybah, Karmashiyah, Ziyada, Tariq Ibn Ziyad, Ayn al-Id and Shihabi.

3. On 10 April 1991 at 0300 hours, three groups of infiltrators of Iranian forces entered Iraqi territory in the direction of the coast road along the Shatt al-Arab waterway, (illegible) and the Shalamjah road, supported by 107 millimetre rocket launchers. From 0920 hours until 1120 hours on the same day, the Iranian side shelled the southern Majnun area of Iraq with heavy artillery.

These violations confirm yet again the persistence of the Iranian Government in breaking the cease-fire agreement between the two countries and its deliberate attempt to infringe the sovereignty and security of Iraq. My Government once again reiterates the responsibility of the Iranian Government for all damages which these violations have caused to Iraq.

91-12096 2252g (E)

/...

0080

I should be grateful if you would have this letter circulated as a document of the Security Council.

(*Signed*) Abdul Amir A. AL-ANBARI
Ambassador
Permanent Representative

0081

UNITED
NATIONS

S

Security Council

Distr.
GENERAL

S/22499
15 April 1991

ORIGINAL: ENGLISH

LETTER DATED 12 APRIL 1991 FROM THE PERMANENT REPRESENTATIVE OF JAPAN TO THE UNITED NATIONS ADDRESSED TO THE SECRETARY-GENERAL

I have the honour to transmit herewith the text of a statement issued on 12 April 1991 by the Press Secretary for Public Information and Cultural Affairs of the Ministry of Foreign Affairs regarding the air drop of relief materials to evacuees stranded in Iraq.

I should be grateful if you would arrange to have the text of this letter and its annex circulated as a document of the Security Council.

(*Signed*) Yoshio HATANO
Ambassador Extraordinary and Plenipotentiary
Permanent Representative of
Japan to the United Nations

91-12102 2186c (E) /...

0082

Annex

Statement of the Press Secretary/Director General for Public Information and Cultural Affairs of the Foreign Ministry on the airdrop of relief materials to evacuees stranded in Iraq

1. On 10 April, the Government of Japan, in response to requests from Iran and Turkey, with which it enjoys friendly relations, and out of humanitarian concern, decided to dispatch a Japanese disaster relief team to Iran and to send emergency relief materials to Iran and Turkey, where a large number of evacuees, most of whom are Kurdish, are entering from Iraq. This is in addition to the financial aid of 10 million dollars it is extending to international organizations concerned through the United Nations Disaster Relief Coordinator's Office (UNDRO).

2. There are still also a large number of evacuees stranded in Iraqi territory. The situation of these evacuees is even more severe than that of the evacuees who have fled to Iran and Turkey, because it is more difficult to get assistance to them. Despite United Nations Security Council resolution 688, which "insists that Iraq allow immediate access by international humanitarian organizations to all those in need of assistance in all parts of Iraq", international humanitarian organizations have thus far been unable to get adequate assistance to the evacuees in Iraq. Several countries, including the United States, the United Kingdom, and France have therefore been airdropping relief materials for them. The actions of these countries will help to alleviate the suffering of the evacuees in Iraq, and the Government of Japan appreciates and firmly supports their humanitarian activities.

0083

UNITED
NATIONS

S

Security Council

Distr.
GENERAL

S/22500
15 April 1991

ORIGINAL: ENGLISH

LETTER DATED 15 APRIL 1991 FROM THE PERMANENT REPRESENTATIVE OF THE ISLAMIC REPUBLIC OF IRAN TO THE UNITED NATIONS ADDRESSED TO THE SECRETARY-GENERAL

Upon instructions from my Government and further to my letter of 12 April 1991 (S/22490), I have the honour to inform that Iraqi violations of the terms of cease-fire and agreements between the two countries are becoming increasingly more serious and in fact quite dangerous. Shelling the territory of the Islamic Republic of Iran, concentration of military personnel at the international borders, and extending support and encouragement to certain elements to launch military operations against the Islamic Republic of Iran from Iraqi territory were among provocative acts the Iraqi military committed during the past three weeks. Such violations have now turned to downright aggression and occupation of the territory of the Islamic Republic of Iran in northern Ghasr-e-Shirin.

Yesterday, 14 April 1991, one Iraqi brigade crossed the international border and made an incursion into the territory of the Islamic Republic of Iran in northern Ghasr-e-Shirin, at Tang Havan (Sutak post) across from Tazeh Abad. The Iraqi brigade occupied an area 3 kilometres deep inside the territory of the Islamic Republic of Iran.

The Foreign Ministry of the Islamic Republic of Iran has strongly protested to the Government of Iraq for this dangerous violation. Note No. 598/4216 dated 15 April 1991 to that effect, addressed to the Embassy of the Republic of Iraq is herewith annexed.

The Government of the Islamic Republic of Iran calls for an immediate withdrawal of all Iraqi forces from the territory of the Islamic Republic of Iran and it cannot but hold the Government of Iraq solely responsible for both losses of life, material damages and all repercussions of this aggressive act. Under the current circumstances, the Iraqi Government is best advised to find a solution other than creation of an external enemy to face up with her internal turmoil.

It would be highly appreciated if this letter and its annex were circulated as a document of the Security Council.

(Signed) Kamal KHARRAZI
Ambassador
Permanent Representative

/...

0085

Annex

The Ministry of Foreign Affairs of the Islamic Republic of Iran presenting its compliments herewith informs:

Following the numerous violations of the terms of the cease-fire and bilateral agreements between the two countries by Iraqi forces during past three weeks, including shelling parts of territory of the Islamic Republic of Iran, concentration of Iraqi military forces behind the international boundaries, embarking on hit and run operations as well as military actions by elements supported by Iraqi Government - some of whose details have been transmitted to that Embassy in previous notes of this Ministry - giving rise to the prediction that these measures were a prelude to another aggression against the territory of the Islamic Republic of Iran, on 14 April 1991, a brigade of Iraqi forces crossing over the international borders of the two countries in the region of north of Ghasr-e-Shirin in Tang Havan (Sutak border post) across Tazeh Abad embarked on a new military aggression against the Islamic Republic of Iran, occupying an area 3 kilometres deep inside Iranian territory.

The Islamic Republic of Iran strongly protesting this hostile act of the Government of the Republic of Iraq calls for the immediate and unconditional withdrawal of all Iraqi forces from the territory of the Islamic Republic of Iran and holds the Government of Iraq fully responsible for all casualties and damages as well as the grave consequences of this aggression.

The Ministry of Foreign Affairs of the Islamic Republic of Iran avails itself of this opportunity to renew its highest consideration.

Hoping for the victory of the oppressed over the oppressors,

Ministry of Foreign Affairs
of the Islamic Republic of Iran

0086

UNITED
NATIONS

S

Security Council

Distr.
GENERAL

S/22502
16 April 1991
ENGLISH
ORIGINAL: ARABIC

LETTER DATED 16 APRIL 1991 FROM THE PERMANENT REPRESENTATIVE OF IRAQ TO THE UNITED NATIONS ADDRESSED TO THE SECRETARY-GENERAL

On instructions from my Government, I have the honour to inform you that Mr. Ali Khamenei, the spiritual leader of the Islamic Republic of Iran, made a provocative speech against Iraq during the Friday prayer on 5 April 1991. In his speech he asked the Iraqi army and its leaders to rise up against the regime and he incited the Iraqi people to engage in acts of sabotage, describing them as "hostile" acts. This provocative act, constituting as it does blatant interference in the internal affairs of Iraq, clearly reveals the involvement of the Iranian leaders in encouraging and aiding the saboteurs and riff-raff who have destroyed civilian property and been bent on killing innocent people, committing their criminal acts of plunder and pillage, burning the property of the Iraqi people and sowing civil strife, as has been their wont since 1980.

We enclose below several passages from that sermon, in which Mr. Khamenei said, "I wish to impress upon the leaders of the regime that it cannot possibly achieve victory through such acts over its people in opposition, for whenever there is a clash between the regime and opponents of the regime, the victor is bound to be the people, and the vanquished, the regime against the people. Similarly, all the leaders of the Iraqi army must know that whenever they go against the Iraqi people a very dire fate shall be theirs, and that the army which joins the people shall be beloved of the people; the army which stands against the people shall be beaten; whenever the people does not wish these officials to be in power, they must not be so. There is no other solution for the leaders of Iraq, from Saddam Hussein to those around him.

"I appeal unambiguously to the Iraqi people. The Iraqi people must realize fully that this is a crucial moment. If they resist, their fate shall be resplendent. Indeed, this path may be difficult and require struggle and self-sacrifice. Without struggle, no goal can be attained. They must assume these difficulties, which will be of short duration. On the other hand, if they back down and submit to this regime, woe betide them from punishment by the regime, for it shall visit upon them incomparably greater cruelty than that experienced hitherto. Should this regime reassert its control over the people (God forbid), it will take a great revenge on the Iraqi people, who will be forced to continue along the same path, relying on God and asking God for help and making the sacrifices of freedom fighters - then God shall make them victorious."

91-12169 2379j (E)

/...

0087

Mr. Khamenei added, "Here I should like to say one word to you, the Iranian people. Note the arrogance, note his anger at and aversion towards the uprising of the vigilant Muslims and the Islamic resurgence. This is what we are witnessing in the events of Iraq. Saddam today, confronting his people in this barbarous fashion, is the same Saddam as two months ago, about whom all the Western newspapers wrote, painting such a cruel picture of him. If this person is really so, why did you deal with him in previous years? And now when the day has come when Saddam is confronting his people, everyone has fallen silent and all this talk which was being heard against Saddam has ceased. All these newspapers, international propaganda services and all these reports have fallen under the arrogant sway of America and Britain. Now, all the propaganda services are working against the cause of Iraq and the Iraqi people, which is fighting for its rights. They turned a blind eye to the murder committed against the Iraqi people at Najaf and Kerbala and Basra and other cities. All of the northern cities have been placed under an umbrella of silence and this cruel figure has ceased to be. Now, when one looks at international newspapers one sees that what these newspapers are writing against the Baathist regime is the same as what they wrote during the imposed war and that the arrogant propaganda is on the side of Iraq ..."

On this occasion I should like to point out that while Mr. Ali Khamenei is the spiritual leader of the Islamic Republic of Iran, he is also its highest official, by virtue of the Iranian Constitution. Therefore my Government interprets his words as constituting an official incitement to the Iraqi army and people to rise up against the regime. It considers this to be blatant interference in the internal affairs of Iraq and incitement to civil strife, on which the leaders of the Iranian regime have been intent ever since 1980.

I should be grateful if you would have this letter circulated as a document of the Security Council.

(Signed) Abdul Amir AL-ANBARI
Ambassador
Permanent Representative

0088

UNITED
NATIONS

S

Security Council

Distr.
GENERAL

S/22503
16 April 1991

ORIGINAL: ENGLISH

LETTER DATED 16 APRIL 1991 FROM THE PERMANENT REPRESENTATIVE OF ROMANIA TO THE UNITED NATIONS ADDRESSED TO THE SECRETARY-GENERAL

Upon instructions from my Government, I have the honour to inform you that pursuant to paragraph 6 of resolution 688 (1991) of the Security Council adopted on 5 April 1991 Romania has decided to contribute to the humanitarian relief efforts for the Iraqi civilian population in various parts of Iraq. The contribution of Romania is estimated at 13 million lei, and will consist of tents, blankets, clothes and other supplies for humanitarian needs. Romania is cooperating with other countries to ensure the transportation of this humanitarian assistance to its destination.

The decision of Romania to extend such humanitarian assistance to the Iraqi population is consistent with resolution 688 (1991) of the Security Council which was supported by Romania and with the general position of my country on the Gulf crisis as expressed by the Romanian delegation in the Security Council since 2 August 1990.

I should be grateful if you would have this letter circulated as a document of the Security Council.

(Signed) Aurel-Dragos MUNTEANU
Ambassador
Permanent Representative

91-12182 2189c (E)

0089

FOR INFORMATION OF UNITED NATIONS SECRETARIAT ONLY
Not for Distribution or Dissemination

5 April 1991

PRESS BRIEFING BY EDOUARD BRUNNER, SPECIAL REPRESENTATIVE TO MIDDLE EAST

Following his recent appointment as the Secretary-General's Special Representative to the Middle East, Ambassador Edouard Brunner of Switzerland briefed correspondents at today's noon briefing.

Mr. Brunner said he was starting his new position with a meeting with the Secretary-General this afternoon, and a round of talks with the representatives of the member States of the Security Council. He would leave tomorrow for Geneva, after which he would visit the capitals of the permanent members of the Security Council. He would not visit the Middle East until May, "most probably with the Secretary-General", he added.

Although much activity at the moment centred around events in the Gulf, he said, the Middle East was still in the minds of many people and he would try and learn more about their thoughts on how to solve the issue during talks in the next weeks.

In reply to a question, Ambassador Brunner said he was not familiar with the plan proposed by the Government of Israel for a preliminary conference between Israel and Arab representatives. However, he would discuss any thoughts on the matter with the parties involved.

Did he see it as his ultimate goal to convene a Middle East peace conference in accordance with Security Council resolutions 242 (1967) and 338 (1973)? Mr. Brunner was asked. The goal for the time being, he said, was to bring peace to the area.

When asked whether the United States was considering convening a conference chaired by the Soviet Union and the United States, not under the United Nations chapeau, to lead to bilateral contacts, he said he had not heard of this.

To a question on what he thought the main difference between his role and that of Gunnar Jarring would be, and whether he expected to play a more active role than his predecessor, Mr. Brunner said events in the region had determined the extent of Mr. Jarring's role. There was much talk now of windows of opportunity, he said, but he did not know "how wide open these windows will be". He would be active in proportion to the possibilities, he added.

He was asked what made him think he could eventually be more active than Mr. Jarring. He did not think that, he answered. He could only hope. Before giving an assessment of any possible activities, he would have to hear from the principal actors in the region on what their thoughts were.

In reply to a question, he said many people realized after the war in the Gulf that a serious effort would have to be made to bring peace to the

(more)

0090

3114B

region. How that should be done, he could not say at this moment. He added that deadlocks had existed within the United Nations and the Security Council on this particular problem until a few months ago, but now a different atmosphere prevailed between the permanent members of the Council, which led to more hope.

He was asked how he thought the Gulf war affected his mission and whether he agreed with the general assessment that it improved the chances of peace in the Middle East. Ambassador Brunner said that before the war, the chances were estimated as being rather slim, and no one was very hopeful. But he had begun to hear from many parts of the world the phrase "window of opportunity" following the Gulf war.

Asked whether his mandate precluded talks with the Palestine Liberation Organization (PLO), he said that was one of the questions he would discuss with the Secretary General this afternoon.

When asked to share some of the thinking of United States Secretary of State James A. Baker, Mr. Brunner said the American approach was a very flexible one, generally speaking, favouring a "double-track" approach, but the details needed to be worked on. What was important was that the United States had shown very quickly after the war its intention to try seriously to bring about peace in the region. He personally believed that something visible had to happen in the next six months to show that there was progress.

A correspondent referred to the provision made for the elimination of Iraq's weapons of mass destruction in setting up a mechanism for regional security, and asked Mr. Brunner whether he could play a role in that wider aim. He replied that there were, besides the question of talks between the interested parties in the region, two other problems which dominated the scene. Those were arms control in the region and the quality of those arms; and, in a very wide sense, the economic approach to the whole region.

If there was a serious attempt at curbing the export of certain types of arms, he said, that could, perhaps, bring about a meeting or conference to look at that problem. However, such an approach would have to be a multilateral one involving countries supplying arms as well as the countries in the region.

Asked what the effects would be if there was no progress in the next six months, Mr. Brunner said it would be a pity after all the efforts that would be made, such as the "troika" of the European Community that travelled around the region and the Italian/Spanish plan for a conference between countries in the Mediterranean.

Would his mandate allow him to implement some of his own ideas? Mr. Brunner was asked. He said he thought the Secretary-General would expect him to make a contribution based on talks in the next weeks.

In reply to a question on what his title implied, he said it was a large mandate, and much would depend on the situation, on what he was invited to do or not to do, and on the role the partners in the region wished the United Nations to play.

(more)

0091

A correspondent said Council resolution 242 (1967) included a formula for peace, and asked Mr. Brunner if he was committed to that formula. "What we are looking for in this region is peace", he replied, adding that there were many ways to bring about peace.

In reply to further questions, he said he had not been in touch with the PLO, and that for the time being he would not be going to Israel.

* *** *

0092

Press Release ND/318
15 April 1991

TWO EMERGENCY APPEALS FOR IRAQI REFUGEES AND VULNERABLE GROUPS IN IRAQ PRESENTED AT UNDRO INFORMATION MEETING

Two international emergency appeals for US $400.2 million and US $178 million respectively to assist 1.5 million Iraqis who are seeking refuge in Iran and Turkey, and to address the needs of vulnerable groups within Iraq, were presented today to representatives of the international donor community at an information meeting convened by the Office of the United Nations Disaster Relief Co-ordinator.

The larger appeal for hundreds of thousands of Iraqi nationals, mainly of Kurdish origin, who crossed the borders into Turkey and Iran in the last week, was presented by the UN Disaster Relief Co-ordinator, M'hamed Essaafi, as the second update of the Regional Humanitarian Plan of Action - a collective effort by HCR, WFP, WHO, UNICEF and the International Organization for Migration (IOM), co-ordinated by UNDRO since last October. Originally, the plan of action was intended to cater to the needs of over one million "third-country nationals" from various Arab and Asian States, who poured into neighbouring countries after Iraq's invasion of Kuwait on 2 August 1990. The first update of the plan of January 1991 assumed that 400,000 additional people would need assistance for three months in the four transit countries: Iran, Jordan, Syria and Turkey.

However, as Mr. Essaafi explained, the plan was overtaken by events as 800,000 Iraqis poured into Iran within a few days. A swift rise in the numbers of asylum-seekers was also registered in Turkey. On 3 April, refugees in Turkey numbered about 10,000. By 12 April, the Turkish authorities reported that approximately 400,000 had reached the border area.

(more)

0093

The Co-ordinator informed the representatives of Permanent Missions in Geneva, United Nations Agencies and Non-Governmental Organizations attending the meeting that due to the changing nature of the emergency, which had clearly become a "refugee situation", UNHCR would be undertaking full operational responsibility, with the other organizations of the UN system and the IOM playing a supportive role. The High Commissioner for Refugees, Mrs. Sadako Ogata, and the Director-General of IOM, Mr. J. Purcell, whose organization has been responsible for repatriating large numbers of third-country nationals, attended the meeting and also stressed the urgency of the needs.

The new plan of action provides for 1.5 million people for three months, mainly in Iran and Turkey, with over half the contributions called for going to UNHCR. Mr. Essaafi specified that the situation would continue to be monitored in Jordan and Syria. He paid tribute to the Governments of Iran and Turkey "who have so admirably responded by alleviating the plight of the refugees with their own resources". The Government of Turkey, he said, had expressed its intention of providing more facilities for the refugees "as and when the international community's contributions were received to increase the capacity of camp, medical and feeding facilities". Mr. Essaafi also thanked the Governments of Canada and Japan for the contributions they had made recently through UNDRO.

Before giving the floor to the newly-appointed Executive Delegate of the Secretary-General, Sadruddin Aga Khan, Mr. Essaafi pointed out that the figures presented in the Regional Humanitarian Plan of Action were only indicative and did not contain unforeseen elements that would undoubtedly arise. He also called on governments to make known their contributions, be they bilateral or through other humanitarian organizations, so that they could be taken into account in the general financial framework of the plan. Finally, he stressed that the Regional Humanitarian Plan of Action appeal related only to activities in or by Iran, Jordan, Syria and Turkey, and not to operations and measures inside Iraq and Kuwait.

The appeal for US $178 million, based on the report of a UN inter-agency mission sent by the Secretary-General to Iraq, from 10 to 17 March, to assess urgent humanitarian needs in that country, following the cessation of hostilities was presented by the Executive Delegate of the Secretary-General. The 52-page document detailed food, agricultural, health, water, sanitation and nutritional requirements for the most vulnerable segments of the population.

The Ambassadors of Iran and Turkey while stressing that their Governments would maintain an "open-door" policy, asked for every possible solution to be examined to allow for the safe return of the refugees to their country. The Permanent Representatives of France, Japan, the United-Kingdom, the United States, as well as the Representative of the EEC reported on the actions already carried out or planned by their Governments.

* *** *

0094

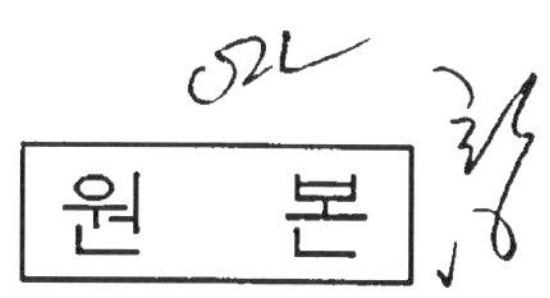

원 본

외 무 부

종 별 :

번 호 : UNW-0989 일 시 : 91 0419 2100

수 신 : 장 관(국연,중동일,기정)

발 신 : 주 유엔 대사

제 목 : 걸프사태(유엔동향)

연: UNW-0954

1. 안보리 제재위원회는 금 4.19 이락의 연호 필수품 긴급수입 및 이를 위한 석유수출 (약10억불 상당)허가신청 문제를 토의하였으나, 여러 이사국들이 본건 필수품목, 석유수출물량 및 수출대상국에 관해 추가 해명을 요구함에 따라 동위원회의장(오지리) 주재 개별협의회를 거쳐 다음주 재 토의 예정임.

2.이락은 안보리 휴전결의 (687) 에 의거 자국의 폐기대상 무기현황 (화학무기, 미상일,핵)을 4.18유엔 사무총장에게 통보 (핵 관련현황은 IAEA에도 제출) 해온바, 이락측이 동 통보문서 배포를 요청하지 않은관계로 유엔문서로 배포되지는않을것이라고함. (보도에 의하면, 화학무기, 스커드미사일 보유는 시인하였으나 핵무기 보유는 부인)

3.안보리는 사무총장이 제출한 이락 무기폐기 업무를 관장할 특별위 설치계획을 NO-OBJECTIONPROCEDURE (일정시점까지 이의제기 이사국이 없는경우 자동승인)에 의거 4.19 오후 승인한바, 당관에서 입수한 동 사무총장 관련 보고서를 별첨송부함.

4.유엔옵서버단 (UNIKOM) 은 본대 (300 명)대부분이 금주 배치완료 예정이며, 다음주까지는 여타 지원병력들도 배치지역에 도착예정이라고 하는바, 동 옵서버단 구성내용은 별첨참조 바람.

5.표제관련 구호업무를 총괄하고있는 S.KHAN유엔대표가 4.19 제네바에서 가진 기자회견 요지를 별첨송부함.

첨부:1.특별위 설치계획복서

2. UNIKOM구성내용

3. S.KHAN 대표기자회견 요지:UNW(F)-177

끝

(미사 고창의-국장)

국기국 1차보 중아국 정문국 청와대 안기부

PAGE 1 91.04.20 10:23 WG

외신 1과 통제관

0095

Distr.
GENERAL 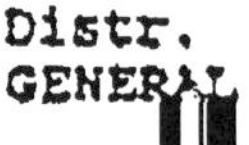

April 1991

ORIGINAL: ENGLISH
PRELIMINARY DRAFT

Report of the Secretary-General

Implementation of paragraph 9 (b)(i)
of Security Council resolution 687 (1991)

1. The present report is submitted in pursuance of Security Council resolution 687 (1991) of 3 April 1991. In paragraph 9 (b) (i) of that resolution the Council decided that the Secretary-General should submit to it for approval a plan calling inter alia for the forming of a Special Commission to carry out the tasks ennumerated in paragraphs 9 (b) (i-iii), 10 and 13.

2. To enable the Special Commission to play its proper part in assessing information and preparing and planning the activities envisaged in Section C of the resolution, including assisting the Director-General of the International Atomic Energy Agency to present a plan within his designated area, there is an urgent need for the Special Commission to be established. The implementation, within or near the timeframes indicated by the resolution, of all the mandates in section C will in fact depend on the existence of the Commission, and its advice in the early stages would be essential.

3. Subject to the approval of the Security Council, it is my intention to set up the Special Commission as described below and

JW-0989
14

7-1

1991-04-10 15:03 212 3701954 P.02

0096

to make all necessary arrangements for it to begin implementation of its tasks.

4. In setting up the structure for the Special Commission I wish to emphasize the need for an efficient and effective executive body. I propose that it should have an Executive Chairman with a Deputy Executive Chairman to assist the Chairman in carrying out his functions. Following the appointment of these two individuals the remainder of the Special Commission would be established on an expanding basis as appropriate individuals are found to fill the positions. Under the Executive Chairman and Deputy Executive Chairman, the planning and operational direction of the functions of the Commission should be carried out by five groups, each under a head of group with appropriate executive experience in the assigned field and each consisting of a small number of experts. The major areas of responsibility would be: biological and chemical weapons; ballistic missiles; nuclear weapons capabilities; future compliance and operations support. Thus the formal membership of the Special Commission would be of the order of 20 to 25 persons.

5. Although the specific timing of the Special Commission's activities have yet to be determined, under the provisions of Section C of the resolution, most of the Commission's functions are time limited. With the accomplishment of the tasks entrusted to four of the five groups, the major active phases would be completed and those four groups would cease to exist. The fifth group would continue in order to implement the activities relating to future compliance.

6. In carrying out its various tasks the Special Commission would be assisted by a number of technical experts serving as inspectors, disposal teams and field support officers. These

7-2

- 3 -

experts would be either specially engaged for this purpose or made available to the Commission by Member States. Their total number would have to be determined in relationship to the size of the task to be carried out. This can be fully assessed only after the baseline field inspections have been completed by the Special Commission, but it is likely that the personnel involved will number in the several hundreds.

7. As soon as the baseline field assignments of the Special Commission and of the International Atomic Energy Agency have been completed, I intend to work out, in consultation with the Commission, a detailed plan for the implementation of the various tasks entrusted to it, and to submit it to the Security Council for its approval.

8. Following the acceptance by the Government of Iraq of the Security Council resolution 687 (1991), expressed in the penultimate provision of the letters addressed respectively to me and to the President of the Security Council on 6 April 1991 by the Minister for Foreign Affairs of the Republic of Iraq, the execution of the baseline field inspections and the subsequent implementation plan is predicated on the assumption of full co-operation by the Iraqi authorities. The Special Commission would enjoy the relevant privileges and immunities provided for in the Convention on the Privileges and Immunities of the United Nations. Members of the Special Commission, experts attached to it and other specialists assigned to assist it in the implementation of Section C of the Security Council resolution 687 (1991), would be regarded as experts on mission within the meaning of Article VI of the Convention on the Privileges and Immunities of the United Nations, relevant Annexes to the Convention on the Privileges and Immunities of the Specialized Agencies and Article VII of the Agreement on the Privileges and

Immunities of the IAEA, respectively. Taking into account the tasks to be performed by the Special Commission, it may be necessary to conclude special agreements covering the status, facilities, privileges and immunities of the Commission and its personnel. The existing agreements mentioned above would equally apply to tasks to be performed in Iraq by the IAEA and could be supplemented by special agreements, should the need arise.

9. While the financial implications relating to the establishment and functioning of the Special Commission cannot at this stage be assessed with accuracy, it is anticipated that certain start up funds will be required. This sum will defray the initial costs of establishing the Headquarters of the Special Commission in New York as well as a field office in the region and the early deployment of advanced elements of the operation in the field. This sum will also defray some of the initial costs to be borne by the IAEA in carrying out the assignments entrusted to it under Section C of the resolution. Comprehensive cost estimates will, of course, be provided to the Security Council as soon as possible. It is my intention, however, to proceed in this regard on the basis of the following principles: (a) that Member States whose nationals will serve on the Commission or assist it in the discharge of its responsibilities should be responsible for their salaries, while the United Nations will bear the costs of travel and daily subsistence, and (b) that the whole exercise will be carried out in the shortest possible time, with a progressive decrease in the number of technical experts and of members of the Special Commission as various operations are completed.

7-4

TOTAL P.25
TOTAL P.05

COMPOSITION OF THE UNITED NATIONS IRAQ-KUWAIT OBSERVATION MISSION (UNIKOM)

19 April 1991

1. <u>Military Observers</u> (300 in all)

Five Permanent Members of the Security Council
Pakistan
Fiji, Ghana, India, Ireland, Kenya, Malaysia, Norway, Uruguay
Argentina, Austria, Bangladesh, Denmark, Finland, Greece, Hungary, Italy, Nigeria, Pakistan, Poland, Romania, Senegal, Singapore, Sweden, Thailand, Turkey, Venezuela
Canada

2. <u>Support Units</u>

Canada: Engineers unit (300 all ranks)
Chile: Helicopter unit (6 choppers; crew of 50)
Switzerland: Fixed Wing unit (2 planes; crew of 3)
Norway: Medical unit (50 all ranks)

3. <u>Logistics units</u>

Denmark: Movement Control and Postal unit (25 all ranks)
Sweden: Supply unit (35 all ranks)

4. <u>Infantry Units</u>

On loan from UNFICYP (Cyprus)--two companies:
Austria
Denmark

On loan from UNIFIL (Lebanon)--three companies plus:
Fiji
Ghana
Nepal
plus Norway/Sweden (composite logistics unit)

ikom-4

7-5

0100

FOR INF[illegible]TION OF UNITED NATIONS SECRETA[illegible]T ONLY
Not for Distribution or Disseminat[illegible]

19 April 1991

PRESS CONFERENCE BY EXECUTIVE DELEGATE TO CO-ORDINATE
UNITED NATIONS INTER-AGENCY HUMANITARIAN ASSISTANCE

Prince Sadruddin Aga Khan, Executive Delegate of the Secretary-General to co-ordinate a United Nations inter-agency humanitarian programme for Iraq, Kuwait and the Turkish and Iranian border areas, briefed journalists at the Palais des Nations in Geneva Friday, 19 April, on his recent trip to Iraq. They had brought back an agreement with Baghdad which would enable them to set in motion the Organization's efforts to promote the voluntary return of Iraqi displaced persons as well as humanitarian measures to avert new flows of refugees.

He said he attached great importance to the co-operation of the Iraqi authorities, who seemed to be very open in this regard. Freedom of movement, of access, of communications, the presence of United Nations staff in the area, the input by the Red Cross, the ICRC and other humanitarian agencies - all these provided a large field for them to operate in order to try to stabilize the situation of an extremely vulnerable population. The agreement had been signed and it was now time to translate it into action. Nonetheless, it was clear that many problems remained to be resolved.

He said he would be meeting shortly with the Secretary-General in Paris to discuss such questions as the practical aspects of implementing the humanitarian assistance programme and fund-raising.

Asked who the "Co-ordinator" was, the Prince replied that that was his counterpart in Iraq, a Swede who was a senior member of the United Nations Development Programme (UNDP). Co-ordination had to be done at the field level and the Co-ordinator would report directly to the Executive Delegate at Geneva.

In response to a question concerning how the United Nations intended to guarantee the safety of the Kurds, the Prince replied that "the United Nations is not a police force". However, it would seek to establish a climate of confidence, among other things, by assisting the returning populations, by setting up relay stations, and assuring that there was no discrimination in assistance to the various groups in the country. It was importent to set up a United Nations radio communciations system on both sides of the border, he added. Iraq's concern for its territorial integrity and sovereignty were also covered by the agreement. The operations to be undertaken should be completed by the end of the year.

The Prince said he saw no reason why reconciliation was not possible. There was no way for the United Nations to establish in a few days' time the sort of humanitarian relief operations needed. "We are no match for hundreds of helicopters and thousands of troops," he noted, referring to the recent relief efforts undertaken by the United States and other allies.

.../...

7-6

0101

Asked whether the United Nations staff in the region intended to co-operate with the allies in this respect, he said that inevitably the United Nations had a presence in the host country, so it was in touch with what was being done there. The United Nations also had to have a very clear idea of what was being done bilaterally in order to avoid duplication of effort. Inevitably there had to be liaison and contacts between the different groups. It was still too early to say how many centres would be needed. The size of a centre would depend on the needs and size of the population in the region to be served by it. These details were being worked out now by his Co-ordinator in Iraq.

However, "all that would remain an empty shell unless we get the money up front and unless bilateral sources can muster the millions of dollars needed for the operation". The international community had to put its money where its mouth was, he added.

In reply to questions, the Prince said he had not met with Saddam Hussein during his visit and furthermore, as he was not a member of the Revolutionary Council, he did not know why the Iraqi authorities had changed their minds about letting foreign forces on their territory. An additional $400 million had to be added to the amounts already announced for United Nations humanitarian programmes in the region, since the situation was constantly evolving there. Asked if he had any money to start relief work or just pledges, the Prince said that the United Nations system had not waited until the signing of the agreement. Relief activities had already begun, but the ongoing process had to be continued and strengthened.

The Executive Delegate said he could not state officially what the Iraqi authorities were going to say or do following the forthcoming meeting between them and the United States military officials. The United Nations efforts were strictly humanitarian. Concerning the situation in the south, the Blue Helmets would have to deal with very sensitive groups. The United Nations had to do everything possible to ensure that no human rights violations or settling of accounts occurred.

Eric Suy said he had nothing to add to what the Prince had already said and made a number of observations concerning conditions in the country. The needs of the refugees, whether in the north or the south, where there were fewer of them, were enormous.

Asked what the Kurds could be offered in order to gain their confidence, the Prince replied that the terms of reference were clear in the agreement and that parameters had been elaborated. He did not want to get involved in the arrangements covering the cease-fire. The United Nations concern in the region was strictly humanitarian, it could not act as a police force there. Personally, he said, if he was a Kurd he would hope to have the right to live in peace in his own country, something anybody would want. There was not just one category of Kurd - not all of them had been involved in the insurgency, so each refugee would have to decide for himself the question of going home.

Asked if the United Nations would agree to the handing over of the camps now being set up by the United States and other allies, he said that such a move could not be made unilaterally; there would have to be very serious discussions about the modalities for such a transfer. As to whether the enormous flow of bilateral aid now headed for the region ought to be multilateral, the Prince said that he worked for a multilateral organization and that in principle aid should be multilateral. However, it also had to be effective

7-7

0102

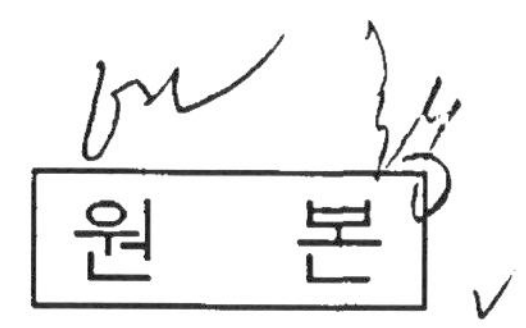

외 무 부

종 별 :

번 호 : UNW-1010 일 시 : 91 0423 1900

수 신 : 장 관(국연,중동일,기정)

발 신 : 주 유엔 대사

제 목 : 걸프사태(유엔동향)

1.금 4.23. 유엔측 발표에 의하면, 지난 4.18 이락난민구호 관련 이락-유엔간 합의 (MOU) 에 의거 UNHCR 선발대 (10-15 명) 가 금주 바그다드 도착예정이며, 동 선발대는 터어키, 이란과의 접경각지역에 현장사무소 (FIELD OFFICES) 를 설치할것이라고 함.또한 UNHCR 은 쿠웨이트와의 접경지역난민 (다국적군 보호하의 약 3 만명) 에대해서도 인도적 지원계획이며, 그동안 동난민의 제3국 정착을 위해 관련국들과 교섭해온 것으로 알 려짐.

2.상기 이락-유엔간 난민구호합의와 관련한 A.HUSSEIN 이락외상 명의 사무총장앞 4.21 자 서한이 금일 안보리문서 (S/22513) 로 배포된바 동서한에서 이락측은 미군등 외국군에 의한 자국북부 ZAKHOU 지역 난민수용소설치 움직임을 주권및 영토 보전 침해행위라고 비난하면서 유엔이동 수용소들을 접수할 것을 요청하였음.금 4.23 정오 브리핑에서 사무총장 대변인 (N.YOUNES) 은상기 이락측 요청을 유럽방문중인 사무총장 (4.24 귀임예정)에게 보고하였으며 유엔은 동 요청을 현재 검토하고 있다고 언급함.

3.한편 안보리 휴전결의에 의거 사무총장은 이락배상기금 및 동기금 운영위 설치계획을 곧안보리에 제출예정인 것으로 알려진바, 동운영위는 집행부 (GOVERNING COUNCIL : 약 15개국참여)및 전문 지원인력 (PANEL OF EXPERTS) 으로 이루어질 것으로 관 측됨.끝

(대사 노창희-국장)

국기국 1차보 중아국 정문국 청와대 안기부

PAGE 1

91.04.24 09:54 WG

외신 1과 통제관

0103

원 본

UN

외 무 부

종 별 :

번 호 : UNW-1050 일 시 : 91 0425 2130

수 신 : 장 관(국연,중동일,기정)

발 신 : 주 유엔 대사

제 목 : 걸프사태(유엔동향)

연: UNW-1010

1. 금 4.25 유엔측 발표에 의하면, 난민구호관련 합동반 (UNHCR, UNV,IMO, UNDP 전문가 약 30명)이 금주발 바그다드 도착예정이라고 하며, 난민구호센타 (HUMANITARIAN CENTERS) 설치 추진과관련 B.BERNANDER 유엔대표 (바그다드 상주)가 현재 이락북부지역 현지조사중이라고함.

2.이락은 연호에이어 4.24 자 유엔사무총장앞 외상명의 서한 (S/22531) 에서 이락 ZAKHO 지역 미군관할 난민수용소를 유엔이 접수해줄것을 재요청해온바, 사무총장은 미, 영, 불 및 이락측과 본건에 관해 협의중인 것으로 알려짐. (별첨안보리문서및 사무총장 기자문답 참조)

3.한편 중국은 이란, 터어키내 이락난민을 위해 270만불 상당의 구호품을 지원키로 결정하였음을 4.24 자 동국대표부 프레스릴리스로 배포하였음.

첨부:1.안보리문서

2.사무총장 기자문답: UNW(F)-182

끝

(대사 노창희-국장)

국기국 1차보 중아국 정문국 청와대 안기부

PAGE 1

91.04.26 10:39 WG

외신 1과 통제관

0104

S/22531
English
Page 2

UNW(FO)-182 10425 2130
(국련. 중동일. 기정)

총 2매

Annex

Letter dated 24 April 1991 from the Minister for Foreign Affairs of Iraq addressed to the Secretary-General

At 1840 hours (local time) on 22 April 1991, the American liaison officer notified our military representative in the town of Zakho that the American forces were to conduct a relief operation and to use helicopters to land military forces in the town of Amadiyah and neighbouring areas on 23 April. The American liaison officer requested that military forces in the area be notified of the action to be carried out there by the American armed forces, in order to avoid any confrontation or friction.

This American measure comes five days after the agreement which I concluded on 18 April 1991, on behalf of the Iraqi Government, with Prince Sadruddin Aga Khan, your Executive Delegate for relief operations. We have already begun, together with the Coordinator appointed by the Executive Delegate, to take immediate practical steps to implement that agreement. This American action constitutes the second precedent set since 20 April as regards persistent flagrant violations of Iraq's sovereignty and territorial integrity.

In protesting this measure, the Government of Iraq once again requests you to ensure that the United Nations takes immediate action to assume its functions of providing relief at the American camps established by force inside Iraq, in accordance with the agreement of 18 April. That agreement covers the relief operations in Iraq, particularly those on behalf of Kurdish Iraqi citizens, in a comprehensive, integrated and balanced manner, ensuring that each and every purported objective of the American measures will be fulfilled. We submit this request at a time when the Coordinator of relief operations appointed by your Executive Delegate is visiting the northern region in order to establish the United Nations Humanitarian Centres, with our full cooperation.

Accept, Sir, the assurances of my highest consideration.

(Signed) Ahmed HUSSEIN
Minister for Foreign Affairs
of the Republic of Iraq

#UNW-1050 의
첨부물

2-1

0105

Remarks by the Secretary-General as he left Security Council consultations on Wednesday 24 April 1991.

Q. How do you interpret the news out of Baghdad today concerning a possible arrangement on the Kurdish situation between Baghdad and the Kurds?

SG. We haven't seen the text, but anything which could help solve the problems of the Kurds is good news for me. I hope that this will be fully confirmed and, what is still more important, fully accepted by the Kurdish people.

Q. Are you satisfied that the UN is moving fast enough to meet the dire crisis of the refugees?

SG. We are going as fast as we can. I heard that there was some criticism, which I could not understand because we could not go any faster and I think we are doing what we have to do. We are constantly in touch with the parties, both in Geneva and in New York. In New York I am going to have a man, Mr. Michael Priestley, who will be the co-ordinator. I have Sadruddin Aga Khan in Geneva and I have Mr. Bernander in Baghdad. I am very pleased that we are acting as soon as we physically can.

Q. The Iraqi Foreign Minister has asked you in your capacity as Secretary-General to oversee the taking over of the so-called allied safe havens in the north of Iraq. Have you yet been able to formulate a response to that, and what is it?

SG. It is something which I am considering. Today I had a meeting with the ambassadors of France, the United Kingdom and the United States, and then tomorrow I am going to have a meeting in the afternoon with Ambassador Al-Anbari in order to see what would be the right moment for us to step in.

Q. In other words you have actually accepted the notion that the UN should take steps to implement that plan?

SG. I think on that everybody is in agreement - the Iraqis, the coalition and myself.

Q. Etes-vous satisfait du travail que vous avez présenté au Conseil de Sécurité sur le Sahara occidental?

SG. Oui, enfin, je suis satisfait. Ce qui est encore plus important, tous les quinze membres du Conseil de Sécurité se sont montrés satisfaits. Alors pour moi c'est un source vraiment de satisfaction, et comme vous savez, lundi on va voter la résolution et je crois que ça va être une résolution unanime. Alors la MINURSO sera prête à se rendre dans le terrain dans les plus courts délais.

2 - 2

0106

주 국 련 대 표 부

주국련 20313- 283　　　　　　　　1991. 4. 25.

수신 장 관

참조 국제기구조약국장, 중동아프리카국장

제목 걸프사태 (안보리)

표제관련 안보리 문서를 별첨과 같이 송부합니다.

첨 부 : 상기 문서.　　　끝.

주 국 련 대 사

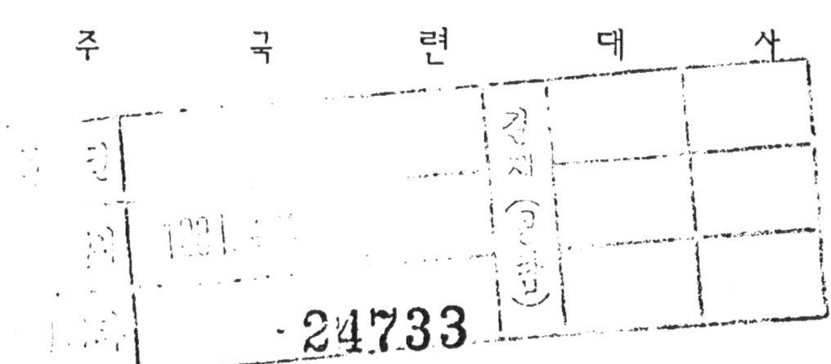

0107

UNITED
NATIONS

S

Security Council

Distr.
GENERAL

S/22475
10 April 1991
ENGLISH
ORIGINAL: ARABIC

LETTER DATED 9 APRIL 1991 FROM THE PERMANENT REPRESENTATIVE OF IRAQ TO THE UNITED NATIONS ADDRESSED TO THE SECRETARY-GENERAL

On instructions from my Government, I have the honour to provide you with the following information:

1. American-Saudi air activity on 7/8 April 1991 amounted to 88 sorties flown by 44 formations.

2. The aircraft, which flew at altitudes ranging from 2 to 9 kilometres and at speeds ranging from 720 to 850 kilometres per hour, were identified as F-14s and F-15s.

3. These hostile flights, which took place mostly over Baghdad, the areas east and west of Baghdad, the central region of the country and kilometre 160, were conducted for the purpose of observation and reconnaissance and for creating a disturbance.

I should be grateful if you would have this letter circulated as a document of the Security Council.

(*Signed*) Abdul Amir AL-ANBARI
Ambassador
Permanent Representative

91-11641 2479b (E)

0108

UNITED
NATIONS

S

Security Council

Distr.
GENERAL

S/22507
18 April 1991
ENGLISH
ORIGINAL: ARABIC

LETTER DATED 18 APRIL 1991 FROM THE PERMANENT REPRESENTATIVE OF IRAQ TO THE UNITED NATIONS ADDRESSED TO THE SECRETARY-GENERAL

On instructions from my Government, I have the honour to inform you of the continued flights of aircraft of the United States Air Force in Iraqi airspace, as follows:

1. American-Saudi air activity on 15/16 April 1991 totalled 138 sorties flown by 68 formations at altitudes ranging from 5,000 to 8,000 metres and at an average speed of 750 kilometres per hour.

2. The aircraft, which were identified as F-14s and F-15s, flew mostly over the areas of Baghdad, Tikrit, Ba'qubah, Kut, Kerbala, Najaf and Ramadi. Their mission was to carry out surveillance and cause disturbance.

I should be grateful if you would have this letter circulated as a document of the Security Council.

(Signed) Abdul Amir AL-ANBARI
Ambassador
Permanent Representative

91-12436 2256g (E)

0109

UNITED
NATIONS

S

Security Council

Distr.
GENERAL

S/22508
18 April 1991

ORIGINAL: ENGLISH

Report of the Secretary-General

Implementation of paragraph 9 (b) (i) of Security Council resolution 687 (1991)

1. The present report is submitted in pursuance of Security Council resolution 687 (1991) of 3 April 1991. In paragraph 9 (b) (i) of that resolution the Council decided that the Secretary-General should submit to it for approval a plan calling *inter alia* for the forming of a Special Commission to carry out the tasks enumerated in paragraphs 9 (b) (i-iii), 10 and 13.

2. To enable the Special Commission to play its proper part in assessing information and preparing and planning the activities envisaged in Section C of the resolution, including assisting the Director-General of the International Atomic Energy Agency to present a plan within his designated area, there is an urgent need for the Special Commission to be established. The implementation, within or near the time-frames indicated by the resolution, of all the mandates in Section C will in fact depend on the existence of the Commission, and its advice in the early stages would be essential.

3. Subject to the approval of the Security Council, it is my intention to set up the Special Commission as described below and to make all necessary arrangements for it to begin implementation of its tasks.

4. In setting up the structure for the Special Commission I wish to emphasize the need for an efficient and effective executive body. I propose that it should have an Executive Chairman with a Deputy Executive Chairman to assist the Chairman in carrying out his functions. Following the appointment of these two individuals the remainder of the Special Commission would be established on an expanding basis as appropriate individuals are found to fill the positions. Under the Executive Chairman and Deputy Executive Chairman, the planning and operational direction of the functions of the Commission should be carried out by five groups, each under a head of group with appropriate executive experience in the assigned field and each consisting of a small number of experts. The major areas of responsibility would be: biological and chemical weapons; ballistic missiles; nuclear-weapons

91-12568 2218i (E) /...

0110

capabilities; future compliance and operations support. Thus the formal membership of the Special Commission would be of the order of 20 to 25 persons.

5. Although the specific timing of the Special Commission's activities have yet to be determined, under the provisions of Section C of the resolution, most of the Commission's functions are time-limited. With the accomplishment of the tasks entrusted to four of the five groups, the major active phases would be completed and those four groups would cease to exist. The fifth group would continue in order to implement the activities relating to future compliance.

6. In carrying out its various tasks the Special Commission would be assisted by a number of technical experts serving as inspectors, disposal teams and field support officers. These experts would be either specially engaged for this purpose or made available to the Commission by Member States. Their total number would have to be determined in relationship to the size of the task to be carried out. This can be fully assessed only after the baseline field inspections have been completed by the Special Commission, but it is likely that the personnel involved will number in the several hundreds.

7. As soon as the baseline field assignments of the Special Commission and of the International Atomic Energy Agency have been completed, I intend to work out, in consultation with the Commission, a detailed plan for the implementation of the various tasks entrusted to it, and to submit it to the Security Council for its approval.

8. Following the acceptance by the Government of Iraq of Security Council resolution 687 (1991), expressed in the penultimate provision of the letters addressed respectively to me and to the President of the Security Council on 6 April 1991 by the Minister for Foreign Affairs of the Republic of Iraq, the execution of the baseline field inspections and the subsequent implementation plan is predicated on the assumption of full cooperation by the Iraqi authorities. The Special Commission would enjoy the relevant privileges and immunities provided for in the Convention on the Privileges and Immunities of the United Nations. Members of the Special Commission, experts attached to it and other specialists assigned to assist it in the implementation of Section C of Security Council resolution 687 (1991), would be regarded as experts on mission within the meaning of Article VI of the Convention on the Privileges and Immunities of the United Nations, relevant Annexes to the Convention on the Privileges and Immunities of the Specialized Agencies and Article VII of the Agreement on the Privileges and Immunities of the IAEA, respectively. Taking into account the tasks to be performed by the Special Commission, it may be necessary to conclude special agreements covering the status, facilities, privileges and immunities of the Commission and its personnel. The existing agreements mentioned above would equally apply to tasks to be performed in Iraq by the IAEA and could be supplemented by special agreements, should the need arise.

9. While the financial implications relating to the establishment and functioning of the Special Commission cannot at this stage be assessed with

0111 /...

accuracy, it is anticipated that certain start-up funds will be required. This sum will defray the initial costs of establishing the Headquarters of the Special Commission in New York as well as a field office in the region and the early deployment of advanced elements of the operation in the field. This sum will also defray some of the initial costs to be borne by the IAEA in carrying out the assignments entrusted to it under Section C of the resolution. Comprehensive cost estimates will, of course, be provided to the Security Council as soon as possible. It is my intention, however, to proceed in this regard on the basis of the following principles: (a) that Member States whose nationals will serve on the Commission or assist it in the discharge of its responsibilities should be responsible for their salaries, while the United Nations will bear the costs of travel and daily subsistence, and (b) that the whole exercise will be carried out in the shortest possible time, with a progressive decrease in the number of technical experts and of members of the Special Commission as various operations are completed.

UNITED
NATIONS

S

Security Council

Distr.
GENERAL

S/22509
19 April 1991
ENGLISH
ORIGINAL: FRENCH

LETTER DATED 19 APRIL 1991 FROM THE PRESIDENT OF THE SECURITY COUNCIL ADDRESSED TO THE SECRETARY-GENERAL

I have the honour to inform you that your report of 18 April 1991 on the implementation of paragraph 9 (b) (i) of Security Council resolution 687 (1991) has been brought to the attention of the members of the Council. They agree to the proposals contained in the report.

(Signed) Paul NOTERDAEME
President of the Security Council

91-12562 2202c (E)

0113

UNITED
NATIONS

S

Security Council

Distr.
GENERAL

S/22510
19 April 1991
ENGLISH
ORIGINAL: SPANISH

LETTER DATED 19 APRIL 1991 FROM THE CHARGE D'AFFAIRES A.I.
OF THE PERMANENT MISSION OF CUBA TO THE UNITED NATIONS
ADDRESSED TO THE PRESIDENT OF THE SECURITY COUNCIL

I have the honour to refer to your note of 18 April transmitting to the members of the Council the preliminary version of the report of the Secretary-General on the implementation of paragraph 9 (b) (i) of Security Council resolution 687 (1991).

As you will recall, Cuba voted against Security Council resolution 687 (1991) and, at the Council's 2981st meeting, Ambassador Ricardo Alarcón de Quesada, Permanent Representative of Cuba to the United Nations, made a statement which made perfectly clear Cuba's position and the reasons for its vote, which included the text's selectiveness on the issue of disarmament when such a measure should have been regional in scope.

Accordingly, while the Republic of Cuba will not obstruct the adoption of the report of the Secretary-General which you have brought to our attention, nor the letter which you propose to send to the Secretary-General, since they derive from a resolution which the Security Council adopted without Cuba's supporting vote, we none the less wish to reaffirm all the elements of our 3 April 1991 statement and to inform you that the Government of the Republic of Cuba does not associate itself with the implications which implementation of this measure could have for the peace, stability and security of the Middle East.

I should be grateful if you would have this letter distributed as a document of the Security Council.

(Signed) Carlos ZAMORA RODRIGUEZ
Ambassador
Chargé d'affaires a.i.

91-12574 2303e (E)

0114

UNITED
NATIONS

S

Security Council

Distr.
GENERAL

S/22512
19 April 1991

ORIGINAL: ENGLISH

LETTER DATED 19 APRIL 1991 FROM THE PERMANENT REPRESENTATIVE OF KUWAIT TO THE UNITED NATIONS ADDRESSED TO THE PRESIDENT OF THE SECURITY COUNCIL

On instructions from my Government, I should like to convey to you our position concerning the failure by Iraq to abide by the terms of relevant Security Council resolutions, which puts into question the credibility and motives of the Iraqi regime.

In the first instance, it should be indicated that a humanitarian but urgent concern is not being addressed by the Iraqi Government, specifically, the commitment by Iraq to abide by the terms of paragraphs 2 (c) and 3 (c) of resolution 686 (1991) and of paragraph 30 of resolution 687 (1991). Iraq is yet to repatriate the remaining Kuwaiti prisoners of war and detainees estimated at 5,433.

Second, Iraq has not to date declared its acceptance under the terms of paragraph 1 (b) of resolution 686 (1991) of its liability for any loss, damage or injury arising in regard to Kuwait and third States, and their nationals and corporations, as a result of the invasion and illegal occupation of Kuwait by Iraq.

Third, in spite of its declared readiness to return property seized in Kuwait, Iraq has not to date returned to Kuwait any of those items seized by it. Iraq has yet to implement faithfully the terms of paragraph 2 (d) of resolution 686 (1991) which demands that Iraq "immediately begins to return all Kuwaiti property seized by Iraq, to be completed in the shortest possible period".

I should appreciate it if you would bring the content of this letter to the attention of the members of the Security Council.

(Signed) Mohammad A. ABULHASAN
Ambassador
Permanent Representative

91-12611 2481b (E)

0115

UNITED
NATIONS

S

Security Council

Distr.
GENERAL

S/22513
22 April 1991
ENGLISH
ORIGINAL: ARABIC

LETTER DATED 21 APRIL 1991 FROM THE PERMANENT REPRESENTATIVE OF IRAQ TO THE UNITED NATIONS ADDRESSED TO THE SECRETARY-GENERAL

On instructions from my Government, I have the honour to transmit herewith the letter dated 21 April 1991 addressed to you by the Minister for Foreign Affairs of Iraq, Mr. Ahmed Hussein, together with its annex containing the memorandum of understanding signed with your representative on 18 April 1991. In the letter, Iraq requests the United Nations, in accordance with the agreement concluded at Baghdad on 18 April 1991 between the Government of Iraq and the United Nations, to assume responsibility for the relief centres established in the Zakhou region in northern Iraq by United States armed forces and the forces of other foreign States cooperating with them.

I should be grateful if you would arrange for the text of this letter and its annex to be circulated as a document of the Security Council.

(Signed) Abdul Amir A. AL-ANBARI
Ambassador
Permanent Representative

91-12741 2483b (E) /...

0116

ANNEX

Letter dated 21 April 1991 from the Minister for Foreign Affairs of Iraq addressed to the Secretary-General

As you are certainly aware, United States armed forces and the forces of other foreign countries cooperating with them have entered the Zakhou region in northern Iraq. The objective of this operation has been stated to be the establishment in Iraqi territory of centres for assisting displaced Iraqi citizens in Turkey. You are also aware that the Government of Iraq is opposed to this measure, since it would constitute a serious, unjustifiable and unfounded attack on the sovereignty and territorial integrity of Iraq.

This measure was announced at a time when the Iraqi Government had made significant progress in its negotiations with Prince Sadruddin Aga Khan, the representative to whom you have entrusted responsibility for relief operations. Steps to carry out the above-mentioned measure were taken on 20 April 1991, even though the Government of Iraq had signed a comprehensive agreement with your representative on 18 April, which provided for the establishment of humanitarian centres throughout Iraq, and in particular in the northern part of the country, with a view to undertaking the assistance operations necessary to induce Iraqi citizens displaced outside Iraq's frontiers to return in complete security to their places of residence in Iraq. It should be pointed out that the Government of Iraq, while opposing the steps taken by United States forces and the foreign forces cooperating with them for the reasons stated above, has not hindered these operations because it is not opposed to the provision of humanitarian assistance to Iraqi citizens who are in need of it and because it wishes to avoid any complication that may prevent the return of all Iraqi citizens in security to their places of residence.

Because the measures taken by the United States forces and the forces cooperating with them constitute a flagrant violation of Iraq's sovereignty and territorial integrity, and bearing in mind our opposition to the creation of centres under United States control inside Iraqi territory and our belief that the agreement which our Government concluded with your representative on 18 April 1991 has made it possible to define all relief operations in Iraq in an integrated and balanced manner, particularly those targeted to Kurds who are Iraqi citizens in such a way as to avoid the realization of the alleged objectives of the United States centres and to remove any justification for the establishment of such centres, which would in one way or another impair Iraq's sovereignty, the Government of Iraq, in pursuance of the above-mentioned agreement, is approaching you to request the United Nations to assume responsibility for the centres referred to above and to have the coordinator appointed by your representative, who is at the present time in Baghdad, immediately to take the measures necessary for the achievement of the purpose which we have described above. I can assure you that my Government

/...

will provide you with all necessary assistance in accordance with the above-mentioned agreement. Please find enclosed the memorandum of understanding signed with your representative on 18 April 1991.

(*Signed*) Ahmed HUSSEIN
Minister for Foreign Affairs of Iraq

Baghdad, 21 April 1991

/...

0118

Enclosure

[Original: English]

Memorandum of Understanding signed on 18 April 1991

This memorandum summarizes the results of discussions held in Baghdad between the Government of the Republic of Iraq, in the context of its request to the Secretary-General of the United Nations in relation to the suffering of the Iraqi population affected by recent events and Security Council resolution 688 of 5 April 1991, which has not been accepted by the Government of Iraq, and:

(a) From 13 to 18 April 1991, the United Nations Mission led by Mr. Eric Suy, Personal Representative of the United Nations Secretary-General, and

(b) From 16 to 18 April, the United Nations Inter-Agency Mission led by Prince Sadruddin Aga Khan, Executive Delegate of the United Nations Secretary-General for the United Nations Humanitarian Programme for Iraq, Kuwait and the Iraq/Iran and Iraq/Turkey Border Areas.

Both Missions have been welcomed by the Government of Iraq.

1. Both sides recognize the importance and urgency of adequate measures, including the provision of humanitarian assistance, to alleviate the suffering of the affected Iraqi civilian population.

2. The Government of the Republic of Iraq welcomes the United Nations efforts to promote the voluntary return home of Iraqi displaced persons and to take humanitarian measures to avert new flows of refugees and displaced persons from Iraq. It pledges its full support to and cooperation with the United Nations and its specialized agencies and programmes in this regard.

3. Both sides agree that the measures to be taken for the benefit of the displaced persons should be based primarily on their personal safety and the provision of humanitarian assistance and relief for their return and normalization of their lives in their places of origin.

4. For this purpose, the Government of the Republic of Iraq agrees to cooperate with the United Nations to have a humanitarian presence in Iraq, wherever such presence may be needed, and to facilitate it through the adoption of all necessary measures. This shall be ensured through the establishment of United Nations sub-offices and Humanitarian Centres (UNHUCs), in agreement and cooperation with the Government of Iraq.

5. Each Centre will be staffed by United Nations civilian personnel which, in addition to the regular staff members of the relevant United Nations agencies, may also include staff co-opted from the non-governmental organizations, the International Committee of the Red Cross and the League of

0119 /...

Red Cross and Red Crescent Societies. The Red Crescent Society of Iraq shall be called upon to play a role in the implementation of humanitarian assistance and relief projects.

6. UNHUCs shall facilitate the provision of humanitarian assistance to the needy and would include, inter alia, food aid, medical care, agricultural rehabilitation, shelter and any other humanitarian and relief measures geared to the speedy normalization of life, in conformity with the principles of this memorandum. UNHUCs shall also monitor the overall situation in this regard to advise the Iraqi authorities regarding measures needed to enhance their work.

7. Routes of return, with relay stations along the way as well as logistic back-up capabilities, will be set up urgently in cooperation with the Iraqi authorities to provide to civilians, particularly the women and children as well as the aged and the sick going back to their home areas, the food aid, shelter and basic health care they will need along the way. United Nations staff will accompany such groups, as required.

8. The United Nations shall take urgent measures, in cooperation with the Government of Iraq, for the early stationing of staff as well as the provision of assistance and relief in all designated centres and, as a matter of priority, those close to the Iraqi borders with its neighbouring countries. For this purpose, the United Nations may, in agreement and cooperation with the Government of Iraq, organize air lifts to the areas concerned, as required, as well as transportation by road of humanitarian assistance and relief goods from and through the neighbouring countries under United Nations or other humanitarian auspices. The Government of the Republic of Iraq shall adopt the necessary measures in order to render such aid in a speedy and effective manner.

9. United Nations humanitarian assistance and relief shall be provided simultaneously to the displaced persons, returnees as well as all other populations covered by the relief Programme in order to encourage a speedy normalization of life.

10. The basic framework for United Nations humanitarian action outlined above is intended to facilitate the task of coordination, effective implementation and monitoring of humanitarian assistance and relief operations. Further specifications are contained in the paragraphs which follow.

11. It is agreed that humanitarian assistance is impartial and that all civilians in need, wherever they are located, are entitled to receive it.

12. All Iraqi officials concerned, including the military, will facilitate the safe passage of emergency relief commodities throughout the country.

0120 /...

13. The Government will establish forthwith, together with the United Nations, a relief distribution and monitoring structure to permit access to all civilians covered by the relief Programme, as soon as possible.

14. A Coordinator, at the Assistant Secretary-General level, has been assigned to Baghdad to coordinate, under the Executive Delegate's direction, the implementation of the Humanitarian Relief Programme. He will have permanent access to a high-level government official responsible for emergency activities in the country, to discuss and resolve policy and operational issues that may arise during the implementation of the Programme.

15. The Government of Iraq shall cooperate in granting United Nations field staff access to the parts of the country requiring relief, by air or road as needed, to facilitate the implementation and monitoring of the Programme.

16. Intergovernmental organizations, NGOs and other relief agencies will be encouraged to participate in the implementation of the Programme, in close cooperation with the United Nations and under clearly defined terms of association agreed with the Government.

17. The Government of Iraq will help in the prompt establishment of United Nations sub-offices in support of UNHUCs and other programmes in towns. These will be selected so as to facilitate the relief Programme when required, to encourage the voluntary return of, and to provide essential assistance to, internally and externally displaced, as well as to local populations covered by the Programme.

18. A United Nations radio communication system which is an indispensable instrument for the success of relief and rehabilitation activities will be set up. The system will cover communications requirements within Baghdad and other cities covered by the relief Programme and within and outside the country, as appropriate.

19. In order to facilitate implementation of, and resource mobilization for, the relief Programme, the Government will make available cash contributions in local currency to help cover in-country operational costs while pursuing discussions regarding the establishment of a special exchange rate for relief operations carried out by the agencies and organizations participating in the Programme.

20. The implementation of the above-mentioned principles shall be without prejudice to the sovereignty, territorial integrity, political independence, security and non-interference in the internal affairs of the Republic of Iraq.

0121

/...

21. The above-mentioned principles shall apply for a period ending on 31 December 1991. Two weeks before the expiration of the said period, the principles and their operational modalities shall be reviewed with a view to assessing any further need for their operation.

Done at Baghdad on 3 Shawal 1411 of the Hijri, corresponding to 18 April 1991 A.D.

FOR THE GOVERNMENT OF
THE REPUBLIC OF IRAQ

(Signed) H.E. Ahmed HUSSEIN
Minister of Foreign Affairs
of the Government of the
Republic of Iraq

FOR THE UNITED NATIONS

(Signed) H.E. Sadruddin Aga KHAN
Executive Delegate of the
United Nations Secretary-General
for the United Nations Humanitarian Programme
for Iraq, Kuwait and the Iraq/Iran
and Iraq/Turkey Border Areas

0122

UNITED
NATIONS

S

Security Council

Distr.
GENERAL

S/22514
22 April 1991
ENGLISH
ORIGINAL: ARABIC

LETTER DATED 21 APRIL 1991 FROM THE PERMANENT REPRESENTATIVE OF IRAQ TO THE UNITED NATIONS ADDRESSED TO THE SECRETARY-GENERAL

On instructions from my Government and further to our previous letters to you, the most recent of which, No. 37, is dated 15 April 1991, I have the honour to bring to your attention details concerning further acts committed by Iran in violation of the cease-fire agreement between Iraq and Iran.

I:

1. On 10 April 1991, at 9 a.m., three groups of Iranians infiltrated into Iraqi territory, taking three different routes (the road along the Shatt al-Arab; the Ataba road; and the Chalamija road). The three groups were supported by vehicles equipped with 107-mm rocket launchers. They later converged and succeeded in taking up a position inside Iraqi territory. Following a skirmish with Iraqi forces, the position was retaken and eight of the Iranian infiltrators were killed.

2. On 10 April 1991, between 9.20 a.m. and 11.20 a.m., Iranians pounded the Majnoon area in Iraq with heavy artillery.

3. On 13 April 1991 at 4.30 a.m. a civilian pick-up carrying four individuals coming from Iranian territory was spotted as it was travelling along the Chalamija road. The vehicle, which remained in Iraqi territory until 4.45 a.m., returned to Iranian territory with the four individuals in question aboard. At 9 a.m. the same day two Iranian armoured vehicles and an Iranian Landcruiser pick-up were spotted as they were travelling along the Doiaji road coming from the Chalamija area and took up a position in Iraqi territory. About a dozen individuals, civilians and military personnel, got out of the vehicles. At 11.15 a.m. that same day the two armoured vehicles and the civilian vehicle took the same road to return to Iranian territory.

4. On 15 April 1991, at 4.35 a.m., a group proceeding from Iranian territory infiltrated into Iraqi territory and fired with light arms on positions occupied by Iraqi forces near the Iraqi post of Moussa Al-Kazem (central sector), wounding five of our soldiers.

91-12735 2298f (E) /...

0123

II. On 18 April 1991, at 6.30 a.m., the Iranians shelled the Faijala region using 107-mm rocket launchers from the Qasr-e-Shirin area in Iran; 12 rockets were fired.

This violation which follows on other Iranian violations confirms once again the Iranian Government's persistence in violating the provisions of the cease-fire concluded between the two countries and its deliberate aim of undermining Iraq's sovereignty and security. The Government of my country reaffirms that it holds the Iranian Government responsible for all the damage caused in Iraq by these violations.

I should be grateful if you would arrange for the text of this letter to be circulated as a document of the Security Council.

(*Signed*) Abdul Amir AL-ANBARI
Ambassador
Permanent Representative

0124

UNITED
NATIONS

S

Security Council

Distr.
GENERAL

S/22515
22 April 1991
ENGLISH
ORIGINAL: ARABIC

LETTER DATED 21 APRIL 1991 FROM THE PERMANENT REPRESENTATIVE OF IRAQ TO THE UNITED NATIONS ADDRESSED TO THE SECRETARY-GENERAL

On instructions from my Government, I have the honour to inform you that United States forces stationed in the northern part of the Rumaila oilfield have prevented the Iraqi personnel who work there from taking the minimum measures to protect property of the Southern Oil Company from sabotage and theft. The United States forces have allowed saboteurs to commit premeditated acts of plunder and destruction, the latter having loaded dozens of large hauling vehicles without licence plates with cement, stocks, supplies and equipment belonging to the above-mentioned company; the vehicles then set out for an unknown destination, apparently Kuwait. Our belief that Kuwait is their destination is reinforced by the fact that the Americans have claimed that the property that was plundered before the eyes of the United States forces belongs to Kuwait. Preliminary estimates place the losses at around 18 million dinars.

These acts, which constitute a flagrant violation of Iraq's sovereignty, were committed with the premeditated aim of plundering Iraqi property. In bringing these acts to your attention, we lodge a most vehement protest against them. We await action on your part to put an end to such acts as required by the principles and provisions of the Charter of the United Nations.

I should be grateful if you would arrange for the text of this letter to be circulated as a document of the Security Council.

(Signed) Abdul Amir AL-ANBARI
Ambassador
Permanent Representative

91-12747 2292h (E)

0125

UNITED
NATIONS

S

Security Council

Distr.
GENERAL

S/22516
22 April 1991
ENGLISH
ORIGINAL: ARABIC

LETTER DATED 21 APRIL 1991 FROM THE PERMANENT REPRESENTATIVE OF IRAQ TO THE UNITED NATIONS ADDRESSED TO THE SECRETARY-GENERAL

On instructions from my Government, I have the honour to inform you that United States Air Force flights continue to violate Iraqi airspace, as follows:

First:

1. On 16 April 1991:

(a) United States air activity in Iraqi airspace totalled 72 sorties flown by 35 formations and 2 single aircraft.

(b) Altitudes ranged between 5,000 and 8,000 metres, and the speed was between 600 and 720 kilometres per hour.

(c) The aircraft were identified as F-14s and F-15s.

(d) The flights focused on the areas of Baghdad, Kirkuk, Kut, Ramadi and Karbala', and their purpose was surveillance and provocation.

2. On 17 April 1991:

(a) United States air activity in Iraqi airspace totalled 67 sorties flown by 33 formations.

(b) Altitudes ranged between 5,000 and 8,000 metres, and the average speed was 750 kilometres per hour.

(c) The aircraft were identified as F-14s and F-15s.

(d) The flights focused on the areas of Baghdad, Kut, Hashimiyah, Ramadi and Samawah, and their purpose was reconnaissance, surveillance and provocation.

91-12753 2435d (E) /...

0126

3. On 18 April 1991:

(a) United States air activity in Iraqi airspace totalled 80 sorties flown by 38 formations.

(b) Altitudes ranged between 4,000 and 8,000 metres, and the average speed was 750 kilometres per hour.

(c) The aircraft were identified as F-14s and F-15s.

(d) The flights focused on the areas of Baghdad, Suwayrah, Hashimiyah and Samawah and the area north of Razzazah, and their purpose was reconnaissance, surveillance and provocation.

Second:

1. On 19/20 April 1991, the number of American/Saudi sorties totalled 92 flown by 46 formations. Altitudes ranged between 4,000 and 8,000 metres, and the speed ranged between 800 and 1,000 kilometres per hour. The flights focused on the areas of Baghdad, Diyala, Suwayrah, Kut, Karbala', Tikrit and Razzazah, and their purpose was surveillance and provocation. The aircraft were identified as F-14s and F-15s.

2. At 1405 hours on 19 April 1991, an American formation consisting of two aircraft flying at an altitude of 7,000 metres and at a speed of 720 kilometres per hour penetrated 2 to 10 kilometres inside Iranian airspace and travelled over a distance of 50 kilometres from the area south of Mandali to the area of Qasr-e-Shirin.

I should be grateful if you would have this letter circulated as a document of the Security Council.

(Signed) Abdul Amir A. AL-ANBARI
Ambassador
Permanent Representative

0127

UNITED NATIONS

S

Security Council

Distr.
GENERAL

S/22517
22 April 1991
ENGLISH
ORIGINAL: ARABIC

LETTER DATED 22 APRIL 1991 FROM THE PERMANENT REPRESENTATIVE OF IRAQ TO THE UNITED NATIONS ADDRESSED TO THE SECRETARY-GENERAL

On instructions from my Government and further to our letters, the most recent being our letter No. 44 of 21 April 1991, I have the honour to submit to you new facts concerning Iranian violations of the cease-fire agreement between Iraq and Iran and concerning Iran's blatant intervention in Iraq's internal affairs, as follows:

First:

1. On 1 April 1991, a group advancing from the Iranian rear fired six rockets from an RPG-7 launcher from the area of Tawilah island in the direction of the Iraqi units in the southern sector.

2. At 1620 hours on 3 April 1991, a force advancing from the Iranian side fired on the Iraqi units in the southern sector with 82 mm mortar artillery, rocket-launchers and medium-sized weapons.

Second:

1. At 1700 hours on 16 April 1991, three groups advancing from the Iranian side launched an offensive against the positions of Iraqi units in the Harithah-Basra area using light weapons and a vehicle carrying a 107 mm rocket-launcher. At 1930 hours on the same day, the Iranian side fired five shells at Iraqi units in the above-mentioned area using mortar artillery. At 2240 hours on the same day, a force advancing from the Iranian side, estimated to number between 20 and 30 men, launched an offensive against Iraqi units in the same above-mentioned area.

2. At 1205 hours on 17 April 1991, the Iranian side dispatched seven Land cruiser vehicles, each carrying 20 men together with a number of men of religion, into Iraqi territory in the Harithah-Basra area. At 1231 hours on the same day, the groups advanced on foot to the right and left of the highway 400 metres into Iraqi territory.

91-12759 2389j (E) /...

0128

These violations once again confirm the Iranian Government's intention to violate the provisions of the cease-fire between the two countries and its deliberate desire to infringe Iraq's sovereignty and security. My country's Government once again affirms the responsibility of the Iranian Government for all damage sustained by Iraq as a result of these violations.

I request you to have this letter circulated as a document of the Security Council.

(Signed) Abdul Amir A. AL-ANBARI
Ambassador
Permanent Representative

0129

UNITED
NATIONS

A S

General Assembly Security Council

Distr.
GENERAL

A/46/158
S/22520
22 April 1991

ORIGINAL: ENGLISH

GENERAL ASSEMBLY
Forty-sixth session
Item 29 of the preliminary list*
THE SITUATION IN AFGHANISTAN AND ITS IMPLICATIONS FOR INTERNATIONAL PEACE AND SECURITY

SECURITY COUNCIL
Forty-sixth year

Letter dated 21 April 1991 from the Permanent Representative of Pakistan to the United Nations addressed to the Secretary-General

I would like to draw your attention to the barbaric Scud attack launched by the Kabul regime on 21 April 1991 against the town of Asadabad, capital of the Kunar Province of Afghanistan, which borders Pakistan.

According to preliminary reports, more than 500 civilians were killed and over 700 injured when two Scud missiles hit the centre of the town around 8 p.m. local time. Hundreds of houses and shops were destroyed and the Asadabad bazaar was completely devastated. Widespread fires caused by the missile blasts compounded the destruction and obstructed rescue work. Bodies of the victims are still being recovered from the debris, and most of them are burnt beyond recognition.

The Government of Pakistan condemns this criminal use of weapons of mass destruction perpetrated by the Kabul regime against the Afghan population. Such acts directly affect Pakistan, producing fresh flows of Afghan refugees. Following the attack on Asadabad, hundreds of injured Afghans and their relatives have started arriving in our border towns and hospitals.

Since the liberation of Khost by the Afghan Mujahidin on the last day of March 1991, the Kabul regime has intensified Scud attacks and aerial bombardment against Mujahidin-controlled towns and other civilian centres.

---

* A/46/50.

91-12720 2931a (E) /...

0130

During April, the town of Khost has been subjected to more than 40 Scud missile attacks and numerous aerial bombings. Even on the day of Id al-Fitr, the day of rejoicing and festivities for Muslims all over the world marking the end of the holy month of Ramadan, Khost was bombed by the regime's aircraft.

While the brutal use of weapons of mass destruction by the Kabul regime against the Afghan population underscores the desperation of the Kabul regime, it also damages the prospects of a political settlement in Afghanistan. It was for this reason that in my letter of 1 April 1991 (A/46/127-S/22428), on behalf of the Government of Pakistan, I had conveyed a request to you to use your influence to stop these brutal attacks, which are taking a heavy toll in human life and causing vast devastation. The Scud attack against Asadabad obliges us to strongly reiterate our request.

I wish to take this opportunity to refer to the baseless allegations, specifically the charge that Pakistani personnel were involved in the Mujahidin operations to liberate Khost, made in the letter from the Foreign Minister of the Kabul regime circulated as the annex to document A/46/140-S/22501 of 12 April 1991. Facts belie these fabrications.

One of the first acts of the Mujahidin commanders' Shura, established immediately after the surrender by the Kabul regime's garrison in Khost, was to invite International Committee of the Red Cross (ICRC) personnel and foreign correspondents. Since then, Khost has been frequently visited by a large number of international observers. Their reports cover every facet of the Mujahidin victory of Khost and the Mujahidin administration of the city, thus providing vivid factual refutation of Kabul's baseless charges.

The letter by the Foreign Minister of the Kabul regime also makes accusations about mistreatment of prisoners of war by the Mujahidin. This charge is equally false, because from the very first day, the Mujahidin commanders' Shura had involved ICRC in providing humanitarian assistance in the area, including the handling of the prisoners of war. ICRC officials remain actively engaged in looking after the prisoners. Representatives of the international media have visited prisoners and have interviewed them. There are no reports of mistreatment of the prisoners of war. On the contrary, the Scud attacks and aerial bombardment by the Kabul regime have complicated the task of shifting them, especially those needing medical care, to safer places.

I once again take this opportunity to reaffirm to you the resolute commitment of the Government of Pakistan to promote a political settlement of the Afghan conflict and our readiness to cooperate with the peace efforts by you.

0131 /...

I should be grateful if the present letter could be circulated as an official document of the General Assembly, under item 29 of the preliminary list, and of the Security Council.

(*Signed*) Jamsheed K. A. MARKER
Ambassador and Permanent Representative

0132

UNITED
NATIONS

S

Security Council

Distr.
GENERAL

S/22518
23 April 1991
ENGLISH
ORIGINAL: ARABIC

LETTER DATED 22 APRIL 1991 FROM THE PERMANENT REPRESENTATIVE OF IRAQ TO THE UNITED NATIONS ADDRESSED TO THE SECRETARY-GENERAL

Upon instructions from my Government, I have the honour to inform you of the continued flights of aircraft of the United States Air Force in Iraqi airspace, as follows:

1. American-Saudi air activity on 20/21 April 1991 totalled 154 sorties flown by 72 formations at a speed of 600 to 850 kilometres per hour and at altitudes ranging between 4,500 and 9,000 kilometres.

2. The aircraft were identified as F-14s and F-15s and flew mostly over the areas of Baghdad, Aziziyah, Hashimiyah, Karbala', Kut, Amarah and Nasiriyah. Their mission was to carry out reconnaissance, surveillance and provocation by flying over residential areas and also by approaching the United Nations aircraft flying from Oman to Kuwait at 1245 hours, when it was in Iraqi airspace in the area to the south of Baghdad.

I should be grateful if you would have this letter circulated as a document of the Security Council.

(Signed) Abdul Amir A. AL-ANBARI
Ambassador
Permanent Representative

91-12788 2227i (E)

0133

UNITED NATIONS

S

Security Council

Distr.
GENERAL

S/22519
23 April 1991
ENGLISH
ORIGINAL: ARABIC

LETTER DATED 21 APRIL 1991 FROM THE PERMANENT REPRESENTATIVE OF IRAQ TO THE UNITED NATIONS ADDRESSED TO THE SECRETARY-GENERAL

On instructions from my Government, I have the honour to inform you that United States military forces are continuing their encroachments on Iraqi territory and their support of saboteur elements in the areas occupied by them, inasmuch as there are United States military forces, consisting of tank units, on both sides of the Safwan-Basra highway, on the earth road through the agricultural area and on the clover-leaf intersection. These forces are offering assistance to saboteur elements and providing them with a refuge, which has encouraged them to carry out acts of theft and plunder in respect of buildings, property and government and private premises. In addition, the United States military presence has enabled the Kuwaitis to circulate in the town of Safwan and seize motor vehicles there on the pretext that the vehicles are Kuwaiti.

The continuation of these acts constitutes a breach of Iraq's sovereignty, an infamous intervention in its internal affairs and an incitement to elements beyond the law to disrupt internal security and stability.

In informing you of these violations, I request you to adopt such measures to put a halt to them as are dictated by the purposes and principles of the Charter of the United Nations.

I should be grateful if you would have this letter circulated as a document of the Security Council.

(*Signed*) Abdul Amir A. AL-ANBARI
Ambassador
Permanent Representative

91-12802 2207c (E)

0134

UNITED NATIONS

S

Security Council

Distr.
GENERAL

S/22521
23 April 1991

ORIGINAL: ENGLISH

LETTER DATED 19 APRIL 1991 FROM THE PERMANENT REPRESENTATIVE OF KUWAIT TO THE UNITED NATIONS ADDRESSED TO THE PRESIDENT OF THE SECURITY COUNCIL

Further to my letter of 14 March 1991, I should like to forward additional information on the Kuwait Airways Corporation properties seized by Iraq since 2 August 1990:

(a) Simulators (see annex I);

(b) Cars - 400 cars;

(c) Computers (see annex II);

(d) Kitchen (see annex III);

(e) Losses of documentation - Revenue (see annex IV).

I should appreciate it if you would arrange for this letter to be circulated as a document of the Security Council.

(*Signed*) Mohammad A. ABULHASAN
Ambassador
Permanent Representative

91-12819 2390j (E) /...

0135

Annex I

Simulators

1. B747 full flight simulator.
2. B747 cockpit procedure trainer and four maintenance system trainers.
3. B727 maintenance system trainers (five).
4. B707 navigation and procedure trainer.
5. B747 and B727 emergency and evacuation trainers.
6. Audiovisual trainers.
7. Miscellaneous training aid.
8. Training centre specialized furnishing.
9. Spares and technical assets and workshop equipment.
10. Airbus cockpit and maintenance system simulator.

0136

/...

Annex II

Computers

	Quantity
A. Hardware	
IBM 4341 mainframe	1
BASF 7/78 mainframe	1
IBM 3350 disk drives	48
BASF disk drives	8
IBM 3420 tape drives	16
IBM 3880 disk controllers	3
BASF disk controller	1
IBM tape controllers	3
IBM power distribution unit	1
IBM 3705 communication controllers	4
Storage Technology 5000 system printer	1
IBM 3203 system printer	1
Channel controllers (remote and local)	15
DOS/VSE consule	4
BASF monitoring consule	1
Resku consules	2
Telex printers	4
Library tapes	5 000
Cathode ray tube Resku	1
IBM 4381	2
IBM 3090 120S	1
IBM 3380 disk drives	8
IBM 3990 disk controller	1
IBM 3745 communication controller	1
IBM 3090 consules	2
ALCS and MVS/ESA operating system	
Automatic cartridge library	1
Tandem non stop (2)	1

0137 /...

	Quantity
Tandem disk drives	4
Tandem tape drive	1
Tandem disk controller	1
Tandem tape controller	1
Tandem system printer	1
Tandem consules	2

B. Software

Reservation system

SAP

CPATA-2

ADABAS

RAS cargo

TAKOF

Time attendance

Job costing

Maxi merlin

MSCS

DCS

C. Other software and hardware

Cathode ray tubes	600
System printers	60
Printers	150
Personal computer hardware	300
Personal computer software	

D. Electrical and communication

KAC telephone exchange

Communication equipment

Uninterrupted power supply (UPS)

Wiring for cathode ray tubes, printers, telephone, etc.

0138

/...

	Quantity
Electrical generator for computer room	
Microfilm machine	2
Microfilm displayer and printer	12
Copier	4
Films	3 000
Film preparation room equipment	

E. Main items

Hardware equipment, excluding MVS/ESA migration and tandem

MVS/ESA migration

Tandem

Software

Other hardware and software

Electrical and communication

Micro film

0139

/...

Annex III

Kitchen

The flight kitchen, where meals for all airlines operating to/from Kuwait International Airport were catered for, plus outside catering, produced up to 20,000 meals per day and of the best standards.

It was equipped with the latest equipment used in the industry for food preparation:

(a) Bakeries, ovens, deep freezers, vast chillers, meal holding rooms, bread cello wrapping machine, cutlery cello wrapping machine, two dish washing machines, trolley washing machine, equipment and food preparation tables and counters, three conveyor belts, etc.;

(b) Mini experimental kitchen;

(c) Fully equipped laboratory;

(d) Trolleys and utensils;

(e) Office furnitures;

(f) Stores with shelf facilities fully airconditioned and temperature control;

(g) One generator, for use in the event of electricity failure.

0140

/...

Annex IV

Passenger documents

Passenger tickets	- Kuwait Airways and other airlines
Excess baggage tickets	- Kuwait Airways and other airlines
Miscellaneous charges, orders and prepaid ticket advise	- Kuwait Airways and other airlines
Airways bills	- Kuwait Airways and other airlines

The above includes:

(a) Other airline documents uplifted, exchanged or refunded by Kuwait Airways and not billed to other airlines; sales made by agents and Kuwait Airways Offices to passengers, local companies and ministries for which payment was not received; and Kuwait Airways blank documents lying in storage in Kuwait;

(b) Other airlines documents refunded by us and not billed for the months of April/May/June 1990;

(c) Sales made by agents during the month of July 1990 (peak season) but payment not received by Kuwait Airlines and most of the unused tickets were refunded by us;

(d) Owing to the suspension of Kuwait Airways flights, partly used tickets were endorsed to other airlines, resulting in revenue losses for Kuwait Airways.

0141

UNITED
NATIONS

S

Security Council

Distr.
GENERAL

S/22522
23 April 1991

ORIGINAL: ENGLISH

LETTER DATED 23 APRIL 1991 FROM THE PERMANENT REPRESENTATIVE OF THE UNITED KINGDOM OF GREAT BRITAIN AND NORTHERN IRELAND TO THE UNITED NATIONS ADDRESSED TO THE PRESIDENT OF THE SECURITY COUNCIL

Further to my letter of 13 February 1991 (S/22218), I have the honour to communicate to you pursuant to paragraph 4 of resolution 678 (1990) a further report on operations in the Gulf.

British Armed Forces played a full part in the 100-hour ground campaign between 24 February and midnight (EST) on 27 February, which led to the liberation of Kuwait. The particular contribution of the British First Armoured Division to the coalition's ground campaign was to engage Iraqi forces to the west of Kuwait. At the end of their advance First Armoured Division troops had reached positions north and north-west of Kuwait City.

The Royal Air Force also continued to contribute to the coalition air campaign. Between 17 January and 27 February the Royal Air Force (RAF) flew over 6,500 sorties, including over 4,000 combat sorties.

The Royal Navy contributed to the maritime campaign and played a leading role in the coalition's mine counter-measures force. Since the end of the hostilities, Royal Navy mine counter-measure vessels have cleared channels into the ports of Ash Shu'aybah and Kuwait City.

The number of prisoners of war taken by British Forces during the ground campaign was some 8,000. All were treated in accordance with the United Kingdom's obligations under the Geneva conventions. Many of those captured had been poorly provided for by the Iraqi authorities, lacking adequate food and clothing. Arrangements were made to supply them with clothing and rations from British stocks before they were evacuated by helicopter from the combat zone for registration under International Committee of the Red Cross (ICRC) procedures. The most extensive medical facilities ever set up by the British Army in the field were used to ensure that the prisoners were properly looked after. They were subsequently passed to the Saudi Arabian authorities.

91-12852 2208c (E) /...

0142

Just under 45,000 British service personnel were deployed to the Gulf in support of the operations. British casualties during the campaign were 25 killed in action and 43 wounded.

The United Kingdom has made a major contribution to the international response to the environmental threat posed by the oil released into the Gulf by Iraq, and by the oil well fires started by Iraq in the closing stages of the conflict. After the oil spills, the United Kingdom responded swiftly to requests for assistance from Gulf States. In particular, the United Kingdom helped with a military air lift of 90 tonnes of anti-pollution equipment, and donated six oil skimmers to Bahrain. It also provided expert advice on oil pollution response and the ecological aspects of the slick. It also offered help in training local volunteers in Saudi Arabia to clean oiled birds. The Royal Air Force and the British Army have helped to clean up debris from some of the offshore islands. On 6 March, the United Kingdom announced a contribution of £1 million to the trust fund established by the International Maritime Organization (IMO) for clean-up operations in the northern Gulf.

In response to the environmental damage caused by the burning oil wells, the United Kingdom has provided the affected States with an initial assessment of the nature and extent of the smoke plumes, their likely evolution, and their possible impact on the environment and human health. Preliminary analysis of data produced by a British research flight in March was incorporated into this report and further information will be provided to the affected States when it becomes available.

I should be grateful if this letter could be circulated as a document of the Security Council.

(Signed) D. H. A. HANNAY

0143

UNITED
NATIONS

S

Security Council

Distr.
GENERAL

S/22523
23 April 1991

ORIGINAL: ENGLISH

LETTER DATED 22 APRIL 1991 FROM THE PERMANENT REPRESENTATIVE OF KUWAIT TO THE UNITED NATIONS ADDRESSED TO THE PRESIDENT OF THE SECURITY COUNCIL

Further to my letter of 14 March 1991 (S/22427, annex) I should like to forward the assessment made by the Ministry of Social Affairs and Labour and its departments of property seized by Iraq since 2 August 1990.

I should appreciate it if you would arrange for this letter to be circulated as a document of the Security Council.

(Signed) Mohammad A. ABULHASAN
Ambassador
Permanent Representative

91-12858 2229i (E) /...

0144

Annex

[Original: Arabic]

Damage sustained by the Ministry of Social Affairs and Labour and its subordinate institutions

1. Furniture and equipment

All office furniture, office equipment, telephone, fax and telex apparatus, equipment for scanning statistics and statistical and representational graphs and television, radio and photographic apparatus.

2. Documentation library

3. Computer apparatus

4. Microfilm apparatus

5. Manuscripts and archives

All files were stolen, as were the official seals of the Ministry.

6. Transport

All 170 vehicles belonging to the Ministry were stolen, as were all spare parts and testing and repair equipment. The stolen vehicles included brand-new vehicles for the transport of the handicapped, whose value is estimated at $30,000 each.

7. Stores

The stores were seized in their entirety and looted of all their contents, including furniture, stationery, foodstuffs, clothing, cleaning materials and utensils, as well as beds, tents and generators used for hikers and youth camps and items needed for children and the handicapped.

8. Social Welfare Homes complex

A major medical clinic, another subsidiary clinic, a dental clinic, a central pharmacy and a medical treatment centre were all seized. Utensils and equipment were also stolen from the complex's central canteen and central laundry.

9. Vocational Training Centre

All contents and equipment, including raw materials and products made by the handicapped and the blind and marketed on their behalf, were looted.

/...

10. Youth centres and recreation centres for mothers and children

The 14 centres were taken over in their entirety, after being stripped of their contents, including children's toys, sports equipment, training workshops for young people's creative activities and the children's library.

11. Sports Captains' Training Centre and Natural Medicine Centre

The centres were looted of all the medical and natural healing equipment which they contained.

12. Scientific Club and branches

All technical apparatus was confiscated and removed. Training workshops were emptied and the scientific inventions of young people were stolen, as well as the contents of the Ajiri Meteorological Station and models used for research.

13. Olympic Committee, sports associations and clubs and all-Asia authorities

There are in all 32 sports clubs and associations, as well as the Olympic Committee and the all-Asia authorities. These establishments and authorities were taken over in their entirety and robbed of all their contents, including furniture, air-conditioning equipment, electric appliances, sports apparatus, audiovisual materials and commemorative and official cups and shields. Horses trained for racing and showjumping were also stolen, as well as yachts, boats and equipment and apparatus used for watersports.

UNITED
NATIONS

S

Security Council

Distr.
GENERAL

S/22526
24 April 1991
ENGLISH
ORIGINAL: ARABIC

LETTER DATED 24 APRIL 1991 FROM THE PERMANENT REPRESENTATIVE OF IRAQ TO THE UNITED NATIONS ADDRESSED TO THE SECRETARY-GENERAL

On instructions from my Government and further to our previous letters to you, the most recent being our letter No. 50 of 22 April 1991, I have the honour to inform you of further violations by Iran of the provisions of the cease-fire between Iraq and Iran. The details are as follows:

1. On 21 April 1991, at 0400 hours, a self-contained unit composed of approximately three infantry regiments proceeding from Iranian territory under cover of two multi-barrelled vehicle-mounted rocket launchers and mortars (120 mm and 60 mm) attacked Iraqi forward units in the southern sector, travelling on the highway along Al Asmak lake. One hundred eighty bombs fell on the area.

2. On 22 April 1991, at 0300 hours, a unit having the strength of an infantry regiment advanced from Iranian territory and attacked Iraqi units in the same sector. At the same time, Iranian forces opened fire on Iraqi forward units in the sector using light arms and mortars (60 mm). A total of 12 bombs were dropped on the sector. At 0430 hours, Iraqi forces in the region were the target of shelling by the Iranians using bazookas and mortars. The shelling lasted for 30 minutes. Thirty rockets were fired.

3. On 22 April 1991, at 0430 hours, a unit having the strength of an infantry regiment advanced on the Iraqi post at Koteiba in the central sector and opened fire on Iraqi units using a variety of weapons. At 1800 hours, a unit proceeding from Iran shelled Iraqi forward units in the southern sector (Harithah-Basra area) using mortars (82 mm). Seven bombs were used.

4. On 23 April 1991, at 1130 hours, Iranian forces fired three shells on Iraqi forward units in the Huwayr Al-Huwaysah area in the southern sector.

These repeated, daily violations perpetrated by the Iranian side in breach of the provisions of the cease-fire between the two countries confirms the Iranian Government's deliberate and persistent desire to infringe Iraq's sovereignty and security. My country's Government once again affirms that it holds the Iranian Government responsible for all damage sustained by Iraq as a result of these violations and for the future consequences of these violations.

I should be grateful if you would arrange for the text of this letter to be circulated as a document of the Security Council.

(*Signed*) Abdul Amir A. AL-ANBARI
Ambassador
Permanent Representative

0148

UNITED
NATIONS

S

Security Council

Distr.
GENERAL

S/22529
24 April 1991
ENGLISH
ORIGINAL: ARABIC

LETTER DATED 24 APRIL 1991 FROM THE PERMANENT REPRESENTATIVE OF IRAQ TO THE UNITED NATIONS ADDRESSED TO THE SECRETARY-GENERAL

On instructions from my Government and further to our previous letters to you, the most recent being our letter No. 56 dated 24 April 1991, I have the honour to inform you of further violations by Iran of the provisions of the cease-fire between Iraq and Iran. The details are as follows:

1. On 16 April at 1900, 1930 and 2000 hours, armed groups riding in vehicles and motorcycles were deployed and opened fire on Iraqi forward units in the Harithah-Basra area, using machine guns, rocket launchers and mortars. The groups later returned to Iranian territory.

2. In the evening of 17 April 1991, the Iranian army pounded with heavy artillery the district of Abu Khasib (Basra governorate), wounding four civilians.

3. At 2400 hours on 18 April 1991 and 1600 hours on 19 April 1991, a self-contained unit whose strength was estimated at three regiments attacked positions of Iraqi forward units under cover of mortar and rocket fire, concentrating their fire on the Chalamija-Tannouma highway (Basra governorate). At 0130 and 0645 hours of the same day (19 April 1991), a group advancing from Iranian territory fired on positions held by Iraqi forward units with light firearms, rocket launchers, multiple rocket projectors (107-mm) and mortars (120-mm and 82-mm). At 1830 hours Iranian forces sporadically shelled positions held by Iraqi forward units in the same area from the neighbouring region of Shatt al-Arab, using 120-mm mortars.

These new violations following on the earlier violations committed by the Iranian side, in breach of the provisions of the cease-fire between the two countries, are fresh proof of the deliberate and persistent intention of the Iranian Government to infringe Iraq's sovereignty and security. My country's Government once again affirms that it holds the Iranian Government responsible for all damage sustained by Iraq as a result of these violations.

91-13006 2273g (E) /...

0149

I should be grateful if you would arrange for the text of this letter to be circulated as a document of the Security Council.

(*Signed*) Abdul Amir A. AL-ANBARI
Ambassador
Permanent Representative

0150

UNITED
NATIONS

S

Security Council

Distr.
GENERAL

S/22530
24 April 1991
ENGLISH
ORIGINAL: ARABIC

LETTER DATED 24 APRIL 1991 FROM THE PERMANENT REPRESENTATIVE OF IRAQ TO THE UNITED NATIONS ADDRESSED TO THE SECRETARY-GENERAL

On instructions from my Government, I have the honour to inform you that United States and American-Saudi aircraft have continued to violate Iraqi airspace, as follows:

I.

1. On 10 April 1991 at 1830 hours, two helicopters of the coalition forces landed at the Jisr checkpoint, near the As Samawah oil refinery. Two groups disembarked and, after ordering the soldiers at the checkpoint to stand clear, took five rifles from a gun rack.

2. On 11 April 1991 at 1200 hours, a United States helicopter violated Iraqi airspace in the Suk-Ashuyukh area and then flew off in the direction of the town of Nasiriyah before returning to the United States forces zone.

II.

1. On 21 April 1991, American-Saudi air activity totalled 163 sorties flown by 80 formations and three solo sorties. The aircraft in question flew at a speed of 720 kilometres per hour and at altitudes ranging between 6,000 and 8,000 metres.

2. The aircraft - F-15s and F-14s - flew mostly over the areas of Baghdad, Ar Ramadi, Hadithah, Tikrit, Karbala', Kut, As Samawah and Nasiriyah. Their mission was to carry out reconnaissance, surveillance and provocation missions, since the aircraft flew over residential areas.

<u>22-23 April 1991</u>

1. American-Saudi air activity totalled 83 sorties flown by 41 formations and one solo sortie. The aircraft in question flew at speeds of between 600 and 720 kilometres per hour and at altitudes ranging from 5,500 to 9,000 metres.

91-13030 2935a (E) /...

0151

2. The aircraft - F-14s and F-15s - flew mainly over northern and eastern Baghdad and the areas of Ar Ramadi, Ar Razzazah, Kut, As Suwayrah and Al Hashimiyah. Their mission was to carry out surveillance and provocation operations.

I should be grateful if you would kindly arrange for the text of this letter to be circulated as a document of the Security Council.

(Signed) Abdul Amir A. AL-ANBARI
Ambassador
Permanent Representative

0152

UNITED
NATIONS

S

Security Council

Distr.
GENERAL

S/22531
24 April 1991
ENGLISH
ORIGINAL: ARABIC

LETTER DATED 24 APRIL 1991 FROM THE PERMANENT REPRESENTATIVE OF IRAQ TO THE UNITED NATIONS ADDRESSED TO THE SECRETARY-GENERAL

On instructions from my Government, I have the honour to transmit herewith a letter dated 24 April 1991 from Mr. Ahmed Hussein, Minister for Foreign Affairs of the Republic of Iraq, requesting that you take immediate action to assume your functions with respect to the provision of relief at the American camps established by force inside Iraq.

I should be grateful if you would have this letter and its annex circulated as an official document of the Security Council.

(Signed) Abdul Amir A. AL-ANBARI
Ambassador
Permanent Representative

91-13036 2272g (E) /...

0153

Annex

Letter dated 24 April 1991 from the Minister for Foreign Affairs of Iraq addressed to the Secretary-General

At 1840 hours (local time) on 22 April 1991, the American liaison officer notified our military representative in the town of Zakho that the American forces were to conduct a relief operation and to use helicopters to land military forces in the town of Amadiyah and neighbouring areas on 23 April. The American liaison officer requested that military forces in the area be notified of the action to be carried out there by the American armed forces, in order to avoid any confrontation or friction.

This American measure comes five days after the agreement which I concluded on 18 April 1991, on behalf of the Iraqi Government, with Prince Sadruddin Aga Khan, your Executive Delegate for relief operations. We have already begun, together with the Coordinator appointed by the Executive Delegate, to take immediate practical steps to implement that agreement. This American action constitutes the second precedent set since 20 April as regards persistent flagrant violations of Iraq's sovereignty and territorial integrity.

In protesting this measure, the Government of Iraq once again requests you to ensure that the United Nations takes immediate action to assume its functions of providing relief at the American camps established by force inside Iraq, in accordance with the agreement of 18 April. That agreement covers the relief operations in Iraq, particularly those on behalf of Kurdish Iraqi citizens, in a comprehensive, integrated and balanced manner, ensuring that each and every purported objective of the American measures will be fulfilled. We submit this request at a time when the Coordinator of relief operations appointed by your Executive Delegate is visiting the northern region in order to establish the United Nations Humanitarian Centres, with our full cooperation.

Accept, Sir, the assurances of my highest consideration.

(Signed) Ahmed HUSSEIN
Minister for Foreign Affairs
of the Republic of Iraq

0154

토

UN

주 국 련 대 표 부

주국련 20313- 284 1991. 4. 25.

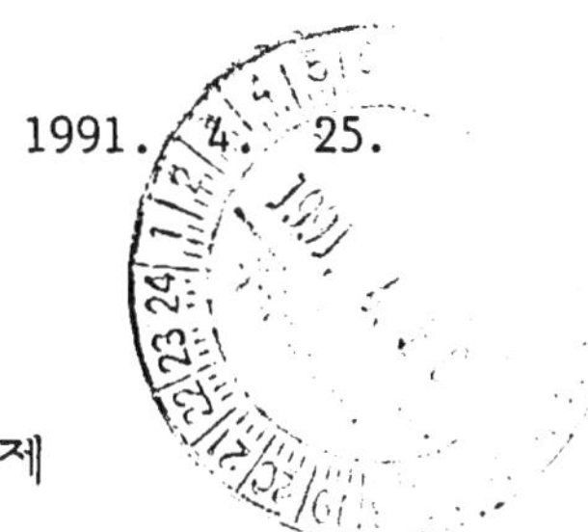

수신 장 관

참조 국제기구조약국장, 중동아프리카국장

제목 걸프사태 관련 경제제재조치 피해국 지원 문제

표제관련 사무총장 명의 서한을 별첨과 같이 송부합니다.

첨 : 상기 서한. 끝. → 별도 보관 문서

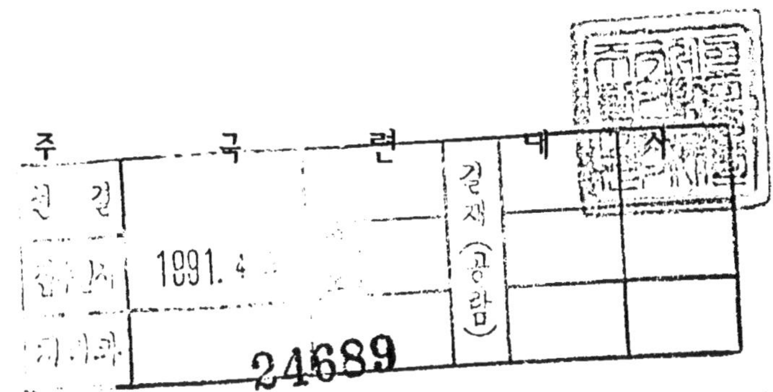

주	국	련	대	사
선 결			결재(공람)	
접수일시	1991. 4.			
처리과	24689			

0155

THE SECRETARY-GENERAL

9 April 1991

Excellency,

I have recently addressed to you communications regarding the recommendations formulated by the Security Council in response to requests for assistance received under the provisions of Article 50 of the United Nations Charter from countries facing special economic problems as a result of their carrying out of the measures adopted by the Council in its resolution 661 (1990).

At this time, I should like to draw your attention to a further communication addressed to me by the President of the Security Council (S/22398) informing me of the recommendations of the Security Council Committee established by resolution 661 (1990) concerning the situation between Iraq and Kuwait, in connection with the requests for assistance from the Syrian Arab Republic and the Republic of Djibouti (S/22021/Add.2). Copies of these documents are attached to this letter. As you know, the Security Council recognized the need for providing urgent assistance to these countries and appealed to all States on an urgent basis to provide them with immediate technical, financial and material assistance to mitigate the adverse impact on their economies of the application by them of the sanctions against Iraq pursuant to Security Council resolution 661 (1990). I should like to express the strongest possible support for this appeal.

In accordance with the recommendation of the Committee, I should be grateful if you could provide me with the relevant information on action taken by your Government to alleviate the special economic problems of these two States. Such information could be made available on a quarterly basis as proposed in my earlier communication of 23 January 1991.

Accept, Excellency, the assurances of my highest consideration.

Javier Pérez de Cuéllar

The Minister for Foreign Affairs
of the Republic of Korea

0156

UNITED
NATIONS

S

Security Council

Distr.
GENERAL

S/22398
22 March 1991

ORIGINAL: ENGLISH

LETTER DATED 21 MARCH 1991 FROM THE PRESIDENT OF THE SECURITY COUNCIL ADDRESSED TO THE SECRETARY-GENERAL

By resolution 669 (1990), adopted by the Security Council at its 2942nd meeting, on 24 September 1990, the Council, recalling its resolution 661 (1990) of 6 August 1990, entrusted the Security Council Committee established by resolution 661 (1990) concerning the situation between Iraq and Kuwait with the task of examining requests for assistance under the provisions of Article 50 of the Charter of the United Nations and making recommendations to the President of the Security Council for appropriate action.

By a letter dated 18 March 1990 (document S/22021/Add.2), the Chairman of the Committee transmitted the recommendations of the Committee with regard to the Syrian Arab Republic and Djibouti.

At consultations of the whole of the Security Council, held on 21 March 1991, it was decided to inform you of the above-mentioned recommendations of the Security Council Committee established by resolution 661 (1990) concerning the situation between Iraq and Kuwait pursuant to resolution 669 (1990) in connection with requests for assistance under the provisions of Article 50 of the Charter of the United Nations and to request you to implement the actions contained in the recommendations.

(*Signed*) Peter HOHENFELLNER
President of the Security Council

91-09300 2830a (E)

외 무 부

종 별 :

번 호 : UNW-1062 일 시 : 91 0426 2030

수 신 : 장 관(국연,중동일,기정)

발 신 : 주 유엔 대사

제 목 : 안보리동향(비공식협의)

안보리는 금 4.26 오전 및 오후 비공식협의를 갖고 엘살바돌, 걸프사태, 차기 사무총장 선출문제를 토의한바, 동결과를 아래보고함.

1. 엘살바돌

사무총장의 평화협상지원 노력을 평가하고, 유엔옵서버단 (ONUSAL) 배치안에도 호의적반응을 보인바, 다음주 재토의 예정임.

2. 이락난민

사무총장은 유엔의 난민구호현황, 미.영.불 군관할 난민수용소 접수교섭에 대하여 설명하고 각국의 재정지원을 촉구함.

3. 걸프사태 경제제재 조치관련 피해국 지원

각국, 유엔및 국제금융기구들의 협조를 촉구하는 안보리의장 명의 성명을 4.29 채택키로함.

4. 차기 사무총장 선출문제

가. 오는 10월 총회에 후보를 추천한다는 목표로 추진한다는데 이론이 없으나, 안보리의장이 각국에 후보추천을 권고하는 서한을 발송하는 문제에 대해서는 다수국이 유보적 입장 (관례나 그필요성에 의문)을 보인바, 추후 재토의 예정임.

나. 상기 서한 발송문제에 오지리, 미, 영이 지지입장을 보였으며, 불.중.에쿠아돌.코트디브와르, 짐바붸.루마니아.쿠바.인도가 유보적 입장을 나타냄. 의장 (벨지움)이 사전에 확인한바에 의하면, 현 총장은 동 서한문제에이의가 없다는 반응을 보였다고함. 끝

(대사 노창희-국장)

국기국 1차보 중아국 정문국 안기부

PAGE 1 91.04.27 10:16 WG

외신 1과 통제관

0158

원 본

UN

외 무 부

종 별 :

번 호 : UNW-1063 일 시 : 91 0426 2030

수 신 : 장 관(국연,중동이,기정)

발 신 : 주 유엔 대사

제 목 : 걸프사태(유엔동향)

1.이락 북부 ZAKHOU 지역 미.영.불군 관할 난민수용소의 유엔접수 교섭과관련, 4.26 J.PEREZDE CUELLAR 사무총장은 기자들에게 곧 합의가 이루어질것 이라고 언급한바, 동 총장 대변인은 금일 정오브리핑시 동합의를 위해서는 여러가지 세부적인 문제들이 남아있음을 시사하였음.

2.한편 J.C.AIME 사무총장 보좌관이 제네바에서 곧 S.KHAN 대표,오가타 유엔난민 고등판무관과회 동예정이며 다음주 터키방면, 바그다드에서 각각발진하는 유엔차량 행열 (UNHCE, UNCEF 의 구호품적재 CONVEY) 이 다음주초 이락북부 지역에 집결예정으로 알려진바,상기 난민수용소의 유엔접수 문제와 관련 주목됨. M.GOULDING사무차장도 다음주 이락-쿠웨이트 접경지역 이락난민들을 방문예정이라고함.

3.일본은 이락난민구호금 0.825 억불 추가공여결정 (현재까지 총액 1 억불)을 안보리문서 및 프레스릴리스로 배포하였으며, 4.25 부시대통령은 유엔사무총장과 통화시 5백 만불 구호금 지원의사를 밝혔다고함.끝

(대사 노창희-국장)

국기국 1차보 중아국 정문국 안기부

PAGE 1

91.04.27 10:17 WG

외신 1과 통제관

0159

외 무 부

종 별 :

번 호 : UNW-1078 일 시 : 91 0429 1900

수 신 : 장 관(국연,중동일,중동이,기정)

발 신 : 주 유엔 대사

제 목 : 안보리(서부사하라, 걸프사태)

2매 특사자료 보완
박사무관
(조서기관)

연: UNW-1030,1062

안보리는 금(4.29) 오후 공식회의 (제 2984-85 차회의) 를 개최하여 서부사하라, 걸프사태관련 의제를 토의한바, 동결과를 아래보고함.

1.서부사하라 주민부표

가.연호 협의결과에 의거, 사무총장의 유엔서부사하라 주민부표 실시단 (MINURSO) 설치계획안 (S/22464) 을 승인하는 결의안 (S/22525) 을 표결한바, 만장일치로 채택됨.(안보리 결의 690 호)

나.표결전 및 표결후 발언국 없었음.

2.걸프사태관련 경제 제재조치 피해국 지원

연호협의시 합의된 별첨 안보리 의장 명의 본건지원 촉구성명을 발표하였음.

첨부:1.서부사하라 관련 결의내용

2.걸프사태관련피해국 지원촉구 의장성명: UNW(F)-186

끝

(대사 노창희-국장대리)

국기국 1차보 중아국 중아국 정문국 청와대 안기부

PAGE 1 91.04.30 09:04 WG

외신 1과 통제관

0160

UNW(F)-186 10429 1900
(국연.중동일.중동이.기정) / 총3매

UNITED NATIONS

S

Security Council

Distr.
GENERAL

S/22525
26 April 1991
ENGLISH
ORIGINAL: FRENCH

Draft resolution

The Security Council,

Recalling its resolution 621 (1988) of 20 September 1988, by which it, inter alia, requested the Secretary-General to transmit to it a report on the holding of a referendum for self-determination of the people of Western Sahara and on ways and means to ensure the organization and supervision of such a referendum by the United Nations in cooperation with the Organization of African Unity,

Recalling also that, on 30 August 1988, the Kingdom of Morocco and the Frente Popular para la Liberación de Saguia el-Hamra y de Río de Oro gave their agreement in principle to the proposals of the United Nations Secretary-General and the current Chairman of the Organization of African Unity in the framework of their joint mission of good offices,

Recalling also its resolution 658 (1990), by which it approved the report of the Secretary-General (S/21360), which contains the full text of the settlement proposals as accepted by the two parties on 30 August 1988, as well as an outline of the plan provided by the Secretary-General in order to implement those proposals, and by which it requested the Secretary-General to transmit to it a further detailed report on his implementation plan containing in particular an estimate of the cost of the United Nations Mission for the Referendum in Western Sahara (MINURSO),

Desirous of reaching a just and lasting solution of the question of Western Sahara,

Having examined the report of the Secretary-General on the situation concerning Western Sahara (S/22464 and Corr.1),

1. Approves the report of the Secretary-General (S/22464 and Corr.1) transmitted to the Security Council in accordance with resolution 658 (1990);

91-13406 3339Z (E) /...

#UNW-1078
첨부물

3-1

0161

2. Expresses its full support for the efforts of the Secretary-General for the organization and the supervision, by the United Nations in cooperation with the Organization of African Unity, of a referendum for self-determination of the people of Western Sahara, in accordance with the objectives mentioned in his report;

3. Calls upon the two parties to cooperate fully with the Secretary-General in the implementation of his plan as described in his report contained in document S/21360 and amplified in his report contained in document S/22464 and Corr.1;

4. Decides to establish, under its authority, a United Nations Mission for the Referendum in Western Sahara (MINURSO) in accordance with the aforementioned report;

5. Decides that the transitional period will begin no later than 16 weeks after the General Assembly approves the MINURSO budget;

6. Requests the Secretary-General to keep the Security Council regularly informed of the implementation of his settlement plan.

3-2

0162

FINAL

Draft statement by the President of the Security Council concerning the States which have invoked Article 50 of the Charter

The members of the Security Council have considered the memorandum dated 22 March 1991 (S/22382) which was addressed to the President of the Security Council by the 21 States which have invoked Article 50 of the United Nations Charter owing to the special economic problems arising from the implementation of the sanctions imposed against Iraq and Kuwait under Council resolution 661 (1990).

The members of the Security Council have taken note of the Secretary-General's oral report to them on 11 April 1991, in which he supported the appeal launched by the 21 States that have invoked Article 50. The Secretary-General further informed the Council on 26 April 1991 of the conclusions reached by the Administrative Committee on Coordination (ACC) at the session it has just held in Paris, where members of ACC agreed to vigorously pursue their efforts to respond effectively to the needs of countries most affected by the implementation of resolution 661. The Secretary-General will coordinate through ACC, within the framework of this assistance, the activities of organizations of the United Nations system.

The members of the Security Council have taken note of the replies from a number of States (Austria, Belgium, Denmark, France, Germany, Greece, Ireland, Italy, Japan, Liechtenstein, Luxembourg, Luxembourg on behalf of the European Community and its 12 member States, Netherlands, Norway, Portugal, Spain, Switzerland, United Kingdom, United States and the USSR) which have furnished specific information on the assistance they have provided to various affected countries; they have also taken note of the replies from officials of international financial institutions, such as those received from the President of the World Bank and the President of IMF. They invite other Member States and international financial institutions and organizations to inform the Secretary-General as soon as possible of the measures that they have taken on behalf of the States which have invoked Article 50.

The members of the Security Council make a solemn appeal to States, international financial institutions and United Nations bodies to respond positively and speedily to the recommendations of the Security Council Committee, established under resolution 661, for assistance to countries which find themselves confronted with special economic problems arising from the carrying out of those measures imposed by resolution 661 and which have invoked article 15.

The members of the Security Council note that the procedure established under Article 50 of the Charter remains in effect.

3187E

3-3

0163

원 본

외 무 부

종 별 :

번 호 : UNW-1096 일 시 : 91 0430 2210

수 신 : 장 관(국연,중동일,기정)

발 신 : 주 유엔 대사

제 목 : 안보리동향(걸프사태,엘살바돌)

1.안보리 제재위원회는 지난 4.19 회의에 이어 금 4.30 회의를갖고 이락측의 석유수출 (약 10억불)허가 요청을 토의하였으나 진전이 없었던 것으로 알려짐.

2.걸프사태관련 ZAKHO 다국적군 관할 난민수용소의 유엔접수 교섭이 진행중인바, 동접수후 난민안전보호문제, 특히 유엔민간경찰 (CIVILIAN POLICE UNIT) 파견, 이를 위한 안보리 승인필요 여부가 주요현안이 되고있다고함.

3.한편 엘살바돌문제관련 안보리는 금일 비공식 협의에서 사무총장의 유엔옵서버단 배치계획을 토의한바, 곧 공식회의에서 승인절차를 밟을 것으로 관측됨.

첨부: 이락난민문제관련 NYT 기자: UNW(F)-188끝

(대사 노창희-국장)

국기국 1차보 중아국 정문국 청와대 안기부

PAGE 1

91.05.01 11:14 WG

외신 1과 통제관

0164

UNW(F)-188 10430 2210
(국연, 중동일, 기2일)

U.N. SEEKS ACCORD ON A POLICE FORCE IN NORTHERN IRAQ

TO REPLACE U.S. TROOPS

Security Council Would Avoid New Debate and Provide Protection for Kurds

By PATRICK E. TYLER
Special to The New York Times

WASHINGTON, April 29 — The five permanent members of the Security Council are seeking agreement on establishing a United Nations police force in the Kurdish region of northern Iraq. The force would take over from American and allied military units, which have set up a refugee zone in the area.

The idea of sending United Nations policemen into northern Iraq, as opposed to a full-fledged peacekeeping force, is intended to avoid a debate in the Security Council over whether such an intervention in Iraq's affairs can be authorized without a request from the Baghdad Government.

Replacing American Soldiers

Sending in a United Nations police force to take over the military security role now being performed by the United States and its allies would save Washington from having large numbers of American soldiers indefinitely committed in northern Iraq.

Those soldiers are there for the time being to provide security against Iraqi forces so that Kurdish families will feel confident enough to come down from the mountains, where they have fled from the army of President Saddam Hussein.

The idea for a police force, as detailed today at the United Nations by the British, who originated it, would be a logical extension of an agreement signed with Iraq on April 18 by the United Nations Secretary General's special refugee envoy, Prince Sadruddin Aga Khan. That agreement authorizes United Nations forces to take over refugee assistance operations in Iraq.

Avoiding a Special Resolution

Since the authorization of a police force for the area flows from this United Nations action, its advocates argue that it would not need any special resolution. From the point of view of the Western allies, this is crucial since it is thought very unlikely that either China or the Soviet Union would allow the adoption of any resolution that sanctioned the presence in Iraq of uninvited foreign military forces.

After the late-afternoon deliberations broke up, a second meeting began tonight in the office of Secretary General Javier Pérez de Cuéllar. It included only representatives from the United States, Britain and France, the nations that now have forces in Iraq.

United Nations peacekeeping forces consist of uniformed soldiers from the military units of member countries. They have automatic weapons, armored vehicles and artillery. The United Nations police are drawn from civilian forces, carry sidearms and wear armbands. They are quicker to deploy but do not use heavy weapons.

Any new security arrangement deemed satisfactory to Washington and its allies would bring about the hoped-for next step — American and allied withdrawal from the northern refugee zone, where commanders worry that they are bring drawn into an open-ended regional occupation to protect the Kurds from further retribution by Baghdad.

But any assumption of a security role by a United Nations force would raise questions of air support and other military backstopping from the allies, who came to the region prepared for confrontations both with the estimated 30,000 Iraqi troops in the north and with thousands of Kurdish guerrillas fighting for autonomy.

Some Official U.S. Views

Today, the White House spokesman, Marlin Fitzwater, suggested that a new assessment would have to be made of the danger in northern Iraq.

At the Pentagon, a senior official said the long-term safety of the Kurds would probably have to be secured politically before a military withdrawal. And such political steps would presumably involve the Iraqi Government and either some agency of the United Nations or representatives of the Kurdish nationalist movements. The Kurdish nationalists are expected to resume talks with Mr. Hussein on greater autonomy.

The official also said he believed that American forces would not be involved in a United Nations police force if one is established in Iraq.

"But whether we would be over the horizon" with back-up forces, "I don't know," he said. "Whether we would continue to have a quick-reaction force or combat air patrols, I don't know."

Mr. Pérez de Cuéllar, commenting in New York today on the concept of a United Nations force said, "Perhaps the Security Council is not needed; that is a possibility."

The American representative to the United Nations, Thomas R. Pickering, said today that Washington is taking "a very positive look" at the idea, adding that such a force is "potentially a very effective way to provide security and to provide protection" for the Kurds.

The first convoys of United Nations relief trucks were scheduled to arrive Tuesday in Zakho "to begin the process of taking over" the Kurdish relief operation, Mr. Fitzwater said. He added that administration of the camps could be turned over in weeks if the security issue was resolved.

Refugee Zone Extended

United States officials announced today that they had extended the refugee security zone well to the east of Zakho to Amadiya, another Kurdish city in northern Iraq. A second refugee center, capable of accommodating 25,000 people, will be built near Amadiya.

Mr. Fitzwater, reflecting the trouble that the American forces have encountered in understanding tribal differences among the Kurds and among their guerrilla movements, said: "Their guerrillas are part of their people, so it's a very difficult situation to sort out, but we are trying as best we can — to get the guerrillas to stop any activities that would thwart the humanitarian relief efforts."

Several hundred Kurdish refugees entered the Zakho area in recent days, and the first families took up residence in the tent city today. United States officials said a major transport effort would begin in a few days to bring 25,000 Kurds down from the mountains to the Zakho site. The total allied relief effort has delivered 10,000 tons of supplies by airdrop and truck.

At a news conference in Baghdad today, a United Nations official said Iraqi Kurdish refugees who fled to the border regions with Turkey and Iran are returning to their homes at the rate of 20,000 a day, a figure that could not be confirmed in Washington.

#UNW-1096 첨부물

0165

외 무 부

종 별 :

번 호 : UNW-1106 일 시 : 91 0501 2000

수 신 : 장 관(국연,중동일,기정)

발 신 : 주 유엔 대사

제 목 : 걸프사태

연: UNW-1096

1. 안보리 제재위원회는 연호 4.30 회의에 이어 5.3(금) 회의개최 예정인바, 오지리 (의장국)G.JANDL 서기관에 의하면 본건관련 지금까지 이락측이 제기해온 요청사항은 다음과같음.

가. 석유수출 (약 9,500 만불 상당)허가

나. 이락 동결자산 (약 1억불상당:미, 영, 스위스, 일은행) 해제

다. 제재조치에 앞서 거래가 이루어진 선적품 (민수용)반입허가

2. 안보리 휴전결의에 의거한 유엔의 이락 특정 무기폐기업무 추진동향에 관해서는 별첨 5.1.자 WP지 기사를 참조바람.

3. 유엔이락, 쿠웨이트 옵서버단 (UNIKOM)배치현황에 관한 4.30 자 유엔 발표내용을 별첨송부함.

첨부:1. 이락무기 폐기관련 WP 기사

2. UNIKOM배치현황: UNW(F)-189

끝

(대사 노창희-국장)

국기국 1차보 중아국 정문국 청와대 안기부 중동일

PAGE 1

91.05.02 10:49 WW

외신 1과 통제관

0166

UNIKOM: 30 APRIL 1991

GENERAL ASSESSMENT: UNIKOM AUGMENTED ITS OPERATIONAL AND LOGISTIC SUPPORT CAPABILITY DESPITE THE TEMPORARY DISLOCATION OCCASIONED BY THE EXPLOSION OF A KUWAITI AMMUNITION SALVAGE VEHICLE IN THE PARKING LOT OF UNIKOM HQ AT THE SAS HOTEL.

PERSONNEL AND LOGISTICS:

AAA PERSONNEL. TOTAL UNIKOM STRENGTH IS 1155. OF THIS NUMBER 1137 ARE IN KUWAIT, NINE (9) IN BAGHDAD, AND THREE (3) IN RIYADH. THE STATUS OF EACH NATION'S CONTINGENT IS NOTED BELOW:

ADVANCE PARTY(ON LOAN FROM OTHER MISSIONS)

AUSTRIA	2	NORWAY	2
FINLAND	2	SWEDEN	2
IRELAND	2		

TOTAL NUMBER OF MILOBS IN ADVANCE PARTY IS 10

UN MILITARY OBSERVERS

ARGENTINA	6	IRELAND	8
AUSTRIA	7	ITALY	6
BANGLADESH	7	KENYA	1
CANADA	1	MALAYSIA	8
CHILE	1	NORWAY	7
CHINA	1	PAKISTAN	9
DENMARK	7	POLAND	7
INDONESIA	7	ROMANIA	7
FIJI	1	SINGAPORE	7
FINLAND	7	SWEDEN	8
FRANCE	20	UK	20
GHANA	1	URUGUAY	1
GREECE	7	USA	20
HUNGARY	7	USSR	20
INDIA	8		

TOTAL NUMBER OF MILITARY OBSERVERS 217

TOTAL SUPPORT UNITS 384

TROOPS ON TEMPORARY ATTACHMENT:

AUSTRIA INFANTRY COMPANY	115
DENMARK INFANTRY COMPANY	115
FIJI INFANTRY COMPANY	105
GHANA INFANTRY COMPANY	105
NEPAL INFANTRY COMPANY	104
TOTAL	544

3-3

0167

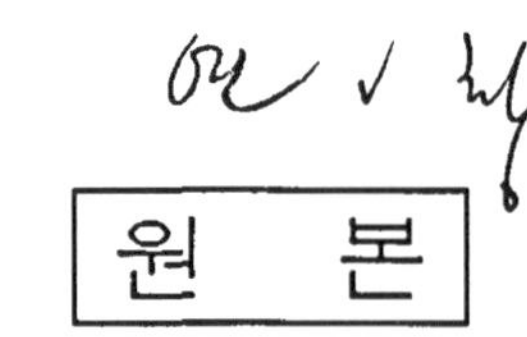

원 본

외 무 부

종 별 :

번 호 : UNW-1117 일 시 : 91 0502 1900

수 신 : 장 관(국연,중동일,기정)

발 신 : 주 유엔 대사

제 목 : 걸프사태(안보리)

1.안보리 휴전결의에 앞서 사무총장은 이락.쿠웨이트 국경획정안 (동결의 본문3항), 배상기금 설치안 (본문 17항)을 안보리에 금명간 제출예정임. 5.2.자 NYT 지 보도에 의하면 동기금충당을 위한 이락 석유수출 수입공제 비율에 대해서는 10 프로이하 (인도, 쿠바, 예멘), 25-30프로 (영국), 40-50프로 (미국)수준이 거론되고 있다함.

2.이락의 특정무기 폐기업무를 관장할 특별위는 5.6-10 간 유엔본부에서 회의를 갖고, 향후 작업계획을 수립할 예정임.

3.다국적군 관할 난민수용소의 유엔이관 교섭과관련, S.KHAN 대표가 바그다드를 곧방문할 예정인 것으로 관측되고 있음.

첨부:1.5.2.자 N.Y.T. 지 기사

2.상기 특별위명단:UNW(F)-190

끝

(대사 노창희-국장)

국기국 1차보 중아국 정문국 안기부

PAGE 1

91.05.03 09:48 WG

외신 1과 통제관

0168

UNW(F)-190 10502 1900
(국연 . 중동일 . 기정) 총고미1

U.S. Wants Iraq to Finance Kurdish Relief Operations

By ELAINE SCIOLINO

Special to The New York Times

WASHINGTON, May 1 — The United States wants Iraq to pay for the American-led effort to help Kurdish refugees in the northern part of the country, senior Bush Administration officials said today.

Although the Administration is uncertain exactly how to require the Baghdad Government to finance the operation, which is expected to cost more than $500 million over six months, one option under consideration would link such payment to approval of Iraqi resumption of oil exports. Linkage would require the approval of the sanctions committee of the United Nations Security Council, which is setting the terms for lifting economic sanctions against Iraq.

The idea of collecting payment from Iraq, initially floated by Britain, reflects the Administration's overall strategy to keep President Saddam Hussein politically and militarily weak, while also searching for new ways to strangle his economy.

Resigned to the prospect that Mr. Hussein may remain President of Iraq for some time and determined that the country not be allowed to rebuild as long as he remains in power, the Administration is preparing a proposal under which Iraq would have to contribute 40 to 50 percent of its oil revenue for reparations from its invasion of Kuwait last August, senior Administration officials said.

> A link between refugee aid and any oil revenue.

But there is considerable skepticism in the Administration that the United States will succeed in convincing the sanctions committee, which includes all 15 members of the Security Council, to require Iraqi financing of the relief effort or to extract such a high percentage of its oil revenue for reparations for damage done to Kuwait during the war.

India, Cuba and Yemen, members of the Security Council, have urged that Iraq pay no more than 10 percent, while Britain proposes that Iraq pay the same amount for reparations as it did for the purchase of weapons over the last decade, a figure equivalent to about 25 to 30 percent of its prewar oil revenue. Under the British plan, these payments would be phased in as Iraqi oil exports come back on line.

The Security Council will begin this week to grapple with the reparations issue. Under the cease-fire resolution adopted by the Council on April 3, Secretary General Javier Pérez de Cuéllar must submit an initial report by Friday with the structure for a fund generated by oil sales. This fund will be tapped for reparations.

Administration officials acknowledge that the American demand for Iraq to pay for the relief effort goes beyond two Security Council resolutions that dictate Iraq's conduct: a cease-fire resolution that sets a series of demands and deadlines that must be met before economic sanctions are lifted, and a resolution giving the Security Council sweeping authority to provide relief to Iraq's refugees. But they argue that these resolutions are flexible enough to take changing circumstances into account.

The United States and Britain take a strict interpretation of the cease-fire resolution in opposing Iraq's requests to sell close to $1 billion of its oil and to gain access to $1 billion of its assets frozen in foreign banks. Baghdad says it needs this money to buy food and medical supplies.

"Everyone in the Council is inclined to be more flexible than us and Britain," a White House official said. "We're motiviated not only by the fact that Saddam is still in power but also that if we open the door a little, he'll find ways to circumvent the sanctions and undermine the coalition aligned against him."

Administration officials argue, for example, that Iraq still has considerable assets in its central bank and sizable gold reserves that it should spend first. Other Security Council members, such as China, are leaning toward aiding Iraq's economy, but the United States remains suspicious of its appeals that its civilian population is in desperate need of food.

The hard line was reflected by Under Secretary of Defense Paul D. Wolfowitz, who said on the "McNeil-Lehrer News Hour" on Monday: "As far as we can tell, some large share of the trucks bringing food in from Jordan get diverted to Iraqi military camps, and as far as we know, the Iraqis still have plenty of assets with which to buy food. So these claims are greeted with considerable skepticism."

U.S. Approach Unavailing

Administration officials acknowledged that their hard line thus far has had no success in dislodging Mr. Hussein. In fact, they said, he is stronger now than he was at the end of the war because he has successfully put down civil insurrections and because the presence of foreign troops on his soil gives him the chance to argue that Iraqi sovereignty is being violated.

These officials acknowledge that there is increasing sympathy in the Security Council for Iraq's economic plight and that the United States may be swimming against the tide.

"There's a new mood that Iraq should be able to get on with their own affairs and recover after the war," an official said. "There's a lot of feeling that 'you destroyed their infrastructure and they've suffered enough.' "

Former United Nations officials question the wisdom of continuing sanctions that might backfire.

"There is a limit beyond which you may not be able to get much out of the Iraqis," said Sir Brian Urquhart, a former Under Secretary General. "If the object of the exercise is to get Saddam to leave, I can't believe this is going to work. There's the danger that you will revive undeserved sympathy and support for the guy."

UNW-1117 의
첨부물

2-1

0169

Press Release

Department of Public Information • News Coverage Service • New York

SG/A/459
IK/19
1 May 1991

SECRETARY-GENERAL APPOINTS MEMBERS OF SPECIAL COMMISSION
PURSUANT TO SECURITY COUNCIL RESOLUTION 687 (1991)

Further to the announcement of 22 April concerning the Special Commission established to carry out the tasks enumerated in paragraphs 9 (b) (i-iii), 10 and 13 of Security Council resolution 687 (1991), the Secretary-General has appointed the following as members of the Special Commission:

Dr. Paal Aas of Norway; Ken Adachi of Japan; Professor B.N.C. Agu of Nigeria; Lt. Col. Andrzej Badek of Poland; Professor Bryan C. Barrass of the United Kingdom; Peter von Butler of Germany; Col. Armando Caputo of Italy; Ronald Cleminson of Canada; Dr. John Gee of Australia; Professor Helmut Hönig of Austria; B.A. Kuvshinnikov of the Soviet Union; Dr. A.J.J. Ooms of the Netherlands; Malmi Marjatta Rautio of Finland; Michel Saint Mleux of France; Lt. Col. Simanjuntak of Indonesia; Miroslav Splino of Czechoslovakia; Emile Vanden Bemden of Belgium; and Yuan Renfeng of China.

An expert from Venezuela is shortly expected to be confirmed as a member of the Special Commission.

On 22 April, Ambassador Rolf Ekeus of Sweden and Robert Gallucci of the United States were appointed by the Secretary-General as Executive Chairman and Deputy Executive Chairman, respectively, of the Special Commission.

* *** *

2-2

20192

For information media—not an official record

0170

UNITED NATIONS

S

Security Council

Distr.
GENERAL

S/22558
2 May 1991

ORIGINAL: ENGLISH

이락-쿠웨이트 국경계획안

REPORT OF THE SECRETARY-GENERAL REGARDING PARAGRAPH 3 OF SECURITY COUNCIL RESOLUTION 687 (1991)

1. The present report is submitted pursuant to Security Council resolution 687 (1991) of 3 April 1991. In paragraph 3 of the resolution, the Security Council called upon me to lend assistance to make arrangements with Iraq and Kuwait to demarcate the boundary between Iraq and Kuwait, drawing on appropriate material, including the map transmitted by Security Council document S/22412, and to report back to the Security Council within one month.

2. In lending my assistance to Iraq and Kuwait with a view to making the arrangements to demarcate the boundary between them, I have borne in mind that, in paragraph 2 of Security Council resolution 687 (1991), the Council demanded "that Iraq and Kuwait respect the inviolability of the international boundary and the allocation of islands set out in the 'Agreed Minutes between the State of Kuwait and the Republic of Iraq regarding the Restoration of Friendly Relations, Recognition and Related Matters', signed by them in the exercise of their sovereignty at Baghdad on 4 October 1963 and registered with the United Nations and published by the United Nations in document 7063, United Nations, Treaty Series, 1964". I have also taken into account that, in a letter dated 4 April 1991 addressed to me by the Deputy Prime Minister and Minister for Foreign Affairs of Kuwait, Kuwait has expressed its intention to scrupulously comply with all the provisions of resolution 687 (1991) and to cooperate with me with a view to ensuring its implementation (S/22457, annex) and that, in accordance with paragraph 33 of Security Council resolution 687 (1991), the Minister for Foreign Affairs of Iraq in the penultimate paragraph of a letter dated 6 April 1991 (S/22456) has notified the Security Council and the Secretary-General of Iraq's acceptance of the provisions of that resolution. The text of the Agreed Minutes referred to in paragraph 2 of Security Council resolution 687 (1991) is contained in Security Council document S/22432.

3. After consultations with the Governments of Iraq and Kuwait, I will now establish an Iraq-Kuwait Boundary Demarcation Commission, to be composed of one representative each of Iraq and Kuwait and three independent experts who will be appointed by me, one of whom will serve as the Chairman. The Council will be informed as soon as the Commission is established. The terms of reference of the Commission will be to demarcate in geographical coordinates of latitude and longitude the international boundary set out in the Agreed

91-13804 2331e (E)

/...

Minutes between Kuwait and Iraq referred to above. In view of the fact that one of the main purposes of the demarcation of the boundary between Kuwait and Iraq is to promote stability and peace and security along the border, the Commission will also make arrangements for the physical representation of the boundary. The coordinates established by the Commission will constitute the final demarcation of the international boundary between Iraq and Kuwait in accordance with the Agreed Minutes of 4 October 1963. They will be lodged in the archives of both Governments and a certified copy will also be submitted to me, which I will communicate to the Security Council and will retain for safe-keeping in the archives of the United Nations.

4. The demarcation of the boundary between Iraq and Kuwait will be accomplished by drawing upon appropriate material, including the map transmitted by Security Council document S/22412, and by utilizing appropriate technology. The physical representation of the boundary will be carried out through the erection of an appropriate number and type of boundary pillars or monuments. The Commission will provide for arrangements for maintenance on a continuing basis and locational accuracy (including repositioning, if necessary) of the surficial boundary representation.

5. As soon as the Commission is constituted and after an initial assessment of the resources required for the demarcation of the boundary has been made, the Commission will transmit to me an estimate of costs, which I will communicate to the Security Council; simultaneously, I will make a proposal that all costs, including the initial costs of the Commission, should be shared between the two interested parties.

6. The Commission will be assisted by a small staff that will adopt its own rules of procedure and working methods and make the necessary arrangements for the identification and examination of appropriate material relevant to the demarcation of the boundary. The Commission will be responsible to me in the conduct of its work and will report regularly to me on the progress of its work with a view to the earliest possible finalization of the demarcation of the boundary. The Commission will take its decisions by majority. Its decisions regarding the demarcation of the boundary will be final.

7. The Commission shall enjoy unimpeded freedom of movement in the area of the demarcation of the international boundary as well as all necessary privileges and immunities for the fulfilment of its task. The three independent experts shall enjoy the status of experts on missions within the meaning of article VI of the Convention on Privileges and Immunities of the United Nations of 1946. 1/

8. In the exercise of its task of demarcating the boundary, with respect to physical security and clearance of mines the Commission will rely on the relevant arrangements made for the United Nations Iraq-Kuwait Observer Mission (UNIKOM).

Notes

1/ General Assembly resolution 22 A (I).

0172 /...

Annex I

Letter dated 19 April 1991 from the Permanent Representative of Kuwait to the United Nations addressed to the Secretary-General

I should like to refer to the report regarding paragraph 3 of Security Council resolution 687 (1991) and to convey the acceptance by the Government of Kuwait of the terms set out in the report and its readiness to cooperate with the United Nations in implementing those terms.

(Signed) Mohammad A. ABULHASAN
Ambassador
Permanent Representative

/...

0173

Annex II

Letter dated 23 April 1991 from the Permanent Representative of Iraq to the United Nations addressed to the Secretary-General

[Original: Arabic]

On instructions from my Government and with reference to the meeting that we held with the Legal Counsel of the United Nations, Mr. Fleischhauer, on 17 April 1991, I have the honour to transmit herewith a letter addressed to you by Mr. Ahmed Hussein, Minister for Foreign Affairs of the Republic of Iraq, dated 23 April 1991 concerning the Iraq-Kuwait Boundary Demarcation Commission.

(Signed) Abdul Amir A. AL-ANBARI
Ambassador
Permanent Representative

0174 /...

Enclosure

Letter dated 23 April 1991 from the Minister for Foreign Affairs of Iraq addressed to the Secretary-General

[Original: Arabic]

With reference to the meeting held between our Permanent Representative and the Legal Counsel of the United Nations on 17 April 1991 and your draft report which you intend to submit to the Security Council concerning paragraph 3 of Security Council resolution 687 (1991) and regarding which you asked for the view of my Government, I have the honour to state the following.

Part I of the letter that I addressed to you on 6 April 1991 explained that, although in its preamble Security Council resolution 687 (1991) affirms that Iraq is an independent sovereign State, many of its iniquitous provisions do not respect this sovereignty but constitute an unprecedented assault on it and on the rights that stem therefrom, embodied in the Charter and in international law and custom. With regard to the question of the boundary, the Security Council has imposed a specific position with regard to the Iraqi-Kuwaiti boundary, whereas the custom in law and in practice in international relations is that boundary questions are left to an agreement between States, because this is the sole basis that can guarantee the principle of the stability of boundaries.

Furthermore, the Council resolution does not take into account the viewpoint of Iraq, namely, that the "Agreed Minutes between the State of Kuwait and the Republic of Iraq regarding the Restoration of Friendly Relations, Recognition and Related Matters" of 4 October 1963 have not yet been subjected to the constitutional procedures required for their ratification by the legislative authority and the President of Iraq, thus leaving the question of the boundary pending and unresolved. The Council has nevertheless imposed on Iraq the line of its boundary with Kuwait. By acting in this strange manner, the Council itself has also violated one of the provisions of resolution 660 (1990), which was the basis for the subsequent resolution adopted by the Council. In its paragraph 3, resolution 660 (1990) called upon Iraq and Kuwait to resolve their differences through negotiations, and the question of the boundary is well known to be one of the main differences. Iraq officially informed the Council that it accepted resolution 660 (1990) and was prepared to implement it, but the Council has disregarded this legal position, contradicting its previous resolutions, and adopted an iniquitous resolution that imposes new conditions on Iraq. It has imposed a border situation on Iraq, an independent sovereign State and Member of the United Nations, and has deprived it of its right to establish its territorial rights in accordance with the principles of international law. Thus the Council would also deprive Iraq of the right to exercise its free choice and to affirm that it accepts that boundary without reservation. Where the question of the boundary is concerned, the Council resolution is an iniquitous resolution, which constitutes a dangerous precedent, a first in the annals of

/...

0175

the international Organization and - as some impartial members of the Council indicated in their statements when the resolution was voted on - an assault on the sovereignty of States.

The Iraqi Government remains convinced of the legitimate character of the position reflected in the above observations. This legitimate character is especially borne out by the mission entrusted to you by virtue of paragraph 3 of resolution 687 (1991). The above-mentioned paragraph calls upon you to lend your assistance to make arrangements with Iraq and Kuwait to demarcate the boundary between Iraq and Kuwait, drawing on appropriate material, including the map transmitted by Security Council document S/22412.

Accordingly, my Government wishes to make the comments set forth below concerning your draft report to which I referred above.

1. My Government wonders on what legal foundation the Council based its resolution 687 (1991) and you your draft report in considering the map that was transmitted by Security Council document S/22412, dated 28 March 1991, at the request of the Permanent Mission of the United Kingdom and which your Legal Counsel described to our Permanent Representative as a United Kingdom map mentioned in the Agreed Minutes of 1963. The Agreed Minutes did not refer to any map, as is clear from the text published in the United Nations Treaty Series, vol. 485, No. 7063. It is blatantly true also that the sole mention of the map in question in paragraph 3 of Council resolution 687 (1991) was introduced without any legal grounds.

The Government of my country was not a party to the drawing of that map. It did not recognize the map, nor is there any proof of its having extended such recognition. Accordingly, the fact that you and the Council consider the map to be a part of the material to be drawn upon for the demarcation process constitutes an iniquitous and unilateral imposition against the will of Iraq, a sovereign State Member of the United Nations, and a prejudgement of the course of the land boundary before any commission embarks on the process of demarcating that boundary.

2. In addition, the assistance that you have offered in making arrangements for the demarcation of the boundary between Iraq and Kuwait must ensure a perfect balance between the positions that either side may adopt with regard to the demarcation process, together with a just and equitable approach to the settlement of any differences that might arise between them concerning technical matters. The Iraqi Government therefore believes that, if the Commission entrusted with the demarcation process is constituted in accordance with your proposal, the result cannot be just and equitable, particularly in view of our comments in paragraph 1 above. You have suggested that the Commission consist of five members, of whom two would represent Iraq and Kuwait respectively, together with three independent experts to be chosen by you, one of whom would be appointed as the Chairman. You have also suggested that the Commission's decisions should be taken by a majority vote. Although it has no doubts as to your credibility with respect to the selection of the three independent experts, my country's Government nevertheless believes that,

0176

/...

since it will play no part in the selection of the three experts, it will have no way of ensuring in advance that they are truly independent. Its views with regard to the demarcation process will thus be represented only by one of the five members.

3. You mention in the draft report that the demarcation of the boundary will be accomplished by drawing upon appropriate material, including the map transmitted by Security Council document S/22412, as referred to in paragraph 3 of resolution 687 (1991). However, you add that the Commission may "utilize appropriate technology" (para. 4 of the draft report) and that it will "make the necessary arrangements for the identification and examination of appropriate material relevant to the demarcation of the boundary" (para. 6 of the draft report). The Government of Iraq believes that the terms "appropriate material", "appropriate technology" and "identification and examination of appropriate material relevant to the demarcation of the boundary" must be explained. This explanation will permit my Government to express its views, if such views are welcome, on a solid basis. The requested explanation will also help to reduce the possibilities of disagreement in the future when the Commission begins its work.

4. You propose in paragraph 5 of the draft report that the costs of the demarcation process should be shared between the two parties. The Government of Iraq fails to understand the basis for this proposal, since the overall thrust of the proposals contained in the draft report amounts - in the opinion of my Government - to a virtual "act of capitulation" in which Iraq is denied any freedom to join in the harmonious agreement on its contents. Accordingly, and in the light of my comments at the beginning of this letter, the suggestion seems to be that Iraq should bear half the costs of the demarcation process without any account being taken of its views on the boundary question as a whole, with respect to either demarcation or delimitation. The Iraqi Government cannot therefore see any justification, based on principles of justice or equity, for bearing any costs relating to a process which is imposed upon it.

I should like, in conclusion, to assure you that the Iraqi Government is fully prepared to consult with you concerning the comments contained in this letter, either in New York or elsewhere. In this connection, I also wish to note that, just as we accepted resolution 687 (1991) despite our objections to and criticism of its provisions, we will cooperate with you and will nominate a representative of our Government to participate in the Demarcation Commission, even if you take no account of the views and comments we have expressed above. We do this because the circumstances forcing our acceptance persist.

(Signed) Ahmed HUSSEIN
Minister for Foreign Affairs
Baghdad, 23 April 1991

0177 /...

Annex III

Letter dated 30 April 1991 from the Secretary-General addressed to the Minister for Foreign Affairs of Iraq

I have the honour to refer to your letter dated 23 April 1991, which was transmitted to me by a letter of the same date from the Permanent Representative of Iraq to the United Nations and which contained comments on the proposals made with regard to the implementation of paragraph 3 of Security Council resolution 687 (1991) and on which I must report to the Security Council no later than 2 May 1991. In informing me of your Government's readiness to cooperate with me and to nominate a representative of Iraq to participate in the proposed Boundary Demarcation Commission, a decision which I welcome, the letter nevertheless contains a number of comments to which I would like to respond.

The first comment of your Government is that, in international law, a boundary demarcation between two States can be carried out only by agreement between the parties and that the Security Council has no competence to impose such a demarcation. In this connection, I would like to recall that, in paragraph 2 of resolution 687 (1991) the Security Council, acting under Chapter VII of the Charter of the United Nations demanded that Iraq and Kuwait respect the inviolability of their international boundary and the allocation of islands "set out in the 'Agreed Minutes between the State of Kuwait and the Republic of Iraq regarding the Restoration of Friendly Relations, Recognition and Related Matters', signed by them in the exercise of their sovereignty at Baghdad on 4 October 1963". In paragraph 3 of that resolution the Council called upon me to lend my "assistance to make arrangements with Iraq and Kuwait to demarcate the boundary between Iraq and Kuwait". In identical letters dated 6 April 1991 addressed to me and to the President of the Security Council (S/22456), your Government formally notified its acceptance of the provisions of that resolution. You further reconfirmed your Government's acceptance of paragraph 3 of resolution 687 (1991) at the end of your letter of 23 April 1991 (see annex II, enclosure). Therefore, the element of agreement as far as Iraq is concerned, is provided by your Government's official notifications of acceptance. Since the Government of Kuwait has also expressed to me its willingness scrupulously to comply with all provisions of the resolution and to cooperate with me to ensure its implementation (S/22457), the necessary element of consent has been provided by the two parties.

Secondly, your Government states that the proposed demarcation would be prejudged by a specific reference to a map made available by the United Kingdom and which, according to the letter, the Legal Counsel described as "a United Kingdom map mentioned in the agreed minutes of 1963". On a purely factual point, I wish to state that the Legal Counsel of the United Nations did not describe the map as having been mentioned in the 1963 agreed minutes. In response to a question as to which map was referred to in document S/22412, your Permanent Representative was informed that the map in question was "a

/...

0178

United Kingdom map". On a substantive level, however, I am obliged to point out that the resolution provides that the demarcation of the boundary should be based on "appropriate material, _including_ the map transmitted by Security Council document S/22412" [emphasis added]. In the light of this wording, I have proposed that the Commission will have to make "necessary arrangements for the identification and examination of appropriate material relevant to the demarcation of the boundary".

Thirdly, your Government queries the independence of the experts to be appointed by me to serve on the Boundary Commission and comments on the proposed decision-making by majority. I would like to assure you that, in appointing the independent experts of the Commission, I shall, as always, base my decisions on the need to ensure independence, competence and integrity. Furthermore, to ensure an equitable approach and the effective functioning of the Commission, I have proposed that neither Government should be able to frustrate the work of the Commission.

Fourthly, your Government has requested me to explain such terms as "appropriate material", "appropriate technology" and "identification and examination of appropriate material relevant to the demarcation of the boundary". It is up to the Commission to examine and identify the relevant documentation and to determine which technology or combination of methods can best be used for the fulfilment of its mandate. In my view it would prejudice the work of the Commission, and even hinder its independence, if at this stage I were to go beyond the level of detail concerning the working methods of the Boundary Commission set out in my draft report.

Finally, your Government objects to paying half of the costs of the demarcation on the ground that its views on the boundary question are not fully being taken into account. However, through your Government's participation in the work of the Boundary Commission its views will find such expression. Together with your Government's acceptance of paragraph 3 of resolution 687 (1991), both in its letter of 6 April 1991 (S/22456) as well as in the letter of 23 April 1991, I can see no basis for objections to the paying of its share of the costs, which will be determined by the Commission.

In the light of your Government's expressed readiness to cooperate with me, I intend to proceed immediately with the establishment of the Commission and will accordingly convey my proposals, together with this exchange of correspondence, to the Security Council.

(_Signed_) Javier PEREZ DE CUELLAR
Secretary-General

0179

원 본

외 무 부

종 별 :

번 호 : UNW-1154 일 시 : 91 0506 1800

수 신 : 장 관(국연,중동일,기정)

발 신 : 주 유엔대사

제 목 : 걸프사태(안보리)

안보리 휴전결의 후속조치 동향에관한 5.6.자 CSM기사를 별첨송부함.

첨부:5.6.자 CSM 기사: UNW(F)-194

끝

(대사 노창희-국장)

국기국 1차보 중아국 정문국 안기부

PAGE 1

91.05.07 08:28 WH

외신 1과 통제관

0180

UNW(F)-194 10506 1800
(국연. 중동일. 기정) 총1매

UN Keeps Economic Grip on Iraq Amid Appeals for Leniency

By Marian Houk

Special to The Christian Science Monitor

UNITED NATIONS, N.Y.

THE United Nations Security Council has decided to keep its economic squeeze on Iraq, hoping that if the Baath Party leadership cannot be ousted, it can at least be forced down the path of political reform.

Western allies say that how hard they push for international policing of Kurdish zones in northern Iraq depends on the outcome of talks being held in Baghdad with Kurdish representatives. Pressure is on the Iraqi government, Western diplomats say, to live up to a 1970s agreement that makes Kurds responsible for their own security, but which was never implemented.

Iraqi diplomats at the UN complain that they face a growing list of United States demands, but say they have no choice but to comply. They privately predict strides toward Iraqi democracy.

The UN's continued squeeze was made clear when Iraq asked permission on April 14 to sell enough oil to buy nearly $1 billion of food and other civilian supplies. The Security Council's sanctions committee, which had previously put off Iraq's request, ruled Friday that, before the appeal can be considered, Iraq will have to account for other assets it might use for such purchases.

"Iraq must have some liquid foreign assets on hand," a US diplomat said Friday. "It must have had them on Aug. 1, before its invasion of Kuwait, and it must still have them."

Mandatory UN sanctions imposed Aug. 6 prohibit trade with Iraq. Under the UN cease-fire resolution, Iraqi oil exports would not resume until arrangements are made for paying war reparations and until Iraq's most dangerous weaponry is destroyed.

One Iraqi, who requested anonymity, says the UN has already been informed that Iraq's Central Bank, where foreign exchange and gold would have been deposited, was destroyed in air raids. Recent reports, however, claim Iraqi president Saddam Hussein, his family, and associates have secret bank accounts. Middle Eastern diplomats have complained about lavish televised celebrations last week for Mr. Hussein's birthday. The Iraqi leader vowed to rebuild a new Iraq, even if UN sanctions were not lifted.

Diplomats said they believe UN and International Committee of the Red Cross reports that the Iraqi population has been badly affected by the war. But, they complained, the Iraqi leadership's posturing is depriving its people of help.

Iraq asked April 28 for $1 billion in frozen assets abroad to be unblocked to finance food and medicine purchases. The next day, Abdul Amir al-Anbari, Iraq's ambassador to the UN, enlarged his appeal, asking the Council to alleviate "the critical situation" he said "threatens to lead to starvation and disease."

Mr. Anbari petitioned the Council for help in releasing food destined for Iraq, but impounded in ports around the world after the UN embargo began. The cargoes, he said, included $19 million of milk for infants, and $45 million of sugar, lentils, meat, fish, eggs, and tea.

The sanctions committee decided Friday that individual governments could release Iraq's frozen assets, under UN monitoring, according to the rules already set down by the Council.

Under these rules, Iraq can buy food if it informs the sanctions committee of its purchases; it can buy other essentials to meet civilian needs if no member of the committee objects; no funds can be unblocked for any other purpose. Under the embargo, Iraq is free to import medicine. Despite these guidelines, US diplomats said, no US-held Iraqi assets would be released.

Iraq last week also asked for a five-year exemption from any payments for war damages. Under the cease-fire terms, Iraq is to pay a percentage of its future oil revenues in reparations.

Anbari said in a letter to UN Secretary-General Javier Pérez de Cuéllar that Iraq's reconstruction and development needs over five years would require $170 billion, but that expected oil revenues would not total more than $20 billion.

Mr. Pérez de Cuéllar has promised to fix a ceiling rate for reparations after further consultations. But, he warned, Iraq's future oil exports will have to be strictly supervised to ensure that accurate reparation payments are made.

#UNW-1154
첨부물

0181

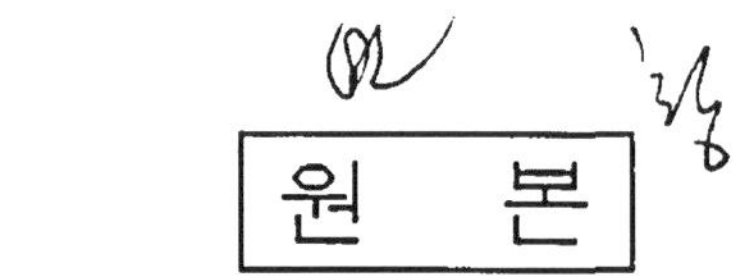

외 무 부

종 별 :

번 호 : UNW-1176 일 시 : 91 0507 2045

수 신 : 장 관(국연,중동일,기정)

발 신 : 주 유엔대사

제 목 : 걸프사태(유엔동향)

1.금 5.7. 사무총장 대변인에 의하면 S.KHAN대표가 5.7-14 간 쿠웨이트, 이란, 이락 ,터어키를 방문한다고 함.

2.한편 유엔옵서버단은 5.6.자로 DMZ 에 배치완료 되었다고 하며, M.GOULDING 사무차장은 현재 바그다드에서 이락당국과 UNIKOM(유엔옵서버단), 북이락 유엔경찰대파견 관련문제를 협의중인것으로 알려짐.

3. J.PEREZ DE CUELLAR 사무총장은 북이락 난민수용소 접수, 특히 유엔경찰력 배치문제와 관련 미,영,불,이락측에 유엔에 대한 요청내용을 보다 분명히 해줄것을 요청하고 그회신을 기다리고있다고함.

첨부:5.7.자 NYT 지 사설 : UNW(F)-196

끝

(대사 노창희-국장)

국기국 1차보 중아국 안기부 정문국

PAGE 1

91.05.08 10:23 WH

외신 1과 통제관

0182

UNW(H)-196 1507 2045 총1여
(유연 . 중동일 . 기전)

Stay In or Get Out of Iraq?

How does one make sense of the conflicting news from Iraq? Down south, in the demilitarized zone on Kuwait's frontier, withdrawing allied forces yesterday formally handed over command to United Nations peacekeepers. Meanwhile, up north, also yesterday, U.S. commanders urged that safe-haven areas for Kurdish refugees be *extended*, all the way to Dohuk, a big provincial city 50 miles within Iraq. Americans may justifiably wonder whether President Bush's victorious coalition is heading into, or out of, a quagmire.

What happened in the south is easier to explain. The handover to the U.N. follows a cease-fire agreement dealing expressly with Saddam Hussein's lawless annexation of Kuwait. But a thin blue-helmeted line of peacekeepers is a symbol of that accord, not its enforcer. The stick is the world's demonstrated ability to close Iraq's ports with strangling economic sanctions.

The allied incursion into northern Iraq stems from Saddam Hussein's ruthless assault on his own Kurdish citizens. President Bush, fearing that help for the Kurds would plunge Americans into an Iraqi civil war, described the humanitarian intervention as "temporary," stressing that he hoped the U.N. would take over the task of protecting refugees in 30 days. His hopes were plainly overoptimistic. But as in Kuwait's demilitarized zone, U.N. sanctions may provide the most practical shield against a vengeful Saddam Hussein.

Understandably, Iraqi Kurds are trying to turn the world's sympathy to their advantage. Their leaders warn that as many as 300,000 Kurds won't come down from nearby mountains unless protected by allied troops.

There's nothing unreasonable about Kurdish pressure to expand this largest, fastest and most complex international relief effort. As even the unsentimental Henry Kissinger acknowledges, the Iraqi Kurds have a special claim "because the violation of human rights occurred under our very eyes, during a cease-fire whose terms we dictated, by a dictator we compared to Hitler and caused by troops it had been in our power to destroy."

But accepting a special responsibility for the suffering of Iraqi Kurds is not the same as favoring statehood for a people scattered through Iraq, Iran, Turkey, Syria and the Soviet Union. That distinction seems to be well understood by leaders of Iraqi Kurds now negotiating with Saddam Hussein for autonomy rights "within the framework of a united, democratic Iraq."

There's no reason for Kurds, or for anyone, to trust this harsh tyrant. But Saddam Hussein, or whoever might supplant him, will still have to contend with a U.N. embargo on Iraqi oil exports and other trade. It can be lifted only with the assent of the Security Council's five permanent members.

Since the sanctions pertain to Kuwait, their use in behalf of the Kurds would require a new Council resolution. It should not be beyond diplomatic wit to find language that would help the Kurds and remove the need for Western forces in northern Iraq. And it should be America's purpose to remain in Iraq only pending creation of convincing security guarantees for an ill-used people.

장관실	차관실	一차보	二차보	기획실	의전장	아주국	미주국	구주국	중아국	국기국	경제국	통상국	정문국	영교국	총무과	감사관	안보원	외연원	청와대	총리실	안기부	공보부

#UNW-1176
첨부물

0183

원 본

외 무 부

종 별 :

번 호 : UNW-1189 일 시 : 91 0508 2030

수 신 : 장 관(국연,중동일,기정)

발 신 : 주 유엔 대사

제 목 : 걸프사태(유엔동향)

금 5.8. 유엔측 발표에 의하면, 유엔옵서버단 배치완료 (5.6.)에 따라 다국적군이 5.9. DMZ지역에서 철군을 완료할것을 예상된다고함.

첨부:상기 유엔측 발표내용: UNW(F)-198

끝

(대사 노창희-국장)

국기국 1차보 중아국 정문국 안기부

PAGE 1 91.05.09 10:02 WG

외신 1과 통제관

0184

UNW(F)-198 2030
(국연.중동일.기조)

총1매

The following was received from the Spokesman of UNIKOM.

UNIKOM was fully deployed in the DMZ on 6 May as expected.

Major-General Greindl was in Baghdad on 6 and 7 May where he met Under-Secretary-General Marrack Goulding. Major-General Greindl also met Iraqi officials of the Coordinating Committee and handed over a letter informing them of the completion of the full deployment of UNIKOM in the DMZ and requesting them to withdraw from the DMZ in compliance with Security Council resolution 687. A similar letter was delivered to the Kuwaiti side.

The coalition troops completed their withdrawal from the northern sector yesterday - 7 May and were continuing this withdrawal today 8 May from the central and southern sectors. It is expected that they will be fully withdrawn by 9 May.

8 May 1991

#UNW-1189
첨부물

0185

UNITED
NATIONS

S

Security Council

Distr.
GENERAL

S/22580
9 May 1991

ORIGINAL: ENGLISH

REPORT OF THE SECRETARY-GENERAL ON THE UNITED NATIONS IRAQ-KUWAIT OBSERVATION MISSION

1. The present report is submitted in pursuance of paragraph 5 of resolution 687 (1991) of 3 April 1991, by which the Security Council established a demilitarized zone (DMZ) along the Iraq-Kuwait border and decided to set up an observer unit to monitor the zone and resolution 689 (1991) of 9 April 1991, by which the Council approved my plan (S/22454 and Add.1-3) for the establishment of the United Nations Iraq-Kuwait Observation Mission (UNIKOM).

2. On 13 April, the UNIKOM advance party, comprising the Chief Military Observer, Major-General Günther Greindl, and a number of military and civilian staff, arrived at Kuwait City, established liaison with the Kuwaiti authorities and set up a temporary headquarters. On 15 April, General Greindl travelled to Baghdad and established liaison with the Iraqi authorities.

3. Over the next three weeks, UNIKOM deployed in the zone assigned to it, with the cooperation of the Governments of Iraq and Kuwait and with substantial logistic support from the forces of Member States cooperating with the Government of Kuwait. As of this date, five observation posts have been established in each of the north, centre and south sectors of the zone, with two additional observation posts planned in the north sector and one additional observation post in the south sector.

4. The Governments of Iraq and Kuwait have both agreed to afford UNIKOM full freedom of movement across the border; the DMZ is thus one undivided area of operation for the Mission. For operational purposes, the DMZ has been organized into three sectors. The headquarters is being readied for occupation at Umm Qasr, as originally envisaged, and a logistic base and liaison office have been established at Doha in Kuwait. UNIKOM also maintains a liaison office at Baghdad.

5. At present, UNIKOM comprises 280 military observers from the following countries:

91-15131 2540b (E) /...

Argentina	7	Nigeria	7
Austria	7	Norway	7
Bangladesh	7	Pakistan	9
Canada	1	Poland	7
China (20) a/	16	Romania	7
Denmark	7	Senegal (7) a/	-
Fiji	8	Singapore	7
Finland	7	Sweden	7
France	20	Thailand	7
Ghana	8	Turkey (7) a/	-
Greece	7	United Kingdom of Great Britain and Northern Ireland	20
Hungary	6	Uruguay	8
India	8	United States of America	20
Indonesia	7	Union of Soviet	20
Ireland	8	Socialist Republics	20
Italy	7	Venezuela	7
Kenya	8		
Malaysia	8		

a/ Figures in brackets indicate planned strength.

An additional five military observers from the United Nations Truce Supervision Organization (UNTSO) are temporarily attached to the Mission.

6. Administrative and logistic support is provided by the following units:

Movement control (Denmark)	20	Post (Denmark)	5	
Engineers (Canada)	297	Medical (Norway)	50	
Logistics (Sweden)	134 a/	Aircraft (Switzerland)	3	
Helicopters (Chile)	47	Total		556

a/ Includes 99 temporarily detached from the United Nations Interim Force in Lebanon (UNIFIL).

United Nations international civilian staff provide transport, communications and administrative support.

7. In addition, UNIKOM is supported by five infantry companies temporarily assigned from UNIFIL (from Fiji, Ghana and Nepal) and the United Nations Peace-keeping Force in Cyprus (UNFICYP) (from Austria and Denmark), one of which is deployed in each of the three sectors, one at the headquarters at Umm Qasr and one at the logistic base at Doha. Their total strength is 544 all ranks. The total strength of military personnel of UNIKOM at present is 1,385.

0187/...

8. UNIKOM's deployment was completed on 6 May. UNIKOM then monitored the withdrawal of the armed forces that were still deployed in its assigned zone. That withdrawal having been completed, the DMZ established by the Security Council came into effect at 2000 hours GMT today, 9 May 1991, and UNIKOM assumed in full the observation responsibilities entrusted to it by the Security Council.

9. I shall present a further progress report to the Security Council in approximately four weeks' time, by when I shall have received from the Chief Military Observer the recommendations foreseen in my report of 5 April 1991 (S/22454, para. 13).

0188

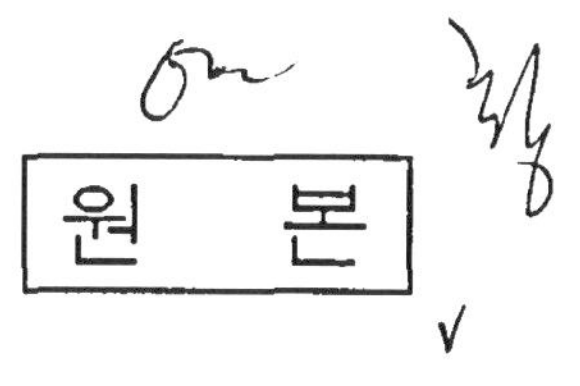

원 본

외 무 부

종 별 :

번 호 : UNW-1214 일 시 : 91 0510 1930

수 신 : 장 관(국연,중동일,기정)

발 신 : 주 유엔 대사

제 목 : 걸프사태(유엔동향)

1.표제관련 케야르 유엔사무총장의 워싱턴방문 (91.5.8-10)동정에 관해서는 별첨 대변인 발표내용 참고바라며, 특히 동방문중 제기된 이락의 유엔경찰력 자국 북부지역 배치반대 문제에 관한 당지 주요기사를 참고로 송부함.

2.안보리휴전 결의 이행을 위한 이락 군비통제특위 작업동향에 관해서는 별첨 5.9.자동위원회 R.EKEUS 의장 (스웨덴)의 유엔출입기자들과의 회견요록 참고바람.

3.5.9. 이락-쿠웨이트 접경 DMZ 에서 유엔옵서버단의 모든 병력 철수가 완료됨에 따라 동일 20:20 (GMT) 를 기해 DMZ 운영이 공식발표되었음.

첨부 FAX:UNW(F)-202

FAX 내역:1.사무총장 워싱톤 방문동정발표내용

2.5.10 자 NYT,WP,WSJ 관련기사

3.상기 특위 의장 기자회견 요록

4. UNIKOM 측 발표내용

끝

(대사 노창희-국장)

국기국 1차보 중아국 정문국 청와대 안기부

PAGE 1 91.05.11 10:27 WG

외신 1과 통제관

0189

UNW(F)-202 10510 1700
(국연 정영된, 개정)

The following was received from a Spokesman accompanying the Secretary-General.

Washington, 10 May 1991.

At 11 a.m. yesterday morning, Thursday 9 May, the Secretary-General met in the Oval Office with President Bush, Secretary of State James Baker, and National Security Adviser Brent Scowcroft. In the course of the discussions the Secretary-General indicated that he had received word from Under-Secretary-General Marrack Goulding in Baghdad that Iraq had given "a very clear rejection" of the idea of a United Nations police presence on Iraqi soil.

The Secretary-General and his senior aides then met in the Cabinet Room with President Bush and a number of senior administration officials, including Ambassador to the United Nations Thomas Pickering and Assistant Secretary of State John Bolton. These discussions covered a broad range of international issues - the situation in the Persian Gulf area, including humanitarian matters and the implementation of resolution 687, El Salvador, Western Sahara, the Middle East, Lebanon, Cyprus, Afghanistan and Bangladesh. President Bush raised the matter of human rights in Cuba. There was also detailed discussion of United Nations finances.

On the subject of the proposed UN police force in northern Iraq, the Secretary-General informed the President that in his view, any United Nations security presence in Iraq would require specific authorization by the Security Council.

In the afternoon, the Secretary-General held a private meeting at Blair House, the presidential guest residence, with General Scowcroft, and then met with IMF Managing Director Michel Camdessus. He then went to Capitol Hill, where he met with members of the Senate Foreign Relations Committee, and later with Speaker of the House Tom Foley for a review of major issues before the United Nations.

In the early evening the Secretary-General greeted United Nations Information Centre staff, representatives of United Nations agencies in Washington and non-governmental organizations at a reception in his honour hosted by the Information Centre.

Before leaving for New York this morning, the Secretary-General met with his Special Representative on the Middle East, Ambassador Edouard Brunner.

* * *

8-1

0190

By R. W. APPLE Jr.

Special to The New York Times

WASHINGTON, May 9 — Secretary General Javier Pérez de Cuéllar of the United Nations told President Bush today that Baghdad had turned down an American-supported proposal for a United Nations police force in northern Iraq, raising the possibility that American troops might have to stay there far longer than the Administration had hoped.

Mr. Pérez de Cuéllar was said by his associates and by American officials to be unwilling to send a United Nations force in the face of Iraqi opposition, unless the Security Council authorized it, which at the moment seems unlikely.

No Lifting of Sanctions

So it appears that President Saddam Hussein of Iraq — defeated in battle, faced with awesome economic and social problems, struggling to hold his country together — has found a way to frustrate the United States, at least for the moment.

But by blocking a United Nations force, Mr. Hussein in effect invites a continuing occupation of part of his country by American and other allied forces. Moreover, until the Kurdish problem is resolved satisfactorily to Americans, the United States has said it would not agree to relaxation of the economic sanctions against Iraq.

Administration officials conceded that Baghdad's action probably means a considerable delay in United States withdrawal from the area. Although the last American troops left southern Iraq on Wednesday, those in the north cannot depart until some other sizable force arrives to screen the new Kurdish refugee camps in the region.

'The Q Word' Is Heard

Last week, important policy makers began to apply what they called "the Q word," meaning quagmire, to the problem developing in the area along Iraq's border with Turkey. Today, they said Mr. Pérez de Cuéllar's report, which was delivered to the President at a White House meeting, represented a major setback to American policy.

Mr. Bush promised last month, when he announced that the United States would aid the Kurds, that American troops would pull back quickly, handing over the camps to United Nations administration. But that plan raised the question of who would make the camps at least symbolically secure enough from possible Iraqi attack to persuade large numbers of Kurds to leave their mountain refuges. And that led to the idea of a United Nations police force.

In company with France and Britain, the United States has insisted the international organization could set up a police force in the area — a less heavily armed force than the peacekeeping force authorized by the United Nations in southern Iraq — without the passage of a new resolution. But Mr. Pérez de Cuéllar, aides said, was worried about bypassing the Security Council.

The three nations hoped, according to Western diplomats, that Iraq would not object to the police force if not specifically asked to approve of it.

'A Very Clear Rejection'

But Mr. Pérez de Cuéllar sent an envoy to Baghdad, where he got the thumbs-down from the Iraqi Government. "Today I have received a very clear rejection from the Iraqi Government," the Secretary General said at the White House. "They do not want a United Nations police force."

John Bolton, the United States Assistant Secretary of State for International Organizations, confirmed that Mr. Pérez de Cuéllar was still pressing for another resolution. The problem with that is that either the Soviet Union or China or both are likely to block a Security Council authorization because they are reluctant to set precedents for interfering in the internal affairs of other countries, such as that between the Kurds and the Baghdad Government.

Some policy makers are hinting about a quagmire.

'Limited in Duration'

Mr. Bush has been emphasizing for weeks that he would do everything possible to avoid getting bogged down in northern Iraq, with American troops stuck there because no replacements were available. At a news conference on Wednesday, he said again that he opposed any permanent commitment. And today he said that the United States still viewed its role in protecting the Kurdish refugees "as limited in duration."

"I think that is the wish of our American friends as well as the United Nations," Mr. Pérez de Cuéllar said, to which Mr. Bush responded, "That's for sure." But then the United Nations official took up again the line that has the White House and the State Department seething with irritation.

"I think we have to be patient," he said.

'Sanctions Will Remain in Place'

According to White House aides, Mr. Bush pressed Mr. Pérez de Cuéllar again today to move faster, as he had done in a telephone call more than two weeks ago.

Richard Haass, Mr. Bush's special adviser on Near Eastern matters, reiterated today the Administration's determination to continue to penalize Iraq until President Hussein is replaced, even though the United Nations resolution setting the terms for ending the war, which was passed April 3, makes no demand for his departure in exchange for relaxing sanctions.

"In our view, Saddam is discredited," Mr. Haass told a group of correspondents. "As a result all possible sanctions will remain in place until he is gone. Iraqis will not participate in the region's post-crisis political, economic and security arrangements until there is a a change in regime."

Eventually, the United States wants private relief agencies and the United Nations to care for the Kurds who have been uprooted by the failed rebellion that followed the Persian Gulf war. But that cannot be done, everyone agrees, until the Kurds' fear of the central government has been overcome, and that may take considerable time.

"The goal is not simply to create a series of camps along the Iraqi border with Turkey and Iran," a senior Administration official said. "The goal is to get the Kurds to return to their place of permanent residence in safety, so the camps are envisioned as a very temporary thing."

New York Times

ß-2

0191

Iraq Rejects U.N. Force To Police Refugee Havens

By David Hoffman and Glenn Frankel
Washington Post Staff Writers

U.N. Secretary General Javier Perez de Cuellar told President Bush yesterday that Iraq has rejected the allied plan for U.N. police to protect the "safe havens" being created for Kurdish refugees in northern Iraq.

"I have received a very clear rejection from the Iraqi government," Perez de Cuellar told reporters at the White House. "They do not want a United Nations police presence in the area."

Administration officials and allied diplomats said the rejection could be a setback to the plan first advanced by British Prime Minister John Major to deploy the U.N. police in northern Iraq under the authority of existing Security Council resolutions. But the officials said they will wait for more information from coming meetings in Baghdad before deciding the next move.

Iraq's tougher stance was also evident on the ground in northern Iraq where special forces have been moved into Dahuk in an apparent challenge to a plan proposed by some U.S. military officers to expand the allied-controlled refugee zone to that provincial capital.

Perez de Cuellar said he had received a message on the Iraqi rejection from Undersecretary General Marrack Goulding, who has been in Baghdad since May 7 negotiating with the Iraqi authorities. Prince Sadruddin Aga Kahn, the secretary general's special envoy for the refugees, is expected to make another visit to Iraq shortly.

Allied officials had hoped that

[illegible]

Iraq could be persuaded to accept the police force because it would make another U.N. resolution mandating a security force unecessary. These officials say they believe that the Soviet Union and China would veto any new resolution. John R. Bolton, assistant secretary of state for international organization affairs, said "the question of the next step" would depend on the coming talks in Baghdad and also on whether Kurdish leaders can come to agreement on autonomy with President Saddam Hussein.

A White House official, after hearing of Perez de Cuellar's remark, said, "We may or may not have hit a snag." He said the deployment of U.N. police could be authorized by consensus within the Security Council if Perez de Cuellar did not favor ordering such action by himself.

But the official, who spoke on condition that he not be named, did not indicate whether he thought such a consensus could be formed soon. "This could possibly last for some time," he said of the U.S. deployment.

He described the deployment of U.S. forces into Dahuk as a "decision that we're thinking about." But he said Bush had held off pending the completion of efforts to persuade Perez de Cuellar to authorize U.N. troops to go there instead.

The proposed U.N. police force is a critical ingredient in the effort to persuade the Kurds to return to their homes. The presence of U.N. police also would permit a more rapid withdrawal of allied forces. Bush, in particular, has been anxious to get U.S. troops out of northern Iraq.

"I don't think we are likely to be put off," a British diplomat said. "We've got to find ways to help these people and they've got to be U.N. ways."

Washington Post

8-3

0192

Baghdad Rejects Proposal to Establish A U.N. Police Force in Northern Iraq

By GERALD F. SEIB
Staff Reporter of THE WALL STREET JOURNAL

WASHINGTON—Iraq rejected a proposal to establish a United Nations police force in northern Iraq, creating new uncertainty about how the Bush administration can extract U.S. troops protecting refugees there.

The Bush administration has been hoping that a civilian U.N. police force could be created informally under an existing U.N. resolution demanding protection for Iraq's Kurdish refugees. It wants such a force to replace U.S. forces guarding refugee camps in northern Iraq.

But Iraq's new stand, one of a series of more hardline gestures Baghdad has taken in recent days, increases the chances the administration may have to take the riskier course of seeking a formal U.N. resolution creating either a military peacekeeping force or a civilian police force for northern Iraq.

Iraq probably would feel compelled to accept a force specifically ordered by a new U.N. resolution. But U.S. officials worry that a new resolution might be vetoed at the Security Council, perhaps by China. China has been cool to the idea of increasing international intervention in Iraq.

The news of Iraq's position was delivered directly to President Bush by U.N. Secretary General Javier Perez de Cuellar at a meeting in the White House. "Today I have received a very clear rejection from the Iraqi government," Mr. Perez de Cuellar told reporters. "They do not want a United Nations police force." He said the message came to him from an Iraqi envoy.

The Iraqi move left U.S. officials uncertain how to arrange for long-term security at the refugee camps being built by U.S. and allied soldiers. It's possible Iraq will be pressured into changing its view, particularly if it sees that the only alternative to a U.N. force is a long-term U.S. presence, officials said. They noted that U.N. envoys still are holding talks with Iraq.

In addition, officials said, the U.S. may informally develop a broader international peacekeeping force, involving fewer U.S. troops and more soldiers from other nations, that could be left in northern Iraq indefinitely. There also is a chance that talks between Iraq's government and Kurdish leaders will produce an agreement on Kurdish autonomy that makes Kurdish refugees feel safe returning to their homes—a development that would eliminate the need for any international force.

Mr. Perez de Cuellar apparently believes, though, that the U.S. may have little choice but to return to the U.N. for another debate if it wants any kind of force to replace U.S. troops. In his meeting with Mr. Bush, the secretary general indicated that he thought another resolution is necessary to authorize either a civilian or military peacekeeping force, John Bolton, an assistant secretary of state, told reporters. "And that's something we're just going to have to discuss further," he said.

President Bush is eager to find a plan for getting U.S. troops out of northern Iraq to avoid the appearance the U.S. is sinking into a long-term "quagmire" there.

The Iraqi refusal to accept a police force is particularly disturbing because it comes at a time when the Iraqi government is being more confrontational in other areas as well. The U.S. has reported in recent days that Iraqi anti-aircraft guns fired at a U.S. reconnaissance flight. And there are reports that Iraq has moved some special forces into the northern Iraqi town of Dahuk, near the refugee camps being built by U.S. forces.

Wall Street Journal

8-4

0193

FOR INFORMATION OF UNITED NATIONS SECRETARIAT ONLY
Not for Distribution or Dissemination

9 May 1991

PRESS BRIEFING BY EXECUTIVE CHAIRMAN OF SPECIAL COMMISSION ON IRAQ

(Revised)

Ambassador Rolf Ekeus of Sweden said this afternoon that the plan for the disposal of Iraq's weapons of mass destruction, contained in Security Council resolution 687 (1991), was "a sound plan" that was being implemented as envisaged by the Council.

Mr. Ekeus made that statement as he briefed correspondents in his capacity as Executive Chairman of a Special Commission set up in that resolution to oversee the destruction, removal or rendering harmless of Iraq's biological, chemical and ballistic missile capabilities. The Commission is to assist the International Atomic Energy Agency (IAEA) in disposing of Iraq's nuclear-weapons capabilities. It is also to submit a plan for the verification of Iraq's undertaking not to acquire such weapons in future.

In introducing him, Yasushi Akashi, Under-Secretary-General for Disarmament Affairs, said that, among other things, Mr. Ekeus had been Chairman of the Ad Hoc Committee on Chemical Weapons at the Conference on Disarmament at Geneva. Also present was Robert Gallucci of the United States State Department, Deputy Executive Chairman of the Commission.

Mr. Ekeus said the elimination of Iraq's weapons of mass destruction was an essential ingredient in achieving a lasting peace in the region. Iraq had accepted the terms of the Council's resolution and he had no complaints about the Iraqi attitude so far, which he described as cooperative. Regarding Iraq's declaration of the locations, amounts and types of all specific weapons, as called for in the resolution, he said the Commission's task was to verify the correctness of that declaration and to designate undeclared sites for inspection as well. The Commission would go to both declared and undeclared sites and would assist and cooperate with IAEA in its tasks.

In the first stage of its work, the Commission would determine the location, quantity and condition of the weapons in question, he said. It would also prepare for their destruction, removal or rendering harmless, and based on information gathered during inspections would plan for the disposal phase. With the Commission's cooperation, IAEA would soon lead a team to Baghdad to begin its work on the ground. In accordance with resolution 687, the plan being developed would be submitted to the Security Council for approval on 18 May. Following approval, Iraq would yield its possession of chemical and biological weapons and installations to the Commission, and its nuclear-weapons materials to IAEA.

The destruction phase, however, would not be easy, Mr. Ekeus said. According to Iraq, some of the munitions in question were under the rubble of bombed buildings and some contained nerve gas. Yet, while the Commission was aware of such possible problems, it could not assess them until it had conducted its own on-site inspections.

(more)

3150B

8-5

0194

A correspondent referred to the timetable outlined in resolution 687. The Council had decided that the plan, once approved, should call for the completion of several acts within 45 days. Those included formation of the Special Commission, which would carry out "immediate on-site inspections of Iraq's biological, chemical and missile capabilities"; the yielding to the Commission by Iraq of the weapons specified and its destruction, under Commission supervision, of all its missile capabilities; and the provision by the Commission of assistance and cooperation to IAEA in its task.

He asked how much would be accomplished in 45 days and how much time would be needed beyond that deadline. Mr. Ekeus said the Commission's task would be to fulfil the requirements outlined by the Council. However, "the Council, in its wisdom, understood well enough you can't destroy those things within the 45 days". Asked how long it would take to destroy those weapons, he said that question could only be answered when the information supplied by Iraq was supplemented by what was received from other Governments and through the Commission's own inspections.

Regarding a statement published in The New York Times that the Council's plan was "unrealistic and unworkable", Mr. Ekeus said: "I declare that this plan is sound". Perhaps that statement had resulted from a hasty reading of the resolution, which did not call for the destruction phase to be completed within 45 days.

Asked how he could be sure that the Commission would have time to reach all the weapons concerned, some of which might be in hiding or inaccessible, Mr. Ekeus said Iraq had declared its acceptance of the resolution. Speedy implementation was in Iraq's own interest, as it was linked to the lifting of the embargo against Iraq's exports.

Did the Commission already have in mind a number of areas it might want to check for undisclosed sites? a correspondent asked. Would Iraq be notified in advance of such inspections? "The name of the game in any arms control is you have to be suspicious", Mr. Ekeus replied. Iraq had made its declaration, "but in all arms control we know what is declared is never enough ... how you work in arms control exercises is always to go to undeclared sites". Such visits would not be announced in advance, but would be on short notice. Such a procedure was not unusual; it was used in bilateral agreements between the United States and the Soviet Union and in many other areas.

"Since there's only one place in the world -- the United States facility in Johnston Island -- where chemical weapons can be destroyed safely, will these weapons be transported there or what? and who's going to pay for it? or are new facilities going to be built?" a correspondent asked. Mr. Ekeus said that was not decided by the Commission. Further, although Johnston Island was "the big one", there were other facilities. He stressed the importance of economy, efficiency, speed and safety, which pointed towards the need for some other solution. As an example, he cited the safety concerns raised by damaged munitions. However, while no options had as yet been excluded prior to on-site inspections, it was the Commission's view at present that "we have to destroy it on the spot".

(more)

8-6

0195

Following up, the correspondent said there was a United Nations convention which had not been agreed upon but which allowed for a 10-year period for safe destruction. Wouldn't immediate destruction be in violation of that convention? she asked. Mr. Ekeus said that, in that case, the Soviet Union had declared some 42,000 tons of chemical weapons and the United States some 35,000 tons. Iraq, however, had declared some 500-600 tons. The 10-year period was simply the time needed to destroy over 40,000 tons in a very complex, very expensive operation.

Asked if Iraq was to pay for the destruction of its own weapons, Mr. Ekeus said the Secretary-General had said the Commission should not address the question of finances. Yet they were very conscious of the need for cost-effectiveness and speed. Speed was essential to maintain the political momentum, "because here we have a high element of intrusiveness", but it was important to balance such considerations with the need to keep costs down. That would call for an innovative approach, perhaps requiring the development of new technologies.

Would the operation be funded by the United Nations or by Iraq? the correspondent continued. Mr. Ekeus said it was his understanding that the costs would be assessed by the General Assembly and, hopefully, that they would be supplemented by voluntary contributions in cash and kind.

Referring to a letter sent by the Commission to some States requesting information, in confidence, on locations of weapons not disclosed by Iraq, a correspondent asked who the letter was sent to and what it said. Mr. Ekeus said the Commission had requested such additional information from many States. "We have thrown a very wide net to get any fish", he said, but the Commission chose "not to bother" Governments having an extremely remote chance of knowing anything.

Continuing, the correspondent asked if they might have been "mostly Governments that might have supplied weapons or ones that have good intelligence". Mr. Ekeus told her those were two good criteria, adding, "you should join the Commission".

Asked if everyone on the Commission was in agreement on the soundness of the Security Council requirements, Mr. Ekeus said he was not a spokesman for the Commission members, but he was convinced that they shared the view that it was a sound plan. He cited the Commission's "enthusiasm and very high, good spirit".

In response to another question, Mr. Ekeus said the Commission's first visit to the area would be announced "very, very soon".

A correspondent said that, in the debate preceding adoption of the Council resolution, attention had focused on concern about the broader regional questions. Did Mr. Ekeus see a broader role for the Commission once its immediate task was completed? He replied that the Commission's future role was very well-defined. It had been called upon to prepare a system for compliance and verification. In fulfiling that task, the Commission would rely heavily on work done by the Conference on Disarmament. He also hoped to glean insight into technical solutions from the papers of the Soviet-United States agreement. Further, there were encouraging recent signs from Geneva on achieving a full, comprehensive chemical weapons ban. Such an agreement would help even out the treatment of Iraq and other parties which would adhere to it. "I feel there is no lasting imbalance in this fundamental field", he said.

* *** *

8-7

0196

Statement attributable to the Spokesman for United Nations Iraq Kuwait Observation Mission (UNIKOM) (released in Kuwait City at 10.00 local time)

Yesterday, Thursday 9 May 1991, the withdrawal of all armed forces from the zone assigned to UNIKOM has been completed. Therefore, the demilitarized zone established by the Security Council came into effect at 20:00 hours G.M.T. yesterday, and UNIKOM assumed in full the observation responsibilities entrusted to it by the Security Council.

The Chief Military Observer, Major-General Günther Greindl infomed all parties concerned about the establishment of the demilitarized zone by letter sent to each of them.

10-May 1991

0197

원 본

외 무 부

종 별 :

번 호 : UNW-1221 일 시 : 91 0513 1830

수 신 : 장 관(국연,중동일,기정)

발 신 : 주 유엔 대사

제 목 : 걸프사태(유엔동향)

1.북부 이락 유엔경찰파견, 중동평화문제에 관한 J.PEREZ DE CUELLAR 사무총장이 5.13. 기자와의 문답내용을 별첨송부함.

2.유엔의 북부이락 ZAKHO 난민촌 인수관련 UNHCR 발표내용은 별첨참조 바람.

첨부:1.사무총장기자 문답

2. UNHCR 발표내용:UNW(F)-203

끝

(대사 노창희-국장)

국기국 1차보 중아국 정문국 청와대 안기부

PAGE 1

91.05.14 09:40 WG

외신 1과 통제관

0198

UNW(F)-203 10513 1830 (국연.중동일.기정) 총3매

Remarks made by the Secretary-General upon entering the Secretariat building on Monday 13 May 1991 at 9:35 a.m.

Q. Could you tell us the latest on Prince Sadruddin's visit to Baghdad?

S-G I have had information that he is making contact with the Iraqi authorities and I hope that he will also make progress. At the same time I understand that the Iraqis and the Kurds are apparently making progress in their talks which are taking place now and I think that is good news. All this information gives me the impression that things are moving ahead.

Q. As we look towards a possible Security Council resolution on the establishment of a police force, could you articulate the fine line between humanitarian support and concern for sovereignty that countries like China and the Soviet Union might have?

S-G I am not sure because I haven't been in touch with them on that so I don't know what the position of China and the Soviet Union would be if a draft resolution is presented to the Council. This is something which the three Western countries might try to obtain, a resolution. Of course, as you know, there is new thinking developing in the sense of seeing how to protect human rights even if there is infringement on the sovereignty of member countries. However, on that I think we have to be very careful for the time being.

Q. Regarding Mr. Baker's trip to the Middle East ....

S-G I am encouraging him to continue his efforts, which I think are excellent, but of course the outcome is not very easy to foresee at this stage.

Q. Do you see a specific role though for the UN in view of the General Assembly resolution equating Zionism with racism?

S-G I think they are two different things. The United Nations has to play a role because it is an international organisation of which Israel is a full member country. As far as the resolution on Zionism is concerned, my position has always been that there was a wrong and unfair interpretation of what Zionism is. Zionism was first of all the need of the Jewish people to preserve their identity and at the same time to try and get a state for their nation. You cannot say that trying to get a territory for your nation is racism, for instance, the Kurds or the Basques in Spain are not racists. These are two different things which should not be mixed up.

Q. There is possible talk of convening a peace conference without Syria's participation. Do you think it is possible?

3-1

0199

- 2 -

S-G I think it would be wrong to exclude any Arab country particularly a country which is so important in the context of the Near East situation.

Q. We understand that Sadruddin Aga Khan is going to make yet another effort to try and convince the Iraqis to accept, if not the police force itself, some sort of non-civilian protection. Have you pursued these options and if so have there been any results?

S-G The main role of Sadruddin Aga Khan is to help the Iraqi population, not only the Kurds but the Shi'ites in the south as well who are often forgotten and the Prince has instructions to raise this question. But if the police force idea does not work as it would appear so far, it confirms my thinking that we need the Iraqi consent since the resolution was adopted under chapter 6 and not chapter 7. Who knows, perhaps we can persuade the Iraqis to accept a police force.

Q. That is my question. Are you intending to make yet another effort to convince the Iraqis to accept the police force?

S-G Oh yes. He (Sadruddin Aga Khan) has to make a new effort and even if the Iraqis accept I have to go to the Council because as you know, a police force even lightly armed needs the Security Council.

Q. Perhaps with a relaxation of some of the sanctions .....

S-G As you know, that is something which is not in my hands. It is the concern of the Security Council.

Q. Regarding the Baker/Bessmertnykh talks, it seems that one of the sticking issues is the United Nations role in a peace conference, how do you feel as head of this organisation, when the UN was so very active on the issue of Iraq and Kuwait and now the problem is whether the UN should be involved in a peace conference?

S-G The UN role is very important because, as you know, it is not a regional problem but a problem of the international community as a whole.

* * *

3-2

0200

ON OPERATIONS WITHIN THE REGIONAL HUMANITARIAN PLAN OF ACTION

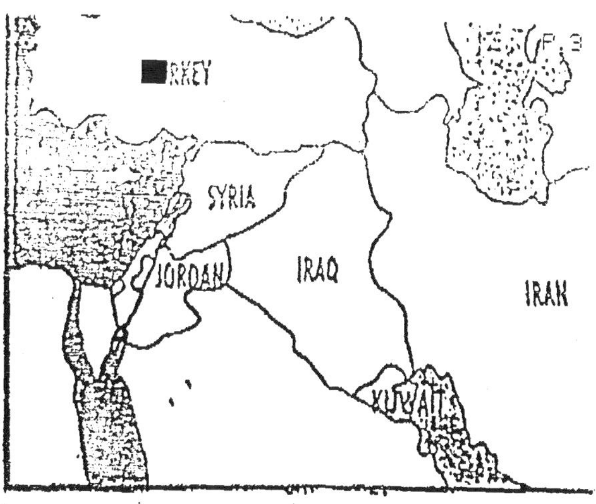

13 May 1991

The United Nations decided to take control Monday of the Zakho transit centre in northern Iraq after determining that the completed camp had been demilitarized and would continue to receive direct relief support from the coalition forces.

Citing the pressing humanitarian needs of hundreds of thousands of refugees and displaced Iraqis, the United Nations High Commissioner for Refugees assumed responsibility for the transit camp on the expectation that the current conditions of security will prevail.

Six UNHCR field officers moved into the camp Monday assuming full responsibility for camp management. UNHCR will also coordinate the relief activities of non-governmental organisations and monitor the assistance which will continue to be provided by the various Allied forces in the sectors of water, food and sanitation facilities.

An estimated 19,000 displaced Iraqis are currently lodged at the centre, about 2.5 kilometres outside the city of Zakho, and another 9,000 are camped a few kilometres away at a still incomplete transit facility.

The return movement among those Iraqis, who sought refuge along the mountainous Turkish-Iraqi border, gained momentum over the weekend. As of May 13, UNHCR field officials estimated that 200,000 people had begun the trek home.

The spontaneous repatriation movement reduced the total population of the eight border camps to 230,000 people, while another 100,000 are scattered outside camps along the Turkish-Iraqi frontier.

An estimated 80,000 of the 1.3 million Iraqi refugees who found sanctuary in Iran have also started for home.

UNHCR currently mans three sub-offices in the northern Iraq towns of Arbil, D'huk and Suleimaniya. In addition, the refugee agency has opened eight field offices in the region to distribute relief supplies and is in the process of deploying 21 mobile units to monitor the well-being of the returnees.

3-3

0201

원 본

외 무 부

종 별 :

번 호 : UNW-1232 일 시 : 91 0514 1800

수 신 : 장 관(국연,중동일,기정)

발 신 : 주 유엔 대사

제 목 : 걸프사태(유엔동향)

5.13 유엔의 북부이락 난민촌 인수에따라 J.PEREZ DE CUELLAR 사무총장은 이락측과 동 난민촌 유엔병력배치 문제를 교섭중인것으로 알려진바, 이에관한 5.14. 자 별첨 사무총장 기자문답요록 참조바람.

첨부:사무총장 기자문답요록: UNW(F)-204

끝

(대사 노창희-국장)

국기국 1차보 중아국 정문국 청와대 안기부

PAGE 1

91.05.15 10:10 WG

외신 1과 통제관

0202

Remarks made by the Secretary-General upon entering the Secretariat building on 14 May 1991 at approximately 3:10 p.m.

Q. Have you reached a tentative agreement with the Iraqis over guards in the refugee camps for the Kurds?

S-G Actually we have to be rather careful because we have agreed on something but so far it is not very clear, very specific. That is why I think it would be only wise not to advance any judgement at this stage.

Q. Can you give us any idea of any of the agreements that have been reached?

S-G I think the word "agreement" is a word which is rather a heavy one. I think Sadruddin Aga Khan, on my behalf, has discussed with the Iraqi authorities the possibilities of a United Nations presence; besides, there is already a United Nations presence but a United Nations presence which could in some way encourage the Kurds to go back to their homes and their villages. So far, we are still discussing this possible presence, and the terms of reference of the presence, that is why I think it is too early to say there is an agreement. We have to be very careful now not to raise too many expectations at this stage.

Q. Are you discussing armed guards amongst the presence?

S-G Some kind of arms, as you say, armed presence, but always light arms.

Q. What about a timetable for what is going on. What about a timetable when you can send your people there?

S-G There couldn't be a timetable as long as there is not an agreement, this is very clear.

Q. So you are not close to establishing a day when you can send the UN forces in?

S-G Not as of today at 3:15 in the afternoon.

Q. So what size armed personnel are you proposing?

S-G It depends, but I think in the case where we embark on some United Nations presence, we have to think, perhaps, in terms of 400 to 500.

Q. Do you have the agreement of the Iraqis on that?

S-G That is what is being negotiated right now. That is why I am very careful in my statements in order not to mislead you or to raise false expectations.

Q. But that is a subsititute for what we know as a police force?

S-G There could be a variation on the same theme, if you wish.

#UNW-1272
첨부물

2-1

..../

0203

Q. Yesterday you mentioned that you opposed the resolution equating Zionism with racism. Do you want that to be scrapped?

S-G It has always been my opinion that the resolution in some way, how can I put it, distorted the meaning of Zionism as it was conceived. I think it is an element which unfortunately has in some way been considered as an obstacle for the peace process, in which the United States now, and some other countries before, have been involved. I think that this resolution has not been helpful as far as the negotiating process is concerned, mainly because now the Israelis consider that because of this resolution the United Nations is not impartial. That is very unfortunate, because Israel owes its very existence to the United Nations. The many resolutions concerning the problem between the Arabs and Israel are United Nations resolutions; the United Nations is an organization which is working for a solution of the Arab/Israeli problem.

Q. Do you want to see it recalled or reversed or scrapped, whatever the procedure is?

S-G It is not for the Secretary-General to ask for such a thing. It is for the Secretary-General to implement resolutions, not to discuss them. Of course if this resolution is rescinded perhaps it could create a better atmosphere in Israel, among all the Israeli friends, for a full United Nations involvement in the peace process.

Q. Is there a relationship between the Iraqis agreeing to an arrangement with military personnel and the possiblity of some easing of the sanctions?

S-G I think it is only normal that in the heads of the Iraqis, they always link the two things. We can not blame them for that.

Q. What is your opinion...

S-G I think that if we can make rapid progress as far as implemention of the resolutions are concerned, it would be only logical that the Security Council start considering the releasing of sanctions.

Q. Secretary of State James Baker in statements he made recently didn't seem to indicate that he was anxious that the United Nations get involved in the process there. How do you respond to that?

S-G It is only logical that the Secretary of State desires to have the United Nations involved. Because, as I have told your colleague, it is only normal that the United Nations, which is the organisation which created the state of Israel, is involved in the security of Israel, the security of all Arab countries and the security of the region as a whole.

* * *

2-2

0204

원 본

외 무 부

종 별 :

번 호 : UNW-1255 일 시 : 91 0515 1920

수 신 : 장 관(국연,중동일,기정)

발 신 : 주 유엔 대사

제 목 : 걸프사태(유엔동향)

1.안보리 휴전결의 (687호) 에 의거 지난 5.2.사무총장이 이락-쿠웨이트 국경획정안 (S/22558)을 제출한것과 관련 안보리 의장은 안보리 이사국들과의 협의를 거쳐 5.13 자 사무총장 앞서한을 통해 동사무총장안의 접수를 확인 (TAKENOTE) 하는 한편 사무총장의 관련 노력에 지지를 표명한바, 이로써 본건 사무총장안대로 추진케됨. (안보리의 별도 승인 절차는 불요)

2.한편 사무총장의 이락 배상 책임 이행안 (S/22559) 과 관련 안보리는 곧 결의안을 채택할것으로 알려지고있음. (동결의안 요지는 UNW-1203 참조), 특히, 휴전결의에 의거 사무총장이 이락 석유 수입 공제상한선을 안보리에 권고토록 되어있는바, 5.15.자 NYT 는 상임이사국들간에 25-30 퍼센트선 (연간 약 5억불수준)에서 합의가 이루어졌다고 보도함.

금 5.15. 정오브리핑시 사무총장 대변인은 사무총장의 동 공제상한선 권고는 다음주 이후에나 가능할 것으로 본다고 언급함.동일자 WP지는 쿠웨이트의 대 이락 청구액이 450 억불에 이를것으로 추정 (여타국들의 배상 청구를 포함하는 경우 1,000 억불 예상)된다고 보도함.

첨부:상기 이락 배상관련 NYT,WP 지 기사:UNW(F)-210

끝

(대사 노창희-국장)

국기국 1차보 중아국 정문국 안기부

PAGE 1

91.05.16 08:51 WG

외신 1과 통제관

0205

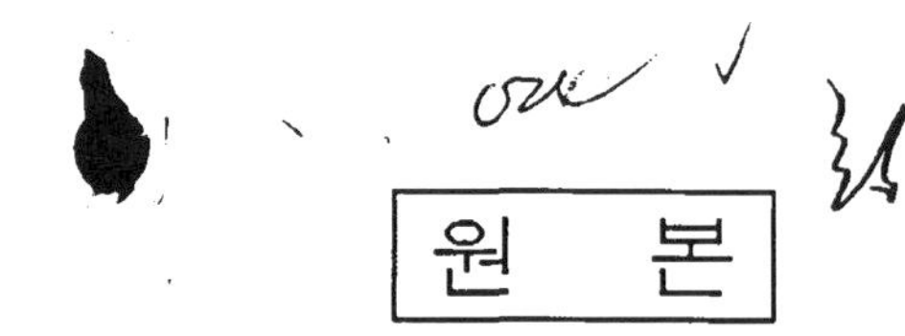

원 본

외 무 부

종 별 :

번 호 : UNW-1270 일 시 : 91 0516 1830

수 신 : 장 관(국연,중동일,기정)

발 신 : 주 유엔 대사

제 목 : 걸프사태(유엔동향)

1.유엔의 북부이락 난민촌 인수에 따른 유엔측과 이락 당사국간 유엔경비인력주둔교섭이 진전을 보이고 있는 것으로 알려짐. 사무총장 대변인에 의하면, 지난번 M.GOULDING 사무차장이 이락측에 타진한것은 평화유지활동과 관련한 유엔경찰력 배치문제였으나, 현재 S.KHAN대표, B.BERNANDEV (바그다드 상주)가 이락정부와 진행중인 교섭은 91.4.18 자 유엔구호활동 관련 양해각서 (MOU) 의 맥락 (CONTEXT) 에서 이루어지고 있다고함.

2.한편 이락은 금 5.16 안보리 문서로 배포된 동국외상 명의 안보리 의장앞 5.12. 자 서한 (S/22599) 을 통해 경찰력 (CIVILIAN POLICE)배치안과 관련 미국을 비롯한 다국적군측을 비난한바, 상세는 별첨 서한내용 참조바람

첨부:1.이락외상 명의서한

2. NYT,WP 지관련기사: UNW(F)-212

끝

(대사 노창희-국장)

국기국 1차보 중아국 정문국 안기부

PAGE 1

91.05.17 08:59 WG

외신 1과 통제관

0206

UNW(FT)-212 10516 1dF
(국연. 중동일. 기차) 총504

Annex

Letter dated 12 May 1991 from the Minister for Foreign Affairs of Iraq addressed to the President of the Security Council

Through its Permanent Representative to the United Nations, at a meeting with our Permanent Representative on the morning of 10 May 1991, the United States of America informed us of its concern at the information that reached it when the United States President had received the Secretary-General of the United Nations on 9 May, namely that the mission of Mr. Marrack Goulding had failed and that Iraq did not accept the Secretary-General's proposal for the deployment of civilian police to assist United Nations relief operations in northern Iraq. The paper read by the Permanent Representative of the United States contained, *inter alia*, the following points, which he said represented the reaction of the United States Administration:

> Taking account of resolution 688, the Government of Iraq must understand that the international community is determined to provide for the necessary protection and security for refugees in Iraq as expressed in that resolution, with which Iraq must comply.
>
> Iraq must prove its intentions by providing the United Nations with all the mechanisms necessary to ensure the complete safety and protection of the operation and by moving rapidly to work with the Secretary-General and his representatives in the appropriate manner in order to implement this task.

The United States reminds Iraq that the provision of a mechanism protecting the humanitarian operation in Iraq will enable the United Nations to be in a position to assume the successful management of the operation. This would help to bring an end to the humanitarian mission of the coalition forces in northern Iraq so as to achieve the goal which Iraq has stated in writing that it is its desire to achieve.

It is clear from the foregoing that the United States of America is treating the matter as if it were speaking on behalf of the Security Council and the international community and as if Security Council resolution 688 had become a cover to permit encroachment on Iraq's sovereignty and territorial integrity and interference in its internal affairs. The United States and the European States cooperating with it, such as the United Kingdom, France and the Netherlands, have brought their armed forces into northern Iraq on the pretext that resolution 688 authorizes them to engage in such obvious military intervention in the internal affairs of Iraq and to violate its territorial integrity. This claim could not be farther from the truth, and the resolution does not grant any party any such authorization. The case is rather that the entire operation constitutes a flagrant violation of the fundamental principle on which the United Nations is based, namely the sovereign equality of all its Members.

UNW-1270
첨부물

5-1

/...

0207

It is clear also that these Western States have resorted to developing the ways and means that they have applied during their known history in the region so as to claim now that they are using force of arms and intervention in the internal affairs of States for purposes of humanitarian assistance. In addition, the position of the United States and the States cooperating with it reveals once again duality in the concepts dealt with by those States in the service of their political objectives. Those who have left their towns and villages in northern Iraq are part of the people of Iraq, and Iraq's concern with returning them to their towns and villages and satisfying their needs is a natural thing and one of the main duties of the government authorities. However, the forces and States that are expressing concern for the security and safety of these Iraqis are the same States that bombarded them and their civilian installations and deprived them of food and medicaments. They are the same States that are still imposing a blockade on the whole Iraqi people, 4 million of whom are living in the city of Baghdad alone and suffering daily from a shortage of food and vital human requirements.

The Iraqi authorities have taken all necessary measures, utilizing all their capacities, for the return of those who have been displaced to their villages and homes, for the restoration of normal life in the northern region, including the amnesty issued in respect of the rebels who engaged in strife and destruction, and for preparing the necessary climate for the safe return of all to their place of residence. A large number of the displaced persons have actually returned without any incident.

It is well known that tens of thousands of those returning have been from areas where the coalition forces maintain no presence, whereas no significant number have returned to areas where those forces maintain a presence.

There are some States that are keeping these displaced persons for dubious political purposes, and that lies outside the responsibility of the Iraqi authorities.

Iraq, for its part, has shown full cooperation with the United Nations and other international organizations in aiding those who were led to emigrate and assuring their return to their homes. The memorandum of understanding of 18 April 1991 was signed with the Executive Delegate of the Secretary-General, Prince Sadruddin Aga Khan, to regulate the efforts and activities of the international agencies concerned with regard to the provision of the required assistance in cooperation with the authorities and the humanitarian organizations in Iraq.

The United States and the States cooperating with it know quite well that, with their armed intervention in northern Iraq, they are acting in a way that violates Iraq's sovereignty and constitutes intervention in its internal affairs. It also violates the principles of the United Nations Charter and the principles of international law and custom. They are now trying to impose a <u>fait accompli</u> on Iraq and to provide a cover of legitimacy for their illegal acts by forcing the Security Council to adopt the United States positions. The present United States demand for the deployment of so-called "civilian"

/...

5-2

0208

police in the place of the United States and other Western forces in northern Iraq is but another example of this new way of exploiting the United Nations based on the logic of force. It has become clear to us now that the more Iraq accepts Security Council resolutions, shows its readiness to implement their provisions, and assumes its responsibilities in that regard, the more these States raise new problems in order to make further attacks on the sovereignty and territorial integrity of Iraq and the more they increase their attempts to intervene in its internal affairs. We hope that the members of the Security Council will be aware of the truth regarding the intentions of the United States of America and the States cooperating with it and will put a halt to the intervention in the internal affairs of Iraq and the use of the Council and the United Nations as a cover for such interventions.

I request you to have this letter circulated as a document of the Security Council.

Ahmed HUSSEIN
Minister for Foreign Affairs
of the Republic of Iraq

0209

Bush May Seek U.N. Ruling For Force in Kurdish Zone

By PATRICK E. TYLER
Special to The New York Times

WASHINGTON, May 15 — President Bush said today that he was willing to seek Security Council authority to create a United Nations security force in northern Iraq that would pave the way for the withdrawal of American and allied military forces from the Kurdish region.

The announcement came a day after the Secretary General of the United Nations, Javier Pérez de Cuéllar, indicated that his envoy in Baghdad was making progress in negotiating conditional Iraqi support for such a security force. The State Department spokesman, Richard A. Boucher, also said today, "There may be some preliminary agreement on some type of guard arrangements to be associated with the U.N. humanitarian effort."

A compromise on the security force issue that is acceptable to Washington and Baghdad could spare Mr. Bush a stalemate in northern Iraq, a development that could turn the humanitarian effort into a political liability at home.

Also, a compromise security force that won Iraq's approval would defuse a potentially bruising dispute between Mr. Bush and the Security Council, where the Soviet Union and China have expressed strong reservations against a United Nations military role in Iraq that is not approved by the Iraqi Government.

In a sign that Mr. Bush may be courting Security Council votes, the President also stated publicly today that he favored renewing China's most-favored-nation trade status, linking his decision to China's cooperation at the United Nations during the Persian Gulf conflict.

Last fall, when Mr. Bush needed critical Chinese and Soviet votes to authorize the use of force against Iraqi troops in Kuwait, the President broke his own ban on high-level visits by Chinese officials imposed after the Tiananmen Square crackdown.

The United Nations police force, if it is approved, would provide protection for the relief operation under way in the Kurdish security zone that stretches from Zakho on the Turkish border to the outskirts of Dohuk, a major Iraqi provincial capital. More than 8,000 American, British and French forces occupy the zone and thousands more are stationed in Turkey and the Eastern Mediterranean as a "quick reaction" force.

Responding to a question about the United Nations police force proposal, Mr. Bush told reporters on the South Lawn of the White House, "We're contemplating going to the United Nations on that to get further authority."

Compromise Possible

Mr. Bush added that, in his opinion, the authority to create such a police force has already been granted "under existing resolutions" of the United Nations that require Iraq to cooperate with humanitarian relief efforts.

But his public remarks indicated that Mr. Pérez de Cuéllar's negotiations with Baghdad may have produced a formula that the United States and its allies will be able to accept.

On Tuesday, Mr. Pérez de Cuéllar said that his special envoy, Prince Sadruddin Aga Khan, was negotiating approval from Iraqi officials to add an armed United Nations security force of 400 to 500 men to the United Nations relief workers already in northern Iraq.

A permanent reconciliation between the Kurds and the Iraqi Government is the subject of separate negotiations now headed by the Kurdish guerilla leader Massoud Barzani. Mr. Bush also said today that these talks "could offer some hope." But Mr. Bush emphasized that until relations between the Kurds and the Iraqi Government are normalized, the United States will adhere to its security commitment. "I don't think we can entrust the fate of the Kurds to the word of Saddam Hussein."

At the State Department, Mr. Boucher said "we don't have the details" of the security force proposal that is emerging from the talks in Baghdad. "But we understand that discussion will continue this week between the U.N. and Iraqi authorities."

5-4

0210

U.N. Experts Set to Inspect Iraq's A-Sites

Visit Is First Step In Arms Destruction

By Jonathan C. Randal
Washington Post Foreign Service

BAGHDAD, Iraq, May 15—A 34-member team of international specialists arrived here today for a week of on-site inspections of nuclear facilities to insure compliance with U.N. resolutions prohibiting Iraqi possession of weapons of mass destruction.

Dimitri Perricos, inspector general of the International Atomic Energy Agency, a U.N. body, told reporters he had "received assurances" his team would see all Iraqi nuclear material, and U.N. disarmament specialist Derek Boothby said Iraqi officials have been "very cooperative in this endeavor."

But Perricos said "no doubt we will have to come back" to complete the mission stemming from U.N. Security Council Resolution 687, adopted last month. It stipulates destruction of Iraq's biological, chemical and nuclear weapons and long-range missiles as part of the allied coalition's terms for a permanent cease-fire ending the Persian Gulf War.

Boothby said inventory and destruction of Iraq's chemical weapons will take place at a later date. It will be "the most difficult" aspect of the mission and physically cannot be completed by July 2, the Security Council's present deadline, he said.

Iraqi President Saddam Hussein's government used poison gas against the country's Kurdish minority in 1988, killing thousands, but it did not carry out threats to use chemical weapons against the allied coalition in the gulf war.

Chemical weapons—such as mustard gas or nerve agents that American officials charged were in the Iraqi inventory—"are difficult to handle, there are more of them and they are extremely difficult to destroy," Boothby said. Iraq last month reported to the United Nations a chemical weapons arsenal considerably larger than estimates given Congress in mid-December by then-CIA director William H. Webster.

Iraq's report listed 1,005 tons of liquid nerve gas stored in vats and 11,381 chemical warheads, 30 of them fitted for Scud missiles and the rest for bombs or artillery shells.

Iraq said at least 2,700 of the chemical warheads are buried under debris from allied missile or air attacks on chemical weapons storehouses.

Other experts will come later, Perricos said, to make an inventory for eventual destruction of Iraq's missiles, both the 200-mile-range Scud and the longer-range Hussein missile used against Israel during the gulf war.

The inspectors also will look into U.S. accusations that Iraq has biological weapons such as anthrax—an accusation Iraq has denied.

The first of an unspecified number of nuclear sites to be visited, Perricos said, will be Iraq's nuclear research institute at Tuwaythah, 20 miles from Baghdad. He said the current trip is solely to take inventory and write a report to the Security Council.

He said he did not expect to meet Iraq's political leadership. The specialists, most of them from the Vienna-based U.N. agency, have often visited Iraqi nuclear facilities checking on safeguards against transforming material into weapons and in the past have given Iraq a clean bill of health.

In 1981, Israeli warplanes bombed and destroyed a French-built nuclear reactor facility near Baghdad and various estimates later said a renewed Iraqi nuclear program was within five to 10 years of producing atomic weapons.

5-5

0211

원 본

외 무 부

종 별 :

번 호 : UNW-1317 일 시 : 91 0521 1945

수 신 : 장관(국연,중동일,기정)

발 신 : 주유엔대사

제 목 : 걸프사태(유엔동향)

1. 안보리 휴전결의(687호)에 의거 케야르 사무총장은 이락-쿠웨이트 국경획정위원회를 설치한바, 동위원회 구성은 다음과 같음.

가. 의장: MOCHTAR KUSUMA-ATMADJA (전 인니외상)

나. 위원: IAN BROOK OF SWEDSURVEY (스웨덴)

WILLIAM ROBERTSON (뉴질랜드)

RIYADH AL-QAYSI (이락)

TARIQ A. RAZOUKI (쿠웨이트)

2. 동위원회는 오는 5.23. 첫회의를 개최할예정이라고함. 끝

(대사 노창희-국장)

국기국 1차보 미주국 중아국 안기부

PAGE 1

91.05.22 09:30 CO

외신 1과 통제관

0212

주 국 련 대 표 부

주국련 20313-387　　　　　　　　　　　1991. 5. 23.

수신 장 관

참조 국제기구조약국장, 중동아프리카국장

제목 걸프사태 (안보리)

표제관련 안보리 문서를 별첨과 같이 송부합니다.

첨 부 : 상기 문서. 끝.

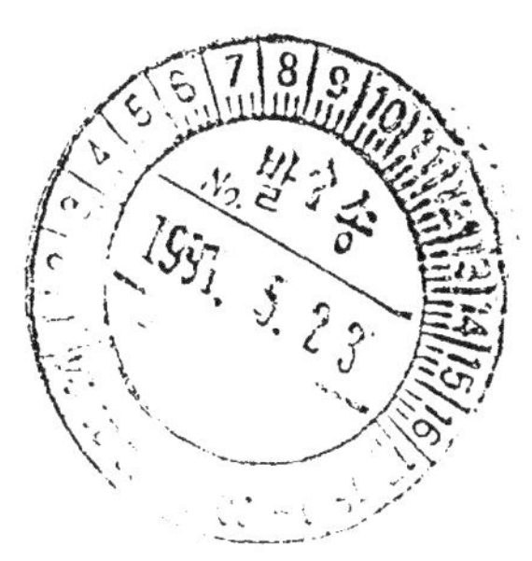

주 국 련 대

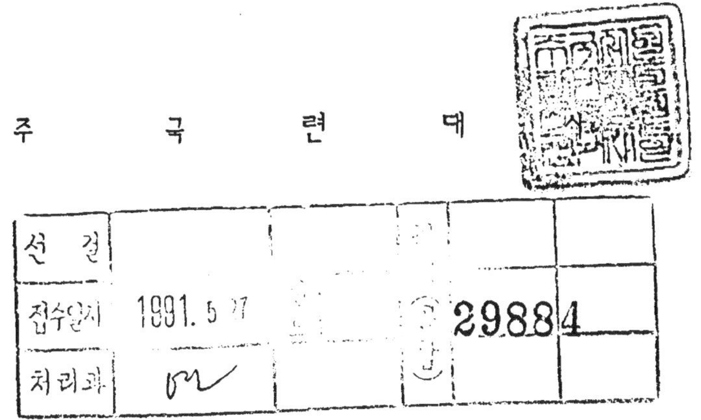

선 결					
접수일시	1991. 5. 27			29884	
처리과					

0213

R090

RX-DDD 0826 FRI 02-MAY-91

175715 UNDRO

175715 UNDRO

02 MAY 91 12:17 GMT
414242 DRO CH
3557944 (UNDRO) GENEVA 02MAY91 1215Z

UNDRO 91/0744A

MIDDLE EAST/PERSIAN GULF - REFUGEE EMERGENCY SITUATION AND REQUIREMENTS
UNITED NATIONS SITUATION REPORT NO. 2 - 2 MAY 1991

PART ONE OF THREE PARTS
::: ::: :: ::: : ::: :

INTRODUCTION
--- --- ---

THIS SITREP IS ISSUED BY UNDRO IN CLOSE CO-OPERATION WITH AND ON BEHALF OF UNHCR AND THE SECRETARY-GENERAL'S EXECUTIVE DELEGATE.

SINCE LAST WEEK'S SITREP, THE UNITED NATIONS HAS SENT TWO ROAD CONVOYS TO NORTHERN IRAQ: ONE LEFT FROM BAGHDAD AND THE OTHER FROM SILOPI, TURKEY. THEY BOTH CARRIED FOOD AND MEDICAL SUPPLIES, ESTABLISHING THE UN PRESENCE IN THAT PART OF IRAQ, AS CALLED FOR BY THE 18 APRIL MEMORANDUM OF UNDERSTANDING. SOME IRAQIS IN THE TURKISH BORDER AREA HAVE STARTED TO RETURN TO ZAKHOU.

THE SAUDI GOVERNMENT ANNOUNCED THAT IT WOULD PROVIDE ASYLUM FOR IRAQIS STRANDED IN DEMILITARIZED ZONE ALONG THE KUWAITI-IRAQ BORDER. THE AIRLIFT OF THE IRAQI REFUGEES TO A CAMP IN RAFHA STARTED ON 28 APRIL. IN ADDITION, THE IRANIAN AUTHORITIES HAVE ALREADY ACCEPTED OVER 2,000 IRAQI ASYLUM SEEKERS BELONGING TO THE SAME GROUP.

TO STRENGTHEN THE UN RESPONSE TO THE EMERGENCY IN THE AREA, THE RELEVANT UN AGENCIES ARE REFINING THE SECOND UPDATE OF THE REGIONAL HUMANITARIAN PLAN OF ACTION TO RESPOND EFFECTIVELY IN ALL THE COUNTRIES CONCERNED. MEANWHILE, THIS REPORT WILL SUMMARIZE PRESENT ACTIVITIES IN IRAQ, IRAN AND TURKEY, AS WELL AS JORDAN AND SYRIA.

0214

ON 26 APRIL THE GOVERNMENT OF JAPAN ANNOUNCED A CONTRIBUTION OF USD 82.5 MILLION TO UNDRO TO PROVIDE ASSITANCE TO THE PEOPLE AFFECTED BY THE AFTERMATH OF THE GULF CRISIS. THIS AMOUNT IS IN ADDITION TO USD 17.5 MILLION ALREADY CONTRIBUTED BY JAPAN IN RESPONSE TO THE APPEAL FOR USD 400.2 MILLION. THE GOVERNMENT OF JAPAN ORGANIZED ALSO SEVERAL RELIEF FLIGHTS TO IRAN AND TURKEY.

SITUATION IN IRAQ

THE SITUATION IN IRAQ IS CHANGING RAPIDLY AND UNHCR, TOGETHER WITH THE REPRESENTATIVE OF THE SECRETARY-GENERAL'S EXECUTIVE DELEGATE AND OTHER AGENCIES CONCERNED ARE TRYING TO ENSURE UN PRESENCE THROUGHOUT THE COUNTRY.

IN THIS CONTEXT, SUB-OFFICES ARE BEING ESTABLISHED IN KEY LOCATIONS. UNICEF IS SETTING UP A UN PRESENCE IN MOSSOUL AND BASRAH WHILE UNHCR IS DOING LIKEWISE IN DOHUK, ARBIL AND SULAIMANYAH. THESE SUB-OFFICES WILL COVER NORTH AND NORTH-WEST IRAQ (MOSSOUL AND DOHUK), NORTH-EAST AND EASTERN IRAQ (ARBIL AND SULAIMANYAH) AND THE SOUTH (BASRAH). IN ADDITION, UNHCR IS ENSURING A PRESENCE IN RAMADI (120 KM NORTH-WEST OF BAGHDAD) WHERE 40,000 IRANIAN REFUGEES ARE BEING ASSISTED. AS REQUESTED BY THE SECRETARY-GENERAL, UNHCR IS PARTICIPATING IN THE UN EFFORT TO ASSIST RETURNEES AND DISPLACED PERSONS WITHIN IRAQ. A KEY CONSIDERATION FOR UNHCR IS THE NEED FOR CONDITIONS FAVOURABLE TO THE SAFE AND DIGNIFIED VOLUNTARY REPATRIATION OF IRAQI REFUGEES AND DISPLACED PERSONS.

IN ORDER TO COPE WITH THE OVERWHELMING TASK AHEAD, THE UNITED NATIONS IS REVISING ITS PLAN OF ACTION FOR IRAQ. THE BASIC ELEMENTS WHICH CAN BE HIGHLIGHTED AT THIS STAGE ARE AS FOLLOWS:

- UNHCR WILL ENSURE THE LARGEST POSSIBLE PRESENCE IN THE COUNTRY (THE NUMBER OF INTERNATIONAL UN STAFF MEMBERS HAS INCREASED TO 57 AND MORE ARE DUE TO REACH IRAQ IN THE NEXT FEW DAYS),

- THROUGH THE FIVE UN SUB-OFFICES, THE UNITED NATIONS WILL COVER REGIONS WHERE FIELD PRESENCE IS BEING ESTABLISHED (PARTICULARLY ALONG THE NORTHERN AND EASTERN BORDERS), ASSISTANCE IS TO BE PROVIDED IN COMMUNITIES FROM WHERE REFUGEES HAVE LEFT IN THE PAST WEEKS AND TO WHICH THEY MAY EVENTUALLY RETURN,

- A LOCAL RADIO COMMUNICATIONS NETWORK IS BEING ESTABLISHED BY UNHCR ON BEHALF OF THE UNITED NATIONS SYSTEM WITH THE SUPPORT OF EXISTING UNIMOG FACILITIES,

- A LOGISTIC BACK-UP STATION IS TO BE SET UP IN AMMAN IN ORDER TO FACILITATE THE PROVISION OF RELIEF THROUGH JORDAN,

- PARTICULAR EFFORT IS BEING UNDERTAKEN BY UNHCR IN ORDER TO FIND DURABLE SOLUTIONS FOR 40,000 IRANIAN REFUGEES PRESENTLY IN AL TASH CAMP NEAR THE CITY OF RAMADI (INCLUDING REPATRIATION AND LOCAL SETTLEMENT).

SPECIFIC ACTIONS ALREADY TAKEN CAN BE SUMMARIZED AS FOLLOWS:

0215

- UNHCR HAS SENT ABOUT ONE HUNDRED TONS OF RELIEF SUPPLIES FROM AMMAN AND DAMASCUS, WHILE 540 MT OF BASIC FOOD HAS BEEN PROVIDED BY WFP FOR VULNERABLE GROUPS,

- IN SPITE OF NUMEROUS DIFFICULTIES, A SURVEY OF VULNERABLE GROUPS' NEEDS IN THE BAGHDAD REGION (WITH SPECIAL ATTENTION TO PARTICULARLY POOR PALESTINIAN COMMUNITIES) HAS STARTED,

- TOGETHER WITH THE IRANIAN AUTHORITIES, REPATRIATION OPERATIONS ARE BEING PREPARED WHILE, THROUGH IOM, OVER 2,000 IRAQI ASYLUM SEEKERS STRANDED ALONG THE KUWAIT-IRAQ BORDER HAVE BEEN RE-SETTLED IN IRAN,

- FOLLOWING THE GENEROUS DECISION OF THE SAUDI AUTHORITIES, SOME 8,000 ADDITIONAL IRAQI ASYLUM SEEKERS ARE BEING PROCESSED AND TRANSFERRED TO SAUDI ARABIA.

CLOSE CO-OPERATION IS BEING MAINTAINED WITH RELEVANT AGENCIES ACCORDING TO THEIR MANDATES SUCH AS: WHO AND UNICEF (FIELD AND STAFFING CO-ORDINATION, I.E. IDENTIFICATION OF BASIC HEALTH, WATER AND SANITATION NEEDS AND RESOURCES REQUIRED), WFP (FOOD PROVISION, DELIVERY AND DISTRIBUTION) WITH THE EVENTUAL PARTICIPATION OF EXPERIENCED NGOS (NEGOTIATIONS ARE TAKING PLACE WITH CARE INTERNATIONAL), ICRC, MSF (PRESENT IN IRAQ SINCE 9 MARCH MSF HAS TEAMS IN THE PROVINCES OF KURDISTAN AND BASRAH AS WELL AS IN THE DISTRICTS OF FALLEYAH AND RAMEDI).

UPON THE RETURN OF THE UNHCR MISSION WHICH PARTICIPATED IN THE UN MEETING HELD IN ZAKHO (NORTHERN IRAQ) ON 30 APRIL WITH COLLEAGUES FROM TURKEY AND BAGHDAD, THE FORESEEN PLAN OF ACTION WILL BE FINALIZED IN THE COMING DAYS.

WHO RE-ESTABLISHED ITS REPRESENTATIVE IN BAGHDAD, WHO IS CO-OPERATING WITH MINISTRY OF HEALTH AND OTHER UN AGENCIES IN MONITORING THE RELATED SECTORIAL NEEDS IN THE COUNTRY.

TO DATE UNICEF HAS DELIVERED IN IRAQ 1,136 TONS OF WATER PURIFICATION MATERIAL, 650 HEALTH KITS AND 29 TONS OF HIGH PROTEIN BISCUITS.

: ESSAAFI UNDRO GENEVA 414242 DRO CH :

UNDRO EMERGENCY TELEPHONE NUMBER: X-41-22-733 20 10

UNDRO TELEX: 414242 DRO CH

UNDRO FAX: X-41-22-733 56 23

UNDRO ELECTRONIC MAIL: UNIENET ID UNX008

END PART ONE OF THREE PARTS

::: ::: ::: :: ::: : ::: :

0216

R091

RX-DDD 1231 FRI 02-MAY-91

175715 UNDRO

175715 UNDRO

02 MAY 91 16:28 GMT
414242 DRO CH
3558529 (UNDRO) GENEVA 02MAY91 1623Z
UNDRO 91/0744B

MIDDLE EAST/PERSIAN GULF - REFUGEE EMERGENCY SITUATION AND REQUIREMENTS
UNITED NATIONS SITUATION REPORT NO. 2 - 2 MAY 1991

PART TWO OF THREE PARTS

SITUATION IN IRAN

AS OF 29 APRIL THERE WERE 1,042,969 IRAQI REFUGEES IN IRAN. UN PLANNING FIGURE, HOWEVER, HAS BEEN INCREASED TO 1,300,000 DUE TO LENGTH OF QUEUES AT ENTRY POINTS. IT MIGHT BE REVIEWED AGAIN IF THE INDICATIONS OF POSSIBLE INFLUX OF 600,000 INTERNALLY DISPLACED SHI'A INTO KHUZISTAN FROM SOUTHERN IRAQ ARE CONFIRMED.

LOCATION OF CASELOAD

PROVINCE	NO OF CAMPS	PRESENT CASELOAD
WEST AZERBAIJAN	17	362,650
KURDISTAN	28	158,670
BAKHTARAN	12	450,500
ILAM	1	2,689
KHUZISTAN	6	68,460

THE PLAN OF ACTION AGREED UPON BY UNHCR AND THE IRANIAN AUTHORITIES ESTABLISHED THAT DURING THE MONTH OF APRIL (PHASE 1) ALL REQUIRED EMERGENCY RELIEF ITEMS SHOULD BE DELIVERED. PHASE 2 (MAY) CALLED FOR MEETING EMERGENCY NEEDS FOR WATER AND SANITATION. PHASE 3 (MAY ONWARDS) WILL LOOK INTO MEDIUM AND LONGER TERM ASPECTS OF THE IRAQI REFUGEE SITUATION IN IRAN.

ASSISTANCE PROGRAMME

0217

5/8

THE FOOD NEEDS OF 1,300,000 REFUGEES DURING THREE MONTHS ARE: MT 40,950 WHEAT, MT 17,550 RICE, MT 3,510 PULSES AND MT 3,510 OIL. AS OF 29 APRIL, WFP (BY REPLENISHING THE STOCKS OF THE GOVERNMENT OF IRAN) HAD PROVIDED MT 32,020 WHEAT, MT 13,600 RICE, MT 3,854 PULSES AND MT 1,844 OIL. IN ADDITION, 750 MT DATES ARE BEING PROCURED LOCALLY TO COMPLEMENT INTERNATIONAL PROCUREMENT OF 654 MT HIGH PROTEIN FOOD.

THE NON-FOOD ITEMS DELIVERY SITUATION IS AS FOLLOWS:

ITEM	TOTAL NEEDS	++PROCURED/ DELIVERED	SHORTFALL
JERRY CANS	520,000	318,386	101,614
COOKING SETS	260,000	167,891	92,109
STOVE	260,000	78,240	181,760
PLASTIC SHEETING/TARP	260,000	95,000	165,000
RUBB HALLS	20	20	-
BLANKETS	2,600,000	2,043,478	556,562
SOAP MT	975	372	603

++ INCLUDES UNHCR AND OTHER SOURCES.

OUT OF A TOTAL NEED OF 260,000 FAMILY TENTS, 36,200 UNITS WERE PROCURED BY UNHCR AND AN ADDITIONAL 50,000 ARE IN THE IN THE PROCESS OF BEING PROCURED, BUT LIMITED AVAILABILITY IN THE MARKET IS HAMPERING SPEEDY PURCHASE. AN ADDITIONAL 21,000 TENTS WERE DONATED/PLEDGED BY OTHER SOURCES.

COOKING FUEL (3 LITRES/PERSON/DAY) IS BEING LOCALLY PROCURED BY THE GOVERNMENT OF IRAN WITH UNHCR FUNDS. MOST HEALTH ITEMS REQUESTED BY UNHCR IRAN HAVE BEEN PROCURED (AND ALL REQUESTED DRUGS AND VACCINES). 100 SURGICAL KITS STILL NEED TO BE PURCHASED.

AS CALLED FOR BY PHASE 2, NGOS ARE BEING IDENTIFIED TO COVER THE MOST URGENT NEED FOR DRINKABLE WATER. A GERMAN NGO WILL COVER THIS SECTOR IN BAKHTARAN PROVINCE AND WILL START OPERATING FIRST WEEK OF MAY. IN THE MEANTIME UNHCR IS PROCURING ON AN URGENT BASIS 10,000 LITRE CAPACITY WATER TANKS.

AS OF 2 MAY UN OPERATIONS IN IRAN HAVE 33 INTERNATIONAL OFFICERS AND 80 LOCALLY RECRUITED STAFF.

: ESSAAFI UNDRO GENEVA 414242 DRO CH :

UNDRO EMERGENCY TELEPHONE NUMBER: X-41-22-733 20 10

UNDRO TELEX: 414242 DRO CH

UNDRO FAX: X-41-22-733 56 23

0218

UNDRO ELECTRONIC MAIL: UNIENET ID UNX008

END PART TWO OF THREE PARTS
::: ::: ::: :: ::: : ::: :

414242 DRO CH

175715 UNDRO

175715 UNDRO

02 MAY 91 16:35 GMT
414242 DRO CH
3559182 (UNDRO) GENEVA 02MAY91 1633Z
UNDRO 91/0744C

MIDDLE EAST/PERSIAN GULF - REFUGEE EMERGENCY SITUATION
AND REQUIREMENTS
UNITED NATIONS SITUATION REPORT NO. 2 - 2 MAY 1991

PART THREE OF THREE PARTS
::: ::: : :: ::: : ::: :

SITUATION IN TURKEY

EXCEPT FOR THE ANNOUNCED RETURN OF SOME IRAQIS AT THE BEGINNING OF THE WEEK, THE REFUGEE SITUATION REMAINS VERY MUCH THE SAME: AS OF 30 APRIL THERE WERE APPROXIMATELY 400,000 IRAQIS AT THE BORDER AREA IN 14 DIFFERENT CAMP SITES AND OTHERS APPROACHING THE BORDER, AS PREVIOUSLY REPORTED.

RESPONDING TO THAT SITUATION, THE TOP PRIORITIES THAT UNHCR IS CONCENTRATING ON ARE DISTRIBUTION NETWORKS, WATER SUPPLY SYSTEMS (IN CO-OPERATION WITH OXFAM AND THE GERMAN RED CROSS) AND

0219

SANITATION. SHELTER MATERIALS ARE STILL URGENTLY NEEDED.

IN ADDITION TO THE ANKARA BRANCH OFFICE, UNHCR'S OPERATIONAL STRUCTURE IS AS FOLLOWS:

DIYARBAKIR:
- OPERATIONS CENTRE
- LIAISON WITH REGIONAL GOVERNOR AND NGOS
- SUPPLY/LOGISTICS UNIT WITH RED CRESCENT.

SILOPI, SIRNAK (ULDERE-ISIKEREN), CUKURCA AND SEMDINLI (TO MOVE TO YUKSEKOVA):
-BORDER OPERATIONAL BASES

ADENA (INCIRLIK BASE):
- LIASON UNIT WITH OPERATION PROVIDE COMFORT (OPC)

HAKKARI AND SIRNAK:
- LIASON UNIT WITH PROVINCIAL GOVERNMENTS AND OPC

VAN:
- LOGISTICS/SUPPLY UNIT WITH RED CRESCENT

AS OF 2 MAY, UN OPERATIONS IN TURKEY HAVE 76 INTERNATIONAL EXPERTS AND 88 LOCALLY RECRUITED STAFF. FIFTEEN ADDITIONAL UNHCR INTERNATIONAL STAFF HAVE ALREADY BEEN IDENTIFIED AND WILL BE DEPLOYED ACCORDING TO NEEDS.

FROM JANUARY TO 30 APRIL, UNHCR DELIVERED:
- 160,240 BLANKETS (26,000 EN ROUTE)
- 12,170 FAMILY TENTS (1,435 EN ROUTE)
- 11,765 PLASTIC SHEETING/TARPAULINS
- 3,000 JERRYCANS
- 1,150 STOVES
- 11,350 KITCHEN SETS (700 EN ROUTE)
- 17 RUBB HALLS
- 84 MT HIGH PROTEIN BISCUITS
- 145 EMERGENCY HEALTH KITS
- 17 VEHICLES.

ON 29 APRIL, THE FIRST 30 FLIGHTS FROM THE KINGDOM OF SAUDI ARABIA TO TURKEY ARRIVED IN DIYARBARKIR WITH A LOAD OF 'CARE PACKAGES' CONTAINING FLOUR, SUGAR, RICE AND BLANKETS WHICH WILL COVER THE NEEDS OF 10,000 FAMILIES.

SINCE FEBRUARY 1991, UNICEF HAS PROCURED OVER USD 2.7 MILLION WORTH EMERGENCY RELIEF SUPPLIES WHICH HAVE ALREADY BEEN DELIVERED BY ROAD OVER THE TURKISH/IRAQI BORDER. UNICEF HAS ALSO DEPLOYED ITS EMERGENCY RAPID RESPONSE TEAM BASED IN KENYE TO THE EASTERN BORDER OF TURKEY, WHERE A DISTRIBUTION SYSTEM FOR HEALTH SUPPLIES HAS BEEN ESTABLISHED.

AT REQUEST OF THE MINISTRY OF HEALTH OF TURKEY, A WHO MULTI-DISCIPLINARY TEAM HAS BEEN ASSIGNED TO THE TURKISH/IRAQI BORDER TO CONDUCT A CRASH COURSE FOR HEALTH PERSONNEL INVOLVED IN REFUGEE OPERATIONS.

0220

SITUATION IN JORDAN
--- --- - -- --- --

FOLLOWING THE LIFTING OF THE STATE OF EMERGENCY AND THE DISMANTLING OF EMERGENCY CAMPS, THE REFUGEE CASELOAD IN JORDAN IS STEADILY DECREASING AND AT PRESENT SHOULD NOT EXCEED SOME 600 CASES AT THE ANDALOUS CAMP. THE AGREEMENT SIGNED BY GOJ WITH THE UN SYSTEM FOR EMERGENCY OPERATIONS WAS FORMALLY TERMINATED ON 30/4/91. UNHCR AND IOM, UNDER THE CO-ORDINATION OF UNDP, ARE FINALIZING THE UN EMERGENCY PROGRAMME IN THE COUNTRY.

THE VOLUNTARY REPATRIATION OF 140 SOMALI INDIVIDUALS TO BERBERA, HARGEISA AND BURAO IS EXPECTED TO TAKE PLACE BEFORE THE END OF THIS WEEK ON AN AIR FLIGHT CHARTERED BY IOM. A SUPPLY OF TENTS WAS ALSO ARRANGED THROUGH GOJ AND THE INTERNATIONAL LEAGUE OF RED CROSS/CRESCENT FOR TEMPORARY ACCOMODATIONS OF THE GROUP UPON ARRIVAL IN SOMALIA.

SITUATION IN SYRIA
--- --- - -- --- -

ABOUT 1,600 IRAQIS ARE PRESENTLY ACCOMODATED AT EL HOL CAMP (NORTH EAST, CLOSE TO THE IRAQI BORDER). ANOTHER GROUP OF 1,300 (IRAQI DEFECTORS, NOT ASSISTED BY UNHCR SO FAR) IS STILL IN ADRA MILITARY PREMISES AND IS EXPECTED TO BE SOON MOVED TO EL HOL. ABOUT 150 URBAN CASES OF DIFFERENT ORIGIN ARE RE-GROUPED IN TARTOUS.

INDEPENDENTLY FROM THESE GROUPS LINKED TO THE POST-WAR EMERGENCY SITUATION, A LIMITED GROUP OF 'PROTECTION CASES' OF VARIOUS ORIGIN IS ASSISTED ON THE CURRENT PROGRAMME.

ARRANGEMENTS FOR THE VOLUNTARY REPATRIATION OF 79 SOMALI CASES TO BERBERA ARE PROGRESSING AND THEIR DEPARTURE IS EXPECTED TO TAKE PLACE AS SOON AS THE CLEARANCE OF THE SOMALI AUTHORITIES IS OBTAINED THROUGH OPERATIONS HANDLED BY IOM.

NEW ARRIVALS FROM IRAQ REMAIN LIMITED TO A FEW INDIVIDUALS PREVIOUSLY STRANDED IN BORDER AREAS. SYRIA IS NOT SIGNIFICANTLY AFFECTED BY THE MOVEMENTS OF THE KURDISH POPULATION TO THE OTHER NEIGHBOR COUNTRIES.

--- --- --- --- --- --- --- --- --- --- --- --- --- --- --- ---

FOR RECORDING OF RELIEF DELIVERIES, ADDRESSEES ARE REQUESTED TO INFORM UNDRO RAPIDLY AS INDICATED BELOW OF THEIR CONTRIBUTIONS WITH INDICATION OF VALUE PER ITEM.

: ESSAAFI UNDRO GENEVA 414242 DRO CH :

UNDRO EMERGENCY TELEPHONE NUMBER: X-41-22-733 20 10

UNDRO TELEX: 414242 DRO CH

0221

1/6

R035

RX-DDD 1113 FRI 03-MAY-91

175715 UNDRO

175715 UNDRO

03 MAY 91 15:05 GMT

414242 DRO CH
3561225 (UNDRO) GENEVA 03MAY91 1501Z
UNDRO 91/0756A

MIDDLE EAST/PERSIAN GULF - EMERGENCY SITUATION
UNDRO FINANCIAL REPORT F1 - 3 MAY 1991

PART ONE OF TWO PARTS

1. AS MENTIONED IN UN SITREP NO.1 OF 26 APRIL 1991, UNDRO IS ISSUING A SEPARATE SERIES OF SITREPS ON THE FUNDING AND CONTRIBUTIONS SITUATION (SERIES F). IT WILL FOCUS ON THE FUNDING OF THE UNITED NATIONS APPEAL WHILE ATTEMPTING TO PROVIDE AN OVERVIEW ON CONTRIBUTIONS CHANNELLED BILATERALLY OR THROUGH ORGANIZATIONS OTHER THAN THAT OF THE UN SYSTEM AND IOM. A FULL LIST OF ALL CONTRIBUTIONS AS REPORTED TO UNDRO WILL BE KEPT SEPARATELY AND WILL BE AVAILABLE ON REQUEST.

OVERVIEW

2. EFFORTS TO PRESENT A COMPREHENSIVE PICTURE OF ALL CONTRIBUTIONS ARE HAMPERED BY LACK OF CONSISTENT REPORTING TO UNDRO, BY LATE REPORTING AND DOUBLE REPORTING.

3. AS OF 1 MAY, THE FOLLOWING TOTALS HAVE BEEN REPORTED TO UNDRO FOR THE REGION:

	USD
GOVERNMENTS	168,223,739
INTERGOVERNMENTAL BODIES	21,439,024
RED CROSS/CRESCENT SYSTEM	11,658,950
NGOS	3,996,226
TOTAL	205,317,939

BREAKDOWN BY COUNTRY AS FOLLOWS:

4. IRAQ

0222

OUT OF USD 205,317,939 ONLY USD 1,006,140 WERE REPORTED ALLOCATED FOR IRAQ. UNHCR AND UNICEF ADVANCED USD 3.5 MILLION FROM THEIR OWN EMERGENCY FUNDS TO SUPPORT RELIEF OPERATIONS INSIDE IRAQ.

5. IRAN

ALLOCATIONS REPORTED FOR IRAN BY DONOR CATEGORY:

	USD
GOVERNMENTS	15,548,276
INTERGOVERNMENTAL BODIES	N/A
RED CROSS/CRESCENT SYSTEM	3,482,982
NGOS	1,090,886
TOTAL	20,122,144

6. TURKEY

	USD
GOVERNMENTS	38,058,314
INTERGOVERNMENTAL BODIES	N/A
RED CROSS/CRESCENT SYSTEM	8,175,968
NGOS	1,880,340
TOTAL	48,114,622

\+ + + + + + +

CONTRIBUTIONS AND PLEDGES TO UN SYSTEM AND IOM FOR PHASE III OF RHPA

7. TOTALS (PERIOD 1-30 APRIL 1991)

		USD
UNDRO		101,661,425
UNHCR		63,701,379
UNICEF		1,923,078
WHO		33,000
WFP	(IN KIND)	9,500,000
IOM		8,755,920
GRAND TOTAL		185,573,920

INTERIM FINANCIAL REPORT BY AGENCY
COVERING PERIOD 1 APRIL - 1 MAY 1991

8. UNHCR

UNHCR HAS RECEIVED PLEDGES AND/OR CONTRIBUTIONS TOTALLING USD 69,251,199 IN CASH AND USD 143,243 CONTRIBUTION IN KIND. USD 63,701,379 CASH HAVE BEEN PLEDGED AND/OR PAID DIRECTLY TO UNHCR WHILE USD 5,971,933 HAVE BEEN RECEIVED THROUGH UNDRO.

0223

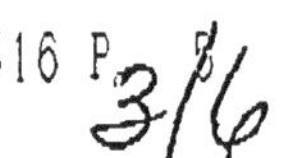

EARMARKINGS REPORTED:

	USD

IRAN	37,217,145
TURKEY	5,230,593
PURCHASE OF DANISH POLYSHEETS	1,083,591
REFUGEES IN IRAN AND TURKEY	14,150,666
MIDDLE EAST AND TURKEY	6,000,000
KURDISH REFUGEES IN THE MIDDLE EAST	488,024
REFUGEES AND DISPLACED IN THE MIDDLE EAST	5,000,000

REMARKS: NO CONTRIBUTIONS WERE EARMARKED FOR IRAQ AND UNHCR ADVANCED USD 1,000,000 FROM ITS EMERGENCY FUND TO SUPPORT RELIEF OPERATIONS IN THE COUNTRY.

: ESSAAFI UNDRO GENEVA +

UNDRO TELEPHONE NO: +41-22-731.02.11
UNDRO EMERGENCY TEL.NO. (OUTSIDE WORKING HOURS): +41-22-733.20.10

UNDRO DESK OFFICER: MS. S. METZNER-STRACK, EXT. 3530
PRESS TO CONTACT UNDRO SPOKESPERSON: M. KHATIB, EXT: 2856

UNDRO TELEX: 414242 DRO CH
UNDRO FAX: +41-22-733.56.23
UNDRO ELECTRONIC MAIL: UNIENET ID UNX008

END PART ONE OF TWO PARTS
::: ::: ::: :: ::: ::: :

414242 DRO CH

175715 UNDRO

.....
1128 05/03
VIA TRT
v^pA
THEY DISCONNECTED

Elapsed time 00:15:12

0224

R097

RX-DDD 1405 FRI 03-MAY-91

175715 UNDRO

175715 UNDRO

SUSPECTED DUPLICATE

03 MAY 91 17:47 GMT
414242 DRO CH
3561604 (UNDRO) GENEVA 03MAY91 1744Z
UNDRO 91/0756B

MIDDLE EAST/PERSIAN GULF - EMERGENCY SITUATION
UNDRO FINANCIAL REPORT F1 - 3 MAY 1991

PART TWO OF TWO PARTS

9. UNICEF

UNICEF HAS RECEIVED PLEDGES AND CONTRIBUTIONS AMOUNTING TO USD 2,823,078. USD 900,000 HAVE BEEN PLEDGED THROUGH UNDRO.

COUNTRY EARMARKINGS REPORTED:

	USD
IRAN	1,386,186
TURKEY	1,436,892
IRAQ 2,500,000 +	

+ ADVANCED FROM UNICEF EMERGENCY FUND

10. WFP

WFP HAS RECEIVED FOOD AID CONTRIBUTIONS WORTH USD 9.5 MILLION, HOWEVER, VALUE OF FOOD AID COMMITTED UNDER WFP OPERATIONS APPROVED IS USD 78,907,768 DIVIDED AS FOLLOWS:

	USD
IRAQ EMOP 4698	17,126,097
IRAQ EMOP 4698/1	25,727,969
IRAN EMOP 4715	23,440,655
TURKEY EMOP 4716	12,013,047
TOTAL	78,907,768

THEREFORE, WFP REPORTS AN OUTSTANDING BALANCE TO COVER

0225

FOOD AID FOR A VALUE OF USD
63,407,768.

11. WHO

TOTAL DIRECT CONTRIBUTIONS RECEIVED BY WHO AMOUNT TO USD 33,000.
ADDITIONAL USD 300,000 HAVE BEEN CONTRIBUTED BY GOVERNMENT OF
DENMARK THROUGH UNDRO FOR HEALTH PROGRAMMES IN TURKEY.

12. FUNDS RECEIVED/PLEDGED TO UNDRO

IN RESPONSE TO THE UN APPEAL FOR USD 400.2 MILLION TO FUND THE
THIRD PHASE OF THE RHPA, UNDRO HAS RECEIVED PLEDGES AND/OR
CONTRIBUTIONS AMOUNTING TO USD 101,161,425 BY FOLLOWING DONORS:

	USD
CANADA	856,780
DENMARK	304,645
JAPAN	17,500,000
JAPAN 82,500,000 + USA (PLEDGE) 500,000	

+ THE JAPANESE CONTRIBUTION OF USD 82.5 MILLION HAS NOT YET BEEN
ALLOCATED PENDING THE RECEIPT OF ADVICE FROM JAPANESE
AUTHORITIES.

FUNDS CHANNELED THROUGH UNDRO, IF NOT SPECIFICALLY EARMARKED, ARE
ALLOCATED TO UN AGENCIES AND IOM ACCORDING TO SHARES REFLECTING
THE MAGNITUDE OF INDIVIDUAL OPERATIONAL RESPONSIBILITIES.

13. IOM

THE FOLLOWING IS AN IOM SUMMARY FINANCIAL REPORT FOR PHASE III
OF RHPA:

	USD
FUNDS PLEDGED/CONTRIBUTED	19,058,927
FUNDS RECEIVED	16,632,021
PAYMENTS MADE	18,753,087

+ + + + + + +

SPECIFIC FINANCIAL REPORTS CAN BE OBTAINED DIRECTLY FROM
CONCERNED UN AGENCIES AND IOM UPON REQUEST.

+ + + + + + +

14. WHILE THE FUNDING SITUATION ALLOWS THE UNITED NATIONS TO
PROCEED AT GOOD PACE WITH EMERGENCY RELIEF ACTIVITIES THE AMOUNTS
RECEIVED FALL FAR SHORT OF THE TOTAL NEEDS. DONORS ARE REQUESTED
TO ADVISE UNDRO OF CONTRIBUTIONS ASAP AND TO EFFECT TRANSFERS
WITH MINIMUM DELAY. TO THE EXTENT POSSIBLE EARMARKINGS SHOULD BE

0226

AVOIDED TO ALLOW FOR MAXIMUM FLEXIBILITY WITH REGARD TO PRIORITIES.

15. ALL DONORS ARE REQUESTED TO USE CONSISTENTLY UNDRO'S STANDARD REPORTING FORMAT AS SUMMARIZED BELOW TO FACILITATE OFFICE'S TASK AND IMPROVE ACCURACY OF FINANCIAL REPORTS:

1. DONOR 2. RECIPIENT COUNTRY 3. DATE OF DECISION TO CONTRIBUTE 4. DESCRIPTION OF EACH RELIEF ITEM 5. QUANTITY PROVIDED (INCLUDING UNIT OF MEASUREMENT) 6. VALUE OF EACH RELIEF ITEM (INCLUDING CURRENCY) 7. TRANSPORT OF RELIEF ITEM (IF ANY: TYPE-AIR/LAND/ SEA AND VALUE OF TRANSPORT) 8. CHANNEL (FOR THOSE CONTRIBUTIONS WHICH ARE CHANNELED THROUGH OR VIA ICRC, RED CROSS/CRESCENT SOCIETIES AND NGOS) 9. LOCAL IMPLETMENTING AGENCY (IN DISASTER-STRICKEN COUNTRY 10. AREA OF DESTINATION OF CONTRIBUTION (IN DISASTER-STRICKEN COUNTRY) 11. PURPOSE OF CONTRIBUTION IN THE AFFECTED COUNTRY 13. BUDGETARY SOURCE OF CONTRIBUTION (I.E. GOVERNMENT, EEC, PRIVATE, ETC.) 14. SPECIFICATION OF TECHNICAL ASSISTANCE PROVIDED.

12. FOR CO-ORDINATION PURPOSES, PLEASE INFORM UNDRO IMMEDIATELY AS INDICATED BELOW OF PLEDGES/CONTRIBUTIONS (SPECIFYING VALUE BY ITEM).

END PART TWO OF TWO PARTS
::: ::: ::: :: ::: ::: :

: ESSAAFI UNDRO GENEVA +

UNDRO TELEPHONE NO: +41-22-731.02.11
UNDRO EMERGENCY TEL.NO. (OUTSIDE WORKING HOURS): +41-22-733.20.10

UNDRO DESK OFFICER: MS. S. METZNER-STRACK, EXT. 3530
PRESS TO CONTACT UNDRO SPOKESPERSON: M. KHATIB, EXT: 2856

UNDRO TELEX: 414242 DRO CH
UNDRO FAX: +41-22-733.56.23
UNDRO ELECTRONIC MAIL: UNIENET ID UNX008

414242 DRO CH

175715 UNDRO

0227

*** END OF DOCUMENT ***

THE SECRETARY-GENERAL

2 May 1991

Dear Mr. President,

In accordance with the request contained in the attached letter of 1 May 1991 from the Permanent Representative of Iraq to the United Nations, I should be grateful if you would bring the contents of the Permanent Representative's letter of 29 April 1991, also attached, to the attention of the members of the Security Council.

Yours sincerely,

Javier Pérez de Cuéllar

His Excellency
Mr. Li Daoyu
President of the Security Council
New York

0228

Translated from Arabic

PERMANENT MISSION OF IRAQ TO THE UNITED NATIONS

No.: 77

Date: 1 May 1991

Sir,

On instructions from my Government, I have the honour to refer to my letter No. 72 of 29 April 1991, to which is annexed a report on the economic situation in Iraq.

I should be grateful if you would kindly bring our above-mentioned letter and the annexed report to the attention of the members of the Security Council.

Accept, Sir, the assurances of my highest consideration.

(Signed) Abdul Amir A. AL-ANBARI
Ambassador
Permanent Representative

His Excellency
Mr. Javier Pérez de Cuéllar
Secretary-General of the United Nations

0229

91-13672/2230c
sm (F)

Translated from Arabic

PERMANENT MISSION OF IRAQ TO THE UNITED NATI...

No.: 72

Date: 29 April 1991

Sir,

On instructions from my Government, I have the honour to transmit herewith a report on the economic situation in Iraq, hoping that its contents will be taken into account in the formulation of the recommendations requested of you by the Security Council in paragraph 19 of resolution 687 (1991) concerning compensation.

Accept, Sir, the assurances of my highest consideration.

Abdul Amir A. AL-ANBARI
Ambassador
Permanent Representative

His Excellency
Mr. Javier Pérez de Cuéllar
Secretary-General of the
United Nations

0230

SUMMARY OF IRAQ'S FINANCIAL OBLIGATIONS AND BASIC REQUIREMENTS

The Iraqi economy has substantial financial obligations and large-scale basic requirements, namely, external debt service, closing the food gap, the domestic demand for foreign commodities and services for consumer purposes, the reconstruction of what was destroyed by the war and investment to guarantee stability and balance the national economy.

We review below briefly Iraq's financial obligations with regard to the servicing of its external debt, its basic foreign currency requirements and the major structural deficiencies suffered by the Iraqi economy under the following basic headings.

I. FINANCIAL OBLIGATIONS

Iraq's total external debt and obligations amount to 13,118 million Iraqi dinars (ID) or the equivalent of $US 42,097 million as of 31 December 1990, excluding interest. 1/

A breakdown of the balances of these debts and obligations by the years in which they fall due is as follows:

Breakdown of the balances of debts and obligations

	Millions of Iraqi dinars	Equivalent in millions of US dollars 2/
Amounts due and not paid up to the end of 1991	7 313.4	23 467.8
1992	1 533.7	4 921.5
1993	1 503.3	4 824.0
1994	1 437.2	4 611.7
1995	919.2	2 949.6
Amounts due after 1995	411.6	1 320.8
	13 118.4	42 097.4

1/ The interest on the balance of the external debt plus the accumulated annual deficit has been estimated at only 8 per cent per year, as indicated in the annexed table.

2/ One Iraqi dinar = 3.208889 US dollars.

/...

0231

The problem of the external debt for the Iraqi economy does not lie solely in its size (which constitutes 65 per cent of the gross domestic product) but extends to servicing difficulties also, since 97 per cent of these debts fall due in the next five years.

II. BASIC REQUIREMENTS

This section covers import programmes, the reconstitution of the stock of foodstuffs and basic commodities, the costs of repairing part of the war damage in the state civilian sector and the continued implementation of development projects that were under way.

The annexed table shows that the total of these obligations for the above-mentioned categories is ID 43.4 billion at an annual rate of ID 8.7 billion during the period 1991-1995, while the estimate of these requirements for 1991 totalled ID 7 billion. These amounts represent the minimum needed to meet Iraqi economic requirements for the restoration of normal life. Below is a brief summary of the main categories of basic requirements:

1. Import programme

Total allocations for import programmes for the next five years are estimated at ID 15.1 billion, including ID 2.4 billion for 1991 alone. The country's import requirements have been estimated on the basis of the 1989 programme, which was characterized essentially by moderation and a focus on basic commodities. Below are the main totals for import programmes over the next few years.

(a) Basic commodities (foodstuffs and medicine)

The sum of ID 4,532 million has been allocated for the categories of foodstuffs and medicine in the import programmes for the next five years, at an annual rate of ID 906 million or the equivalent of 30 per cent of annual allocations for import programmes, as against an allocation of ID 713 million in the 1991 programme for the importation of basic foodstuffs and medicines.

(b) Other consumer goods and raw materials

The sum of ID 7,357 million has been allocated for this group, at an annual rate of ID 1,471 million, which represents 48.7 per cent of the annual allocations for import programmes, as against an allocation of ID 1,158 million in the 1991 programme for the importation of other consumer goods and raw materials.

(c) Production goods

The sum of ID 3,218 million has been allocated, at an annual rate of ID 643.6 million; these allocations represent 21.3 per cent of the total

/...

0232

allocations for the import programme, as against an allocation of ID 507 million in the 1991 programme for the importation of production goods.

2. Reconstitution of stock (foodstuffs and basic commodities)

As a result of the economic embargo, the Government has exhausted its strategic stock of foodstuffs and primary and intermediate goods. Iraq used to keep the equivalent of 25 per cent of its imports as a strategic stock for emergencies, and, in order to reconstitute this stock, the allocation of ID 735 million is required over the period 1991-1995. It is expected that ID 283 million will be allocated during 1991, representing 15 per cent of the volume of imports for 1991.

3. Repair of war damage

The war destroyed infrastructure and enterprises vital to the economic and social life of the country and created a serious case of economic weakness and retardation. It is expected that the situation will remain thus for a long period of time if the repair and reconstruction of war damage to the civilian sector is not expedited.

Our concern will be focused on the costs of reconstructing those of the plants destroyed which are of particular importance for economic and social life, and which bore much of the direct and indirect material damage left by the war.

The cost of reconstructing these plants is estimated at some ID 8.0 billion, 80 per cent of that amount, or ID 6.4 billion, in foreign currency. It is expected that ID 0.6 billion of the total will be allocated during 1991. These costs do not include that of such indirect damage as the stoppage of production, the various forms of social and humanitarian damage, military damage, damage to nuclear-power installations and military industries, damage to private sector establishments or other damage to enterprises located in certain areas of Iraq where there is a foreign military presence.

4. Obligations under the development plan

Total investment allocations for the period 1991-1995 were approximately ID 28.7 billion, and they represent the minimum required to achieve an extremely low rate of growth in non-petroleum GDP of no more than 3.4 per cent a year. This is a paltry figure when account is taken of the population growth rate of 2.8 per cent a year. The foreign currency component of total allocations is approximately ID 17.2 billion, and this represents 60 per cent of all allocations at an annual average of ID 3,447.6 million over the period in question. The breakdown of foreign currency requirements for the economic and social development plan for each year of the plan is as follows:

/...

0233

First year: 19 per cent;

Second year: 18 per cent;

Third year: 20 per cent;

Fourth year: 24 per cent;

Fifth year: 19 per cent.

III. ANTICIPATED REVENUE

Iraq's anticipated oil revenue over the years 1991-1995 are estimated at ID 20 billion. ID 539 million of this amount is for the remainder of 1991, assuming the exportation of only 600,000 barrels of crude oil a day at a rate of $16 per barrel because of the substantial damage caused to oil extraction and exploitation installations. For 1992, oil exports have been estimated at 2 million barrels a day; for 1993, 2.85 million; for 1994, 2.9 million; and for 1995, 2.95 million.

Non-petroleum exports are extremely limited and they are not expected to exceed ID 290 million over the five-year period 1991-1995.

IV. THE GAP BETWEEN REQUIREMENTS AND ANTICIPATED FOREIGN CURRENCY REVENUE

In light of the data presented in sections I and II above, if it is to meet its debt-servicing requirements, instalment payments and interest payments, and to have the minimum necessary to provide for domestic consumption and investment demand, as well as for the repair or reconstruction of those vital enterprises of particular importance for economic and social life which were destroyed by the war, Iraq's total foreign currency needs amount to ID 66.8 billion. Of this amount, ID 23.4 billion would go to service debt instalments and interest payments and ID 43.4 billion to meet the requirements of the national economy. At the same time, Iraq's total revenue are not expected to exceed ID 20.3 billion over the period 1991-1995, a total in which oil would have a 98.6 per cent share, as shown in the accompanying table. Accordingly, the gap between requirements and anticipated foreign currency revenue will reach an accumulated total over the period in question of some ID 46.5 billion at an average of ID 9.3 billion a year. It should be borne in mind that the 1991 deficit is expected to reach ID 14.9 billion. The reason that the size of this deficit is greater than the annual average is the enormous volume of debt instalments falling due this year together with those for previous years. It is because these instalments include all the amounts due for 1991 as well as those for previous years on which no agreement was reached on deferment or on a modality for payment.

/...

0234

The paucity of Iraq's anticipated export revenue over the next five years places the national economy in an unenviable position inasmuch as such revenue do not cover its minimum financial obligations but only its requirements for food and medicine. This conclusion can be drawn from the figures indicating Iraq's anticipated foreign currency expenditures on current debt servicing - instalments and interest payments due and those expected to fall due during the next five years. Its imports of food and medicine alone will amount to ID 20.4 billion, while its total revenue for the period 1991-1995 will be ID 20.3 billion, as set forth below.

1991-1995	Millions of dinars	
Instalments due	12 706	
Interest	2 172	(At a rate of 8 per cent a year on total external debts)
Imports of food and medicine	4 523	(f.o.b.)
Reconstitution of stocks of food and medicine	281	(Three months' consumption of food and medicine only)
Transport and shipping charges	722	(Representing 15 per cent of the value of food and medicine imports only)
Total	20 413	
Export revenue	20 303	
Deficit	110	

/...

0235

V. OTHER KEY PROBLEMS FACING THE IRAQI ECONOMY

The major economic indicators show that there are many economic imbalances and problems which are distorting the allocation of resources and impeding the restoration of economic activity to its normal levels with the necessary speed. The most important of these are as follows:

1. The accumulated deficit in the general state budget

The accumulated deficit in the general state budget is in the order of ID 42 billion, of which ID 35.7 billion is financed by the banking sector at an annual rate of 16.6 per cent, representing 216 per cent of GDP at the present time.

2. Inflation

The increase in prices over the period 1985-1990, as expressed by the consumer price index, was 126 per cent, for an annual inflation rate of 17.7 per cent. This may rise to 23.2 per cent a year, which reflects hidden inflation according to indicators of liquidity or the relation between money supply and GDP.

3. Decline in economic activity

Most of the sectors and activities sharing in the composition of GDP experienced a drop or decline in value added at fixed prices, the rates of real growth of which were close to -0.03, over the period 1985-1989. This situation gave rise to a decline in real per capita income by 2.8 per cent a year, and that decline also had a negative impact on economic activity in terms of investment and real consumption.

4. Balance-of-payments deficit

In the period 1985-1990, the balance-of-payments deficit was about ID 2.6 billion and was financed from external borrowing.

For the same period, the current account deficit is estimated at some ID 8.8 billion.

5. External debts

External indebtedness and external obligations have accumulated, and the total at the end of 1990 was close to $42.1 billion, excluding interest payments due and grants from the Gulf Arab countries.

/...

0236

VI. PROPOSAL OF THE GOVERNMENT OF IRAQ

On the basis of the facts referred to in this note and mentioned above, which clearly reflect the tremendous financial deficit and the great gap between the financial obligations and the financial requirements of Iraq on the one hand and its limited revenue and expected exports for 1991 in particular and for subsequent years on the other hand, and in the light of the conclusions reached by Mr. Ahtisaari, the United Nations Under-Secretary-General dispatched to Iraq, who noted in his report that "... the recent conflict has wrought near-apocalyptic results upon the economic infrastructure ... Now, most means of modern life-support have been destroyed or rendered tenuous. Iraq has, for some time to come, been relegated to a pre-industrial age ...".

With its current financial resources and those expected for 1991 and subsequent years, it is not within the capacity of Iraq alone to restore its economic and social life to that obtaining before the events of 17 January 1991. Intensive international efforts must be exerted in order to help Iraq to accelerate the return to a normal situation. Therefore, Iraq is in no position to bear any deduction from its oil export revenue for 1991 and coming years, which will be meagre and suffice only to finance an extremely small part of its financial obligations and basic requirements, which should be taken into consideration, as stated unambiguously in paragraph 19 of Security Council resolution 687 (1991).

Therefore, the Government of Iraq requests that it should be granted a delay of at least five years for the implementation of paragraphs 18 and 19 of the above Security Council resolution in order to enable it to adjust its economy so as to allow it to meet its international financial obligations and its basic requirements.

/...

0237

Financial obligations and basic foreign-currency requirements of Iraq

(Millions of Iraqi dinars)

Applications							Resources						
	1991	1992	1993	1994	1995	1991-1995		1991	1992	1993	1994	1995	1991-1995
I. External debt service (a + b)	8 363	3 186	3 633	4 056	4 150	23 388	Oil revenues	539	3 640	5 187	5 278	5 369	20 013
(a) Instalments due	7 313	1 534	1 503	1 437	919	12 706							
(b) Interest due	1 050	1 652	2 130	2 619	3 231	10 682	Other exports	20	30	60	80	100	290
II. Economic requirements (1 + 2 + 3 + 4 + 5)	7 046	7 986	9 230	10 389	8 766	43 417							
1. Import programme (a + b + c)	2 378	2 663	2 983	3 341	3 742	15 107							
(a) Foodstuffs	713	799	895	1 002	1 123	4 532							
(b) Other consumer goods and raw materials	1 158	1 297	1 453	1 627	1 822	7 357							
(c) Private-sector production goods	507	567	635	712	797	3 218							
2. Stock reconstitution programme	283	240	63	70	79	735							
3. War damage rehabilitation	640	1 280	1 921	1 921	640	6 402							
4. National development allocations	3 275	3 103	3 448	4 137	3 275	17 238							
5. Net services	470	700	815	920	1 030	3 935							
Total = I + II	15 409	11 172	12 863	14 445	12 916	66 805	Total	559	3 670	5 247	5 358	5 469	20 303
Deficit	14 850	7 502	7 616	9 087	7 447	46 502							

/...

0238

FINANCIAL OBLIGATIONS AND BASIC REQUIREMENTS OF IRAQ

CONTENTS

0239

UNDRO 91/0[illegible]

MIDDLE EAST/PERSIAN GULF - REFUGEE EMERGENCY SITUATION AND REQUIREMENTS
UNITED NATIONS SITUATION REPORT NO. 2 - 2 MAY 1991

INTRODUCTION

THIS SITREP IS ISSUED BY UNDRO IN CLOSE CO-OPERATION WITH AND ON BEHALF OF UNHCR AND THE SECRETARY-GENERAL'S EXECUTIVE DELEGATE.

SINCE LAST WEEK'S SITREP, THE UNITED NATIONS HAS SENT TWO ROAD CONVOYS TO NORTHERN IRAQ: ONE LEFT FROM BAGHDAD AND THE OTHER FROM SILOPI, TURKEY. THEY BOTH CARRIED FOOD AND MEDICAL SUPPLIES, ESTABLISHING THE UN PRESENCE IN THAT PART OF IRAQ, AS CALLED FOR BY THE 18 APRIL MEMORANDUM OF UNDERSTANDING. SOME IRAQIS IN THE TURKISH BORDER AREA HAVE STARTED TO RETURN TO ZAKHOU.

THE SAUDI GOVERNMENT ANNOUNCED THAT IT WOULD PROVIDE ASYLUM FOR IRAQIS STRANDED IN DEMILITARIZED ZONE ALONG THE KUWAITI-IRAQ BORDER. THE AIRLIFT OF THE IRAQI REFUGEES TO A CAMP IN RAFHA STARTED ON 28 APRIL. IN ADDITION, THE IRANIAN AUTHORITIES HAVE ALREADY ACCEPTED OVER 2,000 IRAQI ASYLUM SEEKERS BELONGING TO THE SAME GROUP.

TO STRENGTHEN THE UN RESPONSE TO THE EMERGENCY IN THE AREA, THE RELEVANT UN AGENCIES ARE REFINING THE SECOND UPDATE OF THE REGIONAL HUMANITARIAN PLAN OF ACTION TO RESPOND EFFECTIVELY IN ALL THE COUNTRIES CONCERNED. MEANWHILE, THIS REPORT WILL SUMMARIZE PRESENT ACTIVITIES IN IRAQ, IRAN AND TURKEY, AS WELL AS JORDAN AND SYRIA.

ON 26 APRIL THE GOVERNMENT OF JAPAN ANNOUNCED A CONTRIBUTION OF USD 82.5 MILLION TO UNDRO TO PROVIDE ASSITANCE TO THE PEOPLE AFFECTED BY THE AFTERMATH OF THE GULF CRISIS. THIS AMOUNT IS IN ADDITION TO USD 17.5 MILLION ALREADY CONTRIBUTED BY JAPAN IN RESPONSE TO THE APPEAL FOR USD 400.2 MILLION. THE GOVERNMENT OF JAPAN ORGANIZED ALSO SEVERAL RELIEF FLIGHTS TO IRAN AND TURKEY.

SITUATION IN IRAQ
--------- -- ----

THE SITUATION IN IRAQ IS CHANGING RAPIDLY AND UNHCR, TOGETHER WITH THE REPRESENTATIVE OF THE SECRETARY-GENERAL'S EXECUTIVE DELEGATE AND OTHER AGENCIES CONCERNED ARE TRYING TO ENSURE UN PRESENCE THROUGHOUT THE COUNTRY.

IN THIS CONTEXT, SUB-OFFICES ARE BEING ESTABLISHED IN KEY LOCATIONS. UNICEF IS SETTING UP A UN PRESENCE IN MOSSOUL AND BASRAH WHILE UNHCR IS DOING LIKEWISE IN DOHUK, ARBIL AND SULAIMANYAH. THESE SUB-OFFICES WILL COVER NORTH AND NORTH-WEST IRAQ (MOSSOUL AND DOHUK), NORTH-EAST AND EASTERN IRAQ (ARBIL AND SULAIMANYAH) AND THE SOUTH (BASRAH). IN ADDITION, UNHCR IS ENSURING A PRESENCE IN RAMADI (120 KM NORTH-WEST OF BAGHDAD) WHERE 40,000 IRANIAN REFUGEES ARE BEING ASSISTED. AS REQUESTED

0240

BY THE SECRETARY-GENERAL, UNHCR IS PARTICIPATING IN THE UN EFFORT TO ASSIST REFUGEES AND DISPLACED PERSONS WITHIN IRAQ. A KEY CONSIDERATION FOR UNHCR IS THE NEED FOR CONDITIONS FAVOURABLE TO THE SAFE AND DIGNIFIED VOLUNTARY REPATRIATION OF IRAQI REFUGEES AND DISPLACED PERSONS.

IN ORDER TO COPE WITH THE OVERWHELMING TASK AHEAD, THE UNITED NATIONS IS REVISING ITS PLAN OF ACTION FOR IRAQ. THE BASIC ELEMENTS WHICH CAN BE HIGHLIGHTED AT THIS STAGE ARE AS FOLLOWS:

- UNHCR WILL ENSURE THE LARGEST POSSIBLE PRESENCE IN THE COUNTRY (THE NUMBER OF INTERNATIONAL UN STAFF MEMBERS HAS INCREASED TO 57 AND MORE ARE DUE TO REACH IRAQ IN THE NEXT FEW DAYS);

-THROUGH THE FIVE UN SUB-OFFICES, THE UNITED NATIONS WILL COVER REGIONS WHERE FIELD PRESENCE IS BEING ESTABLISHED (PARTICULARLY ALONG THE NORTHERN AND EASTERN BORDERS); ASSISTANCE IS TO BE PROVIDED IN COMMUNITIES FROM WHERE REFUGEES HAVE LEFT IN THE PAST WEEKS AND TO WHICH THEY MAY EVENTUALLY RETURN;

- A LOCAL RADIO COMMUNICATIONS NETWORK IS BEING ESTABLISHED BY UNHCR ON BEHALF OF THE UNITED NATIONS SYSTEM WITH THE SUPPORT OF EXISTING UNIMOG FACILITIES;

- A LOGISTIC BACK-UP STATION IS TO BE SET UP IN AMMAN IN ORDER TO FACILITATE THE PROVISION OF RELIEF THROUGH JORDAN;

- PARTICULAR EFFORT IS BEING UNDERTAKEN BY UNHCR IN ORDER TO FIND DURABLE SOLUTIONS FOR 40,000 IRANIAN REFUGEES PRESENTLY IN AL TASH CAMP NEAR THE CITY OF RAMADI (INCLUDING REPATRIATION AND LOCAL SETTLEMENT).

SPECIFIC ACTIONS ALREADY TAKEN CAN BE SUMMARIZED AS FOLLOWS:

- UNHCR HAS SENT ABOUT ONE HUNDRED TONS OF RELIEF SUPPLIES FROM AMMAN AND DAMASCUS. WHILE 540 MT OF BASIC FOOD HAS BEEN PROVIDED BY WFP FOR VULNERABLE GROUPS;

- IN SPITE OF NUMEROUS DIFFICULTIES, A SURVEY OF VULNERABLE GROUPS' NEEDS IN THE BAGHDAD REGION (WITH SPECIAL ATTENTION TO PARTICULARLY POOR PALESTINIAN COMMUNITIES) HAS STARTED;

- TOGETHER WITH THE IRANIAN AUTHORITIES, REPATRIATION OPERATIONS ARE BEING PREPARED WHILE, THROUGH IOM, OVER 2,000 IRAQI ASYLUM SEEKERS STRANDED ALONG THE KUWAIT-IRAQ BORDER HAVE BEEN RE-SETTLED IN IRAN;

- FOLLOWING THE GENEROUS DECISION OF THE SAUDI AUTHORITIES, SOME 8,000 ADDITIONAL IRAQI ASYLUM SEEKERS ARE BEING PROCESSED AND TRANSFERRED TO SAUDI ARABIA.

CLOSE CO-OPERATION IS BEING MAINTAINED WITH RELEVANT AGENCIES ACCORDING TO THEIR MANDATES SUCH AS: WHO AND UNICEF (FIELD AND STAFFING CO-ORDINATION, I.E. IDENTIFICATION OF BASIC HEALTH, WATER AND SANITATION NEEDS AND RESOURCES REQUIRED); WFP (FOOD PROVISION, DELIVERY AND DISTRIBUTION) WITH THE EVENTUAL PARTICIPATION OF EXPERIENCED NGOS (NEGOTIATIONS ARE TAKING PLACE WITH CARE INTERNATIONAL); ICRC; MSF (PRESENT IN IRAQ SINCE 9 MARCH MSF HAS
TEAMS IN THE PROVINCES OF KURDISTAN AND BASRAH AS WELL AS IN THE

0241

DISTRICTS OF FALLEYAH AND RAMEDI).

UPON THE RETURN OF THE UNHCR MISSION WHICH PARTICIPATED IN THE UN MEETING HELD IN ZAKHO (NORTHERN IRAQ) ON 30 APRIL WITH COLLEAGUES FROM TURKEY AND BAGHDAD, THE FORESEEN PLAN OF ACTION WILL BE FINALIZED IN THE COMING DAYS.

WHO RE-ESTABLISHED ITS REPRESENTATIVE IN BAGHDAD, WHO IS CO-OPERATING WITH MINISTRY OF HEALTH AND OTHER UN AGENCIES IN MONITORING THE RELATED SECTORIAL NEEDS IN THE COUNTRY.

TO DATE UNICEF HAS DELIVERED IN IRAQ 1,136 TONS OF WATER PURIFICATION MATERIAL, 650 HEALTH KITS AND 29 TONS OF HIGH PROTEIN BISCUITS.

SITUATION IN IRAN

AS OF 29 APRIL THERE WERE 1,042,969 IRAQI REFUGEES IN IRAN. UN PLANNING FIGURE, HOWEVER, HAS BEEN INCREASED TO 1,300,000 DUE TO LENGTH OF QUEUES AT ENTRY POINTS. IT MIGHT BE REVIEWED AGAIN IF THE INDICATIONS OF POSSIBLE INFLUX OF 600,000 INTERNALLY DISPLACED SHI'A INTO KHUZISTAN FROM SOUTHERN IRAQ ARE CONFIRMED.

LOCATION OF CASELOAD

PROVINCE	NO OF CAMPS	PRESENT CASELOAD
WEST AZERBAIJAN	17	362,650
KURDISTAN	26	158,670
BAKHTARAN	12	450,500
ILAM	1	2,689
KHUZISTAN	6	68,460

THE PLAN OF ACTION AGREED UPON BY UNHCR AND THE IRANIAN AUTHORITIES ESTABLISHED THAT DURING THE MONTH OF APRIL (PHASE 1) ALL REQUIRED EMERGENCY RELIEF ITEMS SHOULD BE DELIVERED. PHASE 2 (MAY) CALLED FOR MEETING EMERGENCY NEEDS FOR WATER AND SANITATION. PHASE 3 (MAY ONWARDS) WILL LOOK INTO MEDIUM AND LONGER TERM ASPECTS OF THE IRAQI REFUGEE SITUATION IN IRAN.

ASSISTANCE PROGRAMME
---------- ---------

THE FOOD NEEDS OF 1,300,000 REFUGEES DURING THREE MONTHS ARE: MT 40,950 WHEAT, MT 17,550 RICE, MT 3,510 PULSES AND MT 3,510 OIL. AS OF 29 APRIL, WFP (BY REPLENISHING THE STOCKS OF THE GOVERNMENT OF IRAN) HAD PROVIDED MT 32,020 WHEAT, MT 13,600 RICE, MT 3,854 PULSES AND MT 1,844 OIL. IN ADDITION, 750 MT DATES ARE BEING PROCURED LOCALLY TO COMPLEMENT INTERNATIONAL PROCUREMENT OF 654 MT HIGH PROTEIN FOOD.

THE NON-FOOD ITEMS DELIVERY SITUATION IS AS FOLLOWS:

ITEM	TOTAL NEEDS	*PROCURED/ DELIVERED	SHORTFALL

0242

JERRY CANS	520,000	318,386	101,614
COOKING SETS	260,000	167,891	92,109
STOVE	260,000	78,240	181,760
PLASTIC SHEETING/TARP	260,000	95,000	165,000
RUBB HALLS	20	20	-
BLANKETS	2,600,000	2,043,478	556,562
SOAP MT	975	372	603

* INCLUDES UNHCR AND OTHER SOURCES.

OUT OF A TOTAL NEED OF 260,000 FAMILY TENTS, 36,200 UNITS WERE PROCURED BY UNHCR AND AN ADDITIONAL 50,000 ARE IN THE IN THE PROCESS OF BEING PROCURED, BUT LIMITED AVAILABILITY IN THE MARKET IS HAMPERING SPEEDY PURCHASE. AN ADDITIONAL 21,000 TENTS WERE DONATED/PLEDGED BY OTHER SOURCES.

COOKING FUEL (3 LITRES/PERSON/DAY) IS BEING LOCALLY PROCURED BY THE GOVERNMENT OF IRAN WITH UNHCR FUNDS. MOST HEALTH ITEMS REQUESTED BY UNHCR IRAN HAVE BEEN PROCURED (AND ALL REQUESTED DRUGS AND VACCINES). 100 SURGICAL KITS STILL NEED TO BE PURCHASED.

AS CALLED FOR BY PHASE 2, NGOS ARE BEING IDENTIFIED TO COVER THE MOST URGENT NEED FOR DRINKABLE WATER. A GERMAN NGO WILL COVER THIS SECTOR IN BAKHTARAN PROVINCE AND WILL START OPERATING FIRST WEEK OF MAY. IN THE MEANTIME UNHCR IS PROCURING ON AN URGENT BASIS 10,000 LITRE CAPACITY WATER TANKS.

AS OF 2 MAY UN OPERATIONS IN IRAN HAVE 33 INTERNATIONAL OFFICERS AND 80 LOCALLY RECRUITED STAFF.

SITUATION IN TURKEY
--------- -- ------

EXCEPT FOR THE ANNOUNCED RETURN OF SOME IRAQIS AT THE BEGINNING OF THE WEEK, THE REFUGEE SITUATION REMAINS VERY MUCH THE SAME: AS OF 30 APRIL THERE WERE APPROXIMATELY 400,000 IRAQIS AT THE BORDER AREA IN 14 DIFFERENT CAMP SITES AND OTHERS APPROACHING THE BORDER, AS PREVIOUSLY REPORTED.

RESPONDING TO THAT SITUATION, THE TOP PRIORITIES THAT UNHCR IS CONCENTRATING ON ARE DISTRIBUTION NETWORKS, WATER SUPPLY SYSTEMS (IN CO-OPERATION WITH OXFAM AND THE GERMAN RED CROSS) AND SANITATION. SHELTER MATERIALS ARE STILL URGENTLY NEEDED.

IN ADDITION TO THE ANKARA BRANCH OFFICE, UNHCR'S OPERATIONAL STRUCTURE IS AS FOLLOWS:

DIYARBAKIR:
- OPERATIONS CENTRE
- LIAISON WITH REGIONAL GOVERNOR AND NGOS
- SUPPLY/LOGISTICS UNIT WITH RED CRESCENT

SILOPI, SIRNAK (ULDERE-ISIKEREN), CUKURCA AND SEMDINLI (TO MOVE TO YUKSEKOVA):
-BORDER OPERATIONAL BASES

ADENA (INCIRLIK BASE):

0243

- LIASON UNIT WITH OPERATION PROVIDE COMFORT (OPC)

HAKKARI AND SIRNAK:
- LIASON UNIT WITH PROVINCIAL GOVERNMENTS AND OPC

VAN:
- LOGISTICS/SUPPLY UNIT WITH RED CRESCENT

AS OF 2 MAY, UN OPERATIONS IN TURKEY HAVE 76 INTERNATIONAL EXPERTS AND 83 LOCALLY RECRUITED STAFF. FIFTEEN ADDITIONAL UNHCR INTERNATIONAL STAFF HAVE ALREADY BEEN IDENTIFIED AND WILL BE DEPLOYED ACCORDING TO NEEDS.

FROM JANUARY TO 30 APRIL, UNHCR DELIVERED:
- 160,240 BLANKETS (26,000 EN ROUTE)
- 12,170 FAMILY TENTS (1,435 EN ROUTE)
- 11,765 PLASTIC SHEETING/TARPAULINS
- 3,000 JERRYCANS
- 1,150 STOVES
- 11,350 KITCHEN SETS (700 EN ROUTE)
- 17 RUBB HALLS
- 84 MT HIGH PROTEIN BISCUITS
- 145 EMERGENCY HEALTH KITS
- 17 VEHICLES.

ON 29 APRIL, THE FIRST 30 FLIGHTS FROM THE KINGDOM OF SAUDI ARABIA TO TURKEY ARRIVED IN DIYARBARKIR WITH A LOAD OF "CARE PACKAGES" CONTAINING FLOUR, SUGAR, RICE AND BLANKETS WHICH WILL COVER THE NEEDS OF 10,000 FAMILIES.

SINCE FEBRUARY 1991, UNICEF HAS PROCURED OVER USD 2.7 MILLION WORTH EMERGENCY RELIEF SUPPLIES WHICH HAVE ALREADY BEEN DELIVERED BY ROAD OVER THE TURKISH/IRAQI BORDER. UNICEF HAS ALSO DEPLOYED ITS EMERGENCY RAPID RESPONSE TEAM BASED IN KENYE TO THE EASTERN BORDER OF TURKEY, WHERE A DISTRIBUTION SYSTEM FOR HEALTH SUPPLIES HAS BEEN ESTABLISHED.

AT REQUEST OF THE MINISTRY OF HEALTH OF TURKEY, A WHO MULTI-DISCIPLINARY TEAM HAS BEEN ASSIGNED TO THE TURKISH/IRAQI BORDER TO CONDUCT A CRASH COURSE FOR HEALTH PERSONNEL INVOLVED IN REFUGEE OPERATIONS.

SITUATION IN JORDAN
--------- -- ------

FOLLOWING THE LIFTING OF THE STATE OF EMERGENCY AND THE DISMANTLING OF EMERGENCY CAMPS, THE REFUGEE CASELOAD IN JORDAN IS STEADILY DECREASING AND AT PRESENT SHOULD NOT EXCEED SOME 600 CASES AT THE ANDALOUS CAMP. THE AGREEMENT SIGNED BY GOJ WITH THE UN SYSTEM FOR EMERGENCY OPERATIONS WAS FORMALLY TERMINATED ON 30/4/91. UNHCR AND IOM, UNDER THE CO-ORDINATION OF UNDP, ARE FINALIZING THE UN EMERGENCY PROGRAMME IN THE COUNTRY.

THE VOLUNTARY REPATRIATION OF 140 SOMALI INDIVIDUALS TO BERBERA, HARGEISA AND BURAO IS EXPECTED TO TAKE PLACE BEFORE THE END OF THIS WEEK ON AN AIR FLIGHT CHARTERED BY IOM. A SUPPLY OF TENTS WAS ALSO ARRANGED THROUGH GOJ AND THE INTERNATIONAL LEAGUE OF RED CROSS/CRESCENT FOR TEMPORARY ACCOMODATIONS OF THE GROUP UPON ARRIVAL IN SOMALIA.

0244

SITUATION IN SYRIA
--------- -- -----

ABOUT 1,600 IRAQIS ARE PRESENTLY ACCOMODATED AT EL HOL CAMP (NORTH EAST, CLOSE TO THE IRAQI BORDER). ANOTHER GROUP OF 1,300 (IRAQI DEFECTORS, NOT ASSISTED BY UNHCR SO FAR) IS STILL IN ADRA MILITARY PREMISES AND IS EXPECTED TO BE SOON MOVED TO EL HOL. ABOUT 150 URBAN CASES OF DIFFERENT ORIGIN ARE RE-GROUPED IN TARTOUS.

INDEPENDENTLY FROM THESE GROUPS LINKED TO THE POST-WAR EMERGENCY SITUATION, A LIMITED GROUP OF "PROTECTION CASES" OF VARIOUS ORIGIN IS ASSISTED ON THE CURRENT PROGRAMME.

ARRANGEMENTS FOR THE VOLUNTARY REPATRIATION OF 79 SOMALI CASES TO BERBERA ARE PROGRESSING AND THEIR DEPARTURE IS EXPECTED TO TAKE PLACE AS SOON AS THE CLEARANCE OF THE SOMALI AUTHORITIES IS OBTAINED THROUGH OPERATIONS HANDLED BY IOM.

NEW ARRIVALS FROM IRAQ REMAIN LIMITED TO A FEW INDIVIDUALS PREVIOUSLY STRANDED IN BORDER AREAS. SYRIA IS NOT SIGNIFICANTLY AFFECTED BY THE MOVEMENTS OF THE KURDISH POPULATION TO THE OTHER NEIGHBOR COUNTRIES.

* * * * * * * *

FOR RECORDING OF RELIEF DELIVERIES, ADDRESSEES ARE REQUESTED TO INFORM UNDRO RAPIDLY AS INDICATED BELOW OF THEIR CONTRIBUTIONS WITH INDICATION OF VALUE PER ITEM.

= ESSAAFI UNDRO GENEVA 414242 DRO CH =

UNDRO EMERGENCY TELEPHONE NUMBER: X-41-22-733 20 10

UNDRO TELEX: 414242 DRO CH

UNDRO FAX: X-41-22-733 56 23

UNDRO ELECTRONIC MAIL: UNIENET ID UNX008

0245

Statement by the Secretary-General in Informal Consultations on 26 April 1991

As members of the Council are aware,
I have been deeply concerned by
the suffering of the civilian population in Iraq,
in particular of the most vulnerable groups,
and have been making every effort
to mobilize United Nations assistance to those affected.
In order to ensure the most effective coordination and rapid response
on the part of the United Nations family,
I designated Prince Sadruddin Aga Khan as my Executive Delegate
for a United Nations Inter-Agency Humanitarian Programme
for Iraq, Kuwait and the Iraq/Turkey and Iraq/Iran border areas
on 9 April 1991.

0246

Furthermore, in the context of resolution 688, I designated Mr. Eric Suy as my Personal Representative, to head a team to look into the situation of the civilian population, in particular the Kurdish population as well as the refugees and displaced Iraqi population. Mr. Suy arrived in Baghdad on 13 April.

The Executive Delegate, accompanied by representatives from UNDP, UNICEF, UNDRO, and UNHCR, visited Baghdad with the aim of reaching agreement with the Iraqi Authorities on the execution of his mandate. Following discussions held with Iraqi officials, a memorandum of understanding was signed by Sadruddin Aga Khan and the Iraqi Foreign Minister on 18 April 1991. The terms of the Memorandum of Understanding provide a satisfactory framework to implement an effective United Nations humanitarian relief programme.

0247

Under its terms,

Iraq commits itself to support humanitarian relief efforts and

to assist in the repatriation of refugees and displaced persons.

Furthermore, the United Nations is allowed full latitude for its activities

and the movement of its staff,

including independent communications and logistics.

The United Nations will operate throughout Iraq

and will deliver assistance across borders as required.

The Memorandum of Understanding remains in effect

until 31 December 1991, with provisions for a renewal thereafter.

My Executive Delegate has nominated a Coordinator,

Mr. Bernt Bernander,

who upon assuming his duties in Baghdad on 18 April 1991,

immediately set to work.

Together with the Iraqi authorities and agency colleagues,

Mr. Bernander is undertaking preparatory activities in northern Iraq,

to establish contacts with local officials to survey the situation

and initiate proposals for further action.

0248

In Geneva, a limited non-operational structure

to support the Executive Delegate's activities has been established,

with support from the concerned agencies.

In New York,

a representative will ensure effective liaison

with UN agencies, NGO's and, of course, the permanent missions,

in particular members of the Security Council.

Responsibilities for further United Nations activity in the region

have been entrusted to the agencies, as follows:

UNHCR is assuming the lead role,

supported by UNDRO which will assist

in information gathering, analysis and dissemination of information

to all concerned parties.

UNICEF and WHO are fulfilling their respective roles

in relation to vulnerable groups,

with a focus on health, water, and sanitation.

UNDP, supports the relief operations at the country level.

0249

In view of the installation of relief facilities by American, British and French forces on Iraqi territory, and bearing in mind the letters sent to me by the Foreign Minister of Iraq on 21 and 24 April, it has become imperative that the United Nations be in a position to assume responsibility for the relief operations as soon as possible. In order to expedite this process, it has been decided, with the agreement of the parties concerned, to initiate the following action:

Under the direction of UNHCR, a convoy of relief commodities, accompanied by UN personnel, will cross from Turkey into Iraq on 29 April. The convoy will travel to areas where the largest concentration of Iraqi displaced persons is located. A second convoy will travel to the same region from Baghdad on 29 April. Together, the two convoys will set up facilities for distribution and storage of the relief commodities.

0250

The two teams will also discuss modalities for the take-over, in due course, of the camps presently being set up byAmerican, British and French forces in northern Iraq. On that basis, a plan of action will be prepared for my approval and immediate implementation will follow.

With regard to personnel needed to carry out these challenging tasks, all concerned United Nations organizations have been mobilized and are presently despatching staff to the area. At the moment, there are 67 international staff members in Turkey, 13 international staff in Iran, and 12 international staff in Iraq -- all involved in the humanitarian relief effort. The contingent in Iraq will be joined on 27 April by 35 additional international staff, who will man the UN humanitarian centres.

The efforts in each of these countries

are being assisted by a number of local staff.

New staff and United Nations volunteers are also being recruited,

especially by UNHCR.

Arrangements are, in addition, being made with NGOs so that they,

too,

can work under UN auspices.

The latest figure of displaced persons in Iran is 1,020,000

persons.

As regards Turkey, the figure is 416,000 at the border

and inside that country,

while 200,000 to 400,000 are reported to be on the Iraqi side.

The principal objective before us is therefore to be in a position

to assume responsibility for both the humanitarian centres

and the camps as soon as possible -

in accordance with the wishes of all parties concerned.

We are thus discussing the modalities

by which we can achieve this purpose,

beginning with the most effective integration at the operational level.

Needless to say,

the actual timetable also depends on agreements to be reached

with the US, British and French authorities

and our ability to meet all necessary conditions.

Above all, the United Nations must be assured

of the financial and human resources

which will be indispensable to fulfilling

this most complex and most urgent humanitarian challenge.

Regrettably, until now, the response to the appeals

that have been launched has been very modest,

especially for activities inside Iraq.

If the United Nations is to implement this operation,

as requested by its members states, and to alleviate human suffering

as well as contribute to stabilize a volatile situation,

it is essential that it be given the necessary financial resources

to do so immediately.

0253

In concluding my remarks, Mr. President, I would like to add that, with a view to expediting this process,
I have asked a number of senior officials to travel to Geneva
this weekend for consultations with my Executive Delegate
and the High Commissioner for Refugees.
The aim is to work out a timetable
for the establishment of the UN humanitarian centres
and also to ensure that appropriate arrangements are made to provide
adequate safety and protection to the populations
which will be returning to their home towns and villages.
As you also know, in his letter to me of 24 April,
the Foreign Minister of Iraq
has asked me to ensure that the UN assume responsibility
for the relief centres established in the Zakhou region in northern Iraq
by United States armed forces
and the forces of other foreign States cooperating with them -
this, in accordance with the agreement
concluded at Baghdad on 18 April 1991
between the Government of Iraq and the United Nations.

0254

As already mentioned,

I am taking steps to see to it that this is done as soon as possible.

I shall keep the Council informed of developments.

* * * * *

0255

원 본

외 무 부

종 별 :

번 호 : UNW-1356 일 시 : 91 0524 1540

수 신 : 장 관 (국연,중동일,기정)

발 신 : 주 유엔 대사

제 목 : 걸프사태 (유엔동향)

1.금 5.24. 사무총장 대변인은 5.23. 유엔 B.BERNANDER 대표 (바그다드 상주) 와 이락 당국자간에 지난 4.18.자 양해각서 (MOU) 에 기초한 유엔경비대 이락 배치교섭이 타결되었으며 현재 서명절차 (공한 교환형식)를 밟고 있다고 발표하였음.

2.이와 관련 CUELLAR 사무총장은 5.24. 오전 미, 영, 불 대사들을 면담, 상기 교섭 타결을 정식통보하였다고 하며, 본건 유엔-이락간 합의내용은 서명절차가 끝나는 대로 안보리문서로 배포될 것으로 알려짐. 끝

(대사 노창희-국장)

국기국 1차보 중아국 정문국 안기부

PAGE 1

91.05.25 09:37 WG

외신 1과 통제관

0256

원 본

외 무 부

종 별 :

번 호 : UNW-1428 일 시 : 91 0530 2100

수 신 : 장 관(국연,중동일,기정)

발 신 : 주 유엔 대사

제 목 : 걸프사태(유엔동향)

1. 안보리 휴전결의에 의거 이락군비 통제를 위한 유엔 2차 조사단 (화학무기 전문가 8개 국 35명)이 6.9경부터 이락 방문예정이라고함. 유엔측은 바레인에이락 군비통제를 위한 기지설치를 추진중인 것으로 알려짐.

2. 유엔 이락-쿠웨이트 국경획정 위원회는 지난 5.23-24 당지에서 회의를 가진바, 6월 현지조사활동을 마친다음 7월 제네바 유엔사무소에서 본격적인 작업에 들어갈 예정이라고 함. 끝

(대사 노창희-국장)

국기국 1차보 중아국 외정실 안기부

PAGE 1

91.05.31 10:40 WG

외신 1과 통제관

0257

정 리 보 존 문 서 목 록

기록물종류	일반공문서철	등록번호	2017060008	등록일자	2017-06-05
분류번호	731.33	국가코드	XF	보존기간	30년
명 칭	걸프사태 후 유엔안전보장이사회 동향, 1991. 전3권				
생 산 과	국제연합1과/중동1과	생산년도	1991~1991	담당그룹	
권 차 명	V.2 6-9월				
내용목차	* 8.28 쿠웨이트, 이라크군의 Bubiyan섬 침투사태 관련 항의 안보리 문서 배포 * 이라크의 안보리 휴전 결의 이행 관련 내용 포함				

0001

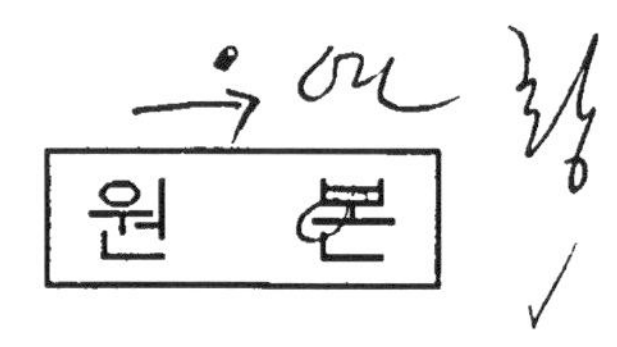

외 무 부

종 별 :

번 호 : UNW-1527 일 시 : 91 0611 1830

수 신 : 장 관(국연,중동일,기정)

발 신 : 주 유엔 대사

제 목 : 걸프사태(안보리)

1.대이락 경제제재 완화문제 정기심사 (휴전결의본문 21항)

가.금 6.11 안보리 비공식 협의에서 본건관련 토의가 있었으나, 특기할 진전은 없었다고함.

나.미, 영, 불은 제재완화에 부정적인 입장을 나타냈으며, 소련은 일부완화 문제에 관심을 보인것으로 알려짐.본건관련 사무총장 보고서 요청문제도 제기되었으며 , 예멘, 쿠바는 공식회의 소집희망을 시사하였다고함.

2.이락 군비통제 문제

가.사무총장의 본건시행안 (UNW-1303) 승인을 위한 안보리 결의안 교섭이 현재 진행 중인바, 동 결의안에는 관련 경비의 이락부담 원칙, 회원국에 대한 기여금등 협조요청이 포함될것이라고함.

나.상기 이락 경비부담원칙과 관련 6.9.자 사무총장앞 서한 (S/22682) 에서 이락측은 유엔주관하의 자국화학무기 폐기경비를 부담할수없다는 입장을 표명함. (유엔 감시하에 자국이 자체적으로 폐기하는 대안제시)

3.이락 남부 쉬아파 주민 공격

이락 정부군이 이락남부 쉬아파 주민을 공격하고 있다고 주장하는 이란측 서한이 유엔에 접수된것으로 알려진바 (6.11. 현재 미배포), 이와관련 사무총장 대변인은 이란측 주장이 아직확인되지않고 있다고 금일 논평하였음.끝

(대사 노창희-국장)

국기국 1차보 중아국 외정실 분석관 청와대 안기부

PAGE 1

91.06.12 09:16 WG

외신 1과 통제관

0002

원 본

외 무 부

종 별 :

번 호 : UNW-1542 일 시 : 91 0612 1900

수 신 : 장 관(국연,중동일,기정)

발 신 : 주 유엔 대사

제 목 : 걸프사태(안보리)

연: UNW-1527

1. 안보리 이락제재위원회 동향

이락의 해외자산 동결 해제요청과 관련 동 위원회는 금 6.12 회의를 가진바, 동 자산 사용이 특정 민수품목수입 목적인 경우 해제가능하다는 기존의 원칙적 입장만을 재확인함. (30 여개이락해외 자산보유국에 동 취지 통보예정)

2. 이락-쿠웨이트 국경 획정

유엔 동 국경 획정위원회 일행은 6.16-19 간 이락, 쿠웨이트 방문예정이며, 7.2 유엔 제네바사무소에서 작업 계획토의 예정이라고함.

3. 이락 남부지역 사태

이란은 연호 6.11 자 안보리문서 (S/22690) 에서, 이락군이 이락남부 지역주민에 대한 대규모 공세를 준비중이며 이로인한 수십만명 난민의 이란 유입이 우려된다고 주장하면서 이와관련 안보리와 사무총장의 즉각적인 조치를 요청하였음.

4. GCC 각료이사회 회의(91.6.2-3)

상기 회의 언론 발표문이 금일 안보리문서 (S/22680) 로 배포된바, 주요내용은 이락내 억류자석방촉구, 미국의 중동평화 노력 (중동평화회의에 GCC 옵서버참가용의) 및 중동지역 대량파괴 무기제거제의 지지, 아랍점령 영토 및 레바논 남부사태 관련 대 이스라엘 비난, GCC-이란협력추진, 소말리아 사태관련 우려 표명등임.

첨부 FAX:1. 이란측 안보리문서

2. WP 지 기고문:UNW(F)-256

끝

(대사 노창희-국장)

국기국 1차보 중아국 외정실 분석관 안기부

PAGE 1

91.06.13 09:07 WG

외신 1과 통제관

0003

UNW(F)-256 10612 1100
(국연. 중동일. 기정) 총2매

UNITED NATIONS

Security Council

Distr.
GENERAL

S/22690
11 June 1991

ORIGINAL: ENGLISH

LETTER DATED 11 JUNE 1991 FROM THE PERMANENT REPRESENTATIVE OF THE ISLAMIC REPUBLIC OF IRAN TO THE UNITED NATIONS ADDRESSED TO THE SECRETARY-GENERAL

Upon instructions from my Government, I have the honour to bring the following urgent issue to your attention.

The Islamic Republic of Iran is gravely concerned over the increasingly momentous reports of developments in southern Iraq which could seriously threaten the national security of the Islamic Republic of Iran on the one hand and further destabilize the entire region on the other. There are credible evidence that Iraqi army is preparing for a general mopping-up operation in the south and the south-east where close to 700,000 Iraqi citizens are contained. Under such circumstances, thousands of Iraqi citizens are feared to get killed while several hundred thousands may flee into Iran.

The Islamic Republic of Iran warns the international community in general and the Security Council of the United Nations in particular that its capacity to care for Iraqi refugees are stretched to the limit and, therefore, it is absolutely unable, with or without international humanitarian assistance, to attend to the needs of another influx of Iraqi refugees. The Islamic Republic of Iran calls upon Your Excellency and the Security Council to adopt immediate measures to avert the risk of recurrence of another tragic incident for Iraqi population and the region as a whole.

It would be highly appreciated if this letter were circulated as a document of the Security Council.

(Signed) Kamal KHARRAZI
Ambassador
Permanent Representative

91-19185 2400f (E)
#UNW-1542
첨부물

2-1

0004

Sadruddin Aga Khan

U.N. Protection Born of Necessity

On May 23 the United Nations secured Iraqi agreement to the deployment of up to 500 U.N. guards, to be assigned wherever a U.N. humanitarian presence is needed. This is not a panacea for the tensions and dangers of the region—and certainly not a means to "monitor all of Iraq," as Jim Hoagland writes [op-ed, June 5]. That was never the intention. But it is a small step for peace, a tentative but instructive idea of how innovation, even within the United Nations' somewhat rigid structures, can unblock the impasse.

The world's media spotlight—dazzlingly effective but lamentably brief—has focused on the grim plight of the Kurdish population in northern Iraq, which should not blind us to the needs of the victims of upheaval in other regions. Coalition forces responded first with a military efficiency that is enviable to traditional relief agencies. And since the signing of our framework agreement in Baghdad on April 18, the United Nations has had underway a humanitarian operation designed to bring succor to vulnerable groups throughout the country. The U.N. high commissioner for refugees has already taken over the Zakho transit camp. But security was hard to address within the confines of a humanitarian program.

Recourse to the Security Council was ruled out at the time. The peace-keeping option was tried to no avail. And indeed traditional U.N. peace-keeping, for all its successes, does have one pitfall: It can freeze a situation in an uneasy stalemate, with the underlying issues conveniently shelved by the parties—a "hard and bitter peace," in the words of John F. Kennedy. Just look at the 33 years of dispute over Kashmir or the 27 years of Cyprus's division.

Another approach was needed. That was why we came up with the "Guards Contingent" formula, blending the disparate humanitarian, political and security elements. A novel if still unproven experiment, the guards' basic mandate is to protect the precious human and material assets deployed in the humanitarian operation. They are neither peace-keepers nor policemen where U.N. resources are not involved. There are no guarantees. But they are there to observe, monitor and report. Any security incidents will be rapidly communicated up the chain of command. In the most direct sense, the guards may be a highly visible but symbolic presence—as indeed are peace-keeping operations themselves, where the "blue helmets" protect more by their color than by their dimension. But the guards ensure the international context. They will bear moral witness and help create confidence. As the eyes and ears of the United Nations, their reports can trigger further action. Moreover, bound as they are to the humanitarian program's time frame, a cutoff date prevents the inertia of the situation in Kashmir or Cyprus.

On first sounding out the concepts in Baghdad, I recalled an earlier idea, which we put forward in a 1981 U.N. report on "Human Rights and Massive Exoduses"—for a corps of "humanitarian observers." These observers were "to monitor situations and contribute through their presence to a de-escalation of tensions," as well as to facilitate humanitarian work. In a refugee context, they could contribute to speedy repatriation. Ahead of their time, they never materialized; however, a decade later the guards represent by another name much of that same philosophy.

The debate over a right of humanitarian intervention has been given a good airing recently. Compassion and self-interest find temporary common cause in international action to alleviate suffering that knows no frontiers. In a vacuum of authority, responsibility must be assumed, and services disrupted by disasters must be restored. Yet imposed concern remains largely unwelcome. Once again, innovation and flexibility are crucial. Life-saving and face-saving may have to go hand in hand.

Critics remind us that the United Nations enjoys no reputation for rapid response to crises: Its potential must indeed be better tapped. Nonetheless it may step in where other powers rightly hesitate to tread. The guards' deployment was risky and cannot shoulder a burden it was never intended to bear, but it deserves its niche in U.N. history. Whatever the outcome, we must not fear to improvise. When hundreds face death each day, as parents bury their children on barren mountaintops, we cannot await the ideal solution. Relief from starvation and disease brooks no bureaucracy.

Complex humanitarian and political challenges defy easy solution. There are no quick fixes: An idea such as the guards contingent for our operation in Iraq can only be part of a broader package. In such situations, where distrust, distress and violence feed upon each other in a poisonous circle, the antidote must have multiple ingredients. First, tensions must be lowered, with the parties agreeing to show some restraint and to support, at the very least, the implementation of the humanitarian program. Specific agreements to that effect should be concluded between all concerned. Second, civilian authority should prevail, reflecting the spirit if not the letter of a demilitarized region. Third, tentative or interim security arrangements might be ensured through a tripartite grouping of both sides together with international representatives associated the humanitarian endeavor. Other assura or leverage may come from outside. tissue of confidence must be rewoven th by thread. One missing strand, one unche incident, will unravel the safety net.

We cut some corners in sending in a guards contingent before the ink dry—in fact before the agreement was signed. And as they had to be part of humanitarian package, their funding is dej dent upon voluntary contributions, in casl in kind. So far the response has fallen shor the needs, estimated at some $35 million the end of the year—about as much as it c the coalition every week, according to p reports, to keep its forces in northern I Give us the means to make this operatio success. As the refugees return down "blue routes," we must keep up the mom tum. Peace comes cheaper than war; it is a good investment. Solidarity today can r stability in a volatile region tomorrow.

The writer is executive delegate of the secretary general for the United Nations inter-agency humanitarian program for Iraq, Kuwait and the Iraq-Turkey and Iraq-Iran border areas.

2-2

0005

UNITED
NATIONS

S

Security Council

Distr.
GENERAL

S/22692
12 June 1991

ORIGINAL: ENGLISH

Report of the Secretary-General on the United Nations Iraq-Kuwait Observation Mission

1. This is a further progress report on the United Nations Iraq-Kuwait Observation Mission (UNIKOM); it follows my report of 9 May 1991 (S/22580).

Organizational aspects

2. Following the arrival of seven observers each from Senegal and Turkey, UNIKOM now has its full complement of military observers, as follows:

Argentina	7	Nigeria	7
Austria	7	Norway	8
Bangladesh	7	Pakistan	9
Canada	1	Poland	7
China	20	Romania	7
Denmark	7	Senegal	7
Fiji	7	Singapore	7
Finland	7	Sweden	7
France	20	Thailand	7
Ghana	8	Turkey	7
Greece	7	Union of Soviet Socialist Republics	20
Hungary	7	United Kingdom of Great Britain and Northern Ireland	20
India	8	United States of America	20
Indonesia	7	Uruguay	8
Ireland	8	Venezuela	7
Italy	7	Total	299
Kenya	8		
Malaysia	8		

91-18250 3052a (E) /...

0006

3. Administrative and logistic support is provided by the following units:

Engineers (Canada)	293
Logistics (Sweden)	31
Movement control/postal (Denmark)	23
Helicopters (Chile)	50
Medical (Norway)	50
Total	447

Two fixed-wing aircraft from Switzerland are operated by civilians. In addition, UNIKOM has had the use of chartered aircraft for the movement of troops and equipment and for communications between Baghdad and Kuwait. The Government of Sweden provided free airlift at the beginning of the Mission.

4. Two infantry companies (Fijian, Nepalese) and one logistic company (Swedish) temporarily assigned from the United Nations Interim Force in Lebanon (UNIFIL) and one infantry company (Danish) from the United Nations Peace-keeping Force in Cyprus (UNFICYP) have returned to their parent missions. Two infantry companies, one from UNFICYP (Austrian) and one from UNIFIL (Ghanaian), remain with UNIKOM; their combined strength is 217 all ranks. As a result, the overall strength of the Mission has been reduced to 963 all ranks.

5. Logistic support for the Mission is still difficult, given the lack of normal infrastructure in the area. However, thanks to assistance from the United States Army and forces of other Member States cooperating with the Government of Kuwait, UNIKOM is now able to meet its requirements as regards rations, vehicles and accommodation. Conditions in the field, however, remain austere, with all personnel living under canvas and subsisting largely on field rations. The situation is expected to improve gradually, with the provision of fresh rations and prefabricated accommodation.

6. UNIKOM headquarters has remained in a hotel annex south of Kuwait City, which was made available by the Government of Kuwait. By 15 June, the headquarters will be moved, as an interim measure, to the logistic base at Doha, pending completion of the necessary refurbishment of the premises at Umm Qasr, which still lack basic facilities such as electricity, water and sewerage.

7. UNIKOM has maintained contact with and provided logistic support to other United Nations missions working in Iraq and Kuwait.

Demilitarized zone

8. The situation in the demilitarized zone (DMZ) has been calm. It is sparsely populated; the main population centres are the towns of Umm Qasr and Safwan, both on the Iraqi side. South of Safwan, on Kuwaiti territory, some 5,000 displaced persons still live in the Abdali camp. They are being

/...

assisted by the International Committee of the Red Cross (ICRC) and the League of Red Cross Societies. The camp is guarded by Kuwaiti police.

9. The Governments of Iraq and Kuwait, which are responsible for civil administration on their respective sides of the DMZ, have deployed border police to maintain law and order. Iraq currently has some 250 police in the DMZ. Kuwait is in the process of restoring its police presence and plans to rebuild and man some 30 police stations along the border. Both Governments have agreed to limit the armament of their police to sidearms.

10. Much of the DMZ is littered with unexploded ordnance and mines, particularly in the south. UNIKOM maintains maps delineating cleared routes; only on these routes is movement authorized.

Deployment and concept of operations

11. For operational purposes, UNIKOM has divided the DMZ into three sectors. Each sector has a headquarters and six observation posts, of which one in the southern sector has not yet been established. The Austrian security company has platoons in the central and northern sectors and at Umm Qasr; the Ghanaian security company has platoons in the southern sector, the Doha Logistic Base and at the temporary UNIKOM headquarters. The deployment of UNIKOM is shown on the attached map.

12. In addition to its fixed observation posts, UNIKOM deploys temporary observation points, mobile patrols (on land and in the air) and investigation teams. The temporary observation points are established from the fixed observation posts, either in areas of particular activity or where roads and tracks enter the DMZ. They are augmented by mobile ground patrols and by aerial reconnaissance. The latter is the only means of maintaining adequate observation of the Khor Abdullah waterway and the southern sector of the DMZ, where mines and unexploded ordnance severely limit UNIKOM's ability to carry out ground patrols. The security companies serve as a quick reaction force and maintain a high state of readiness in order to provide protection to the military observers.

13. UNIKOM maintains close liaison with the Governments of Iraq and Kuwait. Both have given the Mission all the support and cooperation necessary for it to carry out its mandate.

Violations and complaints

14. Since the DMZ was established on 9 May, there have been a number of instances in which personnel of the armed forces of both Iraq and Kuwait and personnel of the Saudi Arabian forces stationed in Kuwait were observed in the DMZ. These observations have been brought to the attention of the parties concerned, which have explained that the majority were due to errors of navigation or misunderstandings over the boundaries of the DMZ. UNIKOM has

/...

posted signs on all major access roads and tracks leading into the DMZ and it is hoped that this will help to prevent future incursions.

15. UNIKOM has also observed a number of overflights of the DMZ by military aircraft. Most of them have been by F-15 and F-16 type aircraft flying along the Iraq-Kuwait border. UNIKOM has brought these overflights to the attention of the Government of Kuwait.

16. Since 9 May, UNIKOM has received two complaints from the Kuwaiti authorities and three from the Iraqi authorities. The complaints of Kuwait arose from reports of Iraqi policemen carrying rifles in the DMZ and of the massing of Iraqi military formations south of Basra. After investigation by UNIKOM both were considered unfounded. Of the Iraqi complaints, one concerned an air violation that could not be substantiated. Another concerned the alleged establishment of a Kuwaiti military checkpoint within the DMZ south of Safwan; this was in fact a police post. The last complaint was that weapons were being kept at the Abdali camp and flags were being flown in a provocative manner. This complaint has been brought to the attention of the Kuwaiti authorities for appropriate action.

Infantry companies

17. The task of the infantry companies temporarily assigned from UNIFIL and UNFICYP was to provide essential security for UNIKOM during the setting-up phase, in view of the uncertainties at that time and the potential risks that might arise (see S/22454, paras. 10 and 13). After 30 days in the Mission, these companies were reduced from 5 to 2. Major General Greindl, the Chief Military Observer, has now recommended that 1 company of some 150 all ranks continue to be assigned to provide security for the Mission; 1 platoon would be deployed to each of the 3 sectors, and 1 at the headquarters in Umm Qasr. This company would also provide the basis for expansion should this be required for security reasons. General Greindl has based his recommendation on his assessment that the area is still in transition and there remains, for the time being, a risk to UNIKOM personnel.

18. I have weighed the above recommendation most carefully. In addition to General Greindl's military assessment, I have taken into consideration the excellent cooperation received from all concerned in the area and the fact that the perceived threats to the security of UNIKOM personnel during the setting-up phase did not in practice materialize. I have also borne in mind the financial implications and the growing financial burden on Member States as a result of the expansion of peace-keeping activities. In the light of these considerations, I have decided not to recommend, in the present circumstances, that UNIKOM be provided with an infantry element on a permanent basis. I intend, however, to explore with Member States the possibilities of rapid reinforcement of UNIKOM in case of emergency. I will monitor developments carefully and revert to the Security Council on this matter, should it become necessary.

/...

0009

Observations

19. As will be apparent from the above report, UNIKOM is now established and fully able to carry out the tasks assigned to it by the Security Council. It only remains for it to occupy its headquarters at Umm Qasr, which will be done as soon as possible. The mission area has now entered the season of great heat and this will be a testing period for UNIKOM's personnel and equipment. In the light of its experience during the remaining months of the current mandate period, I will, in October, undertake a further review of its strength and make appropriate recommendations to the Security Council. Meanwhile I take this opportunity to pay tribute to the determination and professionalism which General Greindl and all under his command have shown in setting up UNIKOM in difficult circumstances.

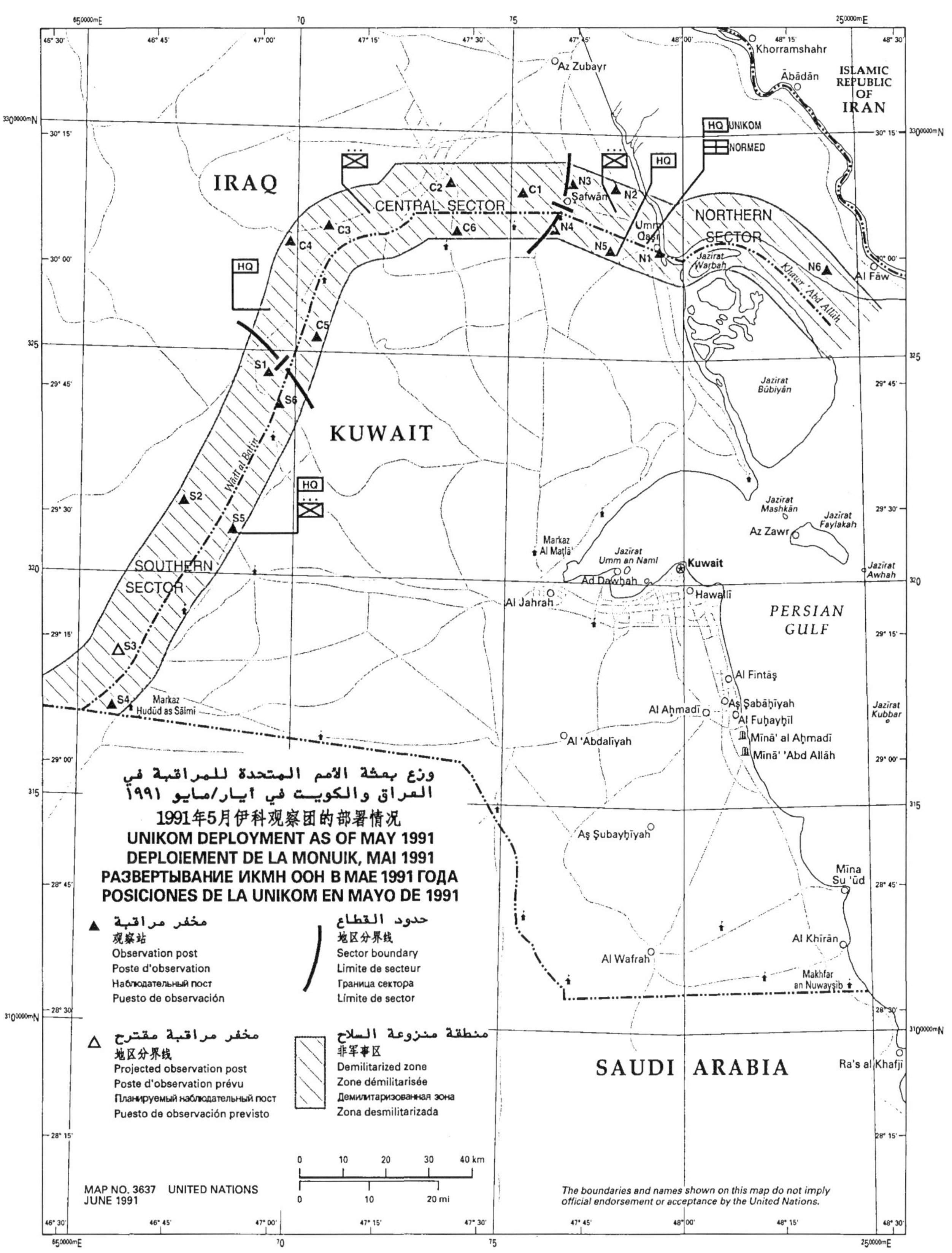

وزع بعثة الأمم المتحدة للمراقبة في العراق والكويت في أيار/مايو ١٩٩١
1991年5月伊科观察团的部署情况
UNIKOM DEPLOYMENT AS OF MAY 1991
DEPLOIEMENT DE LA MONUIK, MAI 1991
РАЗВЕРТЫВАНИЕ ИКМН ООН В МАЕ 1991 ГОДА
POSICIONES DE LA UNIKOM EN MAYO DE 1991
IRAQ
KUWAIT
SAUDI ARABIA
ISLAMIC REPUBLIC OF IRAN
PERSIAN GULF
CENTRAL SECTOR
NORTHERN SECTOR
SOUTHERN SECTOR
HQ UNIKOM
NORMED
Observation post
Poste d'observation
Наблюдательный пост
Puesto de observación
Sector boundary
Limite de secteur
Граница сектора
Límite de sector
Projected observation post
Poste d'observation prévu
Планируемый наблюдательный пост
Puesto de observación previsto
Demilitarized zone
Zone démilitarisée
Демилитаризованная зона
Zona desmilitarizada
MAP NO. 3637 UNITED NATIONS
JUNE 1991
The boundaries and names shown on this map do not imply official endorsement or acceptance by the United Nations.
Kuwait
Al Jahrah
Hawallī
Az Zubayr
Khorramshahr
Ābādān
Umm Qasr
Şafwān
Al Fāw
Jazīrat Būbiyān
Al Aḩmadī
Al Wafrah
Ra's al Khafjī

0011

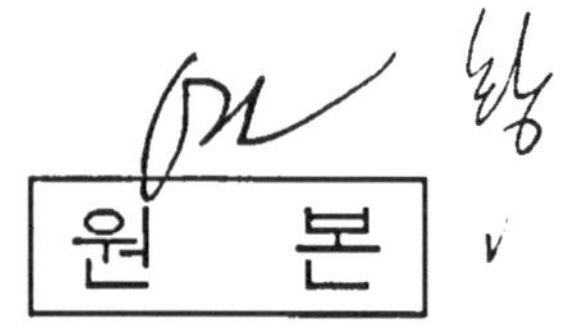

원 본

외 무 부

종 별 :

번 호 : UNW-1550 일 시 : 91 0613 1800

수 신 : 장 관(국연,중동일,기정)

발 신 : 주 유엔 대사

제 목 : 걸프사태(안보리)

연: UNW-1542

1. 이락의 휴전결의(687호) 이행조치

가.이락은 6.8.자 A.HUSSEIN 외상명의 서한을 안보리문서 (S/22689) 로 배포한바, 이락측의 휴전결의 이행과 관련한 제반조치를 설명하고 이러한 자국조치 실적을 안보리의 휴전결의이행 심사과정에서 감안해줄것을 요망하는 요지임.

나.또한 휴전결의 본문 32항과 관련 이락측은 자국의 반테러리즘 공약을 안보리에 6.11 자로 통보해옴.(S/22687)

2.이락남부사태

이락은 연호 이란측주장 (이락 남부 무력탄 압임박)을 부인하는 한편, 이란의 대이락 내정 간섭저의를 비난하는 6.12자 안보리 문서를 배포하였음.(S/22699)

3. 이락보상기금을 위한 이락 석유 수입공제상한선 문제

안보리는 금 6.13 오후 비공식협의에서 본건토의 예정인바 동 토의동향은 추보위계임.

첨부:1.이락측 안보리문서

2. CSM 기사: UNW(F)-260

끝

(대사 노창희-국장)

국기국 1차보 중아국 외정실 분석관 안기부

PAGE 1 91.06.14 09:35 WG

외신 1과 통제관

0012

UNW(FI)-260 10613 1800
(북연. 공동안. 기정) 총5매

Annex

Identical letters dated 8 June 1991 from the Minister for Foreign Affairs of Iraq addressed respectively to the Secretary-General and the President of the Security Council

As you are well aware, the Iraqi Government accepted Security Council resolution 687 (1991) and gave notice of its acceptance in its letter of 6 April 1991 addressed to both the President of the Security Council and the Secretary-General. I should like on this occasion to confirm to you that the Iraqi Government has complied with the said resolution and adopted a positive attitude towards it ever since its adoption. Allow me to review for you the measures taken in this connection by the Government of Iraq.

1. In connection with section A of the resolution, concerning demarcation of the boundary between Iraq and Kuwait, the Iraqi Government has appointed its representatives to the Boundary Demarcation Commission, which held its first session of meetings in New York from 23 to 24 May 1991. Iraq's representative participated actively, in a constructive and cooperative spirit, in the work of that session.

2. In connection with section B of resolution 687 (1991), concerning deployment of the United Nations Iraq-Kuwait Observer Mission, the competent Iraqi authorities have received the Chief Military Observer, Major-General Günther Greindl, on several occasions in Baghdad since his appointment, together with his assistants. Agreement was reached at these meetings on all the requirements for the deployment of the Mission in the demilitarized zone established under the resolution, which came into effect on 9 May 1991.

Cooperation between the competent Iraqi authorities and the Observer Mission continues through the channels designated for that purpose between, respectively, the Iraqi Government, the Mission headquarters and the United Nations Secretariat.

3. In connection with section C of the resolution, which calls for a series of undertakings to dispense with weapons of mass destruction and neither to use, develop, construct nor acquire any such weapons, Iraq has deposited the instrument whereby the Republic of Iraq ratifies the Convention on the Prohibition of the Development, Production and Stockpiling of Bacteriological (Biological) and Toxin Weapons and on Their Destruction, of 10 April 1972. Iraq has also affirmed its unconditional commitment to its obligations under the Geneva Protocol for the Prohibition of the Use in War of Asphyxiating, Poisonous or Other Gases, and of Bacteriological Methods of Warfare, signed at Geneva on 17 June 1925. In addition, the Iraqi Government has provided details of the locations, amounts and types of items relating to chemical weapons and ballistic missiles specified in the resolution and agreed to an inspection of the sites concerned, as laid down in the resolution.

/...

UNW-1550
첨부물

5-1

0013

Iraq has also unconditionally undertaken not to use, develop, construct or acquire any of the items specified in the resolution. It has affirmed its obligations under the Treaty on the Non-Proliferation of Nuclear Weapons of 1 July 1968 and unconditionally agreed not to acquire or develop nuclear weapons or nuclear-weapons-usable material. Iraq informed the International Atomic Energy Agency (IAEA), in a letter dated 27 April 1991 from the Minister for Foreign Affairs, that it was prepared to cooperate with the Agency in implementing the provisions of the resolution: the letter was accompanied by tables providing information on Iraq's nuclear facilities. Iraq has also provided detailed information on the situation with regard to other weapons covered by the resolution to the Special Commission established to implement section C.

In a letter dated 17 May 1991, Iraq agreed to the proposals contained in the Secretary-General's letter of 6 May 1991 concerning the privileges and immunities of the Special Commission and its visiting teams.

The nuclear weapons inspection team visited Iraq from 14 to 22 May 1991. On 23 May 1991, IAEA issued a statement affirming that Iraq had cooperated fully and responded to all the requests submitted by the inspection team. A chemical weapons inspection team, accompanied by the Chairman of the Special Commission, is to visit Iraq from 9 to 15 June in order to begin its mission. Iraq has made all the necessary arrangements to ensure that the inspection team's mission is a success.

4. In connection with section D of the resolution, which relates to the return of Kuwaiti property, Mr. Richard Foran, Assistant Secretary-General and official responsible for coordinating the return of such property, visited Iraq twice during the month of May 1991. The competent Iraqi authorities expressed their readiness to hand over the Kuwaiti property of which Iraq had already notified the Secretariat of the United Nations. A Kuwaiti civilian aircraft was, in fact, handed over at Amman on 11 May 1991. Mr. Foran also undertook a wide-ranging field visit and saw for himself the gold, coins, banknotes, civilian aircraft, museum antiquities and books that will be returned to Kuwait immediately an agreement is reached establishing a location for the handing over, it being understood that it is this property whose handing over Mr. Foran has determined should have priority at the present stage. The same procedures will doubtless be applied to other Kuwaiti property.

5. In connection with sections E and F, which relate to compensation and the lifting of sanctions, no measures are required on the part of Iraq.

6. In connection with section G of the resolution, the competent Iraqi authorities have taken and are continuing to take measures to repatriate all Kuwaiti and third country nationals, and they have provided lists of their names and have facilitated the access of the delegation of the International Committee of the Red Cross (ICRC) in Baghdad to all such persons wherever detained. It should be mentioned that the number of those freed and repatriated has reached 6,366 (6,289 Kuwaitis, 36 Americans, 5 Italians,

/...

5-2

0014

13 Saudis, 17 Frenchmen, 1 Spaniard, 2 Brazilians, 1 Norwegian, 1 Uruguayan and 1 Irishman). The competent Iraqi authorities are still diligently searching for missing subjects of coalition countries with a view to finding them and repatriating them following registration by the ICRC delegation. The competent Iraqi authorities have directly facilitated all matters relating to the work of the ICRC delegation in the registration of Kuwaiti nationals present in Iraq, thereby enabling the delegation to register more than 3,000 Kuwaitis, and they have endeavoured to return the remains of 15 subjects of the coalition countries.

7. In connection with section H, which relates to international terrorism, it should be mentioned that Iraq is a party to the international conventions relating to numerous aspects of this matter and that it abides by the obligations set forth therein. Iraq has not supported any terrorist activities.

In providing you with these clarifications, we are prompted by the hope that you will deem it appropriate to take account of the facts set forth above in any review that the Security Council might intend to make of Iraq's position on the implementation of Security Council resolution 687 (1991).

(Signed) Ahmed HUSSEIN
Minister for Foreign Affairs
of the Republic of Iraq

5-3

0015

Iraqis protest demands as Western members complain of lax compliance with cease-fire

By Marian Houk

Special to The Christian Science Monitor

UNITED NATIONS, N.Y.

THE United Nations Security Council kept the pressure on Saddam Hussein's government in its first periodic review of economic sanctions imposed on Iraq.

But several "nonaligned" council members argued in a meeting Tuesday that political and legal positions should be tempered by moral considerations. Particular concern was expressed for Iraq's children.

Yemeni Ambassador Abdullah al-Ashtal said there was "an evolving consensus that something must be done – not lifting the sanctions altogether ... but possibly a limited lifting." He suggested a limited sale of oil would enable Iraq to buy milk powder and other essentials.

But United States and British diplomats linked the sanctions to the tenacity of Iraq's leadership.

"Saddam Hussein is singularly unlikely to comply fully with the [cease-fire] terms of Resolution 687, and that could lead you to the view, therefore, that the lifting of sanctions is a remote matter," Sir David Hannay, Britain's ambassador, told journalists.

In Tuesday's closed-door session, Western diplomats charged that Iraq has still not complied with the UN's cease-fire terms in several ways. They cited:

- The continued detention of nearly 3,000 Kuwaitis and holding of billions of dollars of stolen Kuwaiti property.
- Inadequate disclosure of Iraq's internally held assets.
- Inadequate disclosure of its weapons of mass destruction.
- Recent public comments by Iraqi Vice President Taha Yassin Ramadan restating Iraq's claim to Kuwait.
- The summary trials and life sentences handed down to two British businessmen. (UN resolutions had ordered Iraq to release all third-country nationals.)
- The absence of any commitment to renouncing terrorism. (After Tuesday's meeting, Iraq's UN mission supplied a letter declaring its rejection of terrorism.)

Western delegates also said Baghdad hadn't done much to reassure civilians in the Kurdish north and Shiite south – or to guarantee the return of those who fled the postwar crackdown.

Kamal Kharrazi, the Iranian ambassador to the UN, circulated a letter citing "credible evidence that the Iraqi Army is preparing for a general mopping-up operation in the south and southeast where close to 700,000 Iraqi citizens are contained." It warned that Iran "is absolutely unable, with or without international humanitarian assistance, to attend to the needs of another influx of Iraqi refugees."

French sources cited as positive developments Iraq's cooperation in establishing a six-mile demilitarized zone along the Iraq-Kuwait border, and in nominating a representative to the boundary demarcation commission. Samir al-Nima, Iraq's chargé d'affaires here, *said* Iraq had "complied fully with whatever was required to meet our obligations as stated by Resolution 687." He contested the right of the US and Britain to decide the sanctions issue, and called on the UN Secretariat to issue an objective report on Iraq's cease-fire compliance.

"We believe Iraq has not been treated fairly," he said, citing recent news-media reports that predict Iraq faces "an imminent disaster unless some step is taken to alleviate the hardship."

UN Secretary-General Javier Pérez de Cuéllar said in late May that no more than 30 percent of Iraq's income should go to the payment of war reparations. The UN chief said he set the figure on the basis of Iraq's estimate that it should be able to resume oil exports at its prewar level by 1993.

Mr. Pérez de Cuéllar projected Iraq's income then would be $21 billion, if oil prices remain steady. Of that amount, he said, 48 percent would go for necessary imports, and 22 percent to service a foreign debt of $42 billion.

Arab diplomats say that without investment funds, Iraq's economy cannot recover. More important, they say, the proposal does not set a cap on Iraq's liability for war damages – and therefore does not limit the number of years Iraq would be required to pay 30 percent of its oil income.

The US State Department has called for a levy of 50 percent, and British sources say 30 percent is the lowest acceptable figure. But France, the Soviet Union, and China say 30 percent is high.

5-4

0016

Rising Demand for Oil May Spell End of Iraq Embargo

By Thomas Stauffer

VIENNA

THE United States faces a Catch-22 dilemma: Iraqi oil may be needed by the end of the year to dampen price increases.

Ironically, the healthier the world economy, the more quickly Iraqi exports will be seen as indispensable, and the US [illegible]ition will have gone full circle: having [illegible]cotted Iraqi oil ostensibly to protect oil consumers, the US may have to allow Iraqi exports in order to protect those same oil consumers.

If the Organization of Petroleum Exporting Countries is correct in its newest calculations, consumers should expect higher oil prices again this year – despite the fact that last week's one-day ministerial meeting in Vienna revealed only deepened divisions and failed to address either pricing or production policy.

"We are trusting to the 'invisible hand' this time," explained Gonzalo Plaza, chairman of OPEC's board of governors. "Thanks to the war, the market is very tight, so we don't need to intervene."

Oil prices have sunk back to prewar lows. Nonetheless, consumers must be wary because the oil industry expects prices to bounce back. There is near consensus that a 20 to 25 percent increase is possible – adding $250 million a day to the world's oil bill.

But OPEC's new optimism is born of weakness, not strength. A "hands-on policy" to control production was not even attempted, because efforts to cut back output by lowering quotas founders on irreconcilable political differences, painfully aggravated by the Gulf war.

Saudi Arabia refuses to intervene. The minister of petroleum, Hisham Muhyi al-Din Nazir, stated categorically, albeit disingenuously, that the kingdom believes in market forces and will not "manipulate" supply. Algeria, reflecting broad concerns, protested that it was almost criminal to sell oil at such distress prices, but was ignored.

Ironically, it is the Gulf war that dealt OPEC its trump cards. The war weakened OPEC politically, rendering any effort to cut production to bolster prices very difficult. It also worsened the recessionary trend that trimmed oil demand.

But the war actually bolstered OPEC's bargaining position. World oil supply is now precariously balanced: without Kuwaiti and Iraqi production, there is no spare capacity.

OPEC reckons that a modest economic recovery will add 1 million to 1.5 million barrels per day (b.p.d.) to world demand, sopping up the small surplus and absorbing the modest extra inventories. OPEC's calculations are supported by the latest market assessment from the International Energy Agency in Paris, a fact that is significant because the IEA has long been suspected of forecasts designed to soften prices and weaken OPEC.

Other signs corroborate OPEC's new confidence in the "invisible hand." Consumers are holding excess inventories, indicating that they, too, expect prices to firm. Indeed, the real fear is that prices will rise too far. Saudi Arabia has increased output again to rebuild stocks overseas – precisely to ensure against a possible shortage and price speculation.

The wild card is production from Iraq and Kuwait. At best, Kuwait will produce 200,000 b.p.d. by the end of the year, largely from the Japanese-controlled offshore concession; its brethren in the Gulf Cooperation Council last week categorically refused to advance or "loan" crude oil to Kuwait from their own production, citing the possible shortfall.

While Kuwait's production is limited by war damage, Iraq is politically constrained. It could quickly export up to 1 million b.p.d., in spite of massive damage, but is totally dependent on US whim to lift the boycott, and then on Saudi Arabia to open the southern pipelines.

Thomas Stauffer is a professorial lecturer, Johns Hopkins University, Baltimore, Md.

5-5

0017

외 무 부

종 별 :

번 호 : UNW-1555 일 시 : 91 0614 1640

수 신 : 장 관 (국연,중동일,기정)

발 신 : 주 유엔 대사

제 목 : 걸프사태 (안보리)

연: UNW-1550

1. 이락 석유수입 공제 상한선 문제

안보리는 6.13. 비공식 협의에서 본건 상한선 (사무총장안 30 퍼센트) 문제를 토의한바, 다음과같이 이사국들이 이견을 보임에 따라 이와관련 안보리 의장 (코트디브아르)이 각이사국들과 개별협의를 가질 예정이라고 함.

1) 미국 50 퍼센트, 영국, 루마니아 30 퍼센트 이상 (단, 구체적 숫자는 미제시), 불란서 30 퍼센트 이하검토 시사

2) 벨지움, 에쿠아돌, 오지리, 짐바붸, 자이르등 30퍼센트

3) 소련 25 퍼센트, 중국, 쿠바 30 퍼센트 이하 (숫자미제시)

4) 예멘 10 퍼센트

2.이락 남부 사태

독일 겐셔 외상은 6.13.자 사무총장앞 서한에서 이락 당국의 남부 주민 탄압으로 난민 대이동 사태위험이 있음을 지적하면서 이와관련 사무총장의 남이락내 유엔인도 지원센타 (HUMANITARIANCENTRES) 설치구상에 지지를 표명하였음. (S/22701)

3. 이락의 휴전결의 이행 여부 논의

쿠웨이트측은 이락이 안보리의 관련 결의들을 이행하지 않고 있다고 주장하는 안보리문서 (S/22702) 를 배포한바, 특히 포로 및 인질의 계속억류 (3,800명), 쿠웨이트 재산 미반환, 쿠웨이트병합 무효화 의문등의 사례를 제기하였음. 끝

(대사 노창희-국장)

국기국 1차보 중아국 의정실 분석관 안기부

PAGE 1 91.06.15 10:01 WG

외신 1과 통제관

0018

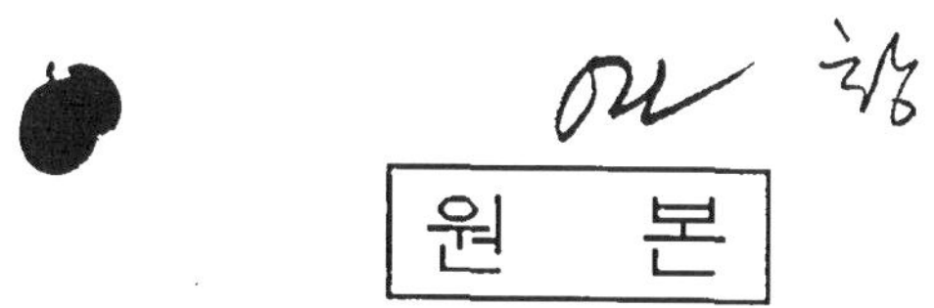

원 본

외 무 부

종 별 :

번 호 : UNW-1605 일 시 : 91 0620 1945

수 신 : 장 관(국연,중동일,기정)

발 신 : 주 유엔 대사

제 목 : 걸프사태(안보리문서 배포)

1.이락측은 6.19 자 사무총장, 안보리의장 앞 서한(S/22693) 에서 최근 N.SCHWARZKOPF 다국적군사령관이 이스라엘군 방송과의 회견에서 이스라엘의 주적(MAJOR ENEMY) 인 이락을 상대로한 걸프전은 이스라엘을 위한 것이었다고 언급하였다고 주장하면서, 다국적군 특히 미측의 저의(반이스라엘 세력 궤멸)를 비난하였음.

2.이에대해 미측은 6.19 자 안보리문서 (S/22722)를 통해 이락의 상기 회견 운운은 완전한 날조(회견사실 부인)이며 회원국의 안보리 문서 배포권 남용이라고 반박하였 음.끝

(대사 노창희-국장)

국기국 1차보 중아국 외정실 청와대 안기부

PAGE 1

91.06.21 10:05 FN

외신 1과 통제관

0019

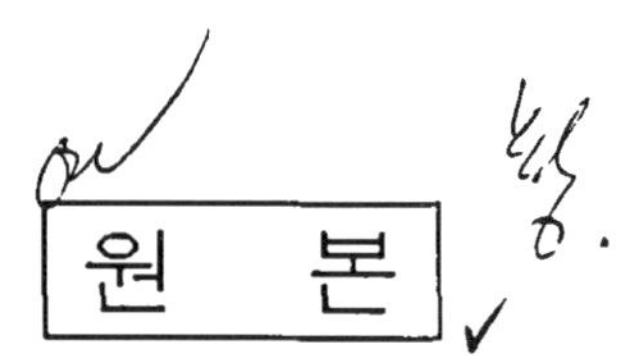

외 무 부

종 별 :

번 호 : UNW-1617 일 시 : 91 0622 0800

수 신 : 장관 (국연,중동일,기정)

발 신 : 주 유엔대사

제 목 : 안보리 비공식협의 (대이락 경제제재조치 완화문제)

연: UNW-1527

1. 안보리는 휴전결의 (본문 21항)에 의거 매 60일마다 대 이락 경제제재 완화문제가 검토되어있는 것과 관련, 연호 6.11. 에 이어 6.20-21 비공식 협의를 가진바, 당관에서 파악한 동 결과는 아래와 같음.

가. 제재조치 완화여부

미. 영을 비롯한 여러나라가 완화에 부정적 입장이며 금번 완화 가능성은 없음.

나. 처리방식 문제

1)쿠바, 예멘은 본건관련 공식회의 개최하자는입장

2) 현제 재수준을 유지한다는 안보리 토의결과를 확인하는 의장 성명 발표문제를 현재 협의중

2.특히 미국은 쿠바가 7월 의장국을 맡기전에 코트디봐르 의장국 재임기간인 6월중 본건 처리를 강력히 희망하고 있는것으로 알려짐.

끝

(대사 노창희-국장)

국기국 1차보 중아국 외정실 분석관 안기부

PAGE 1 91.06.22 23:08 DA

외신 1과 통제관

0020

원 본

외 무 부

종 별 :

번 호 : UNW-1618 일 시 : 91 0622 0800

수 신 : 장관 (국연,중동일,기정)

발 신 : 주 유엔대사

제 목 : 걸프사태 (안보리문서)

연: UNW-1555

1. PLO 측은 쿠웨이트 내 팔레스타인 주민 (약 20만명)에 대한 인권탄압 종식을 위해 유엔사무총장 개입을 요청하는 6.19.자 서한을 안보리 문서로 배포 하였음. (S/22721)

2. 이락 남부주민 탄압문제에 관한 연호 6.13.자 독일 외상의 사무총장앞 서한과 관련 이락외상은 6.19.자 사무총장앞 서한에서 동탄압 사실을 부인하고 이락 국내문제에 간섭하려는 저의라고 독일측을 비난하였음. (S/22723) 또한 이락측은 이락, 쿠웨이트간 비무장지대 (DMZ) 에 유엔 옵서버단이 배치된 이후 쿠웨이트측의휴전위반 사례 (총격, 영공침범)가 여러차례 있었다고 주장하면서 여사한 사례 중지를 위한 사무총장의 조치를 촉구하였음. (S/22719)

끝

(대사 노창희-국장)

국기국 1차보 중아국 외정실 분석관 안기부

PAGE 1

91.06.22 23:11 DA

외신 1과 통제관

0021

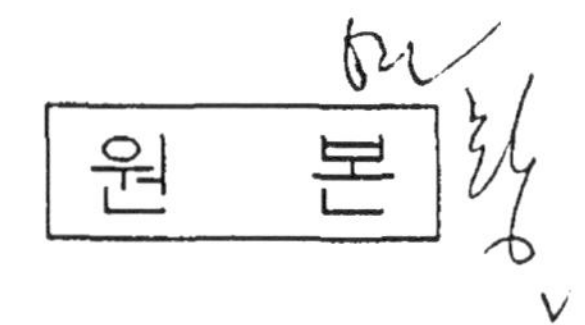

외 무 부

종 별 :

번 호 : UNW-1812　　　　일 시 : 91 0711 2000

수 신 : 장 관(국연,중동일,기정)

발 신 : 주 유엔 대사

제 목 : 걸프사태

연: UNW-1542,1617 ,1691

1. 이락측이 식량, 의료품, 농업용품 긴급수요 (약30 억불) 문제를 제기하면서 식량 및 의료품 수입명목으로 15억불 상당 (당초 10-12 억불)의 석유수출 허가를 안보리 제재위에 7.9 자로 요청해옴에 따라 동위원회는 금 7.11 토의를 가졌으나 진전은 없었다고 함. (SADRUDDIN AGA KHAN대표의 이락 실태보고가 다음주 후반으로 예정되어있고 또 이락측이 외환등 보유현황을 통보해 오지 않고있다는 등의 유에 이유로 거론되었다함.)

2.또한 이락은 7.10 자 안보리 의장앞 서한에서 이락국민이 경제제재 조치로 인해 생존의 위협을 받고있다고 주장하고 특히 연호 제재조치시행 정기심사가 안보리 비공식 협의에서만 거론, 공식적인 결론없이 끝난것을 비난하였음. (안보리측이 휴전 결의상의 임무를 이행치 않고있다고 주장)

3.한편 이란은 이락군당국의 이락 남부지역 주민탄압을 비난하고, 연호 이락남부 HOUR AL-HAMMAR주민 실태조사를 위한 유엔 고위대표단 파견조치를 환영하였음. (S/22776)

첨부: NYT 지 기사및사설: UNW(F)-323

끝

(대사 노창희-국장)

국기국　1차보　중아국　외정실　안기부

PAGE 1　　　　91.07.12　09:46 WG

외신 1과 통제관

0022

UNW(FI)-323 10711 2000
(국연.중동일.기정) 총1매

Iraq's Nuclear Menace

Ever so grudgingly, Iraq now admits that it was conducting a secret uranium enrichment program, thus tacitly conceding it was hellbent on making nuclear arms. Worse yet, it's still trying to conceal a starker truth, that it has come closer to making a bomb than the U.S. suspected.

That shocking news, from knowledgeable Iraqi defectors, reveals that Saddam Hussein remains a regional threat despite the crushing defeat that was supposed to have neutralized him. Even a single nuclear bomb in the hands of a ruthless dictator is menace enough. A nuclear production capability, if undetected, could multiply the risk of attacks and of nuclear blackmail.

The newly understood danger is rightly prompting the U.S. and its Persian Gulf war allies to reconsider how best to disarm Iraq of its terror weapons once and for all. But the dismaying fact is that no sure-fire method exists. Bombing Iraqi nuclear facilities during the war failed to destroy all the nuclear materials.

Trying to eliminate Saddam Hussein might backfire. If he feels himself a target, the Iraqi strongman will have little incentive to hand over his nuclear materials. The best answer is to gain international support for more vigorous inspection and for keeping the pressure on Iraq.

•

The latest revelations surprised many intelligence experts. Before the war, Iraq was judged to be 5 to 10 years away from a full-fledged nuclear arsenal and bomb-making capacity. The more imminent threat came from 100 pounds of known weapons-grade nuclear material that was checked periodically by international inspectors; by worst-case assessment, it could have been turned into a bomb in a year or less.

What's new is that Iraqi informants have told U.S. intelligence of a clandestine electromagnetic process Baghdad was using to separate weapons-grade material. The process has already produced about 90 pounds of uranium, some of it highly enriched. That's enough to make a bomb. And it shows that Baghdad is still lying when it claims to have produced only one pound of enriched uranium clandestinely.

The need to keep nuclear weapons out of Iraq's hands grows more urgent. But none of the three main options look very promising. Bombing nuclear sites, while superficially attractive, is no more likely to eliminate Iraq's nuclear capability than it did during the gulf war. Iraq has been squirreling away uranium and other nuclear material, making it difficult to target. And some of Iraq's nuclear facilities are concealed and hardened.

Another, facile option is to overthrow or kill Saddam Hussein. The U.S. has tried decapitation and failed. And even success wouldn't stop his successor from building the bomb.

The least bad choice is more aggressive use of inspections to find and remove nuclear facilities and material. More inspectors might help. So would rewards for informants. And the international coalition can press Iraq to comply by maintaining tight economic sanctions and, if that fails, threatening renewed bombing of military targets.

Saddam Hussein has to know that the world is ready to resume bombing rather than see him get away with bomb-making.

Last Allied Soldiers In Iraq Kurdish Zone To Leave by Monday

By ERIC SCHMITT
Special to The New York Times

WASHINGTON, July 10 — The United States and its European allies will withdraw their last remaining troops in northern Iraq by Monday, Pentagon officials and European diplomats said today.

To protect Iraqi Kurds from possible retribution by President Saddam Hussein, the officials said the United States and seven European countries have agreed to leave behind a 2,500-member rapid deployment force in southeastern Turkey.

Administration officials said last month that a residual allied force would be stationed along the Turkish border after the withdrawal, but only in the last few days have senior military officials worked out the details of the deployment.

Ground forces equipped with artillery and helicopters from the United States, Britain, France, Belgium, Turkey, Italy, Spain and the Netherlands will be based in Silopi, Turkey, near the Iraqi border, a Pentagon official said.

Dozens of American aircraft, capable of striking targets in northern Iraq, will be stationed at the North Atlantic Treaty Organization base at Incirlik, Turkey, and aboard an American carrier in the Mediterranean.

The withdrawal of the last 3,300 allied troops has raised fears among Kurds that without the coalition's military shield they would soon be targeted for reprisals by Mr. Hussein's army or secret police.

A Pentagon official said today that allied military commanders in the north had told their Iraqi counterparts to stay away from the Kurds once coalition forces leave or risk air strikes and other military intervention.

"It won't be a document like the U.S. Constitution, but the message to Baghdad will be very clear: Don't mess around in northern Iraq or else you'll be in trouble," a European diplomat said.

#UNW-1812
첨부물

1-1

0023

원 본

외 무 부

종 별 :

번 호 : UNW-1876 일 시 : 91 0722 1800

수 신 : 장관(국연,중동일,기정)

발 신 : 주유엔대사

제 목 : 걸프사태(유엔동향)

연: UNW-1835,1869

1. 안보리 제재위 동향

가.동 제재위는 금 7.22 회의를 갖고 SADRUDDIN AGAKHAN 대표로 부터 연호 이락의 인도적 수요실태 보고를 청취하였음.(동 보고요지는 당관에서 입수한 별첨자료참조바람.)

나.동 대표가 이락민의 긴급수요품목 수입을 위한 재원조달 방법으로서 이락산 석유 수출허용 또는 이락해외자산 동결해제 문제를 제기한것과 관련, 금일회의시미,영국등은 본건의 실제적 시행에 따르는 제반통제 및 감시방안에 관심을 보인것으로 알려짐.

다.본건토의를 위해 제재위는 7.24 다시 회의소집 예정이며, 동회의에 앞서 제재위 의장(오지리)이 이사국들과 개별협의를 가질것 이라고함.

2.이락 핵사찰

가. IAEA 측은 지난주 핵사찰반 제3진이 임무를 종료하고 귀환함에 따라 금주중제4진을 이락에 파견 예정이라고함.(제3진 임무종료에 즈음한 IAEA측 발표내용 별첨)

나. IAEA 이사회는 이락의 핵안전협정 불이행을 규탄하는 결의를 7.18채택한바, 동 내용이 7.19 자 총회및 안보리 문서로 배포됨.(A/45/1037,S/22812)

3. 북부 이락사태

가.지난주 북이락 SULAYMANIYAH 에서 발생한 이락군 및 쿠르드족간 유혈충돌사태와 관련 SADRUDDIN AGA KHAN 대표는 양측의 자제를 촉구한것으로 알려짐.

나.한편,금일 안보리 제재위에서 동 대표는 여사한 사태가 신뢰분위기를 저해할것을 우려하였으며,남부지역에 이락군이 재투입되고 있는데 대해서도 유감을

국기국 차관 1차보 중아국 외정실 분석관 정와대 안기부

PAGE 1 91.07.23 08:01 ED

외신 1과 통제관

0024

표시하였음.

첨부:1. KHAN 대표 보고요지,

2.핵사찰관련, IAEA측 안보리문서및 발표내용,

}. NYT 지 W.SAFIRE칼럼기사: UNW(F)-345

끝

(대사 노창희-국장)

원 본

외 무 부

종 별 :

번 호 : UNW-1902 일 시 : 91 0723 2130

수 신 : 장 관(국연,중동일,기정)

발 신 : 주 유엔 대사

제 목 : 걸프사태(대이락 경제제재완화 문제)

1.금 7.23자 NYT 지는 식량.의료품수입.배상책임 이행, 특정무기폐기경비 부담을 위한 재원을 자체적으로 조달할수 있도록 이락의 석유수출을 허용하는 방안을 미국이 적극검토중이라고 보도하였음.

2. NYT 지는 미국이 이락의 석유수출허용을 추진키로 최종 결정하는 경우 이는 미측의 중요한 정책변화를 의미한다고 평가하면서, 미국이 여사한 제재완화 움직임을 보이는 것은 경제제재 조치로 인해 S.HUSSEIN 정권대신 이락주민만이 고통을 받고있고 급양 난 및 질병만연이 우려된다는 비판에 대응하는 한편 제재조치 의 대폭완화내지 해제압력을 견제하려는 것으로 분석하였음.

첨부:상기기사: UNW(F)-349

끝

(대사 노창희-국장)

국기국 1차보 중아국 외정실 분석관 안기부

PAGE 1

91.07.24 10:50 WG

외신 1과 통제관

0026

UNW(F)-349 107ㄴ 2,50
(국연_중동일.기정) 총1매

PLAN WOULD LET BAGHDAD SELL OIL

U.S. Weighs Easing Sanctions to Allow Iraq to Buy Basics

U.S. Policy Change Would Let Iraq Sell Some Oil

By ELAINE SCIOLINO

Special to The New York Times

WASHINGTON, July 22 — The Bush Administration is drawing up a plan to allow the Security Council to remove some sanctions against Iraq to allow Baghdad to sell petroleum, senior Administration officials said today. The profits would be used to pay for food and medicine, war reparations and the destruction of weapons.

The plan, which was drafted by the State Department, is being circulated for review within the department and at the Pentagon, the White House and the Central Intelligence Agency. Officials said that Secretary of State James A. Baker 3d was expected to approve it. It would also need President Bush's approval before it could be presented to the United Nations Security Council as the basis for a resolution.

If the Bush Administration puts the plan forward, as many officials expect, it will represent a major shift in policy. Currently, Iraq is not allowed to sell its oil because of stringent United Nations sanctions imposed after the invasion of Kuwait, and until now the Administration has argued that Iraq had hidden assets in its Central Bank as well as gold reserves that should be used to buy food and medicine, which are not covered by sanctions.

Administration officials said the examination of a new approach reflects a growing realization that the postwar economic strangulation was hurting the Iraqi people rather than weakening President Saddam Hussein's grip on power. The plan is a response to reports by independent medical teams, United Nations officials and the news media of widespread malnutrition and disease in Iraq, as well as an attempt to counter calls for a more sweeping removal of economic sanctions on humanitarian grounds, the officials said.

"We don't want to see more reports about massive starvation and disease in Iraq," said one senior Administration official who is working on the plan. "We know we will eventually have to go this way. We're not there yet, but we'll have to get there." Another senior official described the plan as "a good way to maintain the bulk of sanctions and not be on the wrong side of a potentially emotional issue."

The sanctions review comes at an uncomfortable time for the Administration, which charged again today that Iraq has not disclosed all the details of its secret nuclear program. "We are still very skeptical about their disclosures and believe they have more to tell us," the State Department's deputy spokesman, Richard A. Boucher, said at the State Department briefing today.

Several days ago the five permanent Security Council members — the United States, Britain, France, the Soviet Union and China — gave Iraq until July 25 to declare a final inventory of its nuclear sites. But one senior Administration official today described the date as "an artificial deadline, not necessarily a turning point." The United States had threatened to resume bombing if Iraq did not comply.

'Absurd and Indefensible'

The move to ease sanctions against Iraq was pressed at the United Nations today by Prince Sadruddin Aga Khan, the head of a United Nations Commission that is assessing Iraq's humanitarian needs. The Prince told the Security Council's sanctions committee about a worsening crisis for Iraq's civilian population and suggested that the country be allowed to sell oil to import food, medicine, and some agricultural and industrial materials.

Prince Sadruddin later told reporters that it was "absurd and indefensible" for the United Nations to pay for Iraq's humanitarian needs, "when numerous other urgent crises and disasters, from Bangladesh to the Horn of Africa, cry out for our attention." He added, "Iraq has considerable oil reserves and should pay to meet these needs herself."

The United States has found itself increasingly isolated in the Security Council as other members and officials have made a two-pronged argument: first, that the only way to force Iraq to pay for war reparations and for the elimination of its weapons of mass destruction, both mandated by Security Council resolutions, is with its own oil revenues; and second, that the Security Council should force Iraq to buy much-needed food and medicine with oil profits that could be monitored or even disbursed inside the country through the United Nations.

Special Account Suggested

The first hint of a change in United States policy came in testimony last Thursday by John R. Bolton, the assistant Secretary of State for International Organizations, before a House foreign affairs subcommittee. Mr. Bolton described a new mechanism to provide humanitarian assistance "under a regime of tight controls and strict monitoring." He said that the United States was consulting with members of the Security Council and its coalition partners "on the appropriate operational ways to do this."

One likely scenario would be for the United Nations to control Iraq's oil revenues through a special account or accounts. Thirty percent of the revenues would pay for reparations for Iraq's invasion of Kuwait last August, a formula worked out by the Security Council's sanctions committee, and the rest would pay other bills.

Administration officials stressed that oil sales would go forward only if strict conditions were met, and that the details of the plan still have to be worked out and discussed with coalition partners. Because an international body would control the funds, the officials argued that the plan does not reflect a weakening of international sanctions or of the Administration's resolve to continue to exert maximum pressure on Baghdad.

Policy About-Face

But the plan is a significant departure from public statements by Mr. Bush and some senior officials in recent months that Mr. Hussein had to be punished. On May 7, Robert M. Gates, the deputy national security adviser and the nominee for Director for Central Intelligence, said in a speech that "Iraqis will pay the price while he is in power." Mr. Gates added: "All possible sanctions will be maintained until he is gone." On May 20, Mr. Bush acknowledged to reporters that while there are some instances in which Iraq must sell its oil to comply with United Nations resolutions, "my view is we don't want to lift these sanctions as long as Saddam Hussein is in power."

But Administration officials have said, albeit quietly and reluctantly, that Mr. Hussein has successfully consolidated power since the end of the Persian Gulf war and may remain President of Iraq for years.

UNW-1902 첨부물 1-1

P.4

JUL 23 '91 20:12 KOREAN MISSION

0027

원 본

외 무 부

종 별 :

번 호 : UNW-1910 일 시 : 91 0724 1700

수 신 : 장 관(국연,중동일,기정)

발 신 : 주 유엔대사

제 목 : 걸프사태(안보리동향)

연: UNW-1876

1. 안보리 대이락 제재위 (의장국:오지리)는 지난 7.22 에 이어 금 7.24 회의를갖고 연호 이락의 인도적 긴급수요 및 동 대책문제를 토의한바, 이락의 석유 수출허용 문제는 동 수출수익 안배상 본건 인도적 목적외에도 이락의 손해배상책임, 특정무기폐기, 이락-쿠웨이트국경 획정, 쿠웨이트 재산반환을위한 제반경비 재원조달 문제와 연결되므로 포괄적 검토를 위해 안보리에 회부키로 하였으며, 이에따라 안보리는7.25 비공식 협의 개최예정이라고함.

2.한편 금일 NYT 지는 다음요지로 본건 이락석유 수출허용 움직임에 반대하는 사설을 게재하였음.

가.이락의 핵관련 보유 현황 제출관련 안보리 상임이사국이 설정한 시한(7.25)을바로 앞두고 석유금수 부분해제를 시사하는것은 시기적으로부적절

나.석유수출 허용과 관련한 실제적 통제상의난점

다.석유금수해제 대신 국제적구호 노력전개 (동경비는 추후 이락측에 청구)

첨부: NYT 지 사설.기사및 WP 지기사: UNW(F)-354

끝

(대사 노창희-국장)

국기국 1차보 2차보 중아국 외정실 분석관 안기부

PAGE 1

91.07.25 08:59 CT

외신 1과 통제관

0028

Don't Ease the Squeeze on Iraq

Should Iraq be allowed to resume limited oil exports in order to pay war reparations and finance compelling humanitarian needs at home? Not as long as Saddam Hussein continues to flout the U.N. cease-fire resolution that requires him to disclose all details of Iraq's secret nuclear, biological and chemical weapons programs.

To accept human suffering as a diplomatic lever is tormenting — but preferable to leaving the Persian Gulf allies with no credible way to compel Iraqi compliance except resuming military attacks.

There are other ways to address Iraq's emergency humanitarian needs. With the July 25 allied deadline for full Iraqi nuclear disclosure now at hand, it's exactly the wrong time to be hinting at partial lifting of the oil embargo.

•

Making Baghdad come clean on nuclear supplies won't be easy. The embargo was originally designed for the less ambitious task of containing Iraq's arms buildup. Rolling back existing programs requires greater pressure.

Nor is the alternative of renewed air strikes fully satisfactory. The massive, unopposed air raids of the gulf war apparently failed to destroy Baghdad's nuclear hoard. With allied force levels now reduced, new air raids could involve far greater risk to pilots, with no more success.

The best available course is to maintain maximum economic and political pressure on Baghdad while holding the threat of renewed military action in reserve.

The human suffering Baghdad cites in seeking permission to resume oil sales is real and wrenching. Yet Saddam Hussein's regime showed scant concern for the suffering it caused its own people through eight grueling years of aggressive war against Iran and the devastating defeat in Kuwait.

Honorable arguments can be made for easing the oil embargo. Prince Sadruddin Aga Khan, the U.N. official in charge of monitoring Iraq's humanitarian needs, argues that precious international relief funds needed for Africa and Bangladesh should not be diverted to help oil-rich Iraq.

U.N. diplomats also point out that for Kuwait to receive the reparations it is entitled to, Iraq needs some way to raise funds. And a long series of U.N. resolutions anticipated humanitarian exceptions to the embargo. Limited relief now could help prevent a total erosion of sanctions later on.

The Bush Administration, which long resisted any easing of sanctions, seems to be shifting. The President, declaring that innocent women and children should not suffer, hinted yesterday at possible approval for a U.N. move to allow limited oil sales.

We, too, were once moved by these arguments, but this is the wrong time to relax the embargo. Once Iraqi oil is allowed back on the international market, even if the revenues remain under U.N. control, it will be difficult to make distinctions. How can the immediate needs of food and medicine be distinguished from the longer-term rebuilding of distribution networks and power plants that serve humanitarian needs and the Iraqi economy?

Easing the embargo now would give Baghdad a psychological lift, possibly reinforcing its defiance. A more straightforward way to provide humanitarian relief is to do just that, through an internationally financed effort limited to milk, food and medicine. A bill for the assistance could be presented to Iraq for later payment from oil revenues.

Easing sanctions prematurely could one day leave no choice except winking at Saddam Hussein's defiance or going back to war. There's a wiser course.

0029

U.S. DEFENDS PLAN ON IRAQI OIL SALES

Says Terms of U.N. Embargo Allow Baghdad to Sell for Humanitarian Needs

By ELAINE SCIOLINO

Special to The New York Times

WASHINGTON, July 23 — The White House acknowledged today that it was considering whether to allow Iraq to sell some of its oil to buy food and medicine, but denied that such a move would represent a removal of United Nations-mandated sanctions.

President Bush's spokesman, Marlin Fitzwater, said that sanctions enacted as part of the April 3 Security Council resolution calling for a cease-fire in the gulf war would allow Iraq to sell oil to meet its humanitarian needs. But he emphasized: "There has been no recommendation that has come to the President. There has been no consideration of any of the specifics."

Mr. Fitzwater sought to play down the significance of a deadline set several days ago by the United States and the other permanent members of the Security Council for Iraq to declare an inventory of its nuclear installations.

Last Friday, Thomas R. Pickering, the United States representative at the United Nations, said President Saddam Hussein of Iraq would be given until July 25 to provide a "full, final and complete" inventory, but did not say what the consequences would be if he did not comply. The July 25 date was interpreted as an ultimatum to Iraq: cooperate or face new hostilities.

Today, Mr. Fitzwater said, "There is no deadline as far as we're concerned."

An Awkward Position

In rethinking its position on sanctions, the United States finds itself in the uncomfortable position of wanting to respond to calls by other countries to aid Iraqi civilians while continuing to put pressure on Mr. Hussein.

Mr. Bush summed up the problem in remarks at a photo session with Cabinet members today. He said Iraq had not complied with United Nations resolutions, had not paid reparations to Kuwait or returned gold taken in the occupation, and had not fully disclosed its nuclear technology.

But he said, "The United States is not going to see the suffering of innocent women and children there." He added that his Administration had "not resolved yet exactly what we're going to do at the United Nations."

There is still considerable disagreement in the Administration over the wisdom of even a modest alteration of the sanctions, senior officials say.

A plan drafted by the State Department envisions letting Iraq sell oil to buy food and medicine, and to pay war reparations and the cost of destroying weapons, the officials said.

'Differences of Opinion'

"There are differences of opinion on what resources, what food stocks Saddam has," an official said. "We need to know more about the status of their crop this year, external donations of food, assets inside and outside country, and whether he has things stockpiled that he's parceling out to the army."

Mr. Bush said he spoke about the situation in Iraq today with Prince Sadruddin Aga Khan, the head of a United Nations Commission that is assessing Iraq's needs. Prince Sadruddin said in a telephone interview from New York that he was heartened by the news that the United States is considering allowing Iraq to sell its oil.

"The last thing Americans want to do is to see a lot of kids suffering in Iraq," Prince Sadruddin said. "If things get out of hand and we have a real famine on our hands, a lot of people are going to ask the question, 'Is this what the war was fought for?' "

Although Iraq is forbidden to sell its oil under United Nations sanctions, it delivers about 55,000 barrels a day overland through Jordan, Iraqi and Jordanian reports and international oil experts say. The oil, refined in Jordan and used to meet the country's domestic needs, is a fraction of Iraq's prewar export level of three million barrels a day, but will provide about $400 million in annual revenue.

Reparations Panel Meets

Special to The New York Times

GENEVA, July 23 — A United Nations group began work here today to settle compensation claims arising from the Iraqi invasion of Kuwait.

Representatives of the 15 members of the Security Council, who make up the governing council of the United Nations Compensation Commission, began a session that will end on Aug. 2.

A statement said the governing council would administer the fund, from which compensation for losses caused by the Iraqi occupation would be made. The new council is also charged with establishing guidelines for the presentation and evaluation of claims.

3-2

0030

U.S. Plays Down Idea of New Attack on Iraq

Thursday Is a U.N. Deadline for Information on Nuclear Program, White House Says

By Ann Devroy and John M. Goshko
Washington Post Staff Writers

The Bush administration yesterday soft-pedaled the notion that if Iraq fails to provide required information about its nuclear program to the United Nations by Thursday, the United States might take military action to force Iraqi President Saddam Hussein to comply.

The United States and the four other permanent members of the U.N. Security Council have warned Baghdad privately that they expect a detailed accounting by Thursday of Iraq's nuclear equipment, its other weapons of mass destruction and its plans for destroying them.

Although no one has said so publicly, U.S. officials had hinted broadly that President Bush might order military measures such as air strikes if Iraq fails to provide the accounting. Reports from Baghdad have said that the Iraqi regime regards those hints seriously enough to have increased its antiaircraft defenses.

However, White House press secretary Marlin Fitzwater said yesterday that Thursday is a U.N. deadline "for provision of information," and added that failure to heed it does not mean military force will be used against Baghdad by the United States alone or in conjunction with its allies.

"There is no deadline as far as we are concerned," Fitzwater said in response to questions. "You're implying a deadline for action . . . by the multinational forces which is something quite different. This is a deadline set by the U.N. for information going to them."

U.N. sources, who asked not to be identified, said renewed strikes against Iraq after the Thursday deadline have not been regarded seriously within the world body. They noted that the Soviet Union and China, both permanent Security Council members, oppose that course strongly, and said the United States is regarded as unlikely to endanger the consensus it has built within the council by ignoring the Soviet and Chinese views.

Instead, the sources said, the Thursday deadline appears to be a pressure tactic aimed at reminding Iraq that the countries that defeated it in the Persian Gulf War are not relaxing their insistence that Baghdad comply with all the requirements of the cease-fire. The deadline was part of an effort to remind Iraq that failure to cooperate will not help its efforts to win relief from U.N. economic sanctions and could eventually expose it to further military punishment.

A senior administration official agreed that the July 25 (Thursday) date was part of "a process of putting the pressure on. . . . Whenever we do, [Saddam] comes up with a little more information. The key will be when he quits responding to the pressure. He has not done that yet."

Bush said yesterday that the United States is considering a proposal at the United Nations that would relax the sanctions sufficiently to allow Iraq to sell some of its oil to purchase more food and medicine for its civilian population. Reflecting an internal administration debate and pressure from some U.S. allies, Bush was equivocal when asked whether Iraq should be allowed to sell some of its oil or be given access to its frozen assets in other countries for humanitarian purposes.

The president said that the "machinery is in place" in the Security Council sanctions committee to take care of Iraq's humanitarian needs, "but the United States is not going to see suffering of innocent women or children there. There's all kinds of mechanisms to take care of it. . . . It's a matter that's being discussed at the United Nations."

Spurred by reports that Iraq's food supply is deteriorating, the Security Council is discussing a request by Baghdad to sell $1.5 billion worth of oil. U.N. sources said that request probably will be approved, but added that it will be what one called "a one-shot deal," that the dollar amount of what Iraq can realize from the sale has not been decided and that any approval almost certainly will be contingent on Iraq agreeing to an oversight mechanism to ensure that the food is distributed to those who need it.

The sources said that the United States is particularly insistent that Iraq be given permission only for one sale and that an outside organization such as UNICEF, the International Committee of the Red Cross or a private relief agency such as Caritas supervise the distribution. The senior administration official said Bush wants assurances that Saddam will use the funds for humanitarian purposes and not for his military and industrial apparatus.

A senior diplomatic official at the United Nations said a report by U.N. inspectors investigating Iraq's clandestine nuclear program probably will be released later this week. He said the report will charge that Iraq has not cooperated fully.

The official said Iraq has provided information about its program that develops enriched uranium but was not forthcoming about what use it intends to make of the product. Only after strong U.N. threats did Iraq admit earlier this month that it had a secret nuclear program, including production of enriched uranium that could be used in nuclear weapons.

"The Iraqis still maintain it's a peaceful program, and they haven't explained their multimillion-dollar investments," the official said. "We have no satisfactory answers. . . . As long as we are not satisfied, we won't stop inspecting."

Special correspondent Trevor Rowe contributed to this report from the United Nations.

3-3

0031

원 본

외 무 부

종 별 :

번 호 : UNW-1926　　　　일 시 : 91 0725 1800

수 신 : 장 관(국연,중동일,기정)

발 신 : 주 유엔 대사

제 목 : 안보리 비공식협의(이락제재조치 완화문제)

연: UNW-1910

1. 안보리는 금 7.25 비공식협의를 갖고 대이락제재 위의장 (오지리)으로 부터 연호 7.24 회의결과를 청취한다음 향후 처리 방향에 관해 토의를 가진바, 당관에서 파악한 금일 주요협의 결과는 다음과 같음.

가. 이락의 인도적 긴급 품목수입 필요성, 동 수입및 여타 용도 (연호참조)를 위한 재원확보를 위해 이락석유수출 일부허용 문제검토가 불가피함에 대해 큰 이견이 없었으며 또한 이락의 석유수출을 부분적으로 허용키로하는 경우 석유수출, 인도적 긴급품목 수입, 배분, 여타 용도에의 재원배정의 전과정을 유엔이 통제할수 있는 체제를 만들어야 한다는데 다수이사국이 공감하였음.

나. 상기에 따라 안보리는 관련 결의안을 준비키로하였으며, 이를 위해 안보리 의장(쿠바)이 각이사국및 사무총장과 개별협의를 가질 예정임.

다. 금일 협의시 일부이사국들은 인도적 긴급수요와 관련 제재위에서 신속한 조치를 취하는 문제를 제기하였으나, 상기와 같이 안보리가 결의안을 준비키로 함에따라 본건은 일단 안보리 제재위에서 이사회 본회의로 넘어온 것으로 이해됨.

라. 이사국들은 인도적 긴급 수요에 비추어 상기결의안의 조기타결 필요성에 이의가 없으나, 실제결의안이 포괄적이고 복합적인 통제체제를 포함하게 될것으로 보여 동 타결에는 상당한 시일이 필요할 것이라는 관측이 우세함.

마. 금일 협의중 미.영국은 이락이 동국자산보유현황 명세지출을 계속 미루어오고있음에 큰 불만을 나타냈다고 하며, 예멘은 안보리가 인도적 긴급 수요문제를 다른 문제와 연결시켜 신속한 조치를 취하지 않고 있는것(LINGAGE,PACKAGE 문제)에 유감을 표시하였다고함.

2. 사무총장대변인에 의하면, IAEA 핵사찰반제4진이 7.27 이락도착 예정이라고함.

국기국　1차보　중아국　외정실　분석관　안기부

PAGE 1　　　　91.07.26　08:44 WG

외신 1과 통제관

0032

첨부:상기 안보리비공식협의관련 사무총장기자문답요지: UNW(F)-358
끝.(대사 노창희-국장)

PAGE 2

0033

UNW(F)-358 (국연. 중동일. 기정)

3224

Remarks of the Secretary-General after leaving Security Council Consultations on Thursday 25 July 1991 approximately 12:00 p.m.

Q. What has been decided at the Security Council consultations today?

S-G Nothing so far. They are about to end now. They are considering the situation to see in which way a mechanism can be set up to monitor the use of money, the distribution of food, those kind of things.

Q. Would it require a resolution?

S-G It might.

Q. How urgent is the humanitarian need and how quick will the action of the Security Council be?

S-G We consider the humanitarian needs of the Iraqi population as very urgent and something has to be done. I am glad that the Security Council is considering doing something and allowing Iraq to sell some oil in order to take care of this very serious question. But at the same time, they (Council members) want Iraq to pay other liabilities.

Q. Do you expect to be asked to help in drafting some kind of ......

S-G Yes. Of course. Their pratice is to turn to the Secretary-General and ask him to set up a mechanism to monitor the use of money.

Q. How soon do you think the Council will allow Iraq to export oil again?

S-G I don't know if they are going to meet again tomorrow, but I have the impression that they are not quite ready on the details.

Q. At a time when there is a great humanitarian need in Iraq and when people face starvation, do you think it is appropriate to attach other issues like the disarmament of Iraq and to delay the process?

S-G I don't think that there will be a delay. What has triggered the whole thing is the humanitarian problem - the report of my Executive Delegate who was in Iraq and came back with evidence that the people of Iraq were in great danger not only of famine but of disease. Some delegations, however, consider that it would be inappropriate to allow

#UNW-1926
첨부물

2-1

P.4

JUL 25 '91 16:25 KOREAN MISSION

0034

Iraq not to pay their obligations as far as, for instance, the question of compensation is concerned or the cost of many aspects of Resolution 687.

Q. How do you view all this talk about a deadline for Iraq to declare its nuclear programme?

S-G Of course, I see it with concern. The IAEA considers that unfortunately the Iraqi Government has not revealed all it has as far as its nuclear capabilities are concerned. But I don't have the impression that we are now under an ultimatium. I don't think that is what the Government of the United States has said. They are as concerned as we all are, but they have not threatened, as far as I understand, the use of force.

Q. You don't consider it a deadline then?

S-G I am not particularly concerned because I don't think that the Government of the United States is prepared now to attack again the Iraqi territory together with its allies. Nothing in the statements I have heard indicate that they are about to start tomorrow any military action.

* * *

2-2

JUL 25 '91 15:25 KOREAN MISSION P.5

0035

관리 번호	91 -798

외 무 부

종 별 :

번 호 : UNW-1942 일 시 : 91 0726 1800

수 신 : 장 관(국연,중동일,기정)

발 신 : 주 유엔 대사

제 목 : 안보리동향(이락석유수출 일부허용문제)

연:UNW-1926

1. 연호 이락석유수출 일부허용문제와 관련한 안보리 결의안 교섭동향에 대해 당관 원참사관이 금 7.26 미대표부 J.MANSO 담당관에게 탐문한바, 현재 초안형태로 교섭이 진행되고 있지는 않으며 주요골격 (MAIN ELEMENTS) 에 관한 의견을 나누고있는 단계라고함.

2. 동 담당관에 의하면, 상기 결의안은 인도적 분야외에도 여러 현안문제 (UNW-1910) 를 포괄할 가능성이 크며, 예켄데 배상기금 공제 상한선 문제도 다룰가능성이 있다고함. 앞으로 교섭추이를 보아야 하겠지만 상당히 포괄적이고 통합적인 결의안이 될 전망이라고 하며, 이에따라 교섭에 어느정도 시일이 필요할 것이라고함.

첨부:1.NYT, WP 지 기사,2. 유엔사무총장 기자문답:UNW(F)-363

끝.(대사 노창희-국장)

예고:91.12.31. 일반

국기국	차관	1차보	중아국	분석관	청와대	안기부

PAGE 1

91.07.27 07:52

외신 2과 통제관 BS

0036

JUL 26 '91 16:33 KOREAN MISSION P.1

#별첨 UNW(F)-363 10726 1800 (국연. 중동일. 기정) 총 7 매

U.N. Council Opens Discussion of Iraq Sanctions

By FRANK J. PRIAL

Special to The New York Times

UNITED NATIONS, July 25 — The Security Council began informal discussions today on a plan to remove sanctions against Iraq, enabling it to sell oil to buy food and medical supplies, which United Nations officials say are desperately needed by the Iraqi people.

But diplomats cautioned against expecting any quick response to Iraq's needs. They cited the complex problems in creating and monitoring a program to feed millions of people, as well as the efforts of some Council members, notably the United States and Britain, to link the question of sanctions with other components of the cease-fire agreement ending the Persian Gulf War.

These include full disclosure of Iraq's nuclear program and of its currency and gold reserves, its contributions to a compensation fund to cover the costs of the war, payments to cover the cost of destroying weapons of mass destruction, payments to Kuwait for property stolen during the war, and its share of the cost of a commission determining the Iraq-Kuwait border.

But the Americans and the British, other diplomats said, are not convinced that Iraq really needs a lifting of the sanctions, believing that it has sufficient foreign currency and gold reserves to cover its food and medical requirements for some time.

"How much money they need will, of course, be determined by how much they have," said Sir David Hannay, the British representative to the United Nations. So far, he said, the Iraqis have provided "an incredibly low figure for currency reserves and no figure at all for gold."

A Work in Progress

Thomas R. Pickering, the American representative, added, "I think it's early to talk about a resolution, but people are looking into all the various components that might go into any action by the Council."

Sir David said, however, that "yes, the Council is working on a resolution," and insisted that "the other aspects of 687" — the cease-fire resolution — must be taken into consideration.

Asked about the propriety of linking other aspects of the cease-fire resolution to aid, Sir David replied: "The suffering of the Iraqi people over the sanctions is the fault of Saddam Hussein, and that has been clear from the beginning. There is no question of culpability on the part of the international community, which has been trying to restore international law. The culpability rests quite firmly on the Government of Iraq."

The U.S. and Britain doubt that Baghdad requires relief.

He noted that Prince Sadruddin Aga Khan, who headed a team investigating shortages of food and medicine in Iraq, reported earlier this week that there is not a crisis in Iraq now, but rather an impending one, "and that we need to take action now in order to avert it."

Secretary General Javier Pérez de Cuéllar, who attended the Council's informal meeting, said he would soon set up a commission to work out the details of a program to provide help to Iraq.

This could be highly complex and expensive, other diplomats said. It would involve monitoring the sale of the precise amount of oil permitted, setting up an escrow fund to accept foreign-currency payments, overseeing expenditures for food and medical supplies, and then monitoring the distribution of those supplies to insure that they go to the people who need them most.

Still to be decided is the question of whether any profits from oil sales should be used to satisfy other requirements in the cease-fire resolution. These would include payments for the expenses of the special commission charged with destroying Iraq's nuclear and biological weapons.

Deadline Passes Uneventfully

The Security Council meeting today came on the deadline set by the five permanent members — the United States, the Soviet Union, Britain, France and China — for Iraq to disclose all facets of its nuclear program.

For several weeks, there have been threats of new military action against unspecified Iraqi installations if the deadline was not met.

But the deadline came and went, with the inspection teams of the International Atomic Energy Agency still dissatisfied with the information supplied.

Diplomats here today evaded questions on the deadline without acknowledging that it seemed unenforceable through diplomacy alone.

Mr. Pickering, the United States representative, took shelter behind a statement released by the White House that noted that the deadline had passed.

7-1

0037

U.N. Deadline to Baghdad Passes, But U.S. Rules Out Attack Soon

By ERIC SCHMITT

Special to The New York Times

WASHINGTON, July 25 — A United Nations Security Council deadline for Iraq to provide a detailed list of its weapons of mass destruction expired today, with the Bush Administration charging that Baghdad had failed to comply with it fully.

But despite some earlier threats of retaliation against the Government of President Saddam Hussein, American officials said that no use of force was imminent.

The United States and its allies have been pressing their demand that Mr. Hussein fulfill the terms of the United Nations' resolution adopted at the end of the Persian Gulf war to disclose and ultimately destroy its ballistic missiles, chemical and biological weapons, and nuclear material.

The Security Council's five permanent members — the United States, the Soviet Union, Britain, France and China — ordered Iraq on July 12 to comply by today, and that statement produced speculation that military force might be used in case the deadline was not met.

Today, the Council began considering requests that economic sanctions against Iraq be modified to allow the sale of some Iraqi oil for the purchase of food, medicine and other humanitarian needs. But no immediate action was taken, and it seemed as if the speed at which the Council dealt with ending the sanctions might well depend on Iraq's willingness to disclose its weapons. [Page A8.]

Yet the nations that made up the allied coalition in the gulf war seem to have little appetite for renewed warfare at this time, particularly when an American initiative for a Middle East peace conference is being considered.

For that reason, American and other Western officials said, today's deadline was never a deadline like that on Jan. 15, the coalition's date for Iraq to withdraw from Kuwait.

Rather, it was a "U.N. marker to judge whether or not the Iraqi Government — namely Saddam Hussein — was operating in good faith to meet the requirements of the U.N. resolutions," said a White House spokesman, Roman Popadiuk. "To this moment, as far as I am aware, Iraq had not fully complied."

By threatening renewed air attacks and sending team after team of United Nations inspectors to examine Iraqi installations, the allies hope to browbeat Mr. Hussein into compliance.

Hussein Is Little Help

But the Iraqi leader has been stingy in disclosing information and seems to be hoping that he will ultimately avoid delivering a full account of his nuclear, biological and chemical weapons programs.

The Iraqis have provided several different lists of banned weapons and allowed inspectors to visit some areas. And destruction of some missile sites has begun. But the Americans insist that so far, there are major gaps between what Iraq is providing and what it is known to have.

A group of scientists from the International Atomic Energy Agency in Vienna is scheduled to arrive in Iraq on Saturday to examine known and suspected nuclear installations. Three more teams will be sent in August to deal with chemical and biological weapons and ballistic missiles, the State Department said.

"This July 25 date was never intended as a deadline, after which if we didn't get all the goodies — boom, li we'd go to zap them," a Western diplc mat explained. "So long as we're mak ing good solid progress in wiping ou his means of developing weapons c mass destruction," the coalition wi hold off on military strikes.

Under the truce agreement tha ended the gulf war, Iraq must disclos all aspects of its special weapons prc grams, including their components an production sites.

Iraq has so far released three list detailing its inventory of such weapons as well as its ability to build and de velop the arms. But Administration of ficials say Mr. Hussein continues tc hide some of what he has.

"They have yet to disclose, as required in the resolutions, the purpose and extent of their nuclear, chemical and biological weapons and their ballistic missiles," the Pentagon spokesman, Pete Williams, told reporters today.

"They would have a lot of work to do if they were going to disclose the full extent of their nuclear, chemical and biological warfare weapons, and ballistic missiles," Mr. Williams continued. "It would have to be a very detailed report."

Thousands of Iraqis have left for Jordan in recent weeks, but no air of panic has been reported in Baghdad, and many Western officials said most of the civilians are leaving because travel restrictions have been lifted.

American military officials have said they have "hundreds of targets" in Iraq and are ready to resume bombing if ordered. But political and practical barriers make such action unlikely.

The Administration is drawing up a plan to allow the Security Council to remove some of its sanctions against Iraq, so as to allow Baghdad to sell some petroleum. Under certain constraints, Iraq would be allowed to use the profits to buy food and medicine, and pay war reparations and the cost of destroying its special weapons.

And with Washington in the throes of organizing a Mideast peace conference, unleashing a bombing campaign against Iraq might well upset Arab partners in the peace process.

General Is Vague

The Air Force general who led the allied air campaign in the gulf war said on Wednesday that it would take "several days or weeks" to destroy all of Iraq's suspected nuclear installations.

"Whether it would take one day, two days, 10 days or 100 days would depend on what you want done," the officer, Lieut. Gen. Charles Horner, told reporters.

Other senior military officials have said it would be very difficult to guarantee the destruction of all Iraq's bomb-making equipment and material, much of which can be secretly stored and easily moved.

General Horner said the allies had destroyed about 80 percent of Iraq's nuclear-production and research installations.

U.N. Agency Chief Agrees

In Vienna today, the director general of the International Atomic Energy Agency, Hans Blix, concurred with the Administration's assessment.

"As regards results, we cannot say whether we have seen all," said Mr. Blix, who heads a United Nations specialized agency. "There may be more to declare, especially, the inspectors feel, in the field of centrifuge enrichment."

President Bush on Wednesday declined to discuss the choices he might consider if Iraq continues to defy the United Nations, saying that Iraqi officials "know what they have to do." Asked by reporters if today was a "D-day" for Iraq, Mr. Bush replied, "No."

The Defense Secretary, Dick Cheney, told the Associated Press last week that "there shouldn't be any doubt" in Mr. Hussein's mind "that we're deadly serious about his coming into compliance" with the Security Council resolutions.

7-2

0038

Security Council to Weigh Proposal To Delay Iraqi Food Distribution

U.N. Secretary General's Study Considered Likely to Take 'a Month'

By Trevor Rowe
Special to The Washington Post

UNITED NATIONS, July 25— The Security Council is preparing to consider a proposal to authorize Iraq to sell oil to buy food, but the measure is expected to delay any food distribution by up to a month, sources said today.

Under the proposed resolution expected to be introduced by the United States and Britain, U.N. Secretary General Javier Perez de Cuellar would be asked to provide a report on how the food would be distributed, diplomats said. A Source said such a report might be ready "in a month, perhaps."

Amid mounting international pressure for quick action on humanitarian assistance for Iraq, the United States and Britain continued today to insist on "watertight" controls. They have argued that food distribution and oil sales should be closely monitored to ensure that any aid reaches needy people and that Iraqi President Saddam Hussein does not gain political benefits from such emergency measures. Iraq is barred from selling oil under an international embargo imposed after its Aug. 2 invasion of Kuwait.

The plan to request a report from Perez de Cuellar before allowing food distribution emerged as a deadline for Iraq to divulge full details of its nuclear weapons program passed without any last-minute gesture from Baghdad. The deadline had been set by the Security Council's five permanent members—Britain, China, France, the United States and the Soviet Union.

Officials said the council is not expected to take any immediate action against Iraq on the nuclear weapons issue. However, some diplomats said, the delay in responding to Iraq's request for authorization to sell $2.6 billion in oil to buy food is informally linked to efforts to persuade Baghdad to be more forthcoming on its weapons program.

The effect of the proposal for a report on food distribution, some diplomats said, would be to draw on Perez de Cuellar's expertise. But, they added, the plan also would shift any blame for delaying the food distribution away from Britain and the United States At the same time, a Western diplomat said, the move would maintain pressure on Baghdad to reveal the amount of its gold reserves, which may be available for food or other emergency needs, and to encourage it to accept strict monitoring of food distribution.

A diplomat present during the Security Council consultations said Perez de Cuellar did not seem enthusiastic about his new assignment. One U.N. representative noted "a skeptical expression on the secretary general's face," the diplomat said. Another representative expressed hope that it would not become "a trend of the Security Council to unload its responsibilities on the secretary general," the diplomat added.

Emerging from the meeting, Perez de Cuellar told reporters with a smile that the council members' "practice is always to turn to the secretary general and ask him to set up a mechanism to monitor the use of money."

Sadruddin Aga Khan, who is in charge of U.N. relief efforts in the Persian Gulf area, warned the Security Council last week that action must be taken within the next month if famine is to be averted in Iraq.

Before entering the council meeting, U.S. Ambassador Thomas Pickering reiterated Washington's insistence that Iraq reveal all of its gold holdings.

"I think the Council has a right to know, before it moves ahead, whether the government in question is really hoarding its resources in an effort to punish its own people more—to garner international sympathy—or whether, in fact, thre is a serious capacity on the part of that government to continue to provide more money for food," Pickering told reporters.

Some diplompats warned, however, that any delay would have a harmful impact.

"All this will be too late," said Yemen's U.N. ambassador, Abadalla Saleh Ashtal, whose country was a strong supporter of Iraq during the Persian Gulf War. "By that time, there will be famine. . . . Everybody wants to be away from any blame."

Diplomats are expected to meet Friday to begin crafting the resolution authorizing the Iraqi oil sale.

7-3

0039

Embargo on Iraq

SOONER OR LATER the United Nations will make an exception in its embargo on Iraq to allow it to sell some oil for food and other humanitarian necessities. The current dispute is over timing and conditions—how soon to do it and what questions Iraq has to answer first. The U.N.'s sanctions committee is badly split and has now handed the decision back to the Security Council.

The pressure to act quickly was sharply increased earlier this week when Sadruddin Aga Khan, who has been surveying conditions in Iraq for the U.N., warned it that food shortages are increasing and without prompt aid they will lead to a catastrophe. Some of the governments in the Security Council are prepared to go ahead at once to allow limited oil sales, as long as the process is closely monitored. But other governments, notably the United States', are less eager to act immediately. Distrust of Iraq has been heightened by the past weeks' staggering revelations of the extent of its efforts to build nuclear weapons and of its deceptions to conceal them. Iraq's rulers have not helped their standing by ignoring the U.N.'s latest deadline yesterday for a complete accounting of the nuclear projects.

There is a suspicion within the Bush administration that Saddam Hussein is in effect using his own people as hostages to try to force a partial relaxation of the embargo, in the hope that any exceptions to it will eventually cause the whole complex and costly effort of enforcement to come unraveled. At the U.N. the Americans are pressing the question of Iraq's holdings of gold and cash—its ability to buy whatever its people need out of its present resources, without any oil sales or exceptions to the embargo. The United States is holding up any decision in the Security Council until that question about the cash and gold reserves gets an answer.

Those are serious concerns, but the Security Council is going to have to make a decision very soon. The hunger among the poorest Iraqis is real, and the U.N. cannot allow starvation to undermine the purposes of the embargo. There is still much work of vital importance for the embargo to accomplish. It needs to be held in place until the search for all nuclear, chemical and biological weapons, and the missiles to deliver them, has been completed. That may take many months, and the job of destroying those weapons could take years. In the meantime, the U.N. has the ability to maintain the embargo, to allow limited shipments of oil through it, to supervise the revenue that they earn and to distribute under international supervision the food and medicine that it buys.

It's time to begin that process. The only indispensable condition is absolute international control over both the money and the distribution of the food, and there's not much dissent over that in the Security Council. It would be unwise for the U.N. or the United States to invite a quarrel with Saddam Hussein over who's responsible for starving children. It's infinitely better to prevent hunger—and to let the Iraqi people see who's delivering the food.

7-4

0040

ELIMINATING IRAQ'S WEAPONS OF MASS DESTRUCTION

WHERE THE INTERNATIONAL EFFORT STANDS

The U.N. Security Council voted 12 to 1 on April 3 to compel Iraq's surrender of all weapons of mass destruction, including its stocks of poison gas, biological weapons, nuclear weapons materials and ballistic missiles with a range greater than 95 miles. Iraq was also ordered to forswear any related research and allow destruction of weapons research and production facilities.

Iraq officially accepted terms of the resolution on April 6, enabling the U.N. Special Commission on Iraq to begin implementing the resolution. According to U.N. and U.S. officials, this is where the effort stands to date:

OVERALL COMPLIANCE

■ The White House yesterday said Iraq has not fully complied with the U.N. Security Council requirement for full disclosure of its work on weapons of mass destruction. The International Atomic Energy Agency said in Vienna that it had only a partial picture of the Iraqi nuclear effort. A spokesman for the U.N. Special Commission on Iraq said the group is "far away from a conclusion in any of the fields" because it has not finished on-site inspections.

NUCLEAR RESEARCH

■ Iraq said in April that it had some highly enriched uranium under international safeguards, but no other nuclear weapons-usable materials or related research facilities. Under pressure, it later admitted to possessing substantial stocks of low-enriched and natural uranium, extensive laboratories and three separate programs for uranium enrichment.

■ U.N.-IAEA inspections in May, June and July of major nuclear complexes at Tuwaitha, Tarmiya and Sharqat, plus at least five other sites, revealed extensive Iraqi salvage or concealment efforts, including complete removal of equipment and reinforced, concrete floors from several buildings. They found a small quantity of plutonium and sealed 36 "calutron" devices for uranium enrichment, eight to 10 of which are believed to have been operated. While IAEA officials estimate that at least 6.6 pounds of weapons-grade uranum were made covertly, Iraq has admitted making only one pound. U.S. intelligence officials estimate that Iraq possesses 15-25 pounds, and want Iraq to surrender all of its hidden fissile materials, bomb designs, triggers and any other vital weapons components. Another U.N.-IAEA team will visit Iraq beginning July 27.

CHEMICAL WEAPONS

■ Iraq said in April that it had 355 tons of mustard gas and nerve agents, 650 tons of intermediate chemicals, 6,920 chemical-filled battlefield missile warheads, 1,376 filled aerial bombs and 105 filled artillery shells—almost all at the mammoth Samarra chemical weapons complex west of Baghdad. It also declared that 2,500 filled missile warheads and 200 aerial bombs were buried under debris from allied bombing. Subsequent declarations acknowledged possession of thousands of unfilled chemical munitions.

■ A U.N. inspection team that visited Samarra June 9-14 was able to verify the presence of weapons of the type declared by Iraq. It also found more empty munitions than Iraq had declared. But it did not take a precise inventory, due to the danger posed by extensive contamination and by leaking, damaged or poorly maintained weapons. Another chemical inspection team will visit declared and undeclared sites elsewhere in Iraq in August, and a third team will return to Samarra in September for a more precise inventory. U.N. officials say destruction of the weapons will require at least 18 months, once the means to do it are in place.

BALLISTIC MISSILES

■ Iraq said in April that it possessed 52 ballistic missiles, 38 launchers, 30 chemical-filled missile warheads and 23 conventionally armed warheads at five sites. It subsequently admitted possession of nine additional missiles at one of the sites.

■ In June and July, two U.N. inspection teams visited all the declared sites and witnessed destruction of 61 missiles, 23 conventional warheads and 10 launchers. The other 28 declared launchers were deemed unusable, and the chemical warheads were placed under U.N. control. During a surprise visit last week to an undeclared site near Baghdad, the inspectors found and witnessed destruction of 11 metallic ballistic missile decoys. Another U.N. inspection of suspect sites is planned in August.

BIOLOGICAL WEAPONS

■ During the Persian Gulf War, allied military planes used incendiary bombs to destroy Iraqi scientific research facilities believed associated with germ weapons production. Iraq told the United Nations about five research laboratories it claimed were solely for peaceful research and described an extensive program of vaccine production, but denied making any germ weapons.

■ U.N. germ warfare inspectors are preparing to conduct their first inspection of declared and undeclared sites in Iraq. Officials say their work has been slowed by extensive training of team members and by the need for health precautions, including partial immunization against suspected agents.

—R. Jeffrey Smith

BY MICHAEL DREW—THE WASHINGTON POST

7-5

0041

JUL 26 '91 16:38 KOREAN MIS P.5

Transcript of comments made by the Secretary-General upon entering the Secretariat Building. 9:35 am, 26 July 1991

Q. Given BCCI's alleged funding effort for Argentina, Pakistan and Libya to obtain nuclear arms, do you think the trips you took on the BCCI planes undermine your position as the Secretary-General?

SG: First of all these trips took place about five years ago, around 1986, 1987. You know, you could not guess then whether people are involved or not in this kind of business. But anyway it is something which gives me no concern at all.

Q: There are allegations that the plane was put at your disposal for a five-year period so that you would use your influence to help BCCI gain access to bankers in developing countries.

SG: That is totally false, totally false. I don't know who the novelist is who invented such a thing. This is totally false. This plane was provided to me by one of my assistants, Mr. Hrusovsky, who told me, "Listen, Mr. Secretary-General, there is some danger now in commercial planes, and there is a gentleman who is offering you a plane." That's it.

Q: So the allegation that the plane was provided to you in the hopes that it would provide them access to .....

SG: That is totally false. Anyway, as I didn't keep the plane .....

Q: One other question Sir. In your opinion you did nothing illegal, and exerted no influence on behalf of BCCI?

SG: No, no, no. Don't you have more important news to pass on to people? Isn't it sad to see that you are concentrating so much on such stupid things?

Q: Tell us about how you are going to proceed in determining whether the humanitarian aid reaches Iraq?

SG: Well, I intend to set up a special committee, a small group of officers who will deal specifically with this problem. But still I have to wait for the decision of the Security Council. As you know it met yesterday but they took no decision.

...../

7-6

0042

-2-

Q: Are you concerned that as more time goes by famine will intensify in Iraq?

SG: From the very beginning, from the first mission we sent to the area, we expressed concern over the humanitarian situation of the Iraqi people, regardless of the political implications. It is a humanitarian question, it concerns everybody. When you deal with humanitarian problems you don't think of political criteria, do you. At least I don't think so.

Q: Do you have any ideas on how proceeds from Iraqi oil revenues will be put into escrow and then used to purchase food?

SG: On that the Security Council has to take a decision as well. But so far they are discussing it among members of the Council. Iraq, of course, is against the idea of putting this money into an escrow account. But you see, that is all in the hands of the Council. We are the executors of the decisions of the Council.

* * *

7-7

0043

관리 번호	91/1346

외 무 부

종 별 :

번 호 : UNW-1997　　　　일 시 : 91 0801 2000

수 신 : 장관 (국연,중동일,기정)

발 신 : 주 유엔 대사

제 목 : 안보리 동향 (91.8월주요의제)

1. 금 8.1. 안보리 8 월 의장국으로 취임한 에쿠아돌은 관례에 따라 안보리 이사국들과 당월 주요현안의제에 관해 개별협의에 들어간바, 명일까지 협의진행 예정이라고함.

2. 상기관련 당관 원참사관이 금일 동국 J.VALENCIA 서기관으로 부터 탐문한바 이사국간에 협의중인 금월 주요의제는 다음과 갑다고함.

가. 이락문제

1) 이락 제재조치 시행 정기심사 (안보리 결의 687, 700 호)

가)대 이락금수, 거래금지, 무기공급 차단 관련사항 (687 호 28 항, 700 호 6 항)

나)제재완화 검토 (687 호 21 항)

2)이락 대량파괴무기 폐기 검증시행방안 (687 호 10 항)

나. 회원국 가입신청 처리:4 개국 (아국, 북한, 마샬군도, 마이크로네시아) 신청 내지 신청예상

다. 유엔사무총장의 사이프러스 관련 보고 (8 월말경)

라. 중동평화문제

3. 상기 개별협의 동향중 가입신청처리 관련사항은 별전 보고하며 기타사항은 추보 위계임. 끝

(대사 노창희-국장)

예고:91.12.31. 일반

91.12.31. 일반.

국기국	장관	차관	1차보	2차보	중아국	분석관	청와대	안기부

PAGE 1　　　　91.08.02 10:07

외신 2과 통제관 DO

0044

외 무 부

종 별 :

번 호 : UNW-2002 일 시 : 91 0801 2200

수 신 : 장 관(북미,중동일,국연,기정)

발 신 : 주 유엔대사

제 목 : 미.걸프제국 안보협약교섭 동향(언론보도)

1.금 8.1.자 NYT 지에 의하면 미-걸프제국간 안보협약 교섭 타결이 가까워 졌으며 현 재합동 군사훈련, 무기판매, 공군기지 사용문제가 본격 논의되고 있다고 함.

2.동지는 상기 교섭과정에서 위기발생시에 대비한 미군장비의 역내 사전배치 문제가 특히 정치적으로 민감한 사안의 하나로 볼수있으며 미측은 걸프6개국 각나라에미군장비를 얼마씩 사전 배치해 놓기를 희망하고 있다고 보도함. 끝

(대사 노창희-국장)

첨부: FAX (UNW(F)-378)

미주국 1차보 중아국 국기국 외정실 안기부

PAGE 1

91.08.02 14:02 WH

외신 1과 통제관

0045

UNW(F)-378 10801 2200 처우물 UNW-2002

총 1PH.

U.S. Negotiating New Security Pacts in Gulf

By ERIC SCHMITT

Special to The New York Times

WASHINGTON, July 31 — As the Bush Administration consults with its allies about future military action against Iraq, American officials say they are nearing completion of new long-term security alliances with governments in the Persian Gulf.

Although Arab allies have expressed reservations about renewed bombing of Iraq's nuclear plants, the talks on future security arrangements have steadily advanced.

Administration officials say they are still wrangling over important details like the positioning of military equipment in Saudi Arabia. But American negotiators who met last month with their counterparts in Saudi Arabia, Kuwait, Qatar, Bahrain and the United Arab Emirates said they had made "considerable progress" on a range of issues from joint military exercises to arms sales to the use of air bases.

"There's definitely a willingness by these countries to cooperate and improve the relations," Frederick C. Smith, director of the Defense Department's Near Eastern and South Asian affairs office, said at a recent Congressional hearing.

Administration officials are seeking a strong security pact to prevent a return to the loose arrangements that existed last Aug. 2, when Iraqi forces rolled into Kuwait and threatened Saudi oilfields with virtually no resistance from Arab countries in the region.

The agreement would establish new security arrangements with countries like Kuwait and Qatar, and enhance existing ones with nations like Saudi Arabia and Bahrain.

"We will find that we're able to do regular naval exercises, periodic air deployments and exercise our units with units of governments in the region," Defense Secretary Dick Cheney said recently.

American diplomats in Arab capitals are working to resolve the remaining legal, technical and financial details. Among the most politically sensitive issues, particularly for Saudi Arabia, is the positioning of American military equipment in the region for ready use in future crises.

"It's a balancing act between a desire for better protection on one hand, and not having alien forces present on the other," a Pentagon official said of the Saudi position.

Officials declined to say how much equipment the United States would position in each gulf country, but a Pentagon official familiar with the talks said Washington would have some equipment in each of the six countries in the Gulf Cooperation Council, a regional alliance led by Saudi Arabia. Its other members are Kuwait, Qatar, Bahrain, Oman and the Emirates.

The Pentagon this month asked Congress for about $290 million in additional funds to pay for equipment to be positioned in the gulf.

As the talks near conclusion, the United States military has already withdrawn more than 70 percent of its equipment and all but 44,000 troops from Saudi Arabia and Kuwait, the United States Central Command says.

The Army in particular wants to leave some of its heaviest equipment behind. Mr. Cheney said several weeks ago that the United States would seek to leave behind in Saudi Arabia as much as a division's worth of equipment. A division typically includes as many as 300 M1-A1 tanks and 300 Bradley fighting vehicles.

But in the face of growing opposition from conservative elements in Saudi Arabia to a vivid reminder of Western influence, Administration officials say they are scaling back their goals.

In addition to the fundamental question of what will be positioned where, there are several legal and financial details to be settled.

"We have a lot of equipment just sitting there in desert," a Pentagon official said. "We'll need to build sheds for it. Who will pay for it? Who will provide the security guards for it? Those are the kind of questions to be worked out."

The Administration has emphatically stated that there will be no American ground forces permanently stationed in the region.

Any future regional security arrangements are sure to include arms sales. Many gulf countries have implicitly linked agreements on other security issues to assurances that American arms sales will continue.

(북미·중동일.국연, 기정)

0046

원 본

외 무 부

종 별 :

번 호 : UNW-2020 일 시 : 91 0802 2100

수 신 : 장 관(국연,중동일,기정)

발 신 : 주 유엔대사

제 목 : 걸프사태

1.이락의 쿠웨이트 침공 1주년 반응

가.8.2 유엔사무총장 성명발표: 유엔의 쿠웨이트 전후 복구 노력지원 재확인(SG/SM/4590)

나.언론반응(NYT 지)

1)사설:91.2.28 미국의 휴전조치 옹호

2.안보리 휴전결의 후속조치

가.8.5. 안보리 비공식협의 개최예정

나.안보리 휴전결의(687호 본문 10 항)에 의거 IAEA는 엄격한 핵관련 장기 통제계획안을 제출

(상세 별첨 NYT 지 기사참조)

3.이락 석유수출 일부 허용문제

상임 이사국들간에 금 8.2 현재 결의안 문안 협의중인것으로 알려짐.(UNW-1970참조)

4.쿠웨이트, 이락의 호크 방공미사일포대(당초 쿠웨이트 포대) 배치항의 안보리문서 배포

5.이락의 쿠웨이트 항공기 반환현황

유엔측에 의하면 총15 대중 2대는 반환 완료, 7대는 이락 억류중에 파괴, 6대는이란보유(유엔측이 이란당국과 협의중)

첨부:상기자료: UNW(F)-385 끝

(대사 노창희-국장)

국기국 1차보 중아국 외정실 분석관 안기부

PAGE 1 91.08.03 10:22 WH

외신 1과 통제관

0047 

AUG 02 '91 19:36 KOREAN MISSION

UNW(F)-385 10802 P.1:100
(특연. 중동일.기정)
총3매

United Nations

Press Release

Department of Public Information • News Coverage Service • New York

SG/SM/4590
IK/42
2 August 1991

SECRETARY-GENERAL, ON FIRST ANNIVERSARY OF INVASION OF KUWAIT, SAYS UN REMAINS COMMITTED TO HELPING KUWAITIS REPAIR WAR DAMAGES

The following is attributable to Secretary-General Javier Pérez de Cuéllar:

One year ago, on 2 August 1990, the hopes of a world emerging from the throes of the cold war were severely undermined by an act of international aggression. The occupation of Kuwait, a small and peaceful country, by its large and more powerful neighbour, Iraq, presented a grave challenge to international legitimacy.

Today, one year later, relief that the invasion has been reversed is tempered by the awareness of the enormous tasks now confronting Kuwait and other countries of the region that were adversely affected by the crisis. In the face of continuing suffering by millions of innocent people, various agencies of the United Nations family are working in conjunction with many non-governmental and humanitarian organizations to offer emergency relief and to assist in the process of reconstruction and development.

The people of Kuwait may have confidence that the United Nations will maintain its full commitment to helping them repair the damages of war. It is my heartfelt wish that lasting peace will be established in the region, leading to a new era of justice and harmony, based on the principles of the United Nations Charter.

* *** *

#UNW-2020
첨부물

3-1

For information media—not an official record

0048

Gulf War, and Peace, Revisited

Before 100 hours passed, the ground war had turned into a "turkey shoot." With word from Gen. Norman Schwarzkopf that Saddam Hussein's Republican Guard was shattered and his nuclear capacity "neutralized," the President decided the fighting had gone on long enough. The invasion of Kuwait that horrified the world a year ago today had been undone.

Americans greeted the Feb. 28 cease-fire with relief and pride — relief at miraculously few U.S. casualties and pride in the brilliant performance of the allied forces.

Yet a remorseless Saddam Hussein remains in power, cruelly repressing Kurds and Shiites, defiantly playing nuclear hide-and-seek and maliciously manipulating the Iraqi people's misery. Even liberals who thought Mr. Bush was too quick to pull the trigger in January now wonder if he should have finished off Saddam Hussein and his army when he had the chance.

But the doubters do not do justice to Mr. Bush's restraint. With the benefit of later information showing, for instance, that Iraq's losses had been overestimated, Americans can sensibly wish he had gone on somewhat longer. But even with hindsight, his decision deserves credit.

•

That can be seen by asking what if Mr. Bush had gone all the way, wrecked the rest of Iraq's war machine, marched to Baghdad and overthrown Saddam Hussein?

With no evident successor to restore Iraq's unity, defend its borders or even maintain rudimentary services, there probably would have been a plague of troubles: many more allied and civilian casualties ... protracted civil war, with allied troops by the thousands caught in the middle ..., Americans hated throughout the Arab world as an occupying army.

For all the ugly ambiguities of the actual consequences, Mr. Bush has avoided the quagmire and preserved his two triumphs: the extraordinary cooperation among coalition members and the revived self-confidence of Americans.

This was very much George Bush's war. He defined the options and framed the debate, at home and abroad. He gambled his Presidency on a quick and decisive struggle, and won. In personalizing the conflict, he tended to identify regional security and stability with the end of Saddam Hussein's army and rule. These goals were critical to his contention that the international economic embargo on Iraq would not suffice, necessitating the use of armed force.

But even if Mr. Bush overpersonalized the war, he was careful to defer to his allies. He thereby assured their loyalty and also enhanced the prospects for enduring cooperation in Iraq and for new coalitions in the future. That may disappoint unilateralists in the U.S. who hoped the war would give rise to a Pax Americana. But it's the most promising way to bring a measure of stability and security to this troubled region.

It is obviously impossible to render a final judgment now on Mr. Bush's war policy. We and others argued last fall that it would have been wiser to give the international economic embargo against Iraq more time to deny Iraq its billions in oil revenue. We thought he was in too much of a hurry to start shooting. That said, the President was right to stop it when he did.

By thundering on to Baghdad, Desert Storm might have brought some immediate satisfaction to Americans who have grown increasingly frustrated and furious about Saddam Hussein. But had that happened, just imagine where Americans would be today, a year after the invasion: still in Baghdad, in more danger and more frustration, and with no end in sight.

3-2

0049

3-3

U.N. Nuclear Agency Submits a Plan for Iraq

By FRANK J. PRIAL

Special to The New York Times

UNITED NATIONS, Aug.1 — A tough, all-encompassing plan for long-range monitoring of Iraq's nuclear technology has been submitted to the Security Council by the International Atomic Energy Agency, an arm of the *United Nations*.

The plan, a copy of which was obtained today by The New York Times, would give the agency virtually complete control of Iraq's future nuclear development as well as unlimited right of movement within Iraq and across its borders. Diplomats here said the plan called for the most stringent inspection requirements in the United Nations' history.

Under the long-range plan, Iraq would have to supply the agency with inventories of all nuclear materials and installations and notify the agency of any changes in the inventories a month before they are made.

It would also require complete design information for any planned nuclear installation 180 days before construction begins, as well as all information on changes in Iraq's overall nuclear program one year in advance. It would be required to produce any other information or data the agency says it needs to monitor Iraq's complinace with Security Council Resolution 678, which set terms for a cease-fire in the Persian Gulf war.

The agency would have the right to "full and free" access at any time to "all locations, all persons and all information" it decides is necessary for its verification program. It would have the right to hold unannounced inspections on short notice and would have the right restrict or stop movement of any suspected material and equipment.

It would have freedom of entry and exit to Iraq "without delay" or the need for visas for people travelling on United Nations documents. It would have the right to install equipment and construct inspection installations; to have its own means of transport and communication and unrestriced use of Iraqi communications systems, and to make fixed-wing and helicopter overflights as needed.

If approved by the Security Council, the long-range plan would go into effect once the present phase of inspections, verifications and destruction of weapons-quality nuclear materials has ended. The current phase, begun almost immediately after the gulf war ended, is expected to end sometime this fall.

The duration of the long-range program would be determined by the Security Council, the agency document said.

The long-range plan is subject to modification, the agency proposal made clear.

0050

원 본

외 무 부

종 별 :

번 호 : UNW-2075 일 시 : 91 0807 1900

수 신 : 장 관(국연,중동일,기정)

발 신 : 주 유엔 대사

제 목 : 안보리 동향(비공식협의)

연: UNW-2036

1. 안보리는 금 8.7 안보리 휴전결의 이행문제관련 비공식 협의를 개최한바, 당관에서 탐문한 동 협의 결과를 아래보고함.

가. 대이락 제재조치 정기심사 (결의 687 호 21,28 항,700 호 6항)

연호와같이 다수 이사국들이 현재의 제재조치를 유지해야 한다는 입장임에 따라, 안보리의장 (에쿠아돌)은 '8.5. 비공식 협의결과 제재조치 변경을 위한 필요조건이 충족되었다는데 대해 이사국들간 합의가없었다 ' 는 요지의 언론발표문 (PRESSSTATEMENT) 을 내고 동 발표문을 안보리문서로 배포하는 것으로 일단락 지어짐.

나. 이락 대량파괴 무기 폐기 이행검증 계획안

1)핵관련 계획안 (UNW-2036), 여타대량 파괴무기 관련 계획안 (UNW-2053) 의기술적인 성격에 비추어 충분한 검토후 재토의키로함.

2)단, 조기계획 수립필요성에 대해서는 의견이 합치된바, 본건 계획을 승인하는 결의안 (단일 또는 복수결의안)이 다음주부터 교섭될 것으로 관측됨.

다. 이락 배상기금 (석유수입공제 상한선문제) 및 이락석유수출 일부허용

1)미국은 사무총장안 (30 프로) 수락의사를 표시하여 왔으며, 이에따라 안보리 결정이 가까운 시일안에 있을 전망임.

2)단,미국은 상한선문제를 현재 상임이사국들간에 교섭중인 다음 2개 결의안타결과 연계시키고 있는 것으로 알려짐.

가)이락 석유 수출 일부허용 (UNW-1970 참조)

나)이락의 핵관련 의무이행

2.안보리는 명 8.8 신규회원국 가입신청 처리를 위한 공식회의 개최예정이며, 8.9 에는 비공식협의를 갖고 유엔사무총장의 유엔엘살바돌 옵서버단 (ONUSAL) 관련 보고

국기국 1차보 중아국 외정실 분석관 청와대 안기부

PAGE 1 91.08.08 09:05 WG

외신 1과 통제관

0051

청취예정임.

첨부: NYT 지 사설: UNW(F)-403 끝

(대사 노창희-국장)

PAGE 2

0052

UNW(FI)-403 10807 1900
(국연. 중동일. 기차) 총104

Keep the Heat on Iraq to Disarm

One by one, weapons secrets are being squeezed out of Baghdad. This week, after many lies, Iraq finally acknowledged it was conducting a secret biological weapons program and pursuing yet another nuclear weapons program.

Iraq's grudging revelations confirm that Saddam Hussein intended to arm himself with weapons of mass destruction. They also confirm the need to keep the pressure on him to tell all.

International inspectors must continue to seek what he's trying to hide. Stringent economic sanctions have to remain in force to compel Iraq to submit to inspections. And for long-term security, the United Nations Security Council needs to put in place a tough plan prepared by the International Atomic Energy Agency to keep Iraq from ever acquiring nuclear arms. Similar arrangements are needed for chemical and biological arms.

•

Like nuclear age archeologists, the inspectors charged with enforcing the disarmament provisions of the U.N. cease-fire resolution are still trying to reconstruct Iraq's weapons programs. They had previously discovered three methods Iraq was using to enrich uranium so that it could be used in weapons. Iraq has now admitted trying to build the bomb a fourth way, by reprocessing plutonium from spent nuclear fuel at its Tuwaitha reactor.

But the inspectors can never be sure of what they don't know. And even if they learn everything about Iraq's present programs, they will need to keep it from rearming in the future.

Two policies are essential. One is to keep pressure on Baghdad to comply with the cease-fire resolution. That requires continued economic sanctions despite the Iraqi leader's efforts to get them lifted. No doubt the sanctions hurt ordinary Iraqis more than they hurt Saddam Hussein. But he, not the international community, is the source of their pain. The U.N. dare not let him manipulate his people's misery to escape pressure to comply.

Second, even if he does comply, what's to guarantee that he won't resume arms-making in the future? The I.A.E.A. has proposed a tough program to embargo dangerous nuclear exports to Iraq and require advance notice from states that ship other nuclear material and equipment ostensibly intended for nonmilitary use.

The new rules would allow the I.A.E.A. uninhibited access to "all locations, all persons and all information" needed to verify compliance with the cease-fire resolution. The agency could conduct on-site inspections on short notice, using its own transportation, communication and inspection equipment to avoid depending on its host.

The proposal makes some U.N. members uneasy because they don't want the precedent applied to them. But it's a serious nonproliferation policy that deserves support. If the allies take the heat off Iraq now, they will be asking for trouble from Iraqi terror weapons in the future.

UNW-2075
첨부물

1-1

0053

관리번호	91-891

원 본

외 무 부

종 별 :

번 호 : UNW-2096 일 시 : 91 0808 1930

수 신 : 장관(국연,중동일,기정)

발 신 : 주 유엔 대사

제 목 : 이락 석유수출 일부허용문제(안보리동향)

연:UNW-1970

1. 표제관련 금 8.8 당관 원참사관이 미대표부 B.HANSEN 담당관에게 탐문한바에 의하면, 연호 결의안에 대해 상임이사국들간에 대체적인 합의가 이루어져 현재 여타 이사국들과 문안을 협의중이라고 하며 금일 동 담당관으로 부터 입수한 결의안 초안을 별첨송부함.

2. 상기 초안은 연호 초안을 일부 보완한 것인바, 동 주요 보완내용은 다음과같음.

가. 허용한도액 설정:16 억불 (6 개월기간중 세차례로 나누어 허가)

나. 통제 방법보강

다. 쿠웨이트, 제 3 국인 억류자 및 유해송환 문제 강조

3. 사용허용한도액 16 억불은 일 50 만배럴 생산을 기준으로 한것이며, 이는 걸프전 발발전에 비해 1/6 수준이라고함.

첨부:1. 안보리이사국 초안,

2.NYT 기사:UNW(F)-411 끝

(대사 노창희-국장대리)

예고:91.12.31. 까지

국기국 1차보 중아국 외정실 분석관 안기부

PAGE 1 91.08.09 09:54

외신 2과 통제관 CA

0054

H

#별첨

UNW(F)-411 10808 1930
(국련.중동일.기정)

총9011

7 August 1991
1:00pm

"The Security Council,

A. Recalling its previous relevant resolutions and in particular resolutions 661 (1990), 686 (1991), 687 (1991), 688 (1991), 692 (1991), 699 (1991) and 7.. (1991),

B. Taking note of the report (S/29799) dated 15 July 1991 of the inter-agency mission headed by the executive delegate of the Secretary-General for the United Nations inter-agency humanitarian programme for Iraq, Kuwait and the Iraq/Turkey and Iraq/Iran border areas,

C. Concerned by the serious nutritional and health situation of the Iraqi civilian population as described in this report, and by the risk of a further deterioration of this situation,

D. Concerned also that the repatriation or return of all Kuwaitis and third country nationals or their remains present in Iraq on or after 2 August 1990, pursuant to paragraph 30 of resolution 687 (1991), has not yet been fully carried out,

E. Taking note of the conclusions of the above-mentioned report, and in particular of the proposal for oil sales by Iraq to finance immediate humanitarian relief,

F. Taking note also of the letters dated 14 April 1991, 31 May 1991, 6 June 1991, 9 July 1991 and 22 July 1991 from the Minister of Foreign Affairs of Iraq and the Permanent Representative of Iraq to the Chairman of the Committee established by resolution 661 (1990) concerning the export from Iraq of petroleum and petroleum products,

9-1

.../...

0055

G. <u>Convinced</u> of the need to achieve effective monitoring and transparency in the equitable distribution of humanitarian relief to all segments of the Iraqi civilian population,

H. <u>Recalling and reaffirming</u> in this regard its resolution 688 (1991) and in particular the importance which the Council attaches to Iraq allowing unhindered access by international humanitarian organisations to all those in need of assistance in all parts of Iraq and making available all necessary facilities for their operation, and in this connection stressing the important and continuing role played by the Memorandum of Understanding between the United Nations and the Government of Iraq of 18 April 1991 (S/22663),

I. <u>Recalling</u> that, pursuant to resolutions 687 (1991), 692 (1991) and 699 (1991), Iraq is required to pay the full costs of the Special Commission and the IAEA in carrying out the tasks authorised by section C of resolution 687 (1991), and that the Secretary-General in his report to the Security Council of 15 July 1991 (S/22792), submitted pursuant to paragraph 4 of resolution 699 (1991), expressed the view that the most obvious way of obtaining financial resources from Iraq to meet the costs of the Special Commission and the IAEA would be to authorise the sale of some Iraqi petroleum and petroleum products; recalling further that Iraq is required to pay its contributions to the Compensation Fund and half the costs of the Iraq-Kuwait Boundary Demarcation Commission, and recalling further that in its resolutions 686 (1991) and 687 (1991) the Security Council demanded that Iraq return in the shortest possible time all Kuwaiti property seized by it and requested the Secretary-General to take steps to facilitate this,

9-2

.../...

J. Acting under Chapter VII of the Charter,

1. Authorises all States, subject to the decision to be taken by the Security Council pursuant to paragraph 5 below and notwithstanding the provisions of paragraphs 3(a), 3(b) and 4 of resolution 661 (1990), to permit the import during a period of 6 months from the date of passage of this resolution of petroleum and petroleum products originating in Iraq sufficient to produce a sum to be determined by the Council following receipt of the report of the Secretary-General requested in paragraph 5 of this resolution but not to exceed 1.6 billion US dollars for the purposes set out in this resolution and subject to the following conditions :

(a) approval of each purchase of Iraqi petroleum and petroleum products by the Security Council Committee established by resolution 661 (1990) following notification to the Committee by the State concerned,

(b) payment of the full amount of each purchase of Iraqi petroleum and petroleum products directly by the purchaser in the State concerned into an escrow account to be established by the United Nations and to be administered by the Secretary-General, exclusively to meet the purposes of this resolution,

(c) approval by the Council, following the report of the Secretary-General requested in paragraph 5 of this resolution, of a scheme for the purchase of foodstuffs, medicines and materials and supplies for essential civilian needs as referred to in paragraph 20 of resolution 687 (1991), in particular health related materials, all of which to be labelled to the extent possible as being

9-3

.../...

supplied under this scheme, and for all feasible UN administration, monitoring and supervision to ensure their equitable distribution to meet humanitarian needs in all regions of Iraq and to all categories of the Iraqi civilian population, such UN admistration, monitoring and supervision to be available if desired for humanitarian assistance from other sources,

(d) the sum authorised in this paragraph to be released by successive decisions of the Committee established by resolution 661 (1990) in three equal parts after the Council has taken the decision provided for in paragraph 5 below on the implementation of this resolution, and notwithstanding any other provision of this paragraph, the sum to be subject to review concurrently by the Council on the basis of its ongoing assessment of the needs and requirements,

2. Decides that a part of the sum in the account to be established by the Secretary-General shall be made available by him to finance the purchase of foodstuffs, medicines and materials and supplies for essential civilian needs, as referred to in paragraph 20 of resolution 687, and the cost to the United Nations of administration, monitoring and surveillance and of other necessary humanitarian activities in Iraq,

3. Decides further that a part of the sum in the account to be established by the Secretary-General shall be used by him for appropriate payments to the United Nations Compensation Fund, the full costs of carrying out the tasks authorised by Section C of resolution 687 (1991), the full costs incurred by the United Nations in facilitating the return of all Kuwaiti property seized by Iraq, and half the costs of the Boundary Commission,

9-4

.../...

0058

4. Decides that the percentage of the value of exports of petroleum and petroleum products from Iraq authorized under this resolution to be paid to the United Nations Compensation Fund, as called for in paragraph 19 of resolution 687 (1991) and paragraph 6 of resolution 692 (1991), shall be the same as the percentage decided by the Security Council in paragraph .. of resolution 7.. (1991) for payments to the Compensation Fund, until such time as the Governing Council of the Fund decides otherwise,*

5. Requests the Secretary-General to submit within 20 days of the date of adoption of this resolution a report to the Security Council for decision on measures to be taken in order to implement paragraphs 1 (a), (b) and (c), estimates of the humanitarian requirements of Iraq set out in paragraph 2 above and of the amount of Iraq's financial obligations set out in paragraph 3 above up to the end of the period of the authorisation in paragraph 1 above, as well as the method for taking the necessary legal measures to ensure that the purposes of this resolution are carried out and the method for taking account of the costs of the production and transportation of such Iraqi petroleum and petroleum products,

6. Further requests the Secretary-General in consultation with the International Committee of the Red Cross to submit within 20 days of the date of adoption of this resolution a report to the Security Council on activities undertaken in accordance with paragraph 31 of resolution 687 (1991) in connection with facilitating the repatriation or return of all Kuwaiti and third country nationals or their remains present in Iraq on or after 2 August 1990,

----

* - resolution 7.. (1991) referred to in this paragraph relates to the decision to be taken by the Council upon a recommendation by the Secretary General on the ceiling for the Iraqi contribution to the Compensation Fund; such a resolution should be adopted before this one.

9-5

.../...

0059

7. Requires the Government of Iraq to provide to the Secretary-General and appropriate international organisations on the first day of the month immediately following the adoption of the present resolution and on the first day of each month thereafter until further notice, a statement of the gold and foreign currency reserves it holds whether in Iraq or elsewhere.

8. Calls upon all States to cooperate fully in the implementation of this resolution.

9. Decides to remain seized of the matter.

9-6

0060

5 POWERS AT U.N. DECIDE TO ALLOW IRAQIS TO SELL OIL

NO LIFTING OF SANCTIONS

But Baghdad Representative Criticizes Proposed Limits on Access to Money

By JERRY GRAY

Special to The New York Times

UNITED NATIONS, Aug. 7 — The five permanent members of the United Nations Security Council have decided to continue sanctions against Iraq, but agreed today to allow Baghdad a one-time exception to sell up to $1.6 billion worth of petroleum, with part of the money to be used to buy food and medical supplies.

Along with the permission to sell the oil comes a tough set of restrictions that would keep the revenue out of Iraqi hands and make sure that others, including the United Nations and countries with war-related claims against Iraq, are paid first.

"The United Nations has Iraq spread-eagled against the car and is going through its pockets," a Western diplomat said. "Iraq will never touch any of this money."

Iraqi Leaves in Anger

The head of Iraq's mission to the United Nations, Abdul Amir A. al-Anbari, sat in on the deliberations by the permanent members today but left the meeting in anger after a short while and told reporters that Iraq would denounce the decision.

"Iraq won't accept it both as a matter of principle and as a matter of practice," Mr. Anbari said.

He said the proposed oil sale had become so time-consuming and complicated that "it is simply not going to help us."

'It Benefits Non-Iraqis'

"It benefits non-Iraqis rather than Iraqis," he said. "For all practical purposes, it allows Iraq to buy not one sack of rice or one sack of grain."

There could be room for negotiation on how the rest of the oil money is divided between United Nations expenses and what would go toward food and medicine.

But Western diplomats said there would be no negotiation on the 30 percent chunk for compensation — which already represents a compromise United States — or on giving any of the money directly to Iraq.

Extent of Need Questioned

Security Council members including the United States say they are certain Iraq needs some help, but they question how much. Baghdad had asked to sell $2 billion worth of oil solely to pay for humanitarian aid, but refused demands for a detailed acounting of its gold and foreign currency reserves.

Western diplomats, noting the continued Iraqi importation of goods such as liquor and American-brand soft drinks since the Persian Gulf war ended, have questioned just how desperate Iraqi needs are.

After a week of discussions, the permanent members agreed on a resolution drafted by France that would allow Iraq to pump and sell — in three installments — $1.6 billion worth of oil over the next six months.

One demand in the draft resolution is that the Government of Iraq on the first of each month provide the Secretary General with a statement of its gold and foreign currency reserves.

How much oil Iraq can sell is to be determined by the Security Council after the Secretary General submits a report on the level of Iraq's humanitarian requirements, but the total for the six months cannot exceed $1.6 billion. At current oil prices, that would be about half a million barrels a day, about a sixth of what Iraq produced before the war.

9-7

0061

The draft resolution must still be voted on by the full 15 members of the Security Council, and officials said the vote would occur Friday or early next week. Although some members had favored easing the sanctions further, it is unlikely that the vote will go counter to the decision of the five permanent members — the United States, the Soviet Union, China, Britain and France.

A diplomat who sat in on the Security Council deliberations and spoke on condition that he not be identified said any chances of Iraq's getting easier terms were dashed this week with revelations that Baghdad had secretly extracted small amounts of plutonium and had lied about a biological weapons research plant.

U.S. Threatens Iraq

President Bush and Secretary of Defense Dick Cheney have repeatedly threatened to use military force against Iraq if it did not make full disclosure of its nuclear, chemical and biological weapons programs.

Under the draft resolution, Baghdad would be allowed to sell its oil directly on the open spot market for six months from the date of passage of the resolution. But proceeds from the oil would go into an escrow account controlled by the United Nations Secretary General, Javier Pérez de Cuéllar.

Officials said 30 percent of the oil revenue would be placed into a compensation account to pay governments and individuals who have filed claims against Iraq over war-related losses.

The draft resolution said some of the money would go to meet United Nations costs in Iraq. Those costs include inspections by the International Atomic Energy Agency and the Special Commission that was established to check for weapons of mass destruction, the transfer of all Kuwaiti property seized by Iraq and half the expenses for redrawing the border between Iraq and Kuwait. The United Nations would use the balance of the revenue, expected to be a least half, to buy food and medicine and would monitor the distribution of the goods.

Figures Are Unspecified

But the resolution does not specify a dollar figure or the percentage of revenue that is to go toward compensating the United Nations or to be spent on the humanitarian aid. Diplomats said those expenditures would have to be determined after they get some feeling for how much work has been done and needs to be done.

Iraq, a member of the Organization of Petroleum Exporting Countries, had a prewar daily oil quota of 3.1 million barrels.

Persian Gulf crude was selling at $16.50 a barrel at the end of July, but the price varied according to the field that produced the crude.

The reaffirmation of the sanctions — contained in the so-called cease-fire resolution, number 687 — means that an international ban will continue on the sale of weapons to Iraq and that United Nations observers and inspectors will remain there. The Security Council's permanent members decided Monday at a private meeting to keep the sanctions in place, but that decision was not made public until today.

Under Resolution 687, adopted April 3, the Security Council must meet at least every 60 days to reconsider the sanctions against Iraq. At its first meeting on June 3, the Security Council also refused to remove the sanctions.

The Food and Agriculture Organization of the United Nations reported in July that "Iraq's population is facing a massive famine as a result of the war and a poor harvest."

The F.A.O. said Iraq needed $2.64 billion over the next year to purchase food and $500 million more to rebuild the agricultural sector, replacing machinery, irrigation and drainage systems, fertilizers and animal feed damaged or destroyed during the war.

Even in normal years, the agency said, Iraq produces only about a third of its food needs, with the remainder coming from imports of more than $2 billion annually.

9-A

0062

Iraqis Said to Retrieve Arms in Kuwait

By CHRIS HEDGES

Special to The New York Times

KUWAIT CITY, Aug. 7 — The Iraqi military, in violation of the cease-fire agreement, has made several night raids into Kuwait to retrieve stockpiles, including Silkworm missiles, left behind during their retreat, allied officials here say.

All of the raids have been in the demilitarized zone patrolled by the United Nations, the officials said.

Under the terms of the United Nations cease-fire agreement, the Iraqis are allowed to clear weapons and munitions from dumps on their side of the border. Iraqi soldiers from Iraq are barred from entering the demilitarized zone, although allied officials contend many are entering dressed in civilian clothes to gather war supplies.

The zone runs along the 25 miles of the Khor Abdullah waterway and 125 miles along the common border and extends six miles into Iraq and three miles into Kuwait. The allied forces that pushed back the Iraqis are similarly banned from the sector.

Iraqis Wait Until Dark

And in fact, during the day Iraqi trucks, which often work in groups of four or five, rarely venture into the Kuwaiti part of the zone, allied military officials in Kuwait said. But at night, when the 300 United Nations observers do not patrol, the Iraqi trucks have been sighted inside Kuwait.

"As soon as we turn our lights out they can do what they want," said a European United Nations observer, who occupies one of the 17 posts along the border. "We have no night vision equipment and no night patrols."

Beyond such comments, United Nations officials, including observers interviewed over two days along the border, said they could not discuss any specific incidents of arms scavenging within the zone.

The unarmed observers, part of the United Nations Iraq-Kuwait Observation Mission, are authorized only to record incidents within the zone and pass their reports on to New York.

Huge Pilfering Operation

But allied officials, and the Kuwaiti police who are allowed to operate in the demilitarized zone, described the pilfering operation as "massive."

"It is a bit like mushroom season out there," said a European allied official. "They have just figured out that no one is going to stop them."

The Iraqis reopened 10 police posts and 4 police centers in June along the border, 2 of which are inside Kuwait under the 1963 border agreement between Iraq and Kuwait. The agreement is used by the United Nations to determine the border's location.

A few Iraqi police officers have been seen carrying automatic weapons, a violation of the cease-fire agreement, allied officials said.

The Kuwaitis have not yet established a police presence along the border, and that is compounding the problem of unchecked Iraqi incursions, the officials said.

Allied officials are especially incensed that the Iraqis carted away 15 Silkworm missiles from a bunker complex during the last three days of May. The bunker complex is in the town of Umm Qasr, just inside Kuwait.

Four missiles were inexplicably returned a few days before the July 25 deadline given to President Saddam Hussein to disclose to United Nations officials all of his nuclear plants.

But the missiles are only a small part of the problem, the officials said.

Equipment for Several Thousand

The military stores available to the Iraqis along the border, a desolate expanse of sand where summer temperatures soar above 120 degrees, are enough to equip several thousand troops, allied officials say.

While many of the larger weapons, like tanks and heavy artillery, were destroyed by allied forces, thousands of smaller weapons and truckloads of ammunition were untouched. The Iraqis have also raided stores of uniforms and taken away items like motorboat engines, the officials said.

They said the Iraqi convoys tow damaged vehicles and military equipment like artillery pieces from the zone. The Iraqis are able to get spare parts from the damaged equipment. The embargo against Iraq has made it difficult for Iraqis to find spare parts.

The New York Times

Allied officials say Iraqis have pilfered missiles and other arms in the demilitarized zone of Kuwait.

One week ago, about 15 miles north of the border with Saudi Arabia, an abandoned Iraqi position within the zone had enough servicable ammunition for about three battalions, or 4,500 soldiers. Now there is little left. During the last seven nights Iraqi trucks have hauled away load after load of rocket-propelled grenades, cases full of machine-gun rounds, mortars and stacks of automatic weapons.

Lack of Kuwaiti Police

"Now that they know they can do this with impunity they have sent down convoys of trucks," said a European official. "Since Monday they have been very, very busy."

The debris of war, strewn over hundreds of miles of desert landscape, has attracted various types of scavangers.

Some Iraqi scavangers strip bunkers, filling their vehicles with lumber and tin siding, perhaps for their homes or perhaps for sale.

During a visit along the border Tuesday and Wednesday, some 30 trucks with Iraqi license plates, many laden with ammunition boxes, were seen heading north toward Iraq. Because the border is not marked, and because the Kuwaitis have not re-established their police force, it was often impossible to determine if the trucks were in Iraq or Kuwait.

Two trucks, in addition to carrying green wooden ammunition crates, were towing antiaircraft guns, and a third was towing an armored personnel carrier toward Iraq.

Bedoons, who have established a small sheep market just inside Iraq, appear to loot for profit. They sell the weapons they find, along with bottles of whiskey, in the market.

When the Iraqi police tried to interfere with the commerce about two weeks ago there were shots exchanged. Three people died in the skirmish and three more were severely wounded.

The Iraqi police have since left the Bedoons alone.

There are also reports that groups of Iraqi deserters, who may number as many as 3,000, are coming to the area to search for weapons and ammunition to battle Iraqi soldiers.

'Few of Us Speak Arabic'

"It is hard for us to know who the people are up here," said a United Nations observer. "Few of us speak Arabic and can really question them."

Those in the Iraqi convoys, who handle the bulk of material, are taut young men with closely cropped hair. They go about their work with alacrity.

Despite the heavy Iraqi activity, the number of documented violations by the Iraqis is less than those by the allied forces, both United Nations and allied officials said.

There have been frequent violations of air space by allied planes and allied soldiers have inadvertently wandered into the demilitarized zone.

But allied officials contend that those violations are all accidental, while the Iraqi violations are premeditated.

9-9

0063

원 본

외 무 부

종 별 :

번 호 : UNW-2115 일 시 : 91 0809 2100

수 신 : 장 관(국연,중동일,기정)

발 신 : 주 유엔 대사

제 목 : 걸프사태(유엔동향)

연: UNW(F)-411

이락측이 안보리 휴전결의를 위반하여 쿠웨이트와의 접경 비무장지대 (DMZ) 쿠웨이트지역에서 무기를 수거하고 있다는 연호 NYT 지 보도와 관련 유엔 (UNIKOM) 측은 이에대해 해명한바 동 내용을 별첨송부함.

첨부: UNIKOM 측 발표내용및 NYT 지 사설: UNW(F)-415 끝.

(대사 노창희-국장)

국기국 1차보 중아국 외정실 분석관 안기부

PAGE 1

91.08.10 10:47 WG

외신 1과 통제관

0064

UN-FD-415 10809 2150
(국연. 중동일. 기정) 총 2매

MESSAGE RECEIVED FROM MAJ. GEN. GUNTHER GREINDL

CHIEF MILITARY OBSERVER

UNITED NATIONS IRAQ-KUWAIT OBSERVATION MISSION (UNIKOM)

(selected portions only)

... With respect to night observation, I would like to add that UNIKOM is carrying out night patrols, particularly in the northern sector where most of the civilian activities take place. However, due to vast amounts of "un-"exploded ordnance devices strewn throughout the area, night patrols are limited to hard surface roads.

The headline is totally inaccurate and misleading. All removal activities by the Iraqis are carried out by civilians and are well within the Iraqi side of the DMZ.

I should like to point out that both sides have informed UNIKOM that they want to clear unexploded ordinance from their respective areas of the DMZ. For Iraq this is particularly important since many civilians live in their part of the DMZ. UNIKOM has witnessed uncontrolled explosions and civilian casualties caused by unexploded ordnance.

Concerning the article's last paragraph, UNIKOM has no reason to believe that any of the violations were premeditated. Both sides continue to cooperate with UNIKOM to prevent DMZ violations.

fg3-38

#UNW-2115
첨부물

2-1

0065

Feeding Iraq, Prudently

For weeks the world has been grappling with the problem of how to meet the urgent humanitarian needs of Iraqi civilians without bolstering the outlaw regime of Saddam Hussein. Now it looks as if the major powers at the U.N. have come up with an honorable solution.

A draft proposal being circulated by the five permanent members of the Security Council would allow Baghdad to resume limited sales of its oil under direct U.N. supervision. Revenues would go into a U.N.-administered account to be used for compensating the victims of Iraqi aggression as well as buying food and medicine needed to save Iraqi civilians from starvation and epidemics.

The U.N. would retain direct responsibility for delivering relief supplies inside Iraq, so that Saddam Hussein could not, for example, withhold food from the Kurds or divert civilian supplies to elite military units.

What makes this plan acceptable is that no oil revenues would at any point fall into Baghdad's hands. As a Western diplomat told The Times's Jerry Gray: "The U.N. has Iraq spread-eagled against the car and is going through its pockets."

That's as it should be. Saddam Hussein's regime is, in effect, resisting international arrest by continuing to flout its disarmament responsibilities under the U.N. cease-fire resolution.

Baghdad's nervy insistence that it be permitted to sell oil and have some of the cash put directly in its own hands has attracted almost no diplomatic support. It serves as one more timely reminder of Saddam Hussein's continuing efforts to manipulate the humanitarian issue to his own advantage.

The oil sale plan, assuming it is approved by the full Security Council and accepted by Iraq, will have to be carried out with the utmost strictness. U.N. monitors will have to stay vigilant against potential abuses like covert oil sales or misrepresentation of food supplies already on hand.

There must be absolute assurance that no aspect of the U.N. operation will be used to enhance the authority of the Baghdad regime, or to free strategic resources for non-humanitarian uses.

Only after Baghdad unequivocally complies with its cease-fire responsibilities will it be entitled to ask for the rights normally available to law-abiding members of the international community, like free access to oil markets and sovereign control of its cash receipts. Until then, the U.N. does right to treat it like the outlaw state it is, keeping it spread-eagled and under surveillance.

2-2

0066

원 본

외 무 부

종 별 :

번 호 : UNW-2123 일 시 : 91 0812 1800

수 신 : 장 관(국연,중동일,기정)

발 신 : 주 유엔 대사

제 목 : 걸프사태(유엔동향)

1.유엔 이락.쿠웨이트 옵서버단 (UNIKOM)감축추진

유엔사무총장은 본건 옵서버단측의 건의에 의거 경비절감 및 효율성제고를 위해 인력감축문제를 관련국들과 협의 예정임을 8.9 자로 안보리 의장에게 알려왔음. (S/22916)

가.군요원: 300 명을 250 명으로 감축

나.의료진 축소

다.병참인력 감축및 재배치

라.공병대 감축 (우선 293 명을 85 명으로 감축, 국경획정위 작업종료시 50 명으로 재감축)

2.이락내 억류자 문제

쿠웨이트가 유엔측에 통보해온바에 의하면 현재이락 억류자는 총 2,479 명이며 국별현황은 다음과 같음.

가.쿠웨이트 1,839 명

나. UAE 2, 사우디 66, 시리아 18, 애급 35, 오만 2, 레바논 14, 소말리아 1, 바레인 3, 비율빈 7, 인도 13, 파키스탄 4, 이란 12, 스리랑카 1

다.국적불명 462 명

3.이락 특정무기 폐기관련 고공정찰 추진

유엔이락 특정무기 폐기 특위측은 동 특위임무수행과 관련 이락에 대한 고공관측을 위해 미측으로부터 고공정찰기 1대를 협조받아 이달부터 운용예정이라고 8.7 자로 발표하였음.한편 이락측은 유엔의 정찰비행 자체는 방해하지 않겠다는 입장을 밝혔으나, 미군기를 사용하는것에 대해 불만을 표시하였음.(S/22899) 끝

(대사 노창희-국장)

국기국 1차보 중아국 외정실 분석관 안기부

PAGE 1 91.08.13 08:53 WG

외신 1과 통제관

0067

원 본

암호수신

외 무 부

종 별 :

번 호 : UNW-2163 일 시 : 91 0814 2000

수 신 : 장관(국연,중동일,기정)

발 신 : 주 유엔 대사

제 목 : 안보리 비공식협의(이락문제)

연:UNW-2075,2096

1. 금 8.14 안보리는 비공식협의를 갖고 연호 이락관련 현재 계류중인 결의안문제를 토의한바, 당관에서 탐문한 금일 협의주요결과를 아래보고함.

가. 석유수입 공제상한선 관련 결의안(문안합의)

1)사무총장안대로 30 프로 상한선 설정합의

2)동 상한선 수시 재검토예정

나. 이락의 특정무기폐기 이행위반 규탄결의안(문안합의)

1)안보리 휴전결의상의 의무위반, IAEA 와의 안전협정 상의 의무불이행 규탄

2)관련 자료공개, 사찰협조, 은폐금지, 항공 정찰활동 보장, 의료. 농업.산업목적외의 일체 이락측의 핵관련 활동중지, 사찰요원 특권.면제, 편익 지원보장요구

다. 이락 석유수출 일부허용 결의안

1)상세 연호참조

2)동 연호 문안중 1-2 항 식량및 여타 인도적 필수품목 관련 유엔역할, 특히 통제외에 관리역할 명시문제에 관해 막바지 절충

2. 안보리는 명일 공식회의를 개최, 상기 3 개 결의안 처리예정임.

첨부:상기결의안문안:UNW(F)-432 끝

(대사 노창희-국장)

국기국 1차보 중아국 외정실 분석관 안기부

PAGE 1

91.08.15 09:45

외신 2과 통제관 CE

0068

원 본

외 무 부

종 별 :

번 호 : UNW-2169 일 시 : 91 0816 1800

수 신 : 장 관(국연,중동일,기정)

발 신 : 주 유엔 대사

제 목 : 안보리회의(이락문제)

연: UNW-2163

1. 안보리는 8.15 공식회의에서 연호 3개결의안을 채택함.

가. 이락 석유수출 일부허용 (S/RES/706)

- 부표결과:13-1 (쿠바)-1 (예멘)

- 6개월기간중 16억불 한도내에서 석유수출 허용

- 수출대금은 유엔사무총장 관할하의 특별구좌에입금

- 수출대금 30 퍼센트는 유엔 보상기금에 입금

나. 석유수입공제 상한선 (S/RES/705)

- 부표결과 :전원찬성

- 30 프로 상한선 설정합의

다. 이락의 무기폐기 이행위반 규탄(S/RES/707)

- 부표결과:전원찬성

2. 주유엔 이락대사는 결의 706 은 이락을 식민지와 같은 예속상태로 만든다고 비난하고 이런조건하에서는 석유수출을 하지 않을것이라고 반박함.

첨부: UNW(F)-433 끝

(대사 노창희-국장)

국기국 1차보 중아국 외정실 안기부

PAGE 1

91.08.17 10:03 WG

외신 1과 통제관

0069

UNITED
NATIONS

S

Security Council

Distr.
GENERAL

S/RES/706 (1991)
15 August 1991

RESOLUTION 706 (1991)

Adopted by the Security Council at its 3004th meeting, on 15 August 1991

The Security Council,

Recalling its previous relevant resolutions and in particular resolutions 661 (1990), 686 (1991), 687 (1991), 688 (1991), 692 (1991), 699 (1991) and 705 (1991),

Taking note of the report (S/22799) dated 15 July 1991 of the inter-agency mission headed by the executive delegate of the Secretary-General for the United Nations inter-agency humanitarian programme for Iraq, Kuwait and the Iraq/Turkey and Iraq/Iran border areas,

Concerned by the serious nutritional and health situation of the Iraqi civilian population as described in this report, and by the risk of a further deterioration of this situation,

Concerned also that the repatriation or return of all Kuwaitis and third country nationals or their remains present in Iraq on or after 2 August 1990, pursuant to paragraph 2 (c) of resolution 686 (1991), and paragraphs 30 and 31 of resolution 687 (1991) has not yet been fully carried out,

Taking note of the conclusions of the above-mentioned report, and in particular of the proposal for oil sales by Iraq to finance the purchase of foodstuffs, medicines and materials and supplies for essential civilian needs for the purpose of providing humanitarian relief,

Taking note also of the letters dated 14 April 1991, 31 May 1991, 6 June 1991, 9 July 1991 and 22 July 1991 from the Minister of Foreign Affairs of Iraq and the Permanent Representative of Iraq to the Chairman of the Committee established by resolution 661 (1990) concerning the export from Iraq of petroleum and petroleum products,

Convinced of the need for equitable distribution of humanitarian relief to all segments of the Iraqi civilian population through effective monitoring and transparency,

91-26589 3574Z (E) /...

0070

Recalling and reaffirming in this regard its resolution 688 (1991) and in particular the importance which the Council attaches to Iraq allowing unhindered access by international humanitarian organizations to all those in need of assistance in all parts of Iraq and making available all necessary facilities for their operation, and in this connection stressing the important and continuing role played by the Memorandum of Understanding between the United Nations and the Government of Iraq of 18 April 1991 (S/22663),

Recalling that, pursuant to resolutions 687 (1991), 692 (1991) and 699 (1991), Iraq is required to pay the full costs of the Special Commission and the IAEA in carrying out the tasks authorized by section C of resolution 687 (1991), and that the Secretary-General in his report to the Security Council of 15 July 1991 (S/22792), submitted pursuant to paragraph 4 of resolution 699 (1991), expressed the view that the most obvious way of obtaining financial resources from Iraq to meet the costs of the Special Commission and the IAEA would be to authorize the sale of some Iraqi petroleum and petroleum products; recalling further that Iraq is required to pay its contributions to the Compensation Fund and half the costs of the Iraq-Kuwait Boundary Demarcation Commission, and recalling further that in its resolutions 686 (1991) and 687 (1991) the Security Council demanded that Iraq return in the shortest possible time all Kuwaiti property seized by it and requested the Secretary-General to take steps to facilitate this,

Acting under Chapter VII of the Charter,

1. Authorizes all States, subject to the decision to be taken by the Security Council pursuant to paragraph 5 below and notwithstanding the provisions of paragraphs 3 (a), 3 (b) and 4 of resolution 661 (1990), to permit the import, during a period of 6 months from the date of passage of the resolution pursuant to paragraph 5 below, of petroleum and petroleum products originating in Iraq sufficient to produce a sum to be determined by the Council following receipt of the report of the Secretary-General requested in paragraph 5 of this resolution but not to exceed 1.6 billion United States dollars for the purposes set out in this resolution and subject to the following conditions:

(a) Approval of each purchase of Iraqi petroleum and petroleum products by the Security Council Committee established by resolution 661 (1990) following notification to the Committee by the State concerned;

(b) Payment of the full amount of each purchase of Iraqi petroleum and petroleum products directly by the purchaser in the State concerned into an escrow account to be established by the United Nations and to be administered by the Secretary-General, exclusively to meet the purposes of this resolution;

(c) Approval by the Council, following the report of the Secretary-General requested in paragraph 5 of this resolution, of a scheme for the purchase of foodstuffs, medicines and materials and supplies for essential civilian needs as referred to in paragraph 20 of resolution 687 (1991), in particular health related materials, all of which to be labelled to the extent

0071 /...

possible as being supplied under this scheme, and for all feasible and appropriate United Nations monitoring and supervision for the purpose of assuring their equitable distribution to meet humanitarian needs in all regions of Iraq and to all categories of the Iraqi civilian population, as well as all feasible and appropriate management relevant to this purpose, such a United Nations role to be available if desired for humanitarian assistance from other sources;

(d) The sum authorized in this paragraph to be released by successive decisions of the Committee established by resolution 661 (1990) in three equal portions after the Council has taken the decision provided for in paragraph 5 below on the implementation of this resolution, and notwithstanding any other provision of this paragraph, the sum to be subject to review concurrently by the Council on the basis of its ongoing assessment of the needs and requirements;

2. _Decides_ that a part of the sum in the account to be established by the Secretary-General shall be made available by him to finance the purchase of foodstuffs, medicines and materials and supplies for essential civilian needs, as referred to in paragraph 20 of resolution 687, and the cost to the United Nations of its roles under this resolution and of other necessary humanitarian activities in Iraq;

3. _Decides further_ that a part of the sum in the account to be established by the Secretary-General shall be used by him for appropriate payments to the United Nations Compensation Fund, the full costs of carrying out the tasks authorized by Section C of resolution 687 (1991), the full costs incurred by the United Nations in facilitating the return of all Kuwaiti property seized by Iraq, and half the costs of the Boundary Commission;

4. _Decides_ that the percentage of the value of exports of petroleum and petroleum products from Iraq, authorized under this resolution to be paid to the United Nations Compensation Fund, as called for in paragraph 19 of resolution 687 (1991), and as defined in paragraph 6 of resolution 692 (1991), shall be the same as the percentage decided by the Security Council in paragraph 2 of resolution 705 (1991) for payments to the Compensation Fund, until such time as the Governing Council of the Fund decides otherwise;

5. _Requests_ the Secretary-General to submit within 20 days of the date of adoption of this resolution a report to the Security Council for decision on measures to be taken in order to implement paragraphs 1 (a), (b) and (c), estimates of the humanitarian requirements of Iraq set out in paragraph 2 above and of the amount of Iraq's financial obligations set out in paragraph 3 above up to the end of the period of the authorization in paragraph 1 above, as well as the method for taking the necessary legal measures to ensure that the purposes of this resolution are carried out and the method for taking account of the costs of transportation of such Iraqi petroleum and petroleum products;

/...

0072

6. Further requests the Secretary-General in consultation with the International Committee of the Red Cross to submit within 20 days of the date of adoption of this resolution a report to the Security Council on activities undertaken in accordance with paragraph 31 of resolution 687 (1991) in connection with facilitating the repatriation or return of all Kuwaiti and third country nationals or their remains present in Iraq on or after 2 August 1990;

7. Requires the Government of Iraq to provide to the Secretary-General and appropriate international organizations on the first day of the month immediately following the adoption of the present resolution and on the first day of each month thereafter until further notice, a statement of the gold and foreign currency reserves it holds whether in Iraq or elsewhere;

8. Calls upon all States to cooperate fully in the implementation of this resolution;

9. Decides to remain seized of the matter.

0073

UNITED
NATIONS

S

Security Council

Distr.
GENERAL

S/22957
16 August 1991
ENGLISH
ORIGINAL: ARABIC

LETTER DATED 16 AUGUST 1991 FROM THE PERMANENT REPRESENTATIVE OF IRAQ TO THE UNITED NATIONS ADDRESSED TO THE PRESIDENT OF THE SECURITY COUNCIL

I have the honour to refer to the statement that I made before the Security Council at its meeting held on 15 August 1991. At that time I stated that, because of the time constraint and the length of the statements that I had prepared on the draft resolutions subsequently adopted by the Council on the same day as its resolutions 705, 706 and 707 (1991), I would present only a summary of Iraq's position with regard to resolutions 705 and 707.

Accordingly, I am sending you the full texts of the statements relating to our position on the two aforementioned resolutions.

I should be grateful if you would have these two statements circulated as a document of the Security Council.

(Signed) Abdul Amir A. AL-ANBARI
Ambassador
Permanent Representative

91-26709 2634j (E)

0074 /...

Annex I

Statement by Mr. Abdul Amir A. Al-Anbari to the Security Council at its meeting on 15 August 1991

Mr. President,

I should like to tell you once again how much my delegation appreciates the wisdom with which you have been directing the Council's work since you became President for the month of August.

The Council is meeting today to consider the recommendation made by the Secretary-General in his letter dated 31 May 1991 (S/22661), namely that the contribution to be levied on Iraq's petroleum reserves should be limited to 30 per cent. It also appears that the contribution would begin to be deducted as soon as petroleum exports resume. In this connection, I would like to reiterate what the Iraqi Minister for Foreign Affairs said in the letter which he sent to the President of the Security Council for May 1991, and also what was said in note No. 124 dated 27 May 1991 from the Iraqi Mission, annexed thereto, before explaining to the Council why it should lower the level of the contribution and defer the date on which the contribution would begin to be levied.

The Iraqi Mission has already sent the Secretary-General an official report (annexed to its note No. 72 of 29 April 1991) on Iraq's economic situation, for him to take into account in calculating the contribution referred to in paragraph 19 of Security Council resolution 687 (1991).

The Iraqi Mission also requested the Secretary-General, in its note No. 77 of 1 May 1991, to bring the aforesaid report to the attention of members of the Council. We appreciate the fact that, in proposing a 30 per cent ceiling, the Secretary-General has sought to take account both of the report and of the considerations mentioned in paragraph 19 of resolution 687 (1991). None the less, my Government, which is a daily witness to the sufferings endured by the Iraqi population of all social classes and to the economic difficulties faced by Iraq as a society and a State as a result of the continuation of the embargo imposed on Iraq on 6 August 1990, considers it useful to recall the three considerations which must, according to paragraph 19 mentioned above, be taken into account in determining the level of the contribution, namely:

- the requirements of the people of Iraq;
- Iraq's payment capacity in the light of its external debt service;
- the needs of the Iraqi economy.

0075

/...

These considerations are neither static nor fixed; on the contrary, they are constantly evolving: the situation is in fact becoming increasingly critical and is deteriorating steadily both as a result of the continued embargo on Iraqi imports and on Iraq's petroleum exports and because certain States members of the Sanctions Committee have managed to prevent the implementation of paragraph 23 of resolution 687 (1991) providing for exceptions to be made to the prohibition against the export of Iraqi petroleum in order to finance the purchase of foodstuffs and other products. The international press, in particular The Washington Post of 23 June 1991 and The New York Times of 25 June 1991, and also the study published by a Harvard University medical mission which visited Iraq, the exhaustive report entitled "Modern warfare and the environment: a case study of the Gulf war" published by Greenpeace last May and the even more detailed report of the mission headed by Prince Sadruddin Aga Khan, Executive Delegate of the Secretary-General, have established objectively and impartially, with supporting facts and statistics, that the 42 days of air raids against Iraq inflicted damage on the economic and industrial infrastructure and on the means of modern life which, like the social, economic and health consequences of the bombing, was far more serious than reported in the military communiqués and preliminary assessments issued during and after the cessation of military operations. Likewise, the continuation of economic sanctions despite Iraq's acceptance of all the relevant Council resolutions and its full cooperation with the commissions and missions sent by the United Nations, and the failure of the Sanctions Committee to approve the resumption of petroleum exports under the exception provided for in paragraph 23 of resolution 687 (1991), are likely to perpetuate the consequences of the savage bombing raids on Iraq, thereby affecting future generations, the environment and Iraq's economic means of development. We are forced to ask ourselves, therefore, what is the real purpose of continuing the embargo against the Iraqi people and insisting that Iraq may not benefit from the exception provided for in paragraph 23 of resolution 687 (1991).

It is no exaggeration to say that continuing the embargo goes beyond the goals pursued by the Security Council and that the serious consequences of such a course, which include the spread of epidemics, will sooner or later affect the other countries of the region at the least.

Let me now give a conservative assessment of Iraq's financial obligations with respect to servicing its external debt, as well as of the basic needs of the Iraqi population in terms of food, medical and other supplies and the requirements for the reconstruction of the country's economic infrastructure as provided for in paragraph 19 of resolution 687.

On 31 December 1990, Iraq's external debt and financial commitments amounted to more than 13,118,000,000 dinars or more than $42,097,000,000, not taking into account the interest on these debts, namely an outstanding amount of $3.4 billion (one dinar equals about $3.20 at the official rate). These debts represent for the Iraqi economy 65 per cent of GDP, and 97 per cent of them are scheduled for repayment over the coming five years. For this reason, we have requested - as I shall explain below - a five-year grace period in order to enable us to honour these debts.

0076 /...

As for the basic needs, which relate also to imports or the replenishment of food reserves, primary commodities and the expenditures to be incurred on partially repairing the damaged facilities in the civilian and public sector and relaunching the development projects that were under way before the embargo, these are estimated at $140 billion, or $28 billion a year over the period 1991-1995. This figure represents only 60 per cent of the total expenditure, i.e. solely the portion in foreign currency.

Before concluding, I should like to recall paragraph 21 of resolution 687, which provides that the Security Council shall review the embargo on Iraqi imports, with a view to easing or lifting it in the light of the policies and practices of the Government of Iraq in terms of the implementation of all relevant resolutions of the Security Council. Despite its reservations regarding some of these resolutions, my Government has accepted them all and has sought to implement them in good faith and in full cooperation with the United Nations and the commissions and missions it has sent to Iraq with a view to the implementation of the resolutions in question. My Government has done practically everything called for in these resolutions, although their final implementation depends on the work programmes of the international commissions and missions established for this purpose. This may take a long time where certain aspects are concerned, such as the elimination of weapons of mass destruction, the demarcation of the international frontiers and other issues for which the Security Council has assigned responsibility to the Secretariat or the commissions or other bodies established for this purpose.

The measures taken by my Government in implementation of the Security Council resolutions have been described in detail by the Iraqi Minister for Foreign Affairs in his letter dated 8 June 1991 addressed to the Ministers for Foreign Affairs of some countries members of the Council; that letter is annexed hereto as an integral part of my statement.

Iraq accordingly has high hopes that the Council will review the provisions of the embargo - since more than 130 days have elapsed since the adoption of resolution 687 on 3 April 1991 - and that it will take a decision on this subject in the light of the considerations set forth above.

Annex II

Letter dated 8 June 1991 from the Minister for Foreign Affairs of Iraq addressed to a number of the Ministers for Foreign Affairs of the States members of the Security Council

As you are well aware, the Iraqi Government accepted Security Council resolution 687 (1991) and gave notice of its acceptance in its letter of 6 April 1991 addressed to both the President of the Security Council and the Secretary-General. I should like on this occasion to confirm to you that the Iraqi Government has complied with the said resolution and adopted a positive attitude towards it ever since its adoption. Allow me to review for you the measures taken in this connection by the Government of Iraq.

1. In connection with section A of the resolution, concerning demarcation of the boundary between Iraq and Kuwait, the Iraqi Government has appointed its representative to the Boundary Demarcation Commission, which held its first session of meetings in New York from 23 to 24 May 1991. Iraq's representative participated actively, in a constructive and cooperative spirit, in the work of that session.

2. In connection with section B of resolution 687 (1991), concerning deployment of the United Nations Iraq-Kuwait Observation Mission (UNIKOM), the competent Iraqi authorities have received the Chief Military Observer, Major-General Günther Greindl, on several occasions in Baghdad since his appointment, together with his assistants. Agreement was reached at these meetings on all the requirements for the deployment of UNIKOM in the demilitarized zone established under the resolution, which came into effect on 9 May 1991.

Cooperation between the competent Iraqi authorities and UNIKOM continues through the channels designated for that purpose between, respectively, the Iraqi Government, UNIKOM headquarters and the United Nations Secretariat.

3. In connection with section C of the resolution, which calls for a series of undertakings to dispense with weapons of mass destruction and neither to use, develop, construct nor acquire any such weapons, Iraq has deposited the instrument whereby the Republic of Iraq ratifies the Convention on the Prohibition of the Development, Production and Stockpiling of Bacteriological (Biological) and Toxin Weapons and on Their Destruction, of 10 April 1972. Iraq has also affirmed its unconditional commitment to its obligations under the Geneva Protocol for the Prohibition of the Use in War of Asphyxiating, Poisonous or Other Gases, and of Bacteriological Methods of Warfare, signed at Geneva on 17 June 1925. In addition, the Iraqi Government has provided details of the locations, amounts and types of items relating to chemical weapons and ballistic missiles specified in the resolution and agreed to an inspection of the sites concerned, as laid down in the resolution.

/...

0078

Iraq has also unconditionally undertaken not to use, develop, construct or acquire any of the items specified in the resolution. It has affirmed its obligations under the Treaty on the Non-Proliferation of Nuclear Weapons of 1 July 1968 and unconditionally agreed not to acquire or develop nuclear weapons or nuclear-weapons-usable material. Iraq informed the International Atomic Energy Agency (IAEA), in a letter dated 27 April 1991 from the Minister for Foreign Affairs, that it was prepared to cooperate with the Agency in implementing the provisions of the resolution: the letter was accompanied by tables providing information on Iraq's nuclear facilities. Iraq has also provided detailed information on the situation with regard to other weapons covered by the resolution to the Special Commission established to implement section C.

In a letter dated 17 May 1991, Iraq agreed to the proposals contained in the Secretary-General's letter of 6 May 1991 concerning the privileges and immunities of the Special Commission and its visiting teams.

The nuclear weapons inspection team visited Iraq from 14 to 22 May 1991. On 23 May 1991, IAEA issued a statement affirming that Iraq had cooperated fully and responded to all the requests submitted by the inspection team. A chemical weapons inspection team, accompanied by the Chairman of the Special Commission, is to visit Iraq from 9 to 15 June in order to begin its mission. Iraq has made all the necessary arrangements to ensure that the inspection team's mission is a success.

4. In connection with section D of the resolution, which relates to the return of Kuwaiti property, Mr. J. Richard Foran, Assistant Secretary-General and official responsible for coordinating the return of such property, visited Iraq twice during the month of May 1991. The competent Iraqi authorities expressed their readiness to hand over the Kuwaiti property of which Iraq had already notified the Secretariat of the United Nations. A Kuwaiti civilian aircraft was, in fact, handed over at Amman on 11 May 1991. Mr. Foran also undertook a wide-ranging field visit and saw for himself the gold, coins, banknotes, civilian aircraft, museum antiquities and books that will be returned to Kuwait immediately an agreement is reached establishing a location for the handing over, it being understood that it is this property whose handing over Mr. Foran has determined should have priority at the present stage. The same procedures will doubtless be applied to other Kuwaiti property.

5. In connection with sections E and F, which relate to compensation and the lifting of sanctions, no measures are required on the part of Iraq.

6. In connection with section G of the resolution, the competent Iraqi authorities have taken and are continuing to take measures to repatriate all Kuwaiti and third-country nationals, and they have provided lists of their names and have facilitated the access of the delegation of the International Committee of the Red Cross (ICRC) in Baghdad to all such persons wherever detained. It should be mentioned that the number of those freed and repatriated has reached 6,366 (6,289 Kuwaitis, 36 Americans, 5 Italians,

13 Saudis, 17 Frenchmen, 1 Spaniard, 2 Brazilians, 1 Norwegian, 1 Uruguayan and 1 Irishman). The competent Iraqi authorities are still diligently searching for missing subjects of coalition countries with a view to finding them and repatriating them following registration by the ICRC delegation. The competent Iraqi authorities have directly facilitated all matters relating to the work of the ICRC delegation in the registration of Kuwaiti nationals present in Iraq, thereby enabling the delegation to register more than 3,000 Kuwaitis, and they have endeavoured to return the remains of 15 subjects of the coalition countries.

7. In connection with section H, which relates to international terrorism, it should be mentioned that Iraq is a party to the international conventions relating to numerous aspects of this matter and that it abides by the obligations set forth therein. Iraq has not supported any terrorist activities.

In providing you with these clarifications, we are prompted by the hope that you will deem it appropriate to take account of the facts set forth above in any review that the Security Council might intend to make of Iraq's position on the implementation of Security Council resolution 687 (1991).

(Signed) Ahmed HUSSEIN
Minister for Foreign Affairs
of the Republic of Iraq

0080 /...

Annex III

Statement of the Permanent Representative of Iraq to the United Nations concerning the draft resolution contained in document S/22942 of 14 August 1991, made to the Security Council on 15 August 1991

It is to be noted that the draft resolution is based on two underlying elements which feature in all of its preambular and operative paragraphs and which can be summed up as follows: the circumstances that presented themselves to the second inspection team in the course of its visit to Iraq from 22 June to 3 July 1991, as referred to in the third, fourth, fifth, eighth, ninth and tenth preambular paragraphs; and the resolution of the Board of Governors of the International Atomic Energy Agency (IAEA) of 18 July 1991, as mentioned in the twelfth preambular paragraph.

1. Iraq has already explained in a clear and unequivocal manner and on more than one occasion the circumstances encountered by the second inspection team. The high-level mission led by Mr. Rolf Ekéus was informed during its visit to Iraq of the details of these circumstances, and the Iraqi Government, at the highest levels, provided unambiguous assurances that the Iraqi authorities would provide all possible facilities to the inspection teams. In its report, the high-level mission referred to these assurances and stated that the future would show the extent to which the Government of Iraq would give effect to them. Since that time, several teams have visited Iraq, and a nuclear inspection team and a biological inspection team are still there at this moment. Iraq provided the third nuclear inspection team with all possible facilities and furnished it with an enormous amount of information, as was stated by the Director-General of IAEA at the news conference he held at United Nations Headquarters in New York on 30 July 1991. The leader of the fourth team, Mr. David Kay, has told the news agencies in Baghdad that his team is making progress, that it has obtained much information and that the Iraqis are cooperating with it. The other teams that have visited Iraq have given no indication that they encountered obstacles or any significant problems in their work.

Is it then reasonable, more than a month after the circumstances experienced by the second inspection team and given the excellent experience of cooperation with all the teams that have visited Iraq during this month, to maintain that Iraq is not cooperating and that it is not meeting its obligations? We had been hoping that the Security Council would express its satisfaction at the cooperation that the United Nations teams are receiving from Iraq rather than anticipating that it would adopt a new resolution condemning Iraq because of one incident. Most of the members of the same second inspection team are now in Iraq; they are receiving unparalleled cooperation; information is being exchanged on an immediate basis; and the Council can solicit the opinion of the team leader presently in Baghdad. Is this not one more indication of Iraq's commitment to the Security Council resolution in question? The Council must take this into account.

/...

0081

2. The Board of Governors of IAEA adopted a resolution on 18 July 1991 condemning Iraq for non-compliance with the Agency's safeguards system and informed the Security Council accordingly under the provisions of article XII.C of the Agency's statute. IAEA did not make this notification because it was a task assigned to it under the terms of Security Council resolution 687 (1991), and the notification is therefore no part of that resolution. The situation recorded by the Board of Governors is one that existed before the adoption of Security Council resolution 687 (1991), and that situation came to an end owing to the destruction inflicted on Iraq's nuclear installations. From the legal point of view, therefore, it is not valid that the present draft resolution, which has the appearance of being intended for the purpose of following up the implementation of Security Council resolution 687 (1991), should be based on a situation that existed prior to the adoption of that resolution. In no legal system does a law or a resolution have retroactive effect. The twelfth preambular paragraph cannot therefore be a consideration for the present draft resolution, and the same applies to operative paragraphs 2 and 3.

Moreover, the resolution adopted by the Board of Governors on 18 July contains two operative paragraphs that should be taken into account. The first, paragraph 3, calls upon Iraq to take remedial measures, and it has done this by means of the letters it addressed to the Director-General of IAEA on 10 and 12 July 1991 and the letters exchanged by the chief of the third United Nations inspection team and his Iraqi counterpart. There are no longer in Iraq any nuclear materials, installations or sites that have not been declared. Another operative paragraph of the same resolution, paragraph 7, refers the matter to the next regular session of the IAEA General Conference. This is the supreme authority of the Agency, and most of the world's countries are represented there. Does the present draft resolution seek to prejudge any resolution that might be adopted by the IAEA General Conference and thus deprive the General Conference of the right to decide on a matter that is within its jurisdiction? Under the terms of the Agency's statute, it can take any necessary measures against any of its members. Operative paragraph 2 of the present draft resolution prejudges a matter that is before the next session of the IAEA General Conference by virtue of a resolution of the Board of Governors.

3. With regard to paragraph 3 of the present draft resolution, we should like to assure the Council that the technicians on both sides, the members of the United Nations teams and their Iraqi counterparts, have reached agreement on clear procedures and have put them into effect in such a way as to ensure the convenience of the members of the teams and the speedy completion of the inspection task and to reduce the number of inspection sites to the extent possible so as to facilitate the future task of the teams. Agreement is reached between the two sides on the movement of materials and parts, and times and locations are established before movement is begun. This happened while the third inspection team was there, and it is now taking place while the fourth team is there, without any complications or superfluous bureaucratic formalities. The Council should welcome and record its satisfaction at the establishment of this mechanism, one that is facilitating the work of the inspection teams and reducing the amount of time lost.

/...

4. In light of the foregoing, we feel that the resolution has no substance since it is largely covered by the agreement on the status, privileges and immunities of the Special Commission, IAEA and the inspection teams, an agreement which has been accepted by Iraq. From our point of view, this agreement is workable when the circumstances for cooperation and coordination are present and in our opinion they have come into being and the last month has demonstrated that they have become more firmly established.

5. We should like to ask the Special Commission and the IAEA inspection teams whether they have entered locations that they were previously prohibited from entering or were prevented from inspecting the items that they contain. According to our information, not a single location remains, as is indicated in the reports of the inspection teams, that the teams have not entered and whose contents they have not inspected. More precisely, there was one location around which commotion arose on 28 June 1991. The chief of the third nuclear inspection team agreed to the movement of the items there, equipment and machinery, to the Tuwaitha site. The removal was supervised by two of the members of the United Nations team, the team registered and photographed all of the items, and they were unloaded from the trucks under the supervision of members of the team. The United Nations team released the non-nuclear equipment for use in the reconstruction of basic services in Iraq, and the trucks left the Tuwaitha site under the supervision and with the agreement of the team. All of this is established in the lists and inventories exchanged by the third United Nations team and the Iraqi side. The equipment was stored in an orderly fashion in order to facilitate future inspection by the team. All of this took place quietly and without uproar. So what reason can there now be that the present draft resolution should contain operative paragraph 3? The Council should rather express its satisfaction at the practical steps that have been taken in this regard.

6. With regard to paragraph 3 (v), which refers to the right of inspection teams to use aircraft, we should like to state that Iraq is not against the use of helicopters or fixed-wing aircraft by inspection teams. What it would, however, like to make clear in this respect is that there are difficulties in ensuring the safety of such flights because of the present situation with regard to aspects of logistics, communications and control following the war.

7. Paragraph 4 of the draft resolution determines that Iraq retains no ownership interest in items to be destroyed, removed or rendered harmless. This text is not realistic from the detailed, technical point of view. It is neither wise nor economically feasible to abandon wrecked materials and equipment without returning them to use in other, civilian, industrial roles. Can it be that the scrap metal of a piece of equipment that has been destroyed should be abandoned rather than put to use by melting it down and reusing it for civilian purposes? Can it be that damaged copper piping, for example, should be left lying useless rather than be reused in meeting the Iraqi people's need for basic services? If the inspection teams render a machine harmless, then why cannot Iraq retain its right to use it for another purpose in which there is no harm? From these and other examples, we can see that this paragraph is not realistic and causes unjustifiable material damage to the people of Iraq.

0083 /...

The draft resolution before you not only lacks legal justification but constitutes a fresh violation of Iraq's sovereignty and imposes upon it new burdens under a veil of international legitimacy by seeking to have the Council adopt arbitrary resolutions. This reveals to the entire world that these resolutions are officially adopted by the majority of the Council but are actually part of an iniquitous and hostile policy directed against Iraq by means of which the neo-colonialist States are seeking to make of Iraq a deterrent example to other third world countries and a field of experiment for their schemes to intervene in the affairs of the other countries of the world in order to prevent them from being able to achieve economic development and exercise control over their oil and other natural resources and in order to impose their political hegemony on them.

It is saddening that certain Western States that are permanent members of the Council should make of it an instrument for the pursuit of illegal and hostile actions detrimental to peace and security in the region. They do so under the cover of international legitimacy and by seeking to have new resolutions adopted on one pretext or another in order to tighten their stranglehold on the Iraqi people and hold it hostage to their embargo and their economic sanctions. As long as the Iraqi people does not submit to the wishes of these States, its oil resources are to be held in pawn by them after the countries in question have consolidated their control of other sources of oil in the Arabian Gulf.

COPY

주 국 련 대 표 부

주국련 20313- 656 1991. 8 . 21.

수신 : 장관

참조 : 국제기구조약국장, 중동아프리카국장

제목 : 걸프사태 (안보리)

표제관련 91.8.15 안보리 공식회의록을 별첨과 같이 송부합니다.

첨 부 : 상기 문서(S / PV. 3004). 끝.

주 국 련 대 사

47342

0085

UNITED
NATIONS

S

Security Council

PROVISIONAL

S/PV.3004
15 August 1991

ENGLISH

PROVISIONAL VERBATIM RECORD OF THE THREE THOUSAND AND FOURTH MEETING

Held at Headquarters, New York,
on Thursday, 15 August 1991, at 3.30 p.m.

President:	Mr. AYALA LASSO	(Ecuador)
Members:	Austria	Mr. HAJNOCZI
	Belgium	Mr. van DAELE
	China	Mr. LI Daoyu
	Côte d'Ivoire	Mr. BECHIO
	Cuba	Mr. ALARCON DE QUESADA
	France	Mr. ROCHEREAU DE LA SABLIERE
	India	Mr. GHAREKHAN
	Romania	Mr. FLOREAN
	Union of Soviet Socialist Republics	Mr. LOZINSKY
	United Kingdom of Great Britain and Northern Ireland	Mr. RICHARDSON
	United States	Mr. PICKERING
	Yemen	Mr. AL-ASHTAL
	Zaire	Mr. LUKABU KHABOUJI N'ZAJI
	Zimbabwe	Mr. MUMBENGEGWI

This record contains the original text of speeches delivered in English and interpretations of speeches in the other languages. The final text will be printed in the Official Records of the Security Council.

Corrections should be submitted to original speeches only. They should be sent under the signature of a member of the delegation concerned, within one week, to the Chief, Official Records Editing Section, Department of Conference Services, room DC2-750, 2 United Nations Plaza, and incorporated in a copy of the record.

91-61101/A 5529V (E)

0086

The meeting was called to order at 3.30 p.m.

ADOPTION OF THE AGENDA

The agenda was adopted.

THE SITUATION BETWEEN IRAQ AND KUWAIT

The PRESIDENT (interpretation from Spanish): I should like to inform the Council that I have received letters from the representatives of Iraq and Kuwait in which they request to be invited to participate in the discussion of the item on the Council's agenda. In conformity with the usual practice I propose, with the consent of the Council, to invite those representatives to participate in the discussion without the right to vote, in accordance with the relevant provisions of the Charter and rule 37 of the Council's provisional rules of procedure.

There being no objection, it is so decided.

At the invitation of the President, Mr. Al-Anbari (Iraq) and Mr. Abulhasan (Kuwait) took places at the Council table.

The PRESIDENT (interpretation from Spanish): The Security Council will now begin its consideration of the item on its agenda. The Security Council is meeting in accordance with the understanding reached in its prior consultations.

Members of the Council have before them the following documents: S/22559, which contains a report of the Secretary-General of 2 May 1991 pursuant to paragraph 19 of Security Council resolution 687 (1991); S/22661, which contains a letter dated 30 May 1991 from the Secretary-General addressed to the President of the Security Council; S/22792, which contains a report of the Secretary-General of 15 July 1991 pursuant to paragraph 4 of Security Council resolution 699 (1991); S/22799, which contains a letter dated 15 July 1991 from the Secretary-General addressed to the President of the

(The President)

Security Council transmitting a report by the Executive Delegate of the Secretary-General on humanitarian needs in Iraq; S/22761, which contains a letter dated 4 July 1991 from the Secretary-General addressed to the President of the Security Council; S/22871, which contains a report of the Secretary-General of 1 August 1991 transmitting a plan for future ongoing monitoring and verification of Iraq's compliance with relevant parts of section C of Security Council resolution 687 (1991); S/22872, which contains a note by the Secretary-General of 1 August 1991 transmitting a plan for future ongoing monitoring and verification of Iraq's compliance with paragraph 12 of Security Council resolution 687 (1991).

Members of the Council also have before them three draft resolutions contained in the following documents:

S/22940, containing the text of a draft resolution prepared in the course of consultations;

S/22941, containing the text of a draft resolution submitted by Belgium, France, the Union of Soviet Socialist Republics, the United Kingdom of Great Britain and Northern Ireland and the United States of America. On page 3 of the English version of this document, four lines from the bottom of paragraph 1 (c), a small correction has to be made. The line starts with the words:

(spoke in English)

"regions of Iraq and to all categories of the Iraqi civilian population ...".

(spoke in Spanish)

A comma should appear after the word "population". The Secretary will make the appropriate correction in future editions of this text.

0088

(The President)

Lastly, we have document S/22942 containing the text of a draft resolution submitted by France, the Union of Soviet Socialist Republics, the United Kingdom of Great Britain and Northern Ireland and the United States of America.

The first speaker on my list is the representative of Kuwait, on whom I now call.

Mr. ABULHASAN (Kuwait) (interpretation from Arabic): On behalf of the delegation of Kuwait and on my own behalf, I am happy, Sir, to express our satisfaction at seeing you presiding over the Security Council this month. We have known you as a highly qualified diplomat and as a wise and just person. These qualities will assist the Council and ensure success of its work. Kuwait is grateful for the support of your Government and people, both during the crisis we have endured and during our struggle to eliminate the long-term consequences of that crisis. We are grateful also to the friendly people of Ecuador and wish to express our sincere appreciation.

My delegation also expresses its thanks to your predecessor, Ambassador Ricardo Alarcon de Quesada, the Permanent Representative of Cuba, for the successful manner in which he guided the work of the Council last month.

The Security Council is meeting today, one year after that sad day of 2 August 1990 and more than five months after the liberation of the sacred soil of Kuwait from the forces of aggression and oppression. Therefore, it would not be superfluous to recall the seriousness of Iraq's inhumane aggression against Kuwait and the tragic consequences of oppression, domination, violence and destruction, which are still visible today. The people of Kuwait are suffering from those consequences every day, as are

0089

(Mr. Abulhasan, Kuwait)

people of other nationalities, who had made a good livelihood in Kuwait.

Iraq's aggression against Kuwait was not undertaken in order to settle any political, economic or border dispute, as the Iraqi regime claimed at the beginning. The aggression was an expansionist act. It was methodically planned, using every means of treachery. At the time of its crisis and difficulty, Kuwait, a justice- and peace-loving State, appealed to international legitimacy, represented by the Security Council to offer assistance and save it from the nightmare of occupation and its train of abominable crimes.

The Security Council responded effectively to the crisis and fulfilled its responsibility: it adopted resolutions to halt the aggression and mitigate the consequences of the crisis, to restore usurped rights and to ensure respect for existing conventions and boundaries. As a result, Kuwait is once again a free and independent State - an oasis of peace where justice reigns.

Kuwait has today begun its march towards the reconstruction of the fundamental infrastructure of its country, which was destroyed by the Iraqi aggression. As a country that adheres to universal values and principles, we are deeply appreciative of the preponderantly positive role played by the members of the Security Council. They have followed the path of righteousness and exemplified the international solidarity and support displayed by the entire international community in calling for an end to Iraqi aggression and to the seven-month occupation of Kuwait, which devastated my country.

The Security Council is meeting today to consider three draft resolutions that deal, in essence, with the results of Iraq's aggression against my

0090

(Mr. Abulhasan, Kuwait)

country - aggression which the Council, by the adoption of its historic resolutions, notably resolution 687 (1991), has succeeded in arresting through the use of force within the framework of international legitimacy. Resolutions 686 (1991) and 687 (1991), both of which were adopted after the Iraqi defeat and its forced withdrawal from Kuwait, dealt with ending the consequences of the occupation of my country. The international community, as represented in this Council, has thus called upon Iraq to assume its responsibilities in order to put a complete and total end to its aggression and to safeguard the rights of the countries subjected to its aggression. The Council has called for a restoration of law based on justice and the tenets of the Charter - a system whereby countries would assume legal responsibility for all their actions.

The claims of Kuwait, of the Security Council and of the international community are the basis for lifting the sanctions against Iraq.

(Mr. Abulhasan, Kuwait)

They will deal with the following:

First, the immediate and total return of all prisoners, Kuwaitis and Kuwait residents;

Secondly, all weapons of mass destruction must be eliminated. They must be destroyed, removed or made inoperable;

Thirdly, the boundary between Iraq and Kuwait should be determined in accordance with the 1932 Convention;

Fourthly, Iraq must return all assets stolen by the aggressor regime and its army from Kuwait;

Fifthly, compensation shall be paid for damages incurred by Kuwait and its residents.

The Iraqi regime agreed to those claims by accepting Security Council resolutions, especially resolutions 686 (1991) and 687 (1991). All of us have awaited the complete implementation of those resolutions. However, the Iraqi regime seems not to have learned from the lesson it was given. It has not appreciated the seriousness of the Security Council and that of the international community in the implementation of the Council's resolutions. This might create a dangerous precedent in international relations by allowing an aggressor, after his defeat, to enjoy the fruits of his aggression, or to allow that aggressor to get away without assuming responsibility for that aggression.

Despite everything that the Iraqi people and economy have undergone, the Iraqi regime has pursued a policy of deception and delay. It has refused to assume its obligations. It has used unacceptable pretexts and illegal grounds for its actions, the results of which are, of course, well known. Some of those results are as follows:

0092

(Mr. Abulhasan, Kuwait)

Two thousand four hundred and nine Kuwaiti and non-Kuwaiti prisoners, nationals of 13 countries, are still imprisoned in Iraqi prisons. They have been deprived of their fundamental rights affirmed by Security Council resolutions 686 (1991) and 687 (1991), which call for the immediate return of those people to Kuwait. The prisoners have been used by the Iraqi regime as a means of pressure in future. They have been used for blackmail purposes. One need not be clairvoyant to realize this: those are obvious consequences. The prisoners are innocent. The Iraqi regime must be held responsible for its future actions. The lifting of economic sanctions is closely linked to a number of commitments, in particular the return of prisoners to Kuwait in keeping with paragraphs 21 and 30 of resolution 687 (1991).

The Iraqi regime in its pursuit of its treacherous actions claims that Iraq would return those prisoners but that the Government of Kuwait does not want to accept them. That is a big lie. The Iraqi regime completely ignored the detailed lists of names of Kuwaiti and non-Kuwaiti prisoners when it was submitted to the International Red Cross, which has been trying in every way to learn about their situation. There was no positive response from the Iraqi regime. We transmitted to the International Red Cross information about the locations where those prisoners were being held that had been received from prisoners freed prior to the cease-fire. Iraq claims that there were Kuwaitis and others who were taken prisoner and who wish to be repatriated, but that Kuwait does not want to receive them. That is what the Iraqi regime says. In fact, the truth is as follows:

First, the Iraqi regime deliberately is not drawing a distinction between reunion and prisoners, that is, they are doing the same thing with prisoners

0093

(Mr. Abulhasan, Kuwait)

as they are with those who were in Iraq when hostilities began on 17 January. Their repatriation has nothing whatever to do with those who were taken prisoner in Kuwaiti territory during the occupation and those who were prevented by hostilities from returning to Kuwait. Those people are not considered prisoners. All Kuwaitis wish to return to their country.

Secondly, the Iraqi regime wishes to send agents to Kuwait to implement its own plans under the pretext of repatriating prisoners.

Thirdly, a large number of Iraqis and others wish to flee that nefarious Iraqi regime. After throwing away their identity cards they have gone to the International Red Cross, saying that they were prisoners or people who wish to be repatriated.

Fourthly, the Government of Kuwait received from the International Red Cross the list that the Iraqi regime claims is the list of Kuwaiti and other prisoners who were imprisoned in Kuwait during Iraqi occupation and aggression. We looked at those lists and the names in them. We compared them with the Kuwaiti National Registry, a copy of which has been preserved in the United Nations in keeping with Security Council 679 (1990), which gives a census of all people in Kuwaiti territory up until 1 August 1990. We did not find among all those names what the Iraqi regime claims were Kuwaiti prisoners. We only found 252 names, which were immediately accepted for repatriation into Kuwait.

The clear truth is thus before you: the Iraqi regime is trampling upon human rights and dignity, even if the Iraqi people themselves are paying the price, in terms of their own health and of the famine existing in Iraq.

I urge the entire Council and the international community as a whole to exert pressure on the Iraqi regime to free those innocent people. The Council

(Mr. Abulhasan, Kuwait)

should tell that regime to free those innocent people, because that action would be in the interest of that regime. It would be in the interest of their credibility and of their people, and it would be in the interest of the cause of the lifting of sanctions.

0095

(Mr. Abulhasan, Kuwait)

There is another example of the deception practised by the Iraqi regime to avoid compliance with the Council's resolutions, namely, its possession of weapons of mass destruction - chemical, biological and nuclear. Only when threatened with the use of military force authorized by Security Council resolution 678 (1990) did the Iraqi regime disclose its capabilities.

We receive fresh information daily from the Special Commission on Iraqi practices and they are not those of complete cooperation. It reveals that Iraq has lost its credibility before the international community.

We ask: Is not the Iraqi regime aware of the fact that there is a link between the fulfilment of its obligations and the lifting of sanctions? Did not Iraq agree to those obligations as the basis for the implementation of a cease-fire, or is it just that the Iraqi regime has no respect for its people and its future and does not accept its obligations? Does it wish to maintain its aggression and expansion not only against its neighbours but also against its own people, who have no weapons with which to defend themselves?

In short, mere declarations by Iraq of its acceptance of Security Council resolutions must not make us complacent: we require a guarantee of the complete implementation of international legitimacy as embodied in those resolutions. If we follow the reports of the United Nations we will find wide discrepancies between what the regime says and what it does. In addition, experience teaches that this regime's practices show that it understands only the language of force in the monitoring and controlling of its irresponsible actions.

Despite the humanitarian and material disasters that have befallen Iraq, the policies of the Iraqi Government that led to the crisis are continuing. They are still at the basis of the tragedy of the Iraqi people, which today is

(Mr. Abulhasan, Kuwait)

still the object of aggression by the Iraqi regime, a regime that kills Iraqis both in the north and in the south.

But on the soil of Kuwait we find our oil wells ablaze, destroyed by the Iraqi forces before they retreated. These blazing oil wells are spewing poison and creating further problems. Those oil wells had been the very source of Kuwait's wealth and of the prosperity of other people living in Kuwait. The dimensions of the disaster are huge, and that is why Kuwaitis today feel that the Iraqi aggression against Kuwait, its people and residents of different nationalities, is a crime. Iraq's crimes come within the terms of the Convention on the Non-Applicability of Statutory Limitations to War Crimes and Crimes against Humanity, adopted by the General Assembly on 26 November 1968. That Convention specifically stipulates that the effective punishment of such crimes is an important element in preventing their repetition, in the protection of human rights and fundamental freedoms, the furtherance of cooperation among peoples and the promotion of international peace and security.

It is our hope that the Security Council or an organ of its creation will undertake an inquiry regarding these crimes by the Iraqi regime during its occupation of Kuwait, when it oppressed the Kuwaiti people and wreaked destruction on the environment of the region. These war crimes against mankind are detrimental to peace and are among the worst crimes in international law. We must not forget them.

Today it is not a matter of reciting Iraq's crimes against Kuwait, its people and the people of the Gulf region, and consequently against millions in the world who have suffered great injury. We must unmask Iraq's position which is leading it away from its obligations and from international

0097

(Mr. Abulhasan, Kuwait)

legitimacy. That is why we feel it is important for the Council to monitor closely the attitude of this outlaw regime. It is important that the Council keep Iraq's commitments under constant review in conformity with paragraph 21 of resolution 687 (1991), which states that the Security Council shall every 60 days review the policies and practices of the Government of Iraq, including the implementation of all relevant resolutions of the Security Council.

The sanctions imposed by the Security Council under its resolutions do not constitute war against Iraq nor do they arise out of a vacuum. They represent a legitimate collective action in keeping with the Charter. It has been implemented against a member of the international community whose regime is violating Security Council resolutions. For four months that regime has persisted in refusing to comply with legitimate international resolutions. Kuwait deems that it would be both useful and imperative for the Security Council to consider in detail any steps undertaken before the lifting of the embargo against the Iraqi regime, because we must be precise in the criteria that we have established for lifting the embargo. Iraq's commitment to respect and implement Security Council resolutions and the way in which it cooperates with the Secretary-General and the United Nations in establishing peace and security in the Gulf region on the basis of international legitimacy, as represented by the resolutions of the Security Council, must be scrutinized.

(Mr. Abulhasan, Kuwait)

The Iraqi regime has exposed international peace and security in the Gulf and throughout the world to danger; that danger will continue, and the region will not recover its stability until the current régime is placed under effective international control and its vindictive spirit reined in. The sanctions that have been imposed must not be lifted until the Iraqi regime ceases its actions intended to deceive the international community and violate its resolutions.

Kuwait hopes that today's meeting and the resolutions to be adopted will provide a new glimmer of hope that the ordeal of Kuwaitis and others in detention will come to an end. We hope the resolutions will lead to positive action by consolidating the activities of the Secretary-General and the International Committee of the Red Cross (ICRC), especially since under modern standards the detention of innocent victims in unsafe conditions constitutes a crime against humanity. The vital question of those prisoners is not only of interest to Kuwait and Kuwaitis; it possesses dimensions related to civilization, morality and law, all of which are of concern to the international community as a whole. The families and friends of some 2,400 people today call on this Council to consider its commitments with respect to the Third and Fourth Geneva Conventions.

The Security Council is writing history. It is bringing about a new international order based on justice, law and a commitment to respect international legitimacy. We are seeing a start to the implementation of the Charter purpose "to save succeeding generations from the scourge of war".

God will help us. Together we ask God that all prisoners be freed.

The PRESIDENT (interpretation from Spanish): I thank the representative of Kuwait for the kind words he addressed to me.

The next speaker is the representative of Iraq, on whom I now call.

Mr. AL-ANBARI (Iraq) (interpretation from Arabic): I wish at the outset to congratulate you, Sir, on your assumption of the presidency of the Security Council for this month. Your qualities are well known, and we are confident that your guidance of the Council's work will be a model of judiciousness, fairness and outstanding diplomacy.

I take this opportunity also to express our appreciation and thanks to your predecessor, Ambassador Alarcon de Quesada of Cuba, who presided over the Council last month.

As usual, the representative of the Kuwaiti régime, who spoke before me, employed false and obscene words, but I shall not respond to him, first, because I refuse to stoop to his level and secondly because most of what he said in his boring statement had nothing to do with the item on the Council's agenda.

There are three draft resolutions before the Council today. I want to state the position of my Government on each of those draft resolutions, but to save time for the Council I shall be brief in stating my Government's position on two of those texts, draft resolutions S/22940 and S/22942. But I request that the complete reply of my Government be published in official documents of the Security Council.

My Government's position on draft resolution S/22940 is as follows: Iraq's foreign-currency revenue is almost totally dependent on its oil exports. On the basis of the production capacity of Iraqi oil fields, those

0100

(Mr. Al-Anbari, Iraq)

exports over the next five years will not reach the level defined in July 1990 by the Organization of Petroleum Exporting Countries (OPEC). That is because of the destruction inflicted by aerial bombardment on our oil production and exporting facilities. It is thus anticipated that for the period 1991-1995 Iraq's oil revenues will be $64.2 billion. That projection is on the basis of 600,000 barrels exported in the remainder of 1991, owing to the grave damage inflicted on our oil facilities, and 2 million barrels a day in 1992. An optimistic estimate has it that this could rise to 2.85 million barrels a day in 1993 and 2.9 million in 1994. Those figures presuppose full lifting of the sanctions imposed on Iraq's oil exports and on its import of equipment and other necessities for the refinement, export and shipment of oil.

It is well known that our non-oil exports are extremely limited; in the five-year period 1991-1995 these are not expected to exceed $930.5 million.

A careful examination of the gap between those revenues and our foreign-currency requirements reveals a projected deficit over those five years of $149.2 billion, averaging $29.28 billion a year for that period - although the 1991 deficit is expected to reach $47.8 billion. The reason for the higher 1991 deficit compared with the average annual rate is the enormous cost of servicing the debts incurred this year and last: the installments include all payments due in 1991 and previous years, and no agreement has been reached on deferring these payments. The meagreness of the income Iraq estimates for the next five years will compel it to fall short of its financial obligations and its requirements for food and medicine - and that does not even take into account the deduction of 30 per cent of those revenues.

(Mr. Al-Anbari, Iraq)

That is on the basis of these above-mentioned estimates, which clearly reflect the tremendous deficit and wide gap between Iraq's financial obligations relating to its foreign debt and its basic imports, on the one hand, and its limited revenues from its exports expected in 1991, and especially during subsequent years, and on the basis of Under-Secretary-General Ahtisaari's findings in Iraq, who stated in his report that the conflict had brought near-apocalyptic consequences on the basic economic infrastructure. The report goes on to say that most means of modern life have been destroyed or have become very weak and that Iraq has been returned to the pre-industrial age and will remain so for a period of time.

Hence, Iraq, with its current and expected financial resources during 1991 and subsequently, cannot on its own restore the social and economic life that prevailed before the events of January 1991. Intensive world efforts must be bent to compensate Iraq for the unjust damages inflicted by the aerial bombing of its civilian facilities and economic structure in order to help Iraq to accelerate the restoration of normal life.

My Government has therefore requested that it be given a grace period of five years. Such a period can be arrived at as necessary, on the basis of the statements in the Secretary-General's report which depended on the economic indicators expected for 1993, although the damages that will increase between now and 1993 because of the continued economic embargo will make such estimates much worse than what we have stated.

The premises of the Secretary-General's report before the Council make it necessary to defer the deductions until 1993 at the least, since Iraq's oil revenues during the balance of 1991 and in 1992 will be approximately $13 billion only. This means that the total Iraqi oil revenues during these

(Mr. Al-Anbari, Iraq)

two years are much less than what is required to fulfil the basic requirements estimated at $16 billion for the same two years, although there has been no opportunity until now for Iraq to export oil or oil products. Also, the extensive economic embargo is still being applied and Iraq's assets abroad are still frozen, despite the decision of the Sanctions Committee and the letter of the Chairman of that Committee which theoretically lifted the freezing of these assets but left the States where the Iraqi assets are to be found free to freeze these assets.

In the light of the above-mentioned facts, which any objective observer can ascertain, Iraq requests a grace period in order to allow it to face the major problems stifling its economy which are threatening to weaken the Iraqi people and its future generations. Iraq also requested a decrease in the ceiling of the deduction so as not to exceed 10 per cent of its total oil revenues.

I thank you, Mr. President, for your kind attention to the statement giving my Government's position regarding the first draft resolution on the compensation fund.

Allow me now to indicate in detail my Government's position on the second draft resolution, contained in document S/22941. Although this draft resolution alleges that it is designed to meet the humanitarian requirements of the Iraqi people, it is actually one of the most serious draft resolutions put before the Council since the outbreak of the so-called Gulf crisis. Therefore, allow me first to review the developments pertaining to meeting the humanitarian needs of the Iraqi people, after which I shall explain my Government's position regarding the grave political repercussions aimed at by this draft resolution. And then I shall make Iraq's technical comments on the various items in the draft resolution.

(Mr. Al-Anbari, Iraq)

With regard to the humanitarian requirements of the Iraqi people, members will recall that the mission dispatched to Iraq by the Secretary-General during the period 10 to 17 March 1991, headed by Under-Secretary-General Martti Ahtisaari, which included representatives of the appropriate United Nations agencies and programmes, in its report of 20 March 1991, contained in document S/22366, affirmed the following:

> "there needs to be a major mobilization ... of resources to deal with aspects of this deep crisis in the fields of agriculture and food, water, sanitation and health." (para. 37)

The report concluded:

> "It is unmistakable that the Iraqi people may soon face a further imminent catastrophe, which could include epidemic and famine, if massive life-supporting needs are not rapidly met. The long summer, with its often 45 or even 50 degree temperatures (113-122 degrees Fahrenheit), is only weeks away. Time is short." (ibid.)

In spite of all those warnings, no humanitarian action has so far been taken. It is true that the Council adopted resolution 687 (1991) on 3 April 1991, taking into consideration the recommendations of the United Nations mission when, in paragraph 20 of the resolution, it exempted foodstuffs from the sanctions and provided for streamlining and accelerating the Committee's approval of the exception of basic civilian foodstuffs indicated in the United Nations mission's report.

Paragraph 23 of that resolution provides that the Sanctions Committee may approve exceptions from the ban on importing materials and products from Iraq in order to provide Iraq with sufficient financial resources to import those materials the importation of which into Iraq is approved by the Committee.

0104

(Mr. Al-Anbari, Iraq)

Yet it has been impossible for Iraq, as it has been for the Sanctions Committee, to exercise the powers provided for in paragraphs 20 and 23 of the resolution because of the arbitrary position insisted upon by a small minority of the members of the Sanctions Committee.

Paragraph 21 of resolution 687 (1991) also provided that the Council review the provisions of paragraph 20 of the resolution every 60 days for the purpose of determining whether to reduce or lift the prohibitions referred to in paragraph 21. In spite of the passage of more than 130 days since the adoption of resolution 687 (1991), the Council has not met to reconsider the prohibition measures and to provide the opportunity to the Council members and to Iraq to indicate the extent of its implementation of the Council's resolutions. Rather, the Council confined itself to informal consultations, after which the President issued a presidential statement indicating that the members had failed to agree on any resolution.

Here, I indicate once more that the failure of the Council to meet with the aim of reviewing the sanctions and adopting the necessary resolution is also due to the position of a small minority of its members. This minority is bent on not allowing Iraq to enjoy the exceptions provided for in paragraphs 20 and 23. This minority is also bent on not allowing other member States of the Council that support the lifting of the sanctions to express their views officially and to record their positions publicly.

0105

(Mr. Al-Anbari, Iraq)

Paragraph 22 of resolution 687 (1991) actually provides for the total lifting of the sanctions once the Council takes note of the report of the Secretary-General on the compensation fund - which has actually taken place - and once the Council acknowledges that Iraq has completed all the actions required of it in paragraphs 8 through 13 of the same resolution. That has actually happened, and this fact was communicated to the Council by Iraq.

Yet, the same small minority in the Council prevented the Council from deciding that the second condition - which is necessary for the lifting of all sanctions imposed on Iraq under resolution 661 (1990) of 6 August 1990 - had been met.

In the face of this situation, in a letter dated 7 June 1991, the Iraqi Mission submitted an application to the Sanctions Committee requesting a lifting of the freeze on the Iraqi funds deposited in British, American and other foreign banks - which, as of 31 March 1991, totalled $3,735 million - with a view to purchasing foodstuffs, medicines and basic civilian materials.

However, while the Committee acknowledged the admissibility of unfreezing those deposits, it affirmed that the States in which those Iraqi funds are deposited are not obligated to unfreeze these funds. This has led actually to continued freezing and to depriving Iraq from using its funds with a view to averting the dangers highlighted by the United Nations mission's report.

The States that have kept the Iraqi assets frozen are doing so for political considerations of their own that are irrelevant to Security Council resolutions.

In addition, on 14 March 1991, Iraq requested the Sanctions Committee to allow it to export such quantities of oil as to provide $1.2 billion on the basis of paragraph 23 of the resolution. However, the Committee did not take

(Mr. Al-Anbari, Iraq)

any action on the question. Then, on 9 July 1991, Iraq repeated its request to allow it to export oil to the tune of $1.5 billion for the same purpose. But once again the Committee failed to achieve consensus and the request was shelved.

Iraq once more requested the Committee to approve the export of quantities of oil, with a view to purchasing foodstuffs contracted for with foreign companies, while indicating the quantities and prices of such foodstuffs. Once again, however, the Committee failed to achieve consensus on the request and it was shelved.

The freezing referred to in paragraphs 20, 21, 22 and 23 of Security Council resolution 687 (1991) - each of which provides for exceptions to the sanctions, or for their total lifting - was due to the positions of a small minority which, in fact, does not exceed one State plus three. This minority is also credited with paralysing the work of the Sanctions Committee.

Moreover, that minority takes credit for preventing the Committee from adopting the necessary resolutions to implement the recommendations included in the report of the inter-agency mission, headed by the Executive Delegate of the Secretary-General, Prince Sadruddin Aga Khan, which are included in document S/22799 of 17 July 1991 which it drew up following its visit to Iraq during the period from 29 June until 13 July last.

The report is the most recent of the United Nations Inter-Agency Humanitarian Programme and contains the most accurate information and statistics in its 59 pages. Allow me to quote a number of paragraphs from the aforementioned document:

(Mr. Al-Anbari, Iraq)

(spoke in English)

"We saw with our own eyes the scenes already reported at length ... the children afflicted by malnutrition. Our report is inevitably but a photograph in time, fast obsolete, yet the urgency of relief from suffering remains. Further, the hard statistics speak for themselves. Conditions are already grave in all of the essential sectors assessed and can only worsen in the weeks ahead. We must achieve a breakthrough to avert the looming crisis" (S/22799, para. 131).

(spoke in Arabic)

The report of the mission goes on to say:

(spoke in English)

"This mission has addressed the current humanitarian needs in Iraq and has concluded that their magnitude requires funding that exceeds international aid and short-term palliatives and can be met only from the country's own resources.... On the basis, however, of our deliberations and meetings with the authorities in Iraq, it would appear feasible to institute arrangements whereby Iraq's requests for imports to meet the needs outlined in this report would be submitted to the United Nations and subjected to appropriate monitoring. The precise mechanisms need not be specified here. The formula agreed upon would provide for clear records of all transactions to be furnished to the Organization." (Ibid., para. 137)

(spoke in Arabic)

Finally, I have to remind the Council of the contents of paragraph 138 of the report, because the draft resolution before the Council proceeds in the opposite direction from the one advocated in the report.

(Mr. Al-Anbari, Iraq)

(spoke in English)

"It remains a cardinal humanitarian principle that innocent civilians - and above all the most vulnerable - should not be held hostage to events beyond their control. Those already afflicted by war's devastation cannot continue to pay the price of a bitter peace. It is a peace that will also prove to be tenuous if unmet needs breed growing desperation. If new displacements of Iraq's population result from hunger and disease, if relief is again sought across national frontiers, the region's stability will once more be set at risk with unforeseeable consequences. Humanitarian and political interests converge in the aversion of catastrophe. It is clearly imperative that Iraq's 'essential civilian needs' be met urgently and that rapid agreement be secured on the mechanism whereby Iraq's own resources be used to fund them to the satisfaction of the international community" (Ibid, para. 138).

(spoke in Arabic)

But regrettably, this small minority in the Sanctions Committee succeeded in paralysing the work of the Committee and its ability to adopt a resolution. Hence, the Committee failed to achieve consensus on the recommendations of the mission headed by Prince Sadruddin Aga Khan, which prompted the Chairman of the Committee to refer the matter back to the Security Council for it to take whatever decision it deems appropriate, which was the aim of the small minority in the Sanctions Committee. Why? The secret lies in the provisions of the draft resolution before the Council, which are aimed not at fulfilling the humanitarian needs of the Iraqi people but at exploiting them and imposing on Iraq's economy new financial sanctions and restrictions which had not been mentioned before, and to breach its

0109

(Mr. Al-Anbari, Iraq)

sovereignty contrary to the United Nations Charter and all norms of international law.

For all intents and purposes, the draft resolution is aimed at keeping the economic embargo in place indefinitely, regardless of the provisions of paragraph 22 of Security Council resolution 687 (1991), and confines itself to giving Iraq a minimum of first-aid so that the people will not starve to death, but without providing Iraq with the opportunity to reconstruct its economy, including its oil industry, its agriculture, its irrigation system, its roads, communications, bridges and health facilities.

The Sanctions Committee cannot violate Security Council resolution 687 (1991) or add new requests that were not included in the original resolution and impose them on Iraq. Hence, the Sanctions Committee referred the report of the Secretary-General's Executive Delegate to the Council and we have before us a draft resolution that actually leads to the catastrophe warned against in paragraph 138 of the report, which I quoted earlier.

(Mr. Al-Anbari, Iraq)

The draft resolution before the Council will actually lead to keeping the Iraqi people hostage under the influence of the small minority that claims to defend human rights and democracy in the world but has had no qualms about besieging the entire Iraqi people for more than a year. It has refused to lift the siege unless Iraq agrees to pay the price: relinquish its oil revenues and place its economic requirements and monetary policy in the hands of one State, plus one which has appointed itself as trustee over the Iraqi people, as the European Powers did in the nineteenth century vis-à-vis the Ottoman Empire and with respect to Egypt under the Khedives. What is surprising is that, although the United States and its three allies have announced their rejection of using food as a political weapon, Iraqis, including children, the sick and the elderly continue to die every day as a result of malnutrition, the lack of medicine and the embargo on food, medicine, funds and oil. Every day thousands of people die because the same minority is determined that it, and not Iraq, through United Nations agencies, will market - if not distribute - foodstuffs and medicines and other basic requirements for civilian life in Iraq, although such foodstuffs would be paid for by Iraqi funds and the Iraqi people itself, and not out of the generosity of those States.

In August 1990 the purpose of this inhumane embargo was supposedly to ensure Iraq's withdrawal from the territory of Kuwait, which actually took place last February. The continued embargo affirms what Iraq has always said: that this alliance had the sole aim of destroying Iraq as an effective Arab force influential in determining the fate of the region. Hence, the 30-State alliance did not stop at destroying the infrastructure and the basic civilian structures of Iraq, but persisted in attempting to destroy Iraq by

0111

(Mr. Al-Anbari, Iraq)

continuing the economic embargo and adopting various resolutions, all of which are aimed at putting Iraq forever under the trusteeship of the United States and its allies, on behalf of the Security Council and the committees that it established, in order to administer the affairs of Iraq, control its exports and imports and its internal affairs.

I come now to the political aspects of the draft. Contrary to the United Nations Charter, the draft gravely impinges on Iraq's national sovereignty as a free country and Founding Member of the United Nations, and imposes a foreign guardianship on the free will of the Iraqi people. The draft also deprives the legitimate Government of Iraq of its powers and responsibilities with respect to its citizens and abolishes its role in caring for them and providing for their livelihood, their daily need for foodstuffs and health and medical services.

On the other hand, the draft gives foreign Powers the right to control Iraq's natural resources and allows them to dispose of its wealth and oil revenues as they wish, without the Iraqi people and its Government having any right to invest those resources or funds or to define their own priorities in the elimination of the effects of the unjust aggression by the 30 States against them. The draft also subordinates the humanitarian objective of the report of Prince Sadruddin Aga Khan, to suspect political motives and creates further difficulties for Iraq, although the pretexts that were invoked to impose those sanctions have ceased to exist. The draft actually undermines the provisions of resolution 687 (1990) and converts the partial lifting of the sanctions into colonialist restrictions that would rob Iraq of its right to full sovereignty, interfere in its internal affairs, plunder its oil wealth and usurp its right to dispose of its own funds, even though resolution

0112

(Mr. Al-Anbari, Iraq)

687 (1990) allows Iraq to purchase civilian requirements, such as foodstuffs and medicine without any intervention or trusteeship.

The authors of the resolution have thus wanted to circumvent the report of the international humanitarian organization that undertook field trips throughout Iraq and implicitly uncovered the nature of the brutal crimes perpetrated against Iraq when its infrastructure and national economy were destroyed through a scheme that had nothing to do with the so-called Gulf crisis but was aimed at destroying the potential of Iraq and, isolating its people, overthrowing the symbols of its cultural renaissance and comprehensive progress as an expression of deep-rooted hatred, and to further the aims of world Zionism under the motto of "legitimacy" and a "new world order".

Here I should like to take up the negative aspects of the draft resolution. While the authors claim that their aim is to cope with the grave deterioration in the health and nutritional situation of the Iraqi people and the grim portrait contained in the report of the Executive Delegate, as provided for in preambular paragraphs B and C of the draft, the draft actually imposes conditions on Iraq which lead in the direction opposite to that of the alleged aim of its authors. When we consider the preambular paragraphs of the draft, we see that they shuffle the cards and blur the facts. We note the preambular paragraph that refers to the so-called Kuwaiti detainees in Iraq. That paragraph was superimposed on the draft and was formulated in such a way as to distort the truth.

Those who are impeding the return of Kuwaitis from Iraq are the Government of Kuwait itself. The Iraqi authorities, during the period from 4 March until 14 July 1991, returned 6,133 Kuwaiti captives to Kuwait under the supervision of the International Committee of the Red Cross. Also, that

0113

(Mr. Al-Anbari, Iraq)

Committee recorded 3,400 Kuwaitis residing in Iraq who wished to return to their country, but the Kuwaiti side agreed to accept only 128 individuals and dragged its feet regarding the return of the others, under the pretext of wanting to ascertain their identification. With respect to those so-called missing, the Kuwaiti Government insists on providing lists of names of people whose existence in Iraq has not been borne out by the investigations undertaken by the Iraqi authorities. Perhaps some of them have died as a result of the allied bombardment. Also, the Kuwaiti Government did not bother to inquire about those people in other parts of the world. As is well known, it is not conceivable to expect Iraq to produce someone of whom there is no news. On the other hand, what does this have to do with a draft resolution allegedly dealing with the serious health and nutritional situation of the Iraqi people? The aim behind this artificial inclusion of the so-called Kuwaiti detainees is to create an additional pretext to keep the embargo against the Iraqi people.

Paragraph E of the draft refers to the conclusions of the report of Prince Sadruddin Aga Khan, in particular to the proposal to sell oil to finance urgent humanitarian relief. The draft resolution should have sought to achieve this accommodation, but it could not have been further from that recommendation in letter and spirit. The provisions of the draft do not allow Iraq to sell its oil, but rather allow other States through a slow and complicated mechanism to purchase limited amounts of Iraqi oil. In addition, no stress was laid on the humanitarian relief, but priority was given to the payment of sums to the Compensation Fund and to the expenses of the Commission dealing with the destruction of weapons, the Commission dealing with the restitution of Kuwaiti property, and the Iraq-Kuwait Border Demarcation

0114

(Mr. Al-Anbari, Iraq)

Commission. These provisions include such conditions and costs as would undermine the recommendations of the report of Prince Sadruddin Aga Khan. Preambular paragraph G and operative paragraph (c) indicate the need for the United Nations to intervene in the distribution of foodstuffs, medicines and materials and supplies for essential civilian needs of all categories of the Iraqi people through providing for United Nations administration, monitoring and supervision.

(Mr. Al-Anbari, Iraq)

This concept of the draft resolution runs completely counter to the concept of sovereignty assigned by the Charter of the United Nations. Moreover, it constitutes a grave precedent as regards the humanitarian role of the United Nations. There is in Iraq a just and comprehensive system for the distribution of foodstuffs, which includes all persons, Iraqis and foreigners, residing in Iraq, and allows everyone to obtain basic foodstuffs at subsidized prices. The process of sales is undertaken through an integrated mechanism through the State agents and commercial markets, not through random distribution of assistance. Hence, the attempt to impose a United Nations supervision system, which has no chance of succeeding anyway, is aimed solely at derogating from Iraq's sovereignty, disregarding its organizational, administrative and economic institutions, and adding to the administrative costs of the Iraqi citizen and those taken from Iraq's own resources.

In preambular paragraph H, the draft resolution recalls the importance which the Council attaches to Iraq allowing access by the humanitarian organizations to those in need of assistance in all parts of Iraq and affirms the important role played by the Memorandum of Understanding between the Government of Iraq and the United Nations of 18 April 1991. The reference to this Memorandum in such a manner is invidious to Iraq and its rights. Iraq has been fulfilling its obligations under the Memorandum of Understanding and the United Nations humanitarian programme. Iraq is proceeding according to the agreement and there are no significant problems in this regard. On the other hand, the Memorandum of Understanding relates to a programme of voluntary assistance provided by foreign parties, whereas the draft resolution has to do with foodstuffs and medical supplies paid for and distributed exclusively with Iraqi funds.

(Mr. Al-Anbari, Iraq)

Moreover, preambular paragraph J provides that the Council is acting in accordance with Chapter VII of the Charter. Invoking Chapter VII, regarding sanctions, in this draft resolution, which is alleged to be a humanitarian draft resolution, once again exposes the suspect intent of the authors. Furthermore, it reveals the inhumane and exploitive nature of the draft.

I now turn to the technical and practical aspects of the provisions of the draft resolution. Operative paragraph 1 subordinates the permission of States to import Iraqi oil to seven conditions, including a time condition - six months after the passage of the draft resolution. This condition does not take into consideration the procedure followed in the international oil trade, that is, annual contacting. Hence, the purpose behind the six-month period is to stymie the process of exporting Iraqi oil and to create impediments to the marketing of necessary amounts during the same period, which would definitely lead to a decrease in Iraqi oil. On the other hand, the draft resolution does not allow Iraq to export oil at its own responsibility and to sell it on the free market, as the exception was made exclusively for imports from Iraq and not for exports by the Government of Iraq. Hence, it is not possible for Iraq to sell its oil on the free market, and it allows States to buy oil in very limited quantities and at very low prices. There is a financial condition, which is that the imports from Iraq should not exceed the value of, as it is rumoured, $1.6 billion, which falls short of Iraq's needs to finance its imports. This is all the more serious when we see that the draft resolution gives priority in using the revenues from the imports of Iraqi oil to deducting 30 per cent for the Compensation Fund in addition to the costs of the various conditions established by the Council.

The third condition deals with approval by the Security Council Committee

0117

(Mr. Al-Anbari, Iraq)

on Sanctions of every transaction, which is a waste of time and makes it difficult to pump Iraqi oil systematically because, as members know, the Committee usually meets once a week in a bureaucratic tradition and on a consensus basis so that any member of the Security Council in the Committee can obstruct any transaction for weeks by raising various questions which, whether they are prompted by good will or ill will, have the same effect: of obstructing the marketing of Iraqi oil and of wasting time.

The fourth condition involves placing the oil revenues directly in an escrow account in a bank chosen by the United Nations, to be administered by the Secretary-General. Naturally, the costs of such an account are to be deducted from its assets.

Operative paragraph 1 of the draft resolution provides that the materials needed by Iraq must be defined by the Secretary-General within 20 days after the adoption of the resolution, although the report of Aga Khan defines the type and amounts of the necessary materials to avert epidemics and famine in Iraq. Moreover, the draft makes it conditional that clear markings be placed to indicate that the imports are for humanitarian and civilian requirements, as if they were voluntary contributions by charitable organizations, and not imports financed by Iraqi funds.

Paragraph 1 also subjects the distribution of materials imported by Iraq to the monitoring and supervision of United Nations agencies to ensure their distribution throughout Iraq. This condition disregards the fact that Iraq is a country of 18 million people and that the materials will be distributed by means of ration cards, and not as voluntary grants. This also requires the presence of thousands of United Nations staff, the cost of which will be borne by Iraq indefinitely, which is contrary to the sovereignty of Iraq.

0118

(Mr. Al-Anbari, Iraq)

Finally, unfreezing the balance of the escrow account is also to be carried out through resolutions of the Committee on Sanctions in three equal stages, which would obstruct the import of humanitarian and civilian materials by Iraq. This is contrary to the conditions of paying these sums for imports.

Moreover, paragraph 1 (c) stipulates that the United Nations should provide administration, monitoring and supervision with a view to providing humanitarian assistance from other sources. This provision means that governmental and non-governmental humanitarian organizations and United Nations staff that provided assistance to the Iraqi people in coordination with the Government of Iraq will cease to provide assistance and will be transformed into a machinery of administration, supervision and monitoring, whose costs would be borne by the people of Iraq from their resources, without achieving any gains. Also, under this provision, the United Nations, if it so wishes, can provide more of these from other sources in the numbers it decides, and the people of Iraq have to bear the costs.

In operative paragraph 3 the draft also provides that a portion of the Iraqi oil sales be used to finance Iraq's contribution to the Compensation Fund because of the destruction of the weapons and the restitution of Kuwaiti property. Placing conditions on the export of oil to fill Iraqi humanitarian needs runs counter to resolution 687 (1991), particularly paragraph 19 thereof, which provides that the Iraqi people and their ability to pay must be taken into consideration. These provisions have not been included in the draft resolution. The deductions cannot begin with a partial and conditional lifting, because the limited amount of exported oil, if approved, would not be enough to finance the needs of the Iraqi people. How could it be sufficient after deducting the percentage for the Fund and other costs?

(Mr. Al-Anbari, Iraq)

Fourthly, the draft resolution also breaches the sovereignty of Iraq when it calls upon it to submit monthly reports about its assets in foreign currency and wealth.

In brief, for its part Iraq has prepared and provided all forms of cooperation in seeking to fulfil its obligations under resolution 687 (1991) and has responded fully to the Special Commission and inspection teams in implementing section C of the resolution, the greater part of whose items have been complied with. In addition Iraq has facilitated the restitution of Kuwaiti properties. At present the gold is being returned and preparations are under way to return the museum items; and the Border Demarcation Commission is continuing its work in Geneva with Iraq's active participation. The Council should match responses by Iraq by the full lifting of sanctions. But the will of some of its members runs counter to that; for obvious political reasons not relevant to the Council's resolutions, to international law or to the Charter those States had no qualms about announcing their aims when they tied lifting the sanctions to changing the political régime in Iraq. On the other hand, Iraq is ready to ensure the necessary transparency and has proposed means necessary to inform international agencies of Iraqi imports. Iraq has also undertaken to provide immediately copies of all sales contracts and purchases of foodstuffs and has declared its readiness to sell oil to States permanent members of the Security Council and buy its medical, nutritional and other basic requirements from them so that they may be directly informed of all exports and imports.

The fact that this initiative by Iraq has not been taken into consideration, coupled with the insistence of the authors on their programme, reveals a deliberate attempt to obstruct the lifting of sanctions against

(Mr. Al-Anbari, Iraq)

Iraq. It also constitutes an attempt by some permanent members to evade their responsibility, starve the Iraqi people and blame it on the Iraqi Government by aborting the report of Sadruddin Aga Khan and proposing a complicated and impractical machinery - trusteeship over Iraq. The authors actually want to hold the Iraqi people hostage and to place before it two options: either to allow colonial and neocolonial States to plunder its oil wealth and control it indefinitely, or to keep the state of starvation and life on the brink of disaster. This will not be permitted by Iraq.

I shall now touch briefly on draft resolution S/22942. It should be noted that the draft resolution is based on two points, which are: the circumstance surrounding the second inspection team during its visit from 22 June to 3 July 1991, as indicated in preambular paragraphs c, d, e and f; and the resolution of the Board of Governors of the International Atomic Energy Agency (IAEA) of 18 July 1991.

Iraq has already clearly and unambiguously indicated on more than one occasion the circumstances surrounding the arrival of the second inspection team. The details of those circumstances were communicated to the high-level mission headed by Mr. Ralph Ikeus when that mission visited Iraq. The Iraqi Government provided assurances at the highest level that its authorities would open up all facilities to the inspection teams. The high-level mission mentioned these assurances in its report and indicated that the coming period would begin to show Iraq's fulfilment of those assurances. Since then, more than one team has visited Iraq and a nuclear inspection team and a biological team are still there.

Iraq has opened up all facilities to the third inspection team and provided it with immense quantities of information, as indicated by the

0121

(Mr. Al-Anbari, Iraq)

Director of the IAEA in his press conference at United Nations Headquarters in New York on 30 July 1991. Also, the Chairman of the fourth team, Sir David Kaye, stated before the news agency in Baghdad that his team was making progress and had obtained a great deal of information and that the Iraqis were cooperating with his team. As for the other teams that visited Iraq, they have not indicated the presence of any impediments or significant problems in their work.

Can one truly say, after the passage of more than one month since the circumstances surrounding the second team and after the experience of cooperating with all the teams, that Iraq is uncooperative and not fulfilling its obligations? We had hoped that the Security Council would express its satisfaction with the cooperation enjoyed by the international teams in Iraq, not that it would adopt a new resolution condemning Iraq for an isolated incident.

Most members of the second team are now in Iraq and enjoying unprecedented cooperation. Information is being supplied promptly, and the Council can be guided by the head of the team, who is now in Baghdad. Is this not further evidence of Iraq's abiding by the Council's resolution? This must be taken into consideration by the Security Council.

In spite of the aforementioned we find that the draft resolution does not include any legitimate provisions. Most of it is covered in the agreement on the privileges and immunities of the Special Commission, the IAEA and the inspection teams, which was accepted by Iraq. From our point of view, this agreement is appropriate to the circumstances for cooperation that may be available, and they have now become available as far as Iraq is concerned. Last month proved that they have improved.

0122

(Mr. Al-Anbari, Iraq)

Finally, we should like to inquire of the Special Commission, the teams and the Agency whether they were denied access to certain places or were prevented from inspecting any materials. As far as we know, there is not a single place, as indicated in the reports of the inspection teams, that has not been inspected by them. But, to be more accurate, there was a place over which a clamour was raised on 21 June. The Chairman of the third nuclear inspection team agreed to move the materials found there, and two members of his team supervised the process. The team recorded all the materials, which were photographed and unloaded from trucks under the team's supervision. The international team released the non-nuclear equipment for use in the reconstruction of Iraq. The trucks left there under the supervision and approval of the inspection team. All this is recorded in inventories and lists exchanged between the third inspection team and Iraq. The equipment was stored in warehouses, thus making it easier to be inspected by the team in future. This all took place quietly, so what can be the reason for the current draft resolution including operative paragraph 3? The Council should express its satisfaction with the practical measures taken in this regard instead of trying to condemn Iraq and impose new conditions on it.

I apologize for taking so long. Because of what happened for the first time in the Council, that is, taking up three draft resolutions consecutively for consideration, I was forced to speak at length.

0123

The PRESIDENT (interpretation from Spanish): I thank the representative of Iraq for the kind words he addressed to me.

It is my understanding that the Council is ready to proceed to the vote on the draft resolutions before it. Unless there is any objection, I shall put the draft resolutions to the vote in the following order: S/22940, S/22941 and S/22942.

There being no objection, it is so decided.

I shall first call on members of the Council wishing to make statements before the voting.

Mr. AL-ASHTAL (Yemen) (interpretation from Arabic): At the outset, Sir, I should like to congratulate you heartily on your assumption of the presidency of the Security Council for this month. We know you for your great qualities, qualities which reflect the Latin American heritage of respect for the Charter of the United Nations and international laws and norms. Your presidency also reflects your diplomatic and political qualities and great abilities. I am fully confident that you will lead the work of the Council with success.

I should like also to express my great thanks to the Permanent Representative of Cuba, Ambassador Alarcon de Quesada, who skilfully guided the work of the Security Council last month and who this month has been coordinating the work of the non-aligned caucus in the Security Council.

In my brief statement I shall comment on draft resolution S/22941.

A full year after the imposition of comprehensive sanctions against Iraq, and nearly six months after the end of the war that liberated Kuwait and enabled its legitimate Government to return, the Security Council is facing a

0124

(Mr. Al-Ashtal, Yemen)

humanitarian problem of tragic dimensions. Notwithstanding numerous and continuous reports depicting the suffering of the Iraqi people as a result of the ongoing of the embargo - whose dire consequences could include starvation and death for hundreds of thousands of the most vulnerable members of Iraqi society - the Security Council is still dragging its feet in dealing realistically with the tragedy of the Iraqi people, who were the first victims of the Gulf crisis, and with the resolution by which the Security Council imposed the embargo against Iraq following the war that destroyed Iraq's civilian infrastructure.

On 15 July 1991, Prince Sadruddin Aga Khan, the Secretary-General's Executive Delegate, who headed the inter-agency mission, submitted a comprehensive report on the sad human situation in Iraq. This was the second report, following the one submitted a few months ago by Mr. Martti Ahtisaari.

In its section II, "Summary of main findings and recommendations", the report says,

> "With respect to the possible sale of oil by the Iraqi Government to finance such imports, paragraph 23 of Security Council resolution 687 (1991) empowers the Security Council Committee established by resolution 661 (1990) to approve exceptions to the prohibition against the import of commodities and products originating in Iraq, with the explicit purpose of assuring 'adequate financial resources' on the part of the Iraqi Government to procure medicine and health supplies, foodstuffs and materials and supplies for 'essential civilian needs'". (S/22799, annex, para. 32)

0125

(Mr. Al-Ashtal, Yemen)

Later in the same section, the report says that

"If the Security Council Committee were to decide that Iraq should be allowed to use funds from oil sales or facilitate the use of blocked accounts in order to meet urgent humanitarian needs, the Government indicated that it would cooperate in making available documentation relating to sales of crude oil as well as purchases of the authorized imports. ... [A] suitable device for monitoring such credit balances could be established". (Ibid., para. 34)

It is regrettable that the sanctions Committee, which heard an oral report from Prince Sadruddin and other members of his mission, was unable to take a decision on this matter, which falls within its mandate by the terms of paragraph 23 of resolution 687 (1991). A full month after the submission of Prince Sadruddin's report the Council is seized of draft resolution S/22941, which authorizes the exemption of the sale of some Iraqi oil for a limited period of six months and in the limited amount of $1.6 billion.

Although the draft resolution would ultimately enable needed medicine and food to reach Iraq, it raises many questions of principle. First, what is the justification for submitting a special draft resolution on the humanitarian aspects of the situation in Iraq when the sanctions Committee possesses a mandate under paragraph 23 of resolution 687 (1991) to take decisions on this subject and to permit Iraq to export oil and petroleum products exclusively to meet humanitarian needs? In other words, why was the sanctions Committee not permitted to take the necessary decision immediately after Prince Sadruddin Aga Khan's report was submitted? And why did the Committee and the Security Council not accept the well-considered and reasonable recommendations submitted by Prince Sadruddin in his report?

0126

(Mr. Al-Ashtal, Yemen)

Second, would not these complicated conditions in the draft resolution lead to the creation of bureaucratic mechanisms and procedures which would delay the timely arrival of foodstuffs and medicines to Iraq? And why is the Secretariat involved in technical and commercial operations, something which would add to the burdens of this Organization?

Third, why is this humanitarian draft resolution based on Chapter VII of the Charter? True, the sanctions were imposed against Iraq on the basis of Chapter VII of the Charter; but we are not now dealing with the lifting of the sanctions. We are now dealing with the approval of some exceptions for purely humanitarian reasons. Was it not possible for the Sanctions Committee to allow the same exceptions that would lead to the importation of Iraqi oil for humanitarian needs without any reference to Chapter VII of the Charter? This question acquires a special significance in view of what might happen in the future and the position that the Security Council might take should Iraq reject the export of oil in accordance with the stipulated conditions. This is not a theoretical possibility, for the Prime Minister of Iraq has already rejected the draft resolution since it would not meet the humanitarian needs and would at the same time undermine Iraq's sovereignty.

Fourth, why does the draft resolution confuse the special humanitarian situation of millions of innocent Iraqis with financial matters related to the recovery of the cost of the Special Commission and the IAEA and the Iraq-Kuwait Boundary Demarcation Commission? Does the Security Council equate those Iraqi vulnerable people who could face famine and slow death should sanctions continue with the staff of the international organizations who would not be greatly hurt by the postponement of the receipt of their remunerations? Was it not possible for the Security Council to allow the sale of some shipments of Iraqi oil to meet the costs of international organizations

(Mr. Al-Ashtal, Yemen)

in a specific manner, in addition to the financing of the Compensation Fund, which relates to many innocent people - Kuwaitis and non-Kuwaitis who lost their lives, positions or rights as a result of the war?
How can we interpret this intentional confusion and in the same draft resolution accept that it represents the absence of interest and even the carelessness regarding the fate of millions of innocent Iraqis who are helpless both in war and in peace?

The people and the Government of Yemen are concerned about our brothers in Iraq, especially the vulnerable groups among them, those who would fall as a result of the miserable humanitarian situation in Iraq. United Nations experts have been issuing warnings for a long time and some of them announced that an imminent catastrophe was innevitable. For example, the report of the mission of Medicine for Peace declares, on page 17, that

> "Unless the sanctions are amended, it is probable that the public health system will collapse, which would lead to the death of many children without any justification whatsoever."

Moreover, press reports have indicated that Iraqi civilians with medium incomes have begun to sell their valuable possessions, and even household items, in order to buy the foodstuffs that are sold at astronomical prices. As for those with limited incomes in Iraq, they face want, poverty and famine.

It is expected that, given the Security Council's procrastination, the complications of the draft resolution submitted to us and Iraq's rejection, the blame for the starvation of the Iraqi people will be apportioned here and there. At that time, will it be possible for the Security Council to deny its share of responsibility? The famine that will afflict the children of the Iraqi people will not have been created by nature, and it will not be the

0128

(Mr. Al-Ashtal, Yemen)

result of the scarcity of resources; the continuation of the sanctions will be one of its main reasons.

The Security Council, which is mandated to serve peace and security the world over, should not allow the spread of famine which might lead to massive migrations across international borders, in addition to the possibility of instability and the break-down of internal security. This would ultimately lead to jeopardizing peace and security in the area. Furthermore, the Security Council is responsible for the preservation of the lives and safety of human beings. Everybody says that he is not against the Iraqi people. Why then do some insist on the continuation of its suffering? Why do these people not lift from its shoulders the embargo that is harming and weakening Iraqi society day by day?

It is known that there are political ends that are not declared in the Security Council. But would these ends justify inhuman means?

Each country has the right to impose an embargo against another country in implementation of its own policies and in defence of its interests. But the Security Council should not be used to achieve ends other than those which conform with the Charter and are based on the Charter in letter and in spirit.

The PRESIDENT (interpretation from Spanish): I thank the representative of Yemen for his kind words addressed to me.

Mr. MUMBENGEGWI (Zimbabwe): I should like at the outset, Sir, to congratulate you on your assumption of the presidency of the Council. Your diplomatic skills and wealth of experience have already made their mark on the work of the Council. Your wise guidance of the Council this month will ensure that it discharges its mandate honourably.

Let me also express our deep appreciation to your predecessor, Ambassador Ricardo Alarcon de Quesada of Cuba, for the able and effective manner in which he steered the work of the Council last month. It was indeed a fruitful month, thanks to his distinguished stewardship.

I shall confine my remarks to the draft resolution contained in document S/22941.

The critical humanitarian situation facing the people of Iraq following the end of the Gulf war has been a source of grave concern to Zimbabwe.

Zimbabwe was among the non-aligned members of the Council who submitted a draft resolution last March aimed at relieving the suffering of the civilian population of Iraq. In spite of the detailed report presented to Council members by Mr. Martti Ahtisaari, portraying the distressing humanitarian situation which had arisen in Iraq, the Council was not able to take action on that proposal from the non-aligned members of the Council.

The Executive Delegate of the Secretary-General on humanitarian issues in the Gulf area, Prince Sadruddin Aga Khan, submitted a detailed and comprehensive report last month that carried a timely warning that Iraq was on the brink of famine. He warned that any delay in the Council's taking action might result in a catastrophe in that country.

(Mr. Mumbengegwi, Zimbabwe)

Zimbabwe had therefore expected the Council to respond swiftly through its Committee established by resolution 661 (1990), which, under paragraph 23 of resolution 687 (1991), is empowered to approve exceptions to the prohibition against the import of commodities and products originating from Iraq, when required, to ensure adequate financial resources for purchasing essential civilian needs. It is therefore to be regretted that the Council was not able to take advantage of this more expeditious procedure provided for in resolution 687 (1991).

In the view of my delegation, the principal merit of the draft resolution contained in document S/22941, on which we are about to vote, is that it creates an opportunity for the possibility of generating financial resources to meet the humanitarian requirements of the people of Iraq, as well as compensation for those who suffered loss and hardship as a result of the Gulf war. Zimbabwe therefore welcomes this step about to be taken by the Council to create a mechanism designed to address the needs of the victims of war, in both Iraq and Kuwait, as well as elsewhere.

While welcoming the fact that the Council is taking action to address the needs of the victims of the Gulf war, we cannot fail to register our reservations regarding those provisions of the draft resolution before us which encroach on national sovereignty.

Zimbabwe does recognize the need to ensure transparency in all the transactions to be carried out under the draft resolution before us. However, it is our view that monitoring arrangements could have been put in place that would have ensured transparency without encroaching on sovereignty.

In the final analysis, it is my delegation's view that no opportunity which offers the possibility of alleviating the suffering of innocent civilians should be allowed to slip through our fingers.

<u>The PRESIDENT</u> (interpretation from Spanish): I thank the representative of Zimbabwe for his kind words addressed to me.

<u>Mr. ALARCON de QUESADA</u> (Cuba) (interpretation from Spanish): Mr. President, in one of our private talks, which seem to account increasingly for the bulk of the work of the Council, I have already had an opportunity to say how delighted my delegation and I personally were to see you assume the presidency of the Council. Now that we are meeting formally, let me reiterate that sense of satisfaction and add what I was sure would happen in the first two weeks of August, that is, the manifestation of your competence, your sense of equity, your sense of balance and clear diplomatic skill in your conduct of the work of the Council.

I shall refer to the draft resolution contained in document S/22941. This draft resolution has been identified - and I do not quite know why - as the humanitarian resolution. It evidently has to do with situations with which the members of the Council are familiar, although the Council has not itself formally and expressly considered them.

Information has come to hand over the months reflecting the grave plight of the civilian population of Iraq as a result of the continuation of an ironclad economic sanctions regime. In the opinion of my delegation, the Council should have acted a long time ago in order to put an end completely to the economic sanctions, which cease to be justified at a time when the reasons which had justified them - which are set forth in Security Council resolution 661 (1990) - have been taken care of.

However, the draft resolution which is now before us, and which claims to be humanitarian in connection with the economic sanctions regime, in fact consolidates the sanctions. Indeed, it broadens them, as in the case of medicines and other supplies.

0132

(Mr. Alarcon de Quesada, Cuba)

In resolution 661 (1990), adopted a year ago, before the military clashes took place on Iraqi territory, the Council decided to exclude supplies intended exclusively for medical purposes and, in humanitarian circumstances, foodstuffs. We have received much information, some of it through missions sent by the United Nations itself. From this information, we learned clearly of the existence of humanitarian circumstances. The Council is now invited to add medicine and medical supplies to the sanctions regime, plus foodstuffs, supposedly through an authorization which would be given subject to certain controls for the export of Iraqi oil and the acquisition of some of these supplies, but subject to what we regard as an unjustifiable and strict control system under the sanctions. The Council is considering this draft resolution and two others, one of which has been around for two months, namely, the one setting the ceiling for the Iraqi contribution to the Compensation Fund, and which everyone knows the Council has been unable to consider because one delegation had difficulties with the text. Apparently it has now overcome those difficulties, and again all that was done without debate.

This Council had the opportunity, indeed the mandate pursuant to its own resolutions, to address Iraq's humanitarian needs and to authorize supplies or to slacken the sanctions regime so that those needs could have been better met, thus satisfying the humanitarian concern by which the members of the Council claim to be motivated.

Security Council resolution 687 (1991), paragraph 21, provided that we were to review the provisions every 60 days for the purpose of determining whether to reduce or lift the prohibitions referred to therein. Two 60-day periods have elapsed since the adoption of that resolution and the Council has not strictly determined whether it is appropriate to reduce or lift the

0133

(Mr. Alarcon de Quesada, Cuba)

prohibitions, nor indeed has it been kind enough to meet to carry out such a review.

We are now meeting in certain circumstances, more or less agreed upon in the private consultations to which I referred earlier, in order to adopt, with whatever explanations anyone may wish to make, three draft resolutions. However, we should not suppose that, because in the Council we do not discuss openly the reasons or the non-reasons, as it were, for the continuation of a system that is having a severe impact on the civilian population, there is no such debate. There are public reports, public documents, reports of commissions that have been to Iraq and very interesting debates and discussions.

For example, I have here some documents that show how various committees of the United States Congress considered the same ideas more than a month ago. They considered the same points that we now see in the draft resolution in document S/22941. Indeed, one of those Congressional hearings was held just before the issuance of Prince Sadruddin Aga Khan's report. Obviously, that Congressional meeting took place before the Sanctions Committee's discussion of that report. In other words, the members of the United States Congress and people from the State Department who attended that meeting - the Permanent Representative of the United States, I understand, was among them - discussed with their parliamentary colleagues the ideas which one month later we, the members of the Security Council, are generously informed of and are convened this afternoon kindly to endorse.

So there has been discussion. A representative of UNICEF has drawn attention to a fact that should have prompted more diligent action from the Council a long time ago, action unlike the one that we are required to take now. He stated that he was aware that there were various political

0134

(Mr. Alarcon de Quesada, Cuba)

implications involved in this question, but he also pointed out that no matter what the political implications were, we should not forget that here we are confronting a human calamity whose consequences would rest on the conscience of mankind for a very long time. He emphasized that it was not a natural disaster but rather an entirely man-made disaster.

The representative of UNICEF stated that he personally wished to point out that children were dying every day and that he had to bury too many small children in Iraq to allow him to consider that the situation was acceptable.

This means that we are faced with a situation which clearly suggests the need for the international community to show sensitivity with respect to the various and repeated reports that emphasize the gravity of the humanitarian situation in Iraq. However the draft resolution now before us, far from tackling the humanitarian issue, rather seeks to link it with other elements and to fit it into an overall context which we find unacceptable. It is quite unacceptable to try to use foodstuffs, medicines and medical supplies, which are vital to the health of human beings, as an instrument to attain certain political objectives. We believe that the sanctions against Iraq should have been eliminated at the moment when the causes which were argued in justification of it disappeared, and we feel that the sanctions regime should never have included elements which, from a moral point of view and from the point of view of civilization, cannot be imposed by anyone on anyone else.

My delegation does not believe that Chapter VII of the Charter, or indeed any other Chapter of the Charter, authorizes this Council to take upon itself certain functions and responsibilities, or to entrust them to the Secretary-General, which are clearly a breach of the principle of non-intervention in the internal affairs of States and of the principle of the

0135

(Mr. Alarcon de Quesada, Cuba)

sovereign equality of States. The establishment of the proposed mechanism would really mean appropriating elements of Iraqi sovereignty and would seek to apply to Iraq a type of trusteeship system, which is entirely contrary to the letter and spirit of the Charter.

I feel it appropriate to refer members to Article 78 of the Charter, which states:

> "The trusteeship system shall not apply to territories which have become members of the United Nations, relationship among which shall be based on respect for the principle of sovereign equality".

(Mr. Alarcon de Quesada, Cuba)

In actual fact, in practice, an attempt is being made to continue the war and the confrontation with Iraq after the end of the armed conflict and after the Council adopted various resolutions that claim to have put an end to it, making an improper use of the United Nations for these purposes. For these reasons, the Cuban delegation finds the draft resolution contained in document S/22941 to be unacceptable, and we will vote accordingly.

The PRESIDENT (interpretation from Spanish): I thank the representative of Cuba for his kind words addressed to me.

I shall now put to the vote the draft resolution contained in document S/22940.

A vote was taken by show of hands.

In favour: Austria, Belgium, China, Côte d'Ivoire, Cuba, Ecuador, France, India, Romania, Union of Soviet Socialist Republics, United Kingdom of Great Britain and Northern Ireland, United States of America, Yemen, Zaire, Zimbabwe

The PRESIDENT (interpretation from Spanish): There were 15 votes in favour. The draft resolution has been adopted unanimously as resolution 705 (1991).

I shall now put to the vote the draft resolution contained in document S/22941.

A vote was taken by show of hands.

In favour: Austria, Belgium, China, Côte d'Ivoire, Ecuador, France, India, Romania, Union of Soviet Socialist Republics, United Kingdom of Great Britain and Northern Ireland, United States of America, Zaire, Zimbabwe

Against: Cuba

Abstaining: Yemen

The PRESIDENT (interpretation from Spanish): The result of the voting is as follows: 13 votes in favour, 1 against and 1 abstention. The draft resolution has been adopted as resolution 706 (1991).

I shall now put to the vote the draft resolution contained in document S/22942.

There being no objection, it is so decided.

A vote was taken by show of hands.

In favour: Austria, Belgium, China, Côte d'Ivoire, Cuba, Ecuador, France, India, Romania, Union of Soviet Socialist Republics, United Kingdom of Great Britain and Northern Ireland, United States of America, Yemen, Zaire, Zimbabwe

The PRESIDENT (interpretation from Spanish): There were 15 votes in favour. The draft resolution has been adopted unanimously as resolution 707 (1991).

I shall now call on those members of the Council who wish to make statements following the voting.

Mr. ROCHEREAU DE LA SABLIERE (France) (interpretation from French): First of all, Sir, I should like to say how happy we are to see you as President of the Council. We should also like to thank Ambassador Alarcón de Quesada for the way in which he guided our work last month.

The reasons we are once again meeting in this Chamber, a little more than one year after the invasion of Kuwait by Iraq, and five months after the liberation of Kuwait, are, first of all, to deal with a humanitarian problem; secondly, to respond to the repeated failures of the Iraqi authorities to

0138

(Mr. Rochereau de la Sablière, France)

comply with their obligations under an important section of resolution 687 (1991), calling for the elimination of weapons of mass destruction; and, finally, to complete arrangements for the operation of the Compensation Fund. We have just adopted three draft resolutions on these topics.

The situation created in Iraq, owing to the conduct of the Government of Baghdad, is being followed with great attention in France. Last March, in the light of Mr. Ahtisaari's report, the Sanctions Committee and the Security Council deemed it necessary to ease the embargo so as to allow the civilian population in Iraq easier access to essential materials and supplies. My delegation actively contributed to that effort. In April France alerted the international community to the tragic fate of the civilian populations, in particular the Kurds, who were fleeing from Iraq in the hope of escaping the intolerable oppression to which they had fallen victim. This action led to the adoption of resolution 688 (1991).

Less than one month ago, the report of Prince Sadruddin Aga Khan described to the Council in detail the humanitarian situation in Iraq. It made clear the need to take urgent measures to avoid a serious worsening of the living conditions of the Iraqi population, which could not be held responsible for the faults of a regime that it had not freely chosen. It was necessary to act rapidly on the basis of resolution 687 (1991), which provided that Iraq could be authorized from time to time to export oil to finance the purchase of essential goods. In fact, Iraq had presented several requests of this nature to the Sanctions Committee.

We took these elements as the basis for drafting the text that the Security Council has just adopted. It appeared indispensable to provide very

(Mr. Rochereau de la Sablière, France)

specific modalities for the sale of Iraqi oil, for the use of the resources thus generated and for the distribution of essential goods that could thus be purchased, as it was necessary to have the assurance of achieving the priority goal pursued, namely, to meet the humanitarian needs of the Iraqi population as a whole.

Indeed, we could not trust a Government that attempts to get around Security Council resolutions, practises deception, still prohibits access to certain parts of its territory to United Nations representatives, detains by force Kuwaiti nationals and nationals of other countries and persists in refusing to allow Prince Sadruddin Aga Khan and the High Commissioner for Refugees to open humanitarian centres in those places where they are needed.

(Mr. Rochereau de la Sablière, France)

The text that has been adopted does not aim at establishing definitive rules. It was conceived as a response to an emergency situation for a period of six months. Hence, there was to be no prejudging of the future.

The authorized imports of Iraqi petroleum must produce a sum as determined on the basis of the evaluation of essential needs presented by Prince Sadruddin Aga Khan. One provision allows the Security Council to readjust that sum if it appears, in the light of a report requested of the Secretary-General or of information that might come later on, that that sum does not seem sufficient.

We felt that it was not up to the Security Council to specify either the details or the modalities for commercial and financial transactions authorized by the text nor the modalities for monitoring the distribution of food or medicine in order to ensure their availability to the Iraqi population. We are relying for all this on the Secretary-General, who will present us with his recommendations.

Finally, it was logical to provide, in implementation of prior resolutions, that income received from these exports by Iraq would also generate money for the Compensation Fund and make it possible to finance the operating costs of United Nations bodies set up within the framework of resolution 687 (1991), in particular the Special Commission for the elimination of weapons of mass destruction. The particular provision of the resolution regarding the amount to be levied for the Compensation Fund on the basis of approved authorizations reflects our concern over seeing the Fund built up rapidly. Thereafter the Fund will operate according to the modalities to be decided upon by its Governing Council.

(Mr. Rochereau de la Sablière, France)

The draft resolution on nuclear matters on which we have also just taken a decision is a response to the inadmissible behaviour of the Iraqi authorities. On several occasions, our Council expressed its concern over Iraq's repeated violations of its obligations, either those imposed upon it by resolution 687 (1991) or those deriving from its commitments to the IAEA. Non-compliance with those commitments has been established by the Board of Governors of that Agency. It has also indicated its deep concern over Iraq's attempts at deception. The information made available in recent weeks by the Chairman of the Special Commission for the Elimination of Weapons of Mass Destruction and by the Director General of the IAEA following on-site inspections goes overwhelmingly against the Iraqi Government. It clearly appears that Iraq was involved in a clandestine research programme intended to get nuclear weapons for Iraq, in flagrant violation of its international obligations.

The resolution therefore condemns the failures of Iraq and spells out certain provisions of resolution 687 (1991) regarding the activities of the Special Commission in order to help it carry out the important mission given it by the Security Council.

I shall complete my statement with the draft resolution regarding the percentage of the value of Iraqi petroleum exports within which the Governing Council of the Compensation Fund will have to set the actual amount of Iraq's contribution. The adoption of the proposal made to us by the Secretary-General in this regard, a proposal that takes into account both the needs of the Iraqi people and the need to ensure fair compensation, will complete the work of setting up the Compensation Fund established to compensate the victims of the invasion and occupation of Kuwait. Since the

(Mr. Rochereau de la Sablière, France)

decision has already been taken in Geneva, the Fund will give priority consideration to small requests, essentially those which will be presented by those who lived in Iraq or Kuwait and had to leave those countries and abandon their possessions.

The PRESIDENT (interpretation from Spanish): I thank the representative of France for the kind words he addressed to me.

Mr. PICKERING (United States of America): First of all, I want to congratulate you, Sir, on your assumption of the presidency of the Council and for the work in which you have already led us and to thank your predecessor, Ambassador Alarcon de Queseda, for his work last month.

Once again the Council has convened to take action on problems arising out of Iraq's aggression against Kuwait.

The resolution that we have just approved on compliance with part C of resolution 687 (1991) on inspection and destruction of weapons of mass destruction in Iraq draws the attention of the world to Iraq's failure to comply with resolution 687 (1991) and Iraq's repeated material breaches of its obligations under the nuclear non-proliferation Treaty. I will not detail that list of compliance failures and material breaches, which the International Atomic Energy Agency (IAEA) and the United Nations Special Commission have so well documented in recent weeks, but merely note that we have heard two further reports: the Special Commission's revelation of Iraq's biological weapons violations in its letter of 5 August and evidence of additional nuclear weapons violations contained in the International Atomic Energy Agency's letter to the Secretary-General of 6 August.

The primary purpose behind this resolution is to strengthen the role of the International Atomic Energy Agency and the Special Commission in

0143

(Mr. Pickering, United States)

performing their important task of eliminating Iraq's weapons of mass destruction capability and of assuring that such weapons are not reacquired.

On the one hand, this resolution provides the IAEA and the Special Commission with certain new tools to bolster the effectiveness of their work. On the other hand, the resolution sends a message to Iraq. What is expected, indeed demanded, is Iraq's full compliance with all its obligations under relevant Treaties and Security Council resolutions as well as its complete cooperation with the IAEA and the Special Commission.

The humanitarian resolution that we have just approved intends primarily to get humanitarian assistance to those in Iraq who need it the most. This is not a resolution lifting sanctions. In fact, it will strengthen the sanctions by preventing the Iraqi Government from seeking political and military gains through the misery of the Iraqi people which it has itself caused. Under the exceptions provision of paragraph 23 of resolution 687 (1991), we are making an exception for a special and limited purpose for a limited period of time. With its emphasis on equitable distribution and monitoring, the resolution seeks to ensure that food and other humanitarian assistance reaches those for whom it is most intended. The importance of vigilant monitoring of distribution of humanitarian assistance arising out of this resolution cannot be overemphasized. Careful monitoring is required to deter diversion of food and other humanitarian assistance to privileged sectors of Iraqi society or the misuse of this assistance at the expense of those most in need. Our sad experience has shown that this kind of diversion is a very real possibility unless we take strong steps to prevent it.

In adopting this resolution, the Council has put the Secretary-General and the Secretariat at the centre of the process of providing humanitarian

(Mr. Pickering, United States)

assistance to Iraq. My Government recognizes that the resolution places a heavy burden on the Secretary-General in drawing up his report on a number of highly complex and technical issues never before tackled by the United Nations, but it also gives him the authority to propose whatever additional measures he deems necessary and appropriate to monitor, supervise and manage this operation. Subsequently we will be depending on the Secretary-General and the United Nations to ensure that the goals of the resolution are truly achieved. We stand ready, for our part, to help in any way we can. We appreciate the excellent work the Secretary-General has done throughout the Gulf crisis. We are confident that the United Nations will rise to this challenge once again. I should also note that we have agreed to support the 30-per-cent ceiling imposed by resolution 705 (1991) on the basis that it is fully and directly linked to resolution 706 (1991) and any subsequent Iraqi oil sales.

0145

(Mr. Pickering, United States)

It is important to note that for the past 10 years Iraq itself has spent 28 per cent of its income on military equipment alone.

Finally, I want to mention the pressing and urgent need for Iraq to return all prisoners of war and all captives taken from Kuwait and from other States.

The PRESIDENT (interpretation from Spanish): I thank the representative of the United States for the kind words he addressed to me.

Mr. LI Daoyu (China) (interpretation from Chinese): At the outset, Sir, I should like to congratulate you on your assumption of the presidency of the Security Council for this month and to wish you success in your work.

I should like also to take this opportunity to express my sincere thanks to His Excellency Ambassador Ricardo Alarcon de Quesada, Permanent Representative of Cuba, for the remarkable way in which he handled the work of the Security Council last month.

The Chinese delegation wishes to state its position on resolution 706 (1991), which the Council has just adopted. The ever-deteriorating situation faced by the Iraqi people has for some time been a question of deep concern to the international community, including China. Sound recommendations were made in the report submitted by His Excellency Prince Sadruddin Aga Khan, Executive Delegate of the Secretary-General, but regrettably the Security Council has taken no action on those recommendations.

Resolution 706 (1991), just adopted, permits Iraq to export oil for a given period in order to finance the import of humanitarian goods. That will help alleviate to a certain extent the grave and deteriorating situation faced by the Iraqi people. It is with that in mind that the Chinese delegation voted in favour of resolution 706 (1991).

0146

(Mr. Li Daoyu, China)

But we are of the view that the sovereignty of Iraq must be respected in the implementation of that resolution. Iraq is entitled to play its proper role in the purchase and distribution of the food, medicine and other materials required to meet essential civilian needs.

The designated sum from Iraq's oil income should be used principally for humanitarian relief work. The amount of oil the resolution permits Iraq to export seems insufficient to meet the humanitarian needs of the Iraqi people. For that reason, the Security Council should review this question again at an appropriate time to consider increasing the permitted amount of oil sales and extending the time limit for those sales.

Finally, I would note that it is within the terms of reference of the Governing Council of the United Nations Compensation Commission to decide the percentage of the value of Iraq's oil exports that should be paid into the Compensation Fund.

The Chinese delegation reserves its position on the questions to which I have alluded.

The PRESIDENT (interpretation from Spanish): I thank the representative of China for the kind words he addressed to me.

Mr. RICHARDSON (United Kingdom): It is a pleasure, Sir, to congratulate you on your assumption of the presidency of the Council and at the same time to thank Ambassador Alarcon de Quesada for his effective handling of our affairs last month. Let me add, however, on this occasion, Mr. President, that we have particularly appreciated your patient, skilful and fair handling of our consultations on these important issues over the past two weeks: thank you very much.

(Mr. Richardson, United Kingdom)

My Government welcomes the resolution the Security Council has just adopted setting a ceiling for the hypothecation of Iraq's oil revenues. That decision provides some assurance to the many individuals, companies and institutions which because of the Iraqi invasion and occupation of Kuwait lost their property and in some cases their lives that they will receive some recompense.

I noted sadly, but without surprise, that in the lengthy statement we heard earlier from the representative of Iraq there was not a word of regret for the suffering that Iraq had inflicted on so many innocent people. We tend sometimes to forget about them, and yet they are, of course, one of the main purposes and motivations behind this resolution.

We were pleased by the results of the first session of the Governing Council of the United Nations Compensation Commission, held in July and August, and, in the light of what I have just said, in particular the agreement to establish an expedited procedure for small claimants. We look forward to the continuation of the work of the Compensation Commission in September and October.

I turn now to the resolution we have just adopted on oil sales. As my delegation said in informal consultations among members of the Council on 5 August, when the last review of sanctions took place, my Government does not believe that the time has yet come to lift sanctions. The Iraqi Government has failed to live up to many of its obligations. It has failed, for example, to release Kuwaitis and other foreigners, including a British national, Mr. Ian Richter. There is still a great quantity of Kuwaiti property to return. And more generally, the policies and practices of Iraq have included the oppression of its own people in the north and the south of the country.

(Mr. Richardson, United Kingdom)

But it has never been the aim of my Government to harm the Iraqi people, who after all have no voice of their own in their own country. You cannot deal with the misdeeds of a country's Government without, regrettably, having some impact on the civilian population. But in view of the problems that have been highlighted in the reports by Mr. Ahtisaari and subsequently by Prince Sadruddin, my Government is ready to permit limited sales of Iraqi oil over a six-month period to fund the importation of food, medicine and other humanitarian supplies. A portion of the oil revenues must go to the Compensation Fund and to pay for the Special Commission, the costs of the Iraq-Kuwait Boundary Demarcation Commission and the arrangements for returning Kuwaiti property plundered by Iraq.

In view of the past record of the Iraqi Government, we need an effective United Nations system for monitoring oil sales and for the equitable distribution of humanitarian supplies. These monitoring arrangements, in our view, must ensure that supplies reach the vulnerable segments of the Iraqi population in all parts of Iraq, and we believe there should be provision for random sampling by United Nations officials to that end.

But that said, we shall look forward with keenness to seeing the Secretary-General's proposals in 20 days' time, and we shall take them fully into account in determing what practical steps are needed to fulfil the terms of this resolution.

I turn finally to the resolution we have adopted on the weapons of mass destruction, a resolution of great importance. We believe it is vital that the Special Commission and the International Atomic Energy Agency should

0149

(Mr. Richardson, United Kingdom)

have all the powers they need to carry out their duties under resolution 687 (1991); that, indeed, is one of the main purposes of this resolution.

I mentioned earlier the sad failure of Iraq to carry out all its obligations, and this applies with particular force to the question of weapons of mass destruction. More and more chilling details are being unearthed. We now have confirmation that there was indeed a super-gun project. We now have confirmation that Iraq did indeed have a biological-warfare research programme with an offensive capability. We have confirmation that Iraq held much greater stocks of chemical weapons than it had previously admitted. And finally, we have confirmation that it had separated plutonium from enriched uranium and was developing an industrial-scale facility for enriching its own uranium by using both centrifugal and electro-magnetic isotopic separation processes - the latter, incidentally, in breach of the safeguards of the Treaty on the Non-Proliferation of Nuclear Weapons, of which Iraq is a signatory.

(Mr. Richardson, United Kingdom)

Only yesterday a spokesman of the Secretary-General issued a press release with further details of Iraq's biological weapons research programme. I fear that this is further evidence that the declarations we received earlier fall far short of what is to be desired, and the resolution we have just adopted is wholly appropriate.

In this context, and to conclude, we do also welcome the publication of the plans produced by the Special Commission and the IAEA concerning future compliance. We are studying them carefully and we are sure that all members will be giving them close attention in the weeks to come.

The PRESIDENT (interpretation from Spanish): I thank the representative of the United Kingdom for his kind words.

Mr. HAJNOCZI (Austria): Permit me to congratulate you, Sir, on your assumption of the presidency of the Council for this month. Given your personal and professional qualities and your experience, we are convinced, as we have already seen, that the Council cannot but benefit from your guidance in carrying out its work.

I should also like to thank the Permanent Representative of Cuba, Ambassador Alarcon de Quesada, for the excellent manner in which he presided over the Council last month.

Austria voted in favour of, *inter alia*, resolution 706 (1991), which contains a package of measures aimed at dealing with a number of questions, first and foremost measures to deal with the humanitarian situation in Iraq. We are pleased to note that it has thus been finally possible to transform into a resolution the results of the consultations held by the Chairman of the Security Council Committee established by resolution 661 (1990) as reported by him to the members of the Security Council during informal consultations held on 25 July.

0151

(Mr. Hajnoczi, Austria)

The action initiated today is indeed urgently needed. The latest report on the situation of the Iraqi civilian population, namely the report dated 15 July 1991 of the inter-agency mission headed by the Executive Delegate of the Secretary-General for the United Nations Inter-Agency Humanitarian Programme, presented an alarming picture of the serious nutritional and health situation of the civilian population and the risk of further deterioration.

We hope that the Iraqi Government will - previous statements to the contrary notwithstanding - take full advantage of the opportunity which will be provided to it to earn the necessary revenue for the purchase of foodstuffs, medicines and material and supplies for essential civilian needs of its population. Anything less could lead to serious consequences which should be avoided in the best interest of the Iraqi population.

In this connection the equitable distribution of imports for humanitarian purposes in all regions of Iraq and to all segments of the Iraqi civilian population is of course of paramount importance. We understand the relevant provisions in resolution 706 (1991) as inviting the Secretary-General to submit a plan for an effective United Nations role in this respect to be carried out, by and large, by the United Nations personnel currently in Iraq. Reports to the Security Council on the working of this scheme for ensuring an equitable distribution would enable us to monitor its implementation. Another important element of the report requested of the Secretary-General are the estimates of the humanitarian requirements of Iraq which will be the basis for our final decision.

While resolution 706 (1991) has at its origin our most serious concern regarding the humanitarian situation in Iraq, resolution 707 (1991), but also parts of resolution 706 (1991), address another fundamental problem: Iraq's

(Mr. Hajnoczi, Austria)

failure to comply with or fully carry out its obligations under resolution 687 (1991). By voting in favour of resolution 707 (1991) Austria demonstrates the crucial importance it attaches to full compliance. In this context, I want to stress our support for the activities of the Special Commission and the IAEA with regard to Section C of resolution 687 (1991). The results of their missions undertaken hitherto have shown how significant their activities are. We view resolution 707 (1991) not only as sending a message to Iraq but also as strengthening the hand of the Special Commission and the IAEA.

The PRESIDENT (interpretation from Spanish): I thank the representative of Austria for his kind words.

Mr. LOZINSKY (Union of Soviet Socialist Republics) (interpretation from Russian): I wish to congratulate you, Sir, on your assumption of the high post of President of the Security Council and to express our confidence that you will continue to guide the work of the Council as successfully and outstandingly as you did in the first half of this month. I also wish to thank the Ambassador of Cuba for his successful conduct of the work of the Council in July, which he handled with his customary diplomatic skill.

The Soviet delegation is gratified that the Security Council has adopted three important resolutions - two of them unanimously and the other by an overwhelming majority. Their purpose is to secure the implementation of Security Council resolution 687 (1991), which defined the arrangements for eliminating the consequences of Iraq's aggression against Kuwait and restoring peace and security in that region. The resolutions that have been adopted make it possible for Iraq, in accordance with the arrangements set forth in resolution 687 (1991), to export a certain amount of oil in order to obtain sufficient financial resources with which to acquire foodstuffs, medicines and materials and supplies for basic civilian needs. In addition, the resolutions

(Mr. Lozinsky, USSR)

have triggered the functioning of previous decisions on the financing of the activities of the Compensation Fund, the Special Commission and the Boundary Demarcation Commission and various other relevant United Nations expenses. The Security Council has also emphasized the importance of the need to repatriate all citizens of Kuwait and other countries being held by force in Iraq and also compensation for plundered property - a point which Ambassador Abulhasan of Kuwait rightly emphasized in his important statement at the beginning of our meeting.

The ceiling established by the Council for deductions to be paid into the Compensation Fund, in our view, creates the necessary conditions for compensation for losses sustained by victims of aggression and also for the solution of the pressing humanitarian problems facing the population of Iraq, as well as enabling Iraq to make payments on its external debt. At the same time, the Security Council has condemned Iraq's grave breaches of its obligations as a party to the Treaty on the non-proliferation of nuclear weapons and of various obligations under Section C of resolution 687 (1991).

(Mr. Lozinsky, USSR)

In this connection, the Security Council was obliged to stipulate the adoption of various concrete and effective measures to bring to an end Iraq's breaches of its international obligations. Clearly, many of the provisions of the resolutions we have just adopted would have been quite unnecessary had it not been for Baghdad's persistent attempts to deceive the international community about its military programmes, and in particular with regard to its activities in the nuclear sphere, in addition to the delays Iraq has incurred in the fulfilment of other obligations. We firmly expect Iraq henceforth strictly to fulfil its obligations under all relevant Security Council resolutions.

In the final analysis, that would be in the interests of Iraq itself. Only in this way can it turn a tragic page in its history and take a worthy place in the international community. The complete implementation of Security Council decisions would also bolster the ability of the United Nations to act as a guarantor of peace and security, based on the rule of law, and would help prevent such crises, both in that region and other regions of the world.

The PRESIDENT (interpretation from Spanish): I thank the representative of the Union of Soviet Socialist Republics for his kind words addressed to me.

Mr. VAN DAELE (Belgium) (interpretation from French): Allow me first, Sir, to congratulate you on your assumption of the presidency. The exemplary manner in which you have handled our work so far leaves me convinced that the Council will fulfil its mission completely in the coming weeks.

I also wish to thank Ambassador Alarcon de Quesada for the effectiveness and courtesy with which he presided over the Council's work in July.

(Mr. van Daele, Belgium)

We have just adopted a resolution enabling States to resume, for a period of six months and up to a fixed amount, oil imports from Iraq. That resolution meets the humanitarian concerns voiced on various occasions by my delegation in the Council and in the Sanctions Committee. That is why we decided to become one of the sponsors of the resolution.

The resolution enables Iraq to obtain revenues that will make it possible for it to finance its imports of foodstuffs and essential goods.

Since April my delegation has advocated this option, while making it clear - and this is an important point - that the international community had to make quite sure that the revenues in question were really being used for foodstuffs and essential imports, and that the distribution would be carried out equitably for the benefit of all segments of the population in all regions.

We are gratified that the resolution we have just adopted sets up a workable system that meets that two-fold requirement.

In this respect, the Belgian delegation is grateful to the Secretary-General for kindly agreeing to organizing this supervision and monitoring and making it possible also for the Council to assess Iraq's humanitarian needs, thanks to the excellent report of his special representative, Prince Sadruddin Aga Khan.

Resolution 706 (1991) before us creates the necessary conditions to generate additional revenues, which will make it possible to sustain the compensation fund and finance the cost of the elimination of Iraqi weapons of mass destruction. In this way, the compensation fund will quickly be equipped with funds to provide priority compensation for the individual human cases that its Governing Council, which met recently in Geneva, has rightly identified as being worthy of special attention.

0156

(Mr. van Daele, Belgium)

Similarly, it was, in our opinion, very justifiable for the Council to reach a decision at the same meeting today on the two other resolutions we have just adopted. The compensation fund could not become operational, particularly in order to deal with individual cases until the ceiling for amounts to be withheld from Iraq's oil revenues had been set.

Lastly, I wish to conclude with these remarks: we felt it was necessary for the procedures for inspection of Iraqi weapons of mass destruction to be defined most meticulously at the same time as we were setting the modalities for the financing of the destruction of these weapons, and at the same time we were able to draw all necessary lessons from the reports of the special commission on its mission.

Those are the remarks of my delegation which were prompted by the adoption of these three draft resolutions.

The PRESIDENT (interpretation from Spanish): I thank the representative of Belgium for his kind words addressed to me.

Mr. GHAREKHAN (India): Today is the forty-fourth anniversary of India's independence. On this auspicious day it is my pleasure to extend to you, Sir, my greetings and to express the deep satisfaction of my delegation to see you presiding over the Council. You bring to this high office a long and rich tradition in jurisprudence and diplomacy. These last two weeks you have given more than ample evidence of your skill and wisdom.

I should also like to express my delegation's deep thanks and appreciation to the Permanent Representative of Cuba, Ambassador Alarcon de Quesada, for the manner in which he conducted the proceedings of the Council last month.

(Mr. Gharekhan, India)

I shall confine my remarks to resolution 706 (1991). The events in the Gulf over the last year set in motion the circumstances that the Security Council has been addressing. In recent months, an issue of undoubted importance has been the international community's response to the humanitarian problems in the region. Kuwait's independence and sovereignty have been restored, and we rejoice with the people of Kuwait, but its ordeal is not yet over. Meanwhile, the civilian population in Iraq undergoes suffering and trauma. The latter is our concern here at the moment.

The question, I believe, is not just the need to deal with the humanitarian requirements of those who suffer for no fault of their own. Both the requirements and the need to address them are evident. What is at stake is the manner in which those needs can be met. Several reports, ranging from the former Under-Secretary-General, Martti Ahtisaari's, to various missions by United Nations bodies and non-governmental organizations, down to the latest report by the Secretary-General's Executive Delegate for the United Nations Inter-Agency Humanitarian Programme, Prince Sadruddin Aga Khan, have testified to the wretched condition of the Iraqi civilian population affected by war and sanctions.

My delegation's anxiety to formulate urgent and effective action to alleviate the misery of civilians in Iraq dates back several months. India's view has always been that the Security Council has the obligation to redress the plight of the innocent, just as the international community, as a whole, has partially been doing.

In cooperation with other non-aligned members of the Security Council, my delegation had proposed a draft resolution on this issue right at the beginning, but the Council was not able to adopt it. In the event, the

0158

(Mr. Gharekhan, India)

President of the Council drew attention in a statement to the importance of humanitarian relief for Iraq's civilian population.

In the Sanctions Committee, as well as during informal consultations, India has consistently and repeatedly advocated a generous and effective approach to tackling the humanitarian situation in Iraq. To our regret, our efforts did not receive the unanimous support of Council members. This concern of ours that I have just explained has motivated, and continues to motivate, our position in the Security Council's consideration of the matter.

Needless to say, the United Nations is not unaware of the need to respond. The Sanctions Committee, in particular, has paid considerable attention to the problem. Indeed, the Sanctions Committee devised procedures to expedite certain forms of relief assistance to Iraq.

0159

(Mr. Gharekhan, India)

As a result of the efforts of non-aligned countries, including my own, the Council recognized the need to address this issue in all seriousness and with urgency. My delegation's initial reservations at what we felt were inadequate measures to deal with a problem of considerable magnitude were none the less somewhat allayed by the purposeful manner in which the Sanctions Committee, under the able Chairmanship of Ambassador Hohenfellner of Austria, operated the simplified procedures to clear humanitarian assistance to Iraq. Security Council resolution 687 (1991) subsequently, among other things, defined the humanitarian context in the circumstances then prevailing.

The humanitarian situation in Iraq continues to be grim. The most recent proof of this was Prince Sadruddin Aga Khan's report following his inter-agency mission to Iraq last month. After describing the desperate plight of the Iraqi civilian population, the report concluded that more massive infusion of relief supplies into Iraq was needed than what voluntary international assistance could provide. And for this purpose, he advocated permitting Iraq to utilize some of its oil revenues. We all agree with him on this point.

Resolution 706 (1991), just adopted, tries to meet these concerns to some extent. My delegation supports the idea of permitting oil sales from Iraq to finance, in a certain measure, its humanitarian needs. Paragraph 23 of Council resolution 687 (1991) deserves to be recalled here. That resolution chartered post-war arrangements for Iraq, and paragraph 23 lays down the provisions that should enable a response to the humanitarian circumstances that currently exist and are so acknowledged.

My delegation would have preferred a clear and unambiguous approach to this issue. The simplest and most effective way would have been to take

0160

(<u>Mr. Gharekhan, India</u>)

action under paragraph 23. That, however, was not to be. In the alternative, my delegation would have liked the resolution to deal with the humanitarian aspect on its own. I realize there are other important issues. In particular, the issue of the repatriation of Kuwaiti and third country nationals or their remains must be resolved without delay. But in view of the urgency of providing relief in Iraq, and realizing that this resolution was perhaps the only way of achieving it, my delegation decided to go along with it. I trust that the adoption of the resolution will indeed result in the quick and effective supply of humanitarian assistance to vulnerable sections of Iraqi society.

My delegation's view of the role of the United Nations in the provision of humanitarian relief to Iraq is clear. All would agree with the objective, as my delegation does, that the resources raised by Iraqi oil sales should be deployed for the purposes specified and that foodstuffs and other supplies should be provided equitably in all parts of Iraq and to all segments of the Iraqi civilian population. My delegation firmly believes that this should be sought to be achieved through means which are both consistent with the Charter, particularly the all-important principle of non-interference in the internal affairs of countries, and in as practical and simplified a form as possible. Of cardinal importance in any such exercise is the consent of the country concerned. Lack of consent, or the absence of a specific request that incorporates such consent, will only thwart the effort. My delegation considers it especially important that the measures adopted must not adversely affect or undermine Iraq's sovereignty. Prince Sadruddin Aga Khan himself observed in his report, in the context of equitable distribution, that a functioning food rationing system was already in place in Iraq. The Iraqi

(Mr. Gharekhan, India)

Government's willingness to accept suitable mechanisms for the monitoring of oil revenues as well as their utilization has also been indicated by the Prince. Prince Sadruddin's report in fact made useful suggestions regarding the United Nations monitoring system that could be instituted for the purpose essentially by further developing and strengthening the present monitoring arrangements in the context of the United Nations humanitarian presence in Iraq. It is, therefore, evident that the humanitarian objectives we aim at can be achieved with simple and yet effective arrangements for observation and regular reporting, combined with provisions for review, periodically and as necessary. None of this calls for extensive United Nations machinery for administration or management. Such a United Nations presence, superimposed as it were on Iraq, would be intrusive, cumbersome and expensive. In addition, problems would arise in regard to United Nations expertise and provision of personnel for such a massive operation.

My delegation is of the view that the provisions in the resolution do not call for arrangements of a tutelary kind that might have the effect of interfering in Iraq's internal affairs. The Secretary-General, who is requested to present his considered recommendations in the matter in 20 days' time, will no doubt keep these points in mind.

It is in the light of these considerations, and mindful of our concerns as I have tried to explain them, that we voted in favour of the resolution.

The PRESIDENT (interpretation from Spanish): I should like to congratulate the ambassador of India, on behalf of the Security Council, on the occasion of the anniversary of Indian national independence today. I also thank him for his kind words.

Mr. FLOREAN (Romania): It is a pleasure for the Romanian delegation to congratulate you, Sir, on your assumption of the presidency of the Council for the month of August. As you have proved during these two weeks, we are confident that your efforts will be crowned with success for the benefit of our Council.

I should also like to congratulate Ambassador Alarcon de Quesada of Cuba for the effective manner in which he conducted the business of the Council during the month of July.

The Council has just adopted three resolutions concerning the situation between Iraq and Kuwait, dealing with important aspects of the matter. The first resolution establishes the ceiling of the value of Iraq's petroleum exports to the Compensation Fund established under resolution 687 (1991). The second resolution concerns the plan for the ongoing monitoring and verification of Iraq's compliance with a number of its obligations under the relevant parts of section C of resolution 687 (1991). The third resolution authorizes, under special conditions, the import during a period of six months of petroleum and petroleum products originating in Iraq.

We see these resolutions as an important element in assisting in the normalization of the situation in the Gulf. Kuwait, which suffered so much during the six months of its occupation, and other affected countries and individuals, will start being compensated. The situation of the Iraqi civilian population in all its segments will be improved. We understand that the provisions of resolution 706 (1991), just adopted, are extraordinary ones and the Council was obliged to react in this manner in the light of the Iraqi Government's practices and policies. We should like to stress that the manner in which these resolutions will be implemented will be a test for the Iraqi authorities and will create the grounds for a more positive approach of the

0163

(Mr. Florean, Romania)

Council *vis-à-vis* the future requests of Iraq to ease the sanctions. In this spirit, the Romanian delegation voted in favour of all three resolutions. That is why we make a solemn appeal to the Iraqi Government to fulfil its international obligations and to act in good faith to implement the provisions of the resolutions just adopted.

0164

The PRESIDENT (interpretation from Spanish): I thank the representative of Romania for his kind words addressed to me.

I shall now make a statement in my capacity as representative of Ecuador. I subscribe to all the words of thanks expressed to Ambassador Alarcon de Quesada for the way in which he conducted the Council's work last month, and in fact, I am reiterating what I said before we met on 8 August.

Ecuador voted in favour of the three draft resolutions adopted by the Council. As regards resolution 705 (1991), we did so because it incorporates a recommendation made by the Secretary-General about the percentage of Iraqi oil sales that should be paid into the Compensation Fund. Ecuador endorses the reasons set forth by the Secretary-General in his report for arriving at that recommendation.

With regard to resolution 706 (1991), Ecuador has always upheld the principle whereby the humanitarian needs of the people of Iraq deserve the most favourable and timely consideration. We were among the sponsors of a draft resolution to that end, and we have consistently advocated in the Council and in the Committee provided for in resolution 661 (1991) that the Council should heed the humanitarian needs of the Iraqi people. The measures contained in resolution 706 (1991) will no doubt contribute to the purpose of relieving suffering and meeting the essential needs of the civilian population of Iraq.

Ecuador, however, has previously expressed its doubt about the wisdom of considering the humanitarian situation in Iraq under Chapter VII of the Charter and in connection with various other subjects that have a bearing on obligations assumed by Iraq, which need to be fully discharged, but which have nothing to do with the humanitarian situation. Moreover, Ecuador considers

(The President)

that supervision and monitoring by the United Nations should not lead the Organization to engage in actions at variance with permanent respect for the principles of the Charter, particularly paragraphs 1 and 2 of Article II.

As to resolution 707 (1991), Ecuador considers that, in the light of recent experience, its adoption was entirely justified.

I shall now revert to my role as President of the Council.

The Security Council has thus concluded the present stage of its consideration of the item on its agenda. The Council will remain seized of the matter.

The meeting rose at 6.55 p.m.

0166

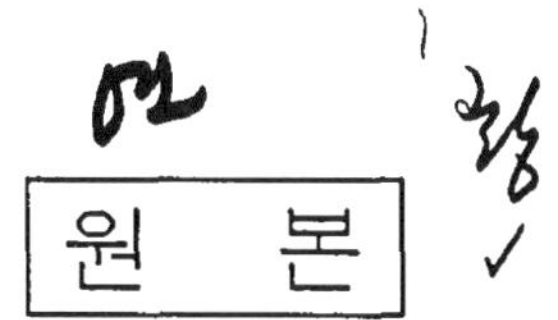

외 무 부

종 별 :

번 호 : UNW-2145 일 시 : 91 0818 1800

수 신 : 장 관(국연,중동일,기정)

발 신 : 주 유엔 대사

제 목 : 걸프사태(유엔동향)

지난 8월초 터어키군의 이락 월경사태 (SEPARATISTTERROISTS 추적을 이유로 이락 영토내 16 KM 까지진입)를 항의하는 이락측 안보리 문서가 금 8.13배포되었음.

첨부:상기기사: UNW(F)-424 끝

(대사 노창희-국장)

국기국 1차보 중아국 외정실 분석관 안기부

PAGE 1

91.08.14 09:00 WG

외신 1과 통제관

0167

UNW(F)-424 10813 1800
(국연 · 중동일 . 기정) 총2매

Iraq Now Faces Very Tall Order: Selling Its Oil

Some Customers Are Wary Of Resuming Business, Even if U.N. Approves

By JAMES TANNER
Staff Reporter of THE WALL STREET JOURNAL

Iraq faces another hurdle in resuming oil exports, even if the United Nations allows it some emergency sales as expected: finding buyers.

One big former purchaser of Iraqi oil refuses even to reply to messages sent by officials of Iraq's State Oil Marketing Organization. Other oil companies that formerly accounted for the bulk of purchases of Iraqi crudes, including several in the U.S., also are wary about a possible renewal of commercial dealings with Baghdad.

"At the present time, we have no plans to buy any Iraqi crude," said a spokeswoman for Chevron Corp., once a major buyer.

The reason is more political than commercial. Even if the U.N. allows Iraq some limited oil sales, U.S. companies would still have to get permission from Washington to buy the crude. The U.N. imposed an embargo on all trade with Baghdad following Iraq's invasion of Kuwait a year ago.

Iraq could still try to sell oil to some developing countries and smaller companies outside the U.S., where the sales wouldn't be politically sensitive. But it could take time for Iraq to line up sufficient small buyers to offset the loss of big purchasers.

The U.N. Security Council is expected to vote this week on a draft resolution that would permit a temporary lifting of economic sanctions and allow an emergency sale of Iraqi oil to finance medical and humanitarian aid for the Iraqi populace. The resolution has been approved by the five permament Security Council members including the U.S., although Baghdad has rejected the proposal because it practically strips Iraq of control over its oil revenue.

The resolution may be amended somewhat to overcome some of Baghdad's objections. As it stands now, Iraq could be allowed to sell $1.6 billion of its oil, or 90 million barrels at current prices, under strict U.N. supervision. The proceeds would be earmarked for purchases of food, medicines, and other emergency supplies for Iraqis.

If spread over six months, the sale might average 500,000 barrels a day. That would be one-fifth of Iraq's former total exports and less than half the amount of oil it was sending to the U.S. in 1990 before the invasion. Iraq then was the U.S.'s No. 2 source of imported oil, behind Saudi Arabia.

Some U.S. oil companies are currently making inquiries to the foreign assets control group of the U.S. Treasury Department, which would handle approvals of oil purchases, probably on a cargo-by-cargo basis as in the case of Iranian oil.

"They would have to have permission to import the oil by going through the licensing process which already exists in foreign assets control," a Treasury spokeswoman said. She added that the companies aren't prohibited from talking to Iraq.

But few companies will confirm that they are even doing that. A spokesman for Coastal Corp., one of the largest buyers of Iraqi oil before the embargo, said the company hasn't made any efforts to line up potential cargoes. "We haven't done anything, and we won't until some rules and regulations are established," he said.

San Francisco-based Chevron was among the biggest buyers of Iraqi oil before the Persian Gulf crisis began last year. The company is said to have had as much as 10 million barrels of Iraqi crude in tankers headed for the U.S. when the U.N. imposed its trade embargo.

Fina Inc., the Dallas-based affiliate of Belgium's Petrofina, was buying 100,000 to 125,000 barrels of Iraqi oil a day, almost two-thirds of its requirements, before the embargo and might consider new purchases.

"We are not actively looking into it," said Michael Couch, vice president, supply and transportation. But, he added, if the U.N. approves the plan, Iraq accepts it, and the U.S. government agrees, "we'd be interested." Still, said Mr. Couch, "we would give consideration to what we think the general public opinion would be."

—Caleb Solomon contributed to this article.

UW-2145
1부득

2-1

0168

U.N. Using U.S. Spy Planes to Monitor Iraqi Arms

By JERRY GRAY

Special to The New York Times

UNITED NATIONS, Aug. 12 — Surprised by disclosures that Iraq conducted clandestine nuclear and biological research despite international monitoring, the United Nations said today that it had started using United States-owned high-altitude spy planes to survey Iraq for nuclear, chemical and biological weapons sites.

A United Nations spokesman said that U-2 flights over Iraq began last weekend under the guidance of the United Nations special commission charged with identifying and eliminating Iraq's weapons of mass destruction. The commission was set up after Iraq's defeat in the Persian Gulf war.

Baghdad agreed to the monitoring, but only after its Foreign Ministry wrote Secretary General Javier Pérez de Cuéllar protesting the flights and the decision to use American aircraft.

"American aircraft have for months been overflying Iraq for purposes of reconnaissance and have photographed virtually every inch of Iraqi territory," said the letter, dated Aug. 6 and signed by Iraq's chief United Nations delegate, Abdul Amir al-Anbari.

The special commission did not say how many U-2 flights it requested. It said Security Council Resolution 687, the cease-fire resolution that ended the gulf war, allowed it to make the aerial surveys to insure that Iraq was complying with the terms of the resolution.

"The special commission will be provided with the photographs on all the sites, locations, facilities and objects which have been surveyed at its request," said a United Nations spokesman, Frederic Eckhard. "This will permit the special commission to arrange for its own independent evaluation."

Mr. Anbari said that Iraq would "not place any obstacle in the way of the proposed reconnaissance flights" by the American planes, but that it would have preferred another nation, specifying the Soviet Union, France or India.

A Pentagon official said the first U-2 flight took place on Sunday. He said the flights were distinct from the reconnaissance missions by American and French jets over northern Iraq since the end of the war to monitor Iraqi military activity in Kurdistan.

The official said the spy plane would provide better coverage of Iraq because spy satellite coverage has been interrupted by cloud cover or haze. The Pentagon said the missions would originate from a base in Saudi Arabia.

2-2

0169

원 본

외 무 부

종 별 :

번 호 : UNW-2319 일 시 : 91 0827 2300

수 신 : 장 관(국연,중동일,기정)

발 신 : 주 유엔 대사

제 목 : 걸프사태(유엔 이락-쿠웨이트 옵서버단)

연: UNW-2123

1. 유엔 사무총장은 표제 옵서버단 (UNIKOM) 이 감축추진을 당분간 보류하는 것이 좋겠다는 의견을 8.23 자로 안보리에제시 하여온바, 안보리는 8.26 자로 이에 동의하였음.(S/22977-78)

2. 사무총장은 상기 보류 이유로서 이락-쿠웨이트 국경간 상황 (8.14 총격사건포함)을 들었음.끝

(대사 노창희-국장)

국기국 1차보 중아국 외정실 분석관 안기부

PAGE 1 91.08.28 13:18 WG

외신 1과 통제관

0170

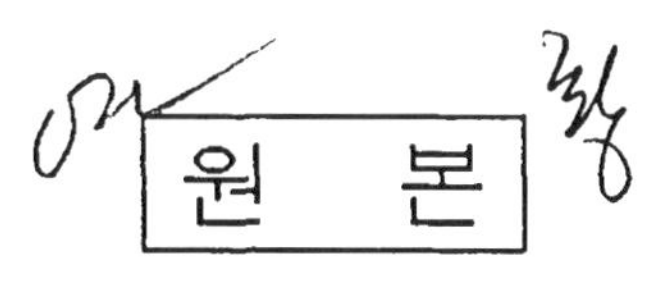

외 무 부

종 별 :

번 호 : UNW-2347 일 시 : 91 0829 1730

수 신 : 장 관(국연,중동일,기정)

발 신 : 주 유엔 대사

제 목 : 걸프사태

1.쿠웨이트는 8.28 이락군의 쿠웨이트 BUBIYAN침부사태 (이락 무장보트 2척이 쿠웨이트 영해를침부, 부비얀섬에 무장인원 상륙및 다수 군용보트합세)를 항의하는 안보리 문서를 배포하였음.(S/22990)

2. 동 문서에서 쿠웨이트측은 여사한 사태의 지지및 재발방지를 위한 안보리의 단호한 조치를 요청하였음.

3.상기사태관련 유엔 이락.쿠웨이트 옵서버단은 양측과 접촉및 현지 정찰활동중이며, 케야르 사무총장은 금 8.29 안보리에 서면 보고예정이라고하는바, 진전사항 추보위 계임.

첨부:상기 안보리문서 및 NYT 지 기사: UNW(F)-479끝

(대사 노창희-국장)

국기국 1차보 중아국 외정실 분석관 안기부

PAGE 1

91.08.30 09:25 WG

외신 1과 통제관

0171

UNW(F)-479 10829 1730
(국연. 중동일. 기정) 총고마

UNITED NATIONS

S

Security Council

Distr.
GENERAL

S/22990
28 August 1991
ENGLISH
ORIGINAL: ARABIC

LETTER DATED 28 AUGUST 1991 FROM THE PERMANENT REPRESENTATIVE OF KUWAIT TO THE UNITED NATIONS ADDRESSED TO THE PRESIDENT OF THE SECURITY COUNCIL

On instructions from my Government, I should like to inform you as follows:

In the morning today, Wednesday, 28 August 1991, at precisely 1140 hours (local time), Iraqi regime forces violated Kuwaiti territorial waters by using two armed boats from which a group of [illegible] the Kuwaiti Island of Bubiyan.

The attackers were immediately surrounded by our forces, and 43 elements, wearing civilian clothes, were taken prisoner. Interrogation of the elements taken prisoner is still going on. There are also a number of Iraqi armed men [illegible] on the island.

The Iraqi attackers used heavy weapons in their attack on the island and were supported by reinforcements of military boats from the Faw peninsula. Our Air Force came out and [illegible] the enemy by striking at these reinforcements, which resulted in the total destruction of seven boats and the flight of five others.

An event of this kind and magnitude cannot be placed in the category of [illegible] recurrent border violations by the Iraqi regime, since it has become clear that it was a premeditated and planned action effected with the support of Iraqi naval forces. The event constitutes a clear confirmation of the nature of the intentions of the Iraqi regime and its aggressive practices, which are aimed at disrupting stability and challenging the will of the United Nations. Accordingly, we request you to take decisive measures to deter the Iraqi regime from such violations and to ensure that they are not repeated in the future.

91-28071 2833b (E) /...

= UNW-2347 첨부물

3-1

0172

S/22990
English
Page 2

I should be grateful if you would inform the members of the Security Council immediately of the contents of this letter and have it circulated as a document of the Security Council.

(Signed) Mohammad A. ABULHASAN
Permanent Representative

3-2

0173

Kuwait Says It Thwarted Iraqi Infiltration of Island

By JERRY GRAY

Special to The New York Times

UNITED NATIONS, Aug. 28 — Kuwait said today that it had thwarted an attempt by a group of heavily armed Iraqis to infiltrate the island of Bubiyan, capturing at least 47 of them and sinking several boats carrying others.

"It's not just a simple border violation," said the spokesman for the Kuwaiti mission to the United Nations, Masoud al-Fehaid. "The forces were quite large, and they had heavy arms with them. I would assume there were casualties on the Iraqi side since several boats were sunk."

Kuwaiti troops were searching for about 40 other Iraqis who were part of the group and believed to be hiding on the island, Kuwaiti officials said.

A spokeswoman for the State Department said Washington was aware of a Kuwaiti border incident involving armed Iraqis, but did not have full information and could not verify all the statements by Kuwait.

"We have initial reports that Iraqis traveling in small watercraft fired on a Kuwaiti helicopter that had observed them in the Bubiyan Island waters," said the spokeswoman, Phyllis Young. "We are now trying to gather more information on the nature and mission of what appears to be a cross-border violation."

A United Nations spokesman said he was awaiting a report by the organization's Iraq-Kuwait observer group.

Bubiyan, which is in the delta of the Shatt al Arab waterway, has in the past been claimed by Iraq. Mr. Fehaid said the island, which is linked to the Kuwait mainland by a bridge, is uninhabited but has Kuwaiti troops stationed there. It was occupied by the Iraqis during the Persian Gulf war.

A senior United Nations official, speaking on condition of anonymity, said he believed that the incident might have stemmed from Iraqi efforts to retrieve weapons left behind by its troops in the war.

The United Nations has confirmed that Iraqis have previously made incursions into the demilitarized zone to haul back caches of weapons. The United Nations says such excursions do not violate the cease-fire so long as the Iraqis are civilians and they travel in civilian vehicles or crafts.

The head of Kuwait's United Nations mission, Mohammed A. Abulhasan, has filed a formal complaint with the Security Council calling for immediate action, Mr. Fehaid said.

Mr. Abulhasan met today with the President of the Security Council, Ayala Lasso of Ecuador, to complain about the reported Iraqi moves.

"I informed the Council President that this dangerous development demonstrates once again the aggressive intentions by Iraq against the security and peace of Kuwait and that Iraq has not learned its lessons," Mr. Abulhasan was quoted as saying by the Kuwait News Agency.

He said later that at least a dozen Iraqi boats were involved in the incident and that Kuwaiti forces had sunk seven of them. He said that although the intruders wore civilian clothes, they had heavy weapons.

"We look at it gravely," Mr. Albulhasan said. "We consider it a military attack."

Mr. Fehaid said: "There were two different movements. We have captured the first one and we have surrounded them. The other ones, who were sent to support the troops who came to the island, were engaged by our air force, and we managed to sink a number of their boats and they just trailed off after that."

3-3

0174

UNITED
NATIONS

S

Security Council

Distr.
GENERAL

S/22992
29 August 1991
ENGLISH
ORIGINAL: ARABIC

LETTER DATED 29 AUGUST 1991 FROM THE CHARGE D'AFFAIRES A.I.
OF THE PERMANENT MISSION OF IRAQ TO THE UNITED NATIONS
ADDRESSED TO THE SECRETARY-GENERAL

On instructions from my Government, I have the honour to transmit a letter dated 29 August 1991 from Mr. Ahmad Hussein, Minister for Foreign Affairs of the Republic of Iraq, addressed to you, concerning the situation of Kuwaiti nationals in Iraq.

I should be grateful if you would have this letter and its annex circulated as a document of the Security Council.

(*Signed*) Sabah Talat KADRAT
Deputy Permanent Representative
Chargé d'affaires a.i.

91-28184 2606e (E) /...

0175

Annex

Letter dated 29 August 1991 from the Minister for Foreign Affairs of Iraq addressed to the Secretary-General

I wish to refer to the letter dated 17 July 1991 from the Permanent Representative of Kuwait to the United Nations, addressed to the President of the Security Council.

I have the honour to notify you of the following information concerning the situation of Kuwaiti nationals in Iraq since the end of the Gulf War.

1. The competent Iraqi authorities repatriated to Kuwait 6,328 Kuwaitis and 5 persons not of Kuwaiti nationality under the supervision of the delegation of the International Committee of the Red Cross (ICRC) during the period from 4 March to the present.

2. The ICRC delegation registered 3,400 Kuwaitis comprising 606 families who were in Iraq in addition to 159 individuals.

3. The Kuwaiti side agreed to the repatriation of 170 of the Kuwaitis referred to in paragraph 2 above. The Kuwaiti side is now attempting to delude Arab and international public opinion into believing that Iraq is concealing large numbers of Kuwaitis.

4. The Kuwaiti authorities are constantly endeavouring to impede the return of Kuwaitis to Kuwait on the pretext that verification procedures have not been completed. They have made a number of errors as testified by ICRC, the most recent of which was on 13 July when it had been decided to hand over a group of Kuwaitis but the Kuwaiti representative did not come to the Ar'ar area in Saudi Arabia to receive them. The handing over operation was postponed until 14 July, the ICRC delegation having confirmed that it had informed the Kuwaiti side of the time of the handing over.

We believe that the delay in the repatriation of the Kuwaitis who are still in Iraq, of which ICRC is aware, was directly caused by the Kuwaiti authorities who bear full responsibility for it.

Iraq is cooperating fully on this matter with ICRC and once again affirms its readiness to hand over all Kuwaitis who are in Iraq to the Kuwaiti side through ICRC. I should like the Secretary-General to exert pressure on the Kuwaiti side to receive them and not to exploit this matter for dishonourable publicity purposes.

I should be grateful if you would have this letter circulated as a document of the Security Council.

(*Signed*) Ahmad HUSSEIN

0176

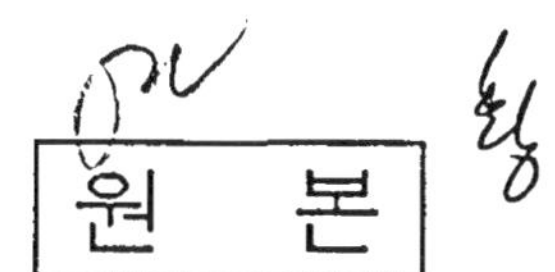

관리 번호	91 -1017

외 무 부

종 별 :

번 호 : UNW-2372 일 시 : 91 0830 2100

수 신 : 장관(국연,중동일,기정)

발 신 : 주 유엔 대사

제 목 : 안보리 비공식협의(이락-쿠웨이트 충돌사태)

연:UNW-2347

안보리는 연호 BUBIYAN 섬 충돌사태 관련 금 8.30 오후 비공식협의를 개최한바, 당관 원참사관이 관련 대표부들로부터 탐문한 동협의 결과를 아래보고함.

1. 케야르 사무총장의 보고를 청취한 다음토의가 있었는바, 미, 영, 불만이발언하였으며 동국들은 모두 사태의 심각성을 강조하였음.

2. 유엔 이락, 쿠웨이트 옵서버단의 현지조사를 기초로 사무총장이 사태진상을 안보리에 추보키로함.

첨부 FAX:UNW(F)-487 끝

(대사 노창희-국장)

예고:91.12.31. 까지

국기국	장관	차관	1차보	2차보	중아국	분석관	청와대	안기부

PAGE 1

91.08.31 16:34

외신 2과 통제관 CE

0177

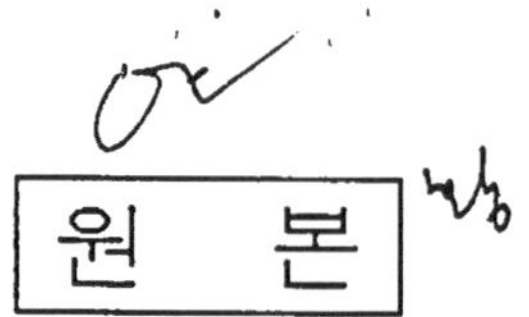

외 무 부

종 별 :

번 호 : UNW-2427 일 시 : 91 0904 1800

수 신 : 장 관(국연,중동일,국기,기정)

발 신 : 주 유엔 대사

제 목 : 걸프사태(안보리동향)

연: UNW-2347

1.BUBIYAN 섬 출돌사건

가.케야르 사무총장은 유엔 이락.쿠웨이트 옵서버단 (UNIKOM) 활동 정기보고서를 안보리에 9.3.자로 제출해온바, 동보고서 (S/23000) 에 포함된 연호 BUBIYAN 섬 충돌사건 관련 내용을 별첨송부함.

나.상기 보고서에 의하면 지난 8.28 오후 쿠웨이트 하안경비대가 이락어선 11척, 스피드보트 1척, 승선자 45명을 부비안섬앞 해상에서 나포하였으며, 동승선자 일부가 부비안섬에서 탄약등을 수거하였음은 확인되었으나, 부비안섬으로부터의 총격, 이락해군 스피트보트 출동, 부비안섬앞 보트잔해 발생경위 등에 대해서는 확인되지 않고있다함.

2.이락 핵사찰

핵문제 관련 안보리의 이락 규탄결의 (707 호) 를 반박하는 A.HUSSEIN 이락외상의 8.28 자 사무총장앞 서한이 금 9.4. 안보리문서로 배포됨.(S/22998)

첨부:사무총장보고서 및 이락측 안보리문서:UNW(F)-499 끝

(대사 노창희-국장)

국기국 1차보 중아국 국기국 외정실 분석관 안기부

PAGE 1 91.09.05 09:28 WG

외신 1과 통제관

0178

UNITED NATIONS

S

Security Council

Distr.
GENERAL

S/23000
3 September 1991

ORIGINAL: ENGLISH

REPORT OF THE SECRETARY-GENERAL ON THE
IRAQ-KUWAIT OBSERVATION MISSION

1. The present further interim report on the United Nations Iraq-Kuwait Observation Mission (UNIKOM) contains a summary of events since my last report dated 12 June 1991 (S/22692).

2. UNIKOM continued to monitor the demilitarized zone (DMZ) established by the Security Council. This was generally respected and the number of violations decreased. The following violations of the DMZ were recorded:

(a) UNIKOM observed a number of minor incursions by armed and unarmed military personnel. The Iraqi forces accounted for 6, and the Kuwaiti and allied forces for 36 such incursions;

(b) UNIKOM observed 10 violations by Iraqi police and 5 by Kuwaiti police of the limitation on the arms that they are permitted to carry in the DMZ. As previously reported (S/22692, para. 9), both Iraq and Kuwait have agreed to limit such armaments to sidearms only;

(c) UNIKOM observed 36 violations of the DMZ by military aircraft of the type used by the forces allied with Kuwait.

3. UNIKOM raised the violations of the DMZ with the party concerned, usually in writing, with a view to having action taken to prevent a recurrence. Both Iraq and Kuwait gave repeated assurances to this effect and, in UNIKOM's judgement, they continued to extend their cooperation to the Mission.

4. Both sides indicated misgivings about the limitation on the armament of the police. They pointed out that that made it difficult for the police to deal effectively with smugglers or others who were better armed. While acknowledging that difficulty, UNIKOM nevertheless considered it necessary to maintain the limitation for the time being in order to reduce the potential for serious incidents.

5. UNIKOM received eight written complaints from Iraq and six from Kuwait. It investigated those complaints and was able in 11 cases to establish the facts through its own observations and informed the complaining party accordingly.

91-28546 2565g (E) /...

0179

6. One of the purposes of UNIKOM is to deter violations of the boundary between Iraq and Kuwait through its presence in and surveillance of the DMZ. Pending demarcation of that boundary by the Iraq-Kuwait Boundary Demarcation Commission established under paragraph 3 of resolution 687 (1991) and in order to avoid friction and incidents, UNIKOM has established the principle that Iraqi and Kuwaiti officials, including police, should maintain a reasonable distance of about 1,000 metres from the boundary line shown on UNIKOM maps. UNIKOM is using a British map, which it has given to both sides for reference. They have agreed to work with it as a practical arrangement to facilitate UNIKOM's task and without prejudice to their positions concerning the boundary.

7. During the reporting period, Iraq deployed 4 border police centres and 10 border police posts in the DMZ. Five of the posts are on the Kuwaiti side of the boundary line shown on UNIKOM's map; 2 are closer to it than 1,000 metres, on the Iraqi side. UNIKOM made lengthy and intensive efforts to have Iraq move the seven posts further back. However, the Iraqi authorities maintained that those posts had been in place before 2 August 1990 and that pulling them back would prejudice Iraq's position regarding the demarcation of the border. Once the demarcation had taken place, Iraq would comply with the "reasonable distance" principle.

8. Apart from a border post on the main road south of Safwan, Kuwait has deployed only one police post, in the southern sector. The Kuwaiti authorities maintained contact with UNIKOM regarding the deployment of additional posts and reiterated their willingness to comply with the "reasonable distance" principle, if the Iraqi authorities did so too.

9. UNIKOM recorded the following shooting incidents involving Iraqi and Kuwaiti military and police personnel:

(a) On 28 July 1991, three Kuwaiti soldiers in uniform fired a light machine-gun from a military vehicle at an Iraqi police centre in the central sector. The vehicle left when a UNIKOM patrol appeared. The Iraqis did not return fire and there were no casualties;

(b) On 31 July 1991, a Kuwaiti police patrol reported to UNIKOM observers that its vehicle was stuck in the sand about 1 kilometre north-east of an Iraqi police post. The UNIKOM observers found that the vehicle carried two rifles, hand grenades and ammunition. Iraqi police, who had approached the vehicle, claimed that the Kuwaiti personnel had fired at them;

(c) On 14 August 1991, an incident developed between Iraqi personnel stationed at a police post in the southern sector and a convoy of Kuwaiti police and senior officials accompanied by UNIKOM observers on a joint reconnaissance of proposed police posts. This incident was the subject of a communication from the Permanent Representative of Kuwait to the President of the Security Council (S/22950). A UNIKOM team investigated the incident and questioned persons involved on both sides. The Iraqi policemen claimed that the incident began when their post came under fire from the Kuwaiti convoy.

/...

0180

The UNIKOM observers accompanying the convoy, which was stretched out over a long distance, were at its very end and did not notice any firing. The investigating team was unable to confirm that the Iraqi post had been fired upon. It was also unable to establish which side opened fire in an exchange that took place when two of the Kuwaiti vehicles became bogged down in the sand, were left behind and were then approached by a group of 12 to 15 Iraqi policemen. The firing at that location was heard by the personnel of UNIKOM observation post No. S6. There were no casualties and the Kuwaiti policemen were able to depart in one vehicle. UNIKOM observers came to the spot and informed the Iraqi policemen that they were on Kuwaiti territory and should return to Iraqi territory. The Iraqis initially rejected this and attempted to take possession of the remaining Kuwaiti vehicle, but they withdrew upon the arrival of a UNIKOM patrol and helicopter. The disabled vehicle was returned to the Kuwaiti authorities. The UNIKOM team was not able to establish who initiated the exchange of fire. However, UNIKOM has protested to the Iraqi authorities the violation of Kuwaiti territory and of the limitation on the arms to be carried in the DMZ.

10. The maintenance of law and order, notably the enforcement of laws regulating the movement of persons and goods across the border, is the responsibility of the government authorities concerned. However, as a result of illegal movement across the border, some tension has arisen during the reporting period, which has been of concern to UNIKOM.

11. One source of tension and the site of several shooting incidents was an illegal market, which was held in the southern sector of the DMZ. It is known by UNIKOM as the "sheep market", although alcohol and arms are traded as well as livestock. When UNIKOM first discovered the market in May it was located in Iraq. Following a shooting incident on 27 June, in which three Iraqi policemen were fatally injured, the market ceased for two weeks, after which it reappeared in a new location closer to the border. In mid-August, it moved to the Kuwaiti side of the DMZ. UNIKOM has reported its observations to the Governments of Iraq and Kuwait and both have taken measures to curb access to the market.

12. In a new development since the beginning of August, UNIKOM observed on several occasions groups of Iraqis, apparently civilians, collecting weapons, ammunition and other battlefield items on the Kuwaiti side of the DMZ. In addition, UNIKOM was informed by the Kuwaiti authorities that a number of such persons were arrested well inside Kuwaiti territory. UNIKOM raised the matter with the Iraqi authorities, who denied any involvement by Iraqi officials or soldiers but could not exclude the possibility that civilians had crossed the border. The Iraqi authorities explained that they had offered a financial reward to their citizens for the delivery of ammunition and other military items that were still scattered throughout large areas and posed a danger to the population. The Iraqi authorities undertook to do what they could to curb crossings into Kuwait. For their part, the Kuwaiti authorities informed UNIKOM that they had arranged to have the southern sector cleared of military items and were considering a similar project for the islands of Bubiyan and Failaka.

/...

0181

13. In the afternoon of 28 August 1991, UNIKOM was informed by a Kuwaiti army liaison officer that there had been an incident involving firing between Iraqi and Kuwaiti personnel on, and in the vicinity of, the Kuwaiti island of Bubiyan, outside the DMZ. The incident has been the subject of communications addressed to the President of the Security Council by the Permanent Representative of Kuwait (S/22990) and by the Chargé d'affaires a.i. of the Permanent Mission of Iraq (S/22993).

14. UNIKOM has carried out an investigation, in the course of which Bubiyan Island was visited and some of the Kuwaiti military personnel directly involved, as well as some of the Iraqis taken into custody during the incident, were questioned by the investigating team. The UNIKOM team also visited the Al Faw peninsula in Iraq. The following is a summary of its findings:

(a) In the afternoon of 28 August 1991, a Kuwaiti Coast Guard detachment comprising 4 boats took custody of 11 Iraqi fishing boats and 1 speedboat in the waters off Bubiyan Island and of their crews, 45 persons in all. No one was taken from Bubiyan, and UNIKOM received no further information regarding earlier reports that some Iraqis had hidden on Bubiyan;

(b) According to its commander, the Kuwaiti detachment came under small arms fire from Ras al Qaid and Ras al Barshah on Bubiyan. The UNIKOM team was not able to find evidence of firing at those locations. There were no injuries and none of the vessels showed signs of having been hit;

(c) The crew of the speedboat and at least some of the crews of the fishing boats had collected ammunition and other items (e.g. military-style blankets) on Bubiyan. They stated that they had done so for financial gain. UNIKOM has had independent reports of trading in ammunition in southern Iraq. The UNIKOM team did not find, nor was it shown, evidence that there had been weapons on the Iraqi boats;

(d) A senior Kuwaiti army liaison officer stated that, during the incident on 28 August, 12 Iraqi navy speedboats left the Al Faw jetty to come to the assistance of the Iraqi boats off Bubiyan. The jetty mentioned by the Kuwaiti officer is the only marine facility that UNIKOM has observed on the southern shore of the Al Faw peninsula. It offers no protection and can be used only by small craft, which are grounded at low tide. The jetty is about 13 kilometres from UNIKOM observation post No. 6 and is visited by daily patrols from there. Those patrols have not, so far, observed any naval presence. Similarly, the UNIKOM personnel observing the access to the Khowr Abd Allah south of Umm Qasr had not observed any movement of Iraqi vessels;

(e) The UNIKOM team interviewed Kuwaiti airforce pilots, who stated that on the day of the incident, at 1710 hours local time and after the Coast Guard detachment had left the area with the captured vessels, they had engaged and sunk seven boats off Bubiyan. They did not know from where those boats had come. The UNIKOM team saw from the air the wrecks of two boats in the

0182 /...

vicinity of Ras al Qayd but was not able to establish their identity or when they had been sunk.

15. Major-General Greindl and his staff are conscious of the implications of the incidents described in this report. They will continue to maintain a high level of vigilance in the performance of the tasks entrusted to them by the Security Council.

0183

주 국 련 대 표 부

주국련20313- 682 1991. 9. 5.

수신 장 관

참조 국제기구조약국장, 중동아프리카국장

제목 이락석유수출 일부허용(안보리 결의706호)

표제관련 안보리 문서를 별첨과 같이 송부합니다.

첨 부 : 상기 사무총장 서한. 끝.

주 국 련 대

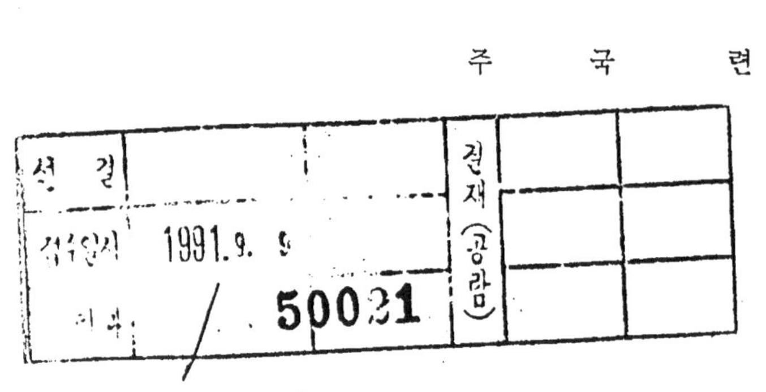

선 결		결재(공람)		
접수일시	1991.9. 9			
처 리	50031			

0184

UNITED ⁻TIONS NATION ═UNIES

POSTAL ADDRESS—ADRESSE POSTALE UNITED NATIONS, N.Y. 10017
CABLE ADDRESS—ADRESSE TELEGRAPHIQUE UNATIONS NEWYORK

REFERENCE: SCPC/7/91(5)

The Secretary-General of the United Nations presents his compliments to the Permanent Observer of the Republic of Korea to the United Nations and has the honour to transmit herewith resolution 706 (1991), adopted by the Security Council at its 3004th meeting, on 15 August 1991, in connection with its consideration of the item entitled "The situation between Iraq and Kuwait".

The Secretary-General wishes, in particular, to draw attention to paragraphs 1 and 8, which read as follows:

"The Security Council,

...

"Acting under Chapter VII of the Charter,

"1. Authorizes all States, subject to the decision to be taken by the Security Council pursuant to paragraph 5 below and notwithstanding the provisions of paragraphs 3 (a), 3 (b) and 4 of resolution 661 (1990), to permit the import, during a period of 6 months from the date of passage of the resolution pursuant to paragraph 5 below, of petroleum and petroleum products originating in Iraq sufficient to produce a sum to be determined by the Council following receipt of the report of the Secretary-General requested in paragraph 5 of this resolution but not to exceed 1.6 billion United States dollars for the purposes set out in this resolution and subject to the following conditions:

"(a) Approval of each purchase of Iraqi petroleum and petroleum products by the Security Council Committee established by the resolution 661 (1990) following notification to the Committee by the State concerned;

"(b) Payment of the full amount of each purchase of Iraqi petroleum and petroleum products directly by the purchaser in the State concerned into an escrow account to be established by the United Nations and to be administered by the Secretary-General, exclusively to meet the purposes of this resolution;

Annex enclosed

0185

UNITED NATIONS  NATIONS UNIES

-2-

"(c) Approval by the Council, following the report of the Secretary-General requested in paragraph 5 of this resolution, of a scheme for the purchase of foodstuffs, medicines and materials and supplies for essential civilian needs as referred to in paragraph 20 of resolution 687 (1991), in particular health related materials, all of which to be labelled to the extent possible as being supplied under this scheme, and for all feasible and appropriate United Nations monitoring and supervision for the purpose of assuring their equitable distribution to meet humanitarian needs in all regions of Iraq and to all categories of the Iraqi civilian population, as well as all feasible and appropriate management relevant to this purpose, such a United Nations role to be available if desired for humanitarian assistance from other sources;

"(d) The sum authorized in this paragraph to be released by successive decisions of the Committee established by resolution 661 (1990) in three equal portions after the Council has taken the decision provided for in paragraph 5 below on the implementation of this resolution, and notwithstanding any other provision of this paragraph, the sum to be subject to review concurrently by the Council on the basis of its ongoing assessment of the needs and requirements;

...

"8. Calls upon all States to cooperate fully in the implementation of this resolution".

19 August 1991

M. R.

0186

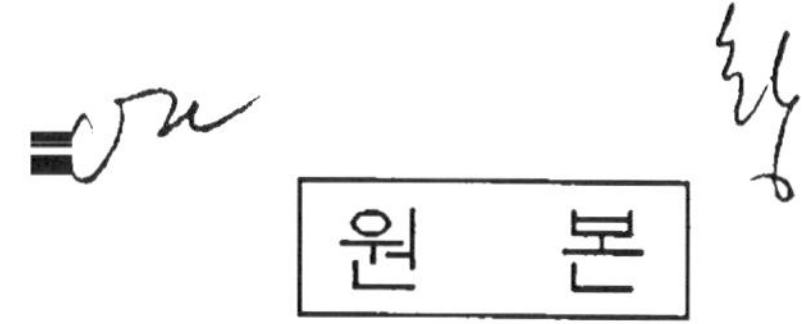

원 본

외 무 부

종 별 :

번 호 : UNW-2505　　　　일 시 : 91 0907 1800

수 신 : 장 관(국연,중동일,기정)

발 신 : 주 유엔 대사

제 목 : 이락 석유 수출 일부 허용 문제(안보리)

1. 이락민 구호지원 및 동재원 확보를 위한 동국석유 수출일부 허용(6개월간 16억한도)에 관한안보리 결의 706호 (본문5항)에 의거,유엔사무총장이 안보리에 제출해온 동 결의 이행계획안이 금 9.7 안보리 문서(S/23006) 로배포된바,주요 특기 사항은다음과 같음

가.수출 한도 상향 조정 필요

1)동기간 수입이 필요한 인도적 품목 수요는 17.3억불이나,수출 허용액 16억불에서 다른 용도분을공제하고 나면 약 8억불 부족 예상

2)향후 적절한 시기에 안보리에 상향 조정 권고예정

나.1차 허용분(전체는 3차)에 대해서는 조기허가:적립에 따른 시차 문제 해결

다.보충 재원 문제 제기:이락 AK결 자산,자발적기여금의 예치 운영

라.송유 경비 조달

1)이락-터키간 송유관(KIRKUK-YUMURTALIK) 을이용하되,동수송대금은 터어키측에현찰,현물(석유)로 공히 지불가능

2)동대금 충당을 위한 추가 석유 수출 허용 문제제기

2.안보리의 본건 사무총장 보고서에 관한 토의동향은 추보 위계임

첨부(FAX): 사무총장 보고서(S/23006)(발췌)끝

(대사-국장)

국기국　1차보　2차보　중아국　외정실　안기부

PAGE 1　　　　91.09.08 17:04 FO

외신 1과 통제관

0187

UNW(F)-514 10907 1800
(국연, 중동일, 기정)

(총 3매)

V. RECOMMENDATIONS

A. General recommendations

57. The Secretary-General wishes to recommend the following for consideration and decision by the Security Council with a view to facilitating smooth and secure realization of the objectives and purposes of the relevant provisions of resolution 706 (1991):

(a) Problems would arise if the decisions to release the tranches came only at the end of the process of selling a quantity of oil. Authorization of the release of the first tranche by the Committee established by resolution 661 (1990) immediately after the passage of the enabling resolution should resolve this difficulty;

(b) Paragraph 1 (d) of resolution 706 (1991) provides for a regular review by the Security Council of the ceiling of $1.6 billion. In the light of the estimates contained in the reports of his Executive Delegate, the Secretary-General will at the appropriate time recommend to the Council to use its powers under this provision to increase the maximum figure;

(c) The Security Council may wish to address the question of allowing assets held in favour of Iraq or any voluntary contributions to be deposited into the escrow account as a sub-account to be used exclusively in the manner and for the purposes stipulated in paragraph 20 of resolution 687 (1991);

(d) In response to the request to the Secretary-General to find a method for taking account of the costs of transportation of Iraqi petroleum and petroleum products, it is suggested that the transportation costs payable to Turkey be met in cash or kind. For this purpose, the Secretary-General considers that an additional amount of oil may be permitted to be exported from Iraq over and above the quantity necessary to meet the requirements of resolution 706 (1991). The actual transportation costs to BOTAS will have to be established by negotiations on an ad hoc basis. The value of any such oil is to be subject to the requirement that 30 per cent of its value should be paid directly to the Compensation Fund.

B. Specific measures for the implemention of the relevant provisions of Security Council resolution 706 (1991)

58. In accordance with the basic structure set out in section IV of the present report, the Secretary-General recommends the following specific measures for implementing the relevant provisions of resolution 706 (1991) in a manner that would effectively promote and satisfy the objectives and purposes of the resolution:

(a) Iraq, through its oil authority, SOMO, will market and sell the petroleum, f.o.b. Ceyhan;

UNW-2505
철부

/...

3-1

0188

(b) Every contract must include the following terms:

(i) The contract enters into force only after it has received the approval of the Committee established by resolution 661 (1990), following notification to the Committee by the State in which the purchaser is based;

(ii) The full proceeds from the sale of petroleum are to be deposited by the purchaser into the escrow account established by the United Nations and administered by the Secretary-General, in accordance with the Financial Regulations and Rules of the United Nations;

(iii) The purchaser must open a letter of credit for each transaction providing for payment into the United Nations escrow account;

(iv) The oil will be shipped via the Kirkuk-Yumurtalik pipeline from Iraq to Turkey;

(c) The Security Council Committee established by resolution 661 (1990) will have ultimate responsibility for monitoring the sale of Iraqi oil. It will be assisted in this function by independent inspection agents appointed by the United Nations, who will verify that the above terms are included in every contract and that the price of the oil is reasonable in light of prevailing market conditions. The Committee may also be assisted by other experts as appropriate in all aspects of its work deriving from Security Council resolution 706 (1991);

(d) The Committee established by resolution 661 (1990) should adopt procedures by which approval of each contract can be obtained promptly. Submissions for approval to the Committee can be made only by the Government of the State of the purchaser concerned. The Governments of States where purchasers are located should, where necessary, establish procedures that facilitate prompt submission of the contracts to the Committee for approval;

(e) Inspection agents will be appointed by the United Nations to ensure that the quantity and quality of oil delivered accords with the contract terms and that no oil is delivered without the requisite approval. They will be stationed at the Iraqi access points to the Kirkuk-Yumurtalik pipeline, at the border between Iraq and Turkey to the extent possible and at the loading terminal in Yumurtalik;

(f) The purchaser will open a letter of credit, issued by a reputable bank engaged in international banking, for each transaction providing for payment into the United Nations escrow account;

(g) Explicit language should be included in the Security Council resolution approving the present report setting forth the immunity of the oil. Iraq should be required, in the same resolution, to take all steps necessary to accord immunity to the oil. Additionally, Turkey should be called upon by the resolution to ensure that, while in Turkish jurisdiction, the oil will not be subjected to legal proceedings;

/...

3-2

0189

(h) The escrow account should be set up as a United Nations account and as such will be fully protected by the immunities of the United Nations. Additional protection would follow from establishing the escrow account in a bank of a country which, under the national laws of that country, enjoys the maximum protection from third-party claims. It would also come from including language in the Security Council resolution approving the present report reiterating that the escrow account is to be considered a United Nations asset and therefore enjoys the privileges and immunities of the United Nations;

(i) Purchases of the supplies to meet humanitarian needs in Iraq will be undertaken by Iraq. Monitoring of the purchases and deliveries will be undertaken by the Secretariat with the assistance of United Nations-appointed inspection agents;

(j) The Office of the Executive Delegate will receive a list of humanitarian requirements from Iraq and, after revising the list, if necessary, submit it to the Committee established by resolution 661 (1990) for approval;

(k) The Committee established by resolution 661 (1990) should adopt procedures for approving the submitted list. Upon approval, the Committee shall so notify the Secretary-General, who shall authorize payments from the United Nations escrow account. The Office of the Executive Delegate will then notify Iraq that it may commence procedures for the purchases and for arranging deliveries of the goods;

(l) Inspection agents appointed by the United Nations will evaluate, verify and monitor every element of the transaction up to entry points to Iraq. Part-payment may be made to suppliers at the time of delivery. The remainder will be paid after the Office of the Executive Delegate has submitted a report confirming compliance with the terms of the supply contract to the Committee established by resolution 661 (1990) and the Committee approves such payment;

(m) Movement of goods to designated centres and commencement of in-country distribution will be arranged by the government agencies concerned, which will notify the Office of the Executive Delegate of the proposed distribution of incoming consignments in order to enable the United Nations agencies to put in place effective monitoring arrangements;

(n) Monitoring of in-country distribution will be undertaken in accordance with the proposals submitted by the Executive Delegate of the Secretary-General on 27 August 1991, reproduced in annex II to the present report.

/...

3-3

0190

관리번호	91/1613

외 무 부

종 별 :

번 호 : UNW-2674 일 시 : 91 0913 2130

수 신 : 장관(연일,중동일,기정)

발 신 : 주 유엔 대사

제 목 : 안보리동향 (비공식협의)

안보리는 금 9.13 비공식 협의를 개최한바, 당관 원참사관이 관련 대표부들로 부터 탐문한 금일 협의 주요 결과를 아래 보고함.

1. 유엔 레바논 평화유지군(UNIFIL) 요원 피격사건

의장(불란서)이 사건경위, 조치현황에 관한 사무국측의 통보내용을 이사국들에게 설명하였으나, 특기할 그이상의 토의는 없었음.

2. 이락의 인도적 긴급수요와 관련한 석유수출 일부허용 결의안 이행에 관한 사무총장 보고서(S/23006)

다음주중 동 보고서 승인결의안 채택예정

3. 유엔 이락 특정무기 폐기특위(UNSCOM) 자체 헬기 사용 불허문제

본건을 이락의 중대한 안보리 결의(707 호) 위반행위로 보는 이사국들의 입장을 우선 의장이 이락측에 구두로 전달예정

4. 과테말라의 베리즈 승인조치

동 조치에 대한 이사국들의 환영의 뜻을 의장이 언론에 표명(에쿠아돌제외)끝

(대사 노창희-국장)

예고:91.12.31. 까지

91.12.31. 일반

국기국 안기부	장관	차관	1차보	2차보	중아국	외정실	분석관	청와대

PAGE 1 91.09.14 13:12

외신 2과 통제관 BN

0191

UNITED
NATIONS

S

Security Council

Distr.
GENERAL

S/23012
12 September 1991

ORIGINAL: ENGLISH

REPORT OF THE SECRETARY-GENERAL SUBMITTED IN ACCORDANCE WITH PARAGRAPH 6 OF SECURITY COUNCIL RESOLUTION 706 (1991)

1. The following report is submitted in accordance with paragraph 6 of Security Council resolution 706 (1991), which was adopted on 15 August 1991. Paragraph 6 reads as follows: "Further requests the Secretary-General in consultation with the International Committee of the Red Cross (ICRC) to submit within 20 days of the date of adoption of this resolution a report to the Security Council on activities undertaken in accordance with paragraph 31 of resolution 687 (1991) in connection with facilitating the repatriation or return of all Kuwaiti and third country nationals or their remains present in Iraq on or after 2 August 1990."

2. It will be recalled that in the months since the adoption of Security Council resolution 687 (1991) on 3 April 1991, the Secretary-General and the President of the Security Council have received a number of communications regarding the repatriation or return of Kuwaitis and third country nationals or their remains present in Iraq since 2 August 1990. For ease of reference, those communications which have been issued as documents of the Security Council are reprinted as annexes at the end of this report.

3. In a meeting with the President of the ICRC in Geneva on 28 August 1991, the Secretary-General drew attention to paragraph 6 of Security Council resolution 706 (1991). He recalled also the text of paragraph 31 of Security Council resolution 687 (1991), which reads: "Invites the International Committee of the Red Cross to keep the Secretary-General apprised as appropriate of all activities undertaken in connection with facilitating the repatriation or return of all Kuwaiti and third country nationals or their remains present in Iraq on or after 2 August 1990."

4. The ICRC has conveyed to the Secretary-General the following information for inclusion in this report:

91-29789 2681j (E) /...

0192

A. Repatriation of former residents of Kuwait from Iraq to Kuwait

		Prisoners of war	Civilian internees
Operation no. 1:	6 March 1991	1	
Operation no. 2:	7 March 1991		1 174
Operation no. 3:	21-27 March 1991	4 176	862
Operation no. 4:	6 April 1991	1	20
		4 178	2 056

The ICRC points out that all but the second of the above repatriation exercises took place under its auspices. The 1,174 individuals that returned to Kuwait on 7 March 1991 were not registered with the ICRC.

B. Registration and repatriation of persons wishing to return to Kuwait

From the beginning of April to 18 August 1991 the ICRC registered in Iraq 3,506 names of civilians, civilian internees or prisoners of war wishing to return to Kuwait. Some prisoners of war and civilian internees were registered by ICRC delegates in detention centres. The large majority of the 3,506 persons came spontaneously to the ICRC office in Baghdad where ICRC delegates recorded their personal data for transmission to the Kuwaiti authorities who, in turn, determine eligibility for repatriation. As of 29 August 1991, Kuwait has authorized the return of 206 persons registered by the ICRC (41 prisoners of war, 53 civilian internees and 112 civilians), all of whom have been repatriated to Kuwait under ICRC auspices.

C. Repatriation of third country nationals

The ICRC has supervised the repatriation of 23 prisoners of war of the United States, 12 prisoners of war of the United Kingdom and 2 prisoners of war of Italy. The ICRC has also supervised the repatriation to Saudi Arabia of 28 prisoners of war, 33 civilian internees and 49 civilians.

D. Kuwaiti list of civilians and military personnel missing since 2 August 1990

On 9 September 1991, the Kuwaiti authorities handed over to the ICRC Delegation in Kuwait a list containing 2,242 names of civilians and military personnel missing since 2 August 1990, and whom they presume have been arrested by the Iraqi authorities. The ICRC is transmitting this list to the Iraqi authorities.

0193

/...

Annex I

Letter dated 19 April 1991 from the Permanent Representative of Kuwait to the United Nations addressed to the President of the Security Council 1/

On instructions from my Government, I should like to convey to you our position concerning the failure by Iraq to abide by the terms of relevant Security Council resolutions, which puts into question the credibility and motives of the Iraqi regime.

In the first instance, it should be indicated that a humanitarian but urgent concern is not being addressed by the Iraqi Government, specifically, the commitment by Iraq to abide by the terms of paragraphs 2 (c) and 3 (c) of resolution 686 (1991) and of paragraph 30 of resolution 687 (1991). Iraq is yet to repatriate the remaining Kuwaiti prisoners of war and detainees estimated at 5,433.

Second, Iraq has not to date declared its acceptance under the terms of paragraph 1 (b) of resolution 686 (1991) of its liability for any loss, damage or injury arising in regard to Kuwait and third States, and their nationals and corporations, as a result of the invasion and illegal occupation of Kuwait by Iraq.

Third, in spite of its declared readiness to return property seized in Kuwait, Iraq has not to date returned to Kuwait any of those items seized by it. Iraq has yet to implement faithfully the terms of paragraph 2 (d) of resolution 686 (1991) which demands that Iraq "immediately begins to return all Kuwaiti property seized by Iraq, to be completed in the shortest possible period".

1/ *See* document S/22512, dated 19 April 1991.

/...

Annex II

Letter dated 3 June 1991 from the Chargé d'Affaires a.i. of the Permanent Mission of Kuwait to the United Nations addressed to the President of the Security Council 2/

On instructions from my Government, I should like to bring to your attention the following:

First, in spite of the provisions of paragraphs 2 (c) and 3 (c) of Security Council resolution 686 (1991), that Iraq immediately release under the auspices of the ICRC all Kuwaiti and third country nationals and arrange for immediate access to all POWs, Iraq is yet to release around 3,800 POWs and detainees of which around 700 are women and 730 are children 15 years old and below. Iraq has also been found wanting in allowing access to all POWs and detainees. Concern about their fate had been communicated to the Security Council in our letter of 20 May 1991.

Second, notwithstanding the provision of paragraph 2 (d) of resolution 686 (1991) that Iraq immediately begin to return all Kuwaiti property seized by Iraq, to be completed in the shortest possible period, to date, the only item returned to Kuwait is a single aircraft that the Iraqis had kept in Jordan.

Third, while Iraq has declared, in accordance with the provision of paragraph 2 (a) of resolution 686 (1991), that it has rescinded decisions regarding the annexation of Kuwait, recent statements by the Iraqi Vice-President (S/22655) clearly contradict the aforementioned declaration. These statements emphasize that implementation of Security Council resolutions is but a tactical move rather than a change of policy by Iraq.

Lastly, it should be emphasized that failure, to date, to return all POWs and detainees, return property seized from Kuwait, and cease hostile statements are indications that the "policies and practices of the Government of Iraq" are not in implementation of relevant Security Council resolutions. What is required of Iraq is not merely acceptance, but, as described in resolution 686 (1991), implementation of its acceptance of Security Council resolutions.

2/ See document S/22702 (annex), dated 13 June 1991.

Annex III

Letter dated 2 July 1991 from the Permanent Representative of Saudi Arabia to the United Nations addressed to the Secretary-General 3/

I have the pleasure, further to letter dated 11 June 1991 (S/22689) addressed to Your Excellency from the Chargé d'affaires a.i. of the Permanent Mission of Iraq to the United Nations, in which he transmitted a letter dated 8 June 1991 from the Minister for Foreign Affairs of Iraq, whereby he confirmed the Iraqi Government's undertaking to accept and comply with all the provisions of Security Council resolution 687 (1991) that are linked with the cease-fire in the Gulf War, to convey to Your Excellency, upon instructions from my Government, that Iraq has not complied with the provisions of section G of resolution 687 (1991) concerning the repatriation of all Kuwaitis and third country nationals, including Saudi Arabian nationals.

According to the information that the Saudi Arabian authorities concerned received from previously released prisoners and Iraqi refugees that are now in Saudi Arabia, it has been confirmed, without doubt, that there are at least 15 Saudi Arabians who have not been repatriated to Saudi Arabia until now.

3/ *See* document S/22760, dated 3 July 1991.

/...

0196

Annex IV

Letter dated 15 July 1991 from the Permanent Representative of Iraq to the United Nations addressed to the Secretary-General 4/

With reference to the letter of the Permanent Representative of the Kingdom of Saudi Arabia to the United Nations, document S/22760 dated 3 July 1991, I wish to explain to you that the competent Iraqi authorities have advised in respect of the contents of the above-mentioned letter that they have notified the mission of the International Committee of the Red Cross (ICRC) in Baghdad of the arrest of 10 Saudi Arabian civilians because they contravened Iraqi laws and that they have been registered with ICRC. The Iraqi authorities have expressed their readiness to repatriate these 10, whose names are annexed hereto, once the above-mentioned authorities have issued them a pardon.

4/ See document S/22793, dated 15 July 1991.

Annex V

Letter dated 17 July 1991 from the Permanent Representative of Kuwait to the United Nations addressed to the President of the Security Council 5/

On instructions from my Government I should like to draw your attention to the failure by Iraq to abide by the terms of relevant Security Council resolutions, in particular those pertaining to the urgent humanitarian demand that Iraq immediately release under the auspices of the ICRC all Kuwaiti and third country nationals and arrange for the ICRC immediate access to all POWs and detainees. In this regard, I should like to convey the following:

First, there are around 1,890 Kuwaiti POWs and detainees still held by Iraq, in addition to 1,990 non-Kuwaiti POWs and detainees.

Second, a number of the above were detained at a restricted area in Baghdad, Al-Rahwaniya, near the International Airport. Others were detained at General Intelligence (Al-Mukhabarat) building in Al-Athimiya district in Baghdad.

Third, the ICRC confirmed our information on some locations of POWs and detainees, a matter which was brought to the attention of the members of the Council on 20 May 1991.

Fourth, POWs and detainees have recently been transferred to undisclosed locations. The ICRC have been denied information of, let alone access to, these new locations.

Fifth, since the cease-fire formally came into effect on 11 April 1991 only 68 POWs and detainees of different nationalities have been repatriated in five phases, on 15 and 25 May, 12 and 27 June and 14 July.

Sixth, it is noteworthy that before the cease-fire formally came into effect on 11 April 1991, Iraq had released through the ICRC 5,060 POWs and detainees of different nationalities. Around 1,498 more persons of different nationalities have escaped Iraq through various routes.

Seventh, Iraq includes those returned under family reunion in the total number of POWs and detainees thus inflating the number of repatriated POWs and detainees. To illustrate, 56 persons were released to Kuwaiti authorities on 14 July 1991, of which 53 persons qualified for family reunion, 2 were Kuwaiti POWs and the last was a Syrian detainee.

5/ See document S/22809, dated 18 July 1991.

0198 /...

While bringing the above to your attention, Kuwait wishes to emphasize its deep concern at the fate of those still held by Iraq. Our concern is compounded due to the recent transfer of POWs and detainees to undisclosed locations. Lastly, the Iraqi pattern of release of POWs and detainees puts into question the credibility and motives of the regime vis-à-vis a humanitarian matter of no apparent strategic asset to it.

0199

/...

Annex VI

Letter dated 5 August 1991 from the Permanent Representative of Kuwait to the United Nations addressed to the Secretary-General 6/

On instructions from my Government, I wish to inform you that the Iraqi regime, in an attempt to mislead the international community and to divert attention from the fact that it is detaining thousands of Kuwaiti and non-Kuwaiti prisoners of war in flagrant violation of Security Council resolutions 686 (1991) and 687 (1991), as well as of the third Geneva Convention, has persisted in submitting requests to the International Committee of the Red Cross (ICRC) on behalf of individuals it claims to be Kuwaiti citizens seeking to leave and return to Kuwait for the purpose of "reunion". In all, there have been 697 requests, listing 3,458 (three thousand four hundred and fifty-eight) individuals. Kuwait has approved the return of 252 (two hundred and fifty-two) Kuwaitis and non-Kuwaitis among those on the list after checking their identities and nationalities and verifying that they were included, before 1 August 1990, in the civilian population register of the State of Kuwait, a copy of which is deposited with the United Nations in accordance with Security Council resolution 677 (1990). The individuals concerned left Kuwait of their own accord during the brutal Iraqi occupation. They are not detained in Iraq, as may be seen from the fact that they applied to the ICRC office in Baghdad. Approval was given for the return of those whose identities were verified. Needless to say, their situation is entirely unrelated to that of the prisoners of war whose return has been requested by Kuwait and of whose names a full list was submitted to ICRC and transmitted to the authorities of the Iraqi regime. In attempting to mingle the former cases with those of Kuwaiti prisoners and detainees, the Iraqi regime's intention is simply to procrastinate and to confuse international public opinion with respect to Iraq's inhumane practices and failure to comply with the 1949 Geneva Convention relative to the Treatment of Prisoners of War.

We call upon you to draw the regime's attention to these blatant violations of the third Geneva Convention and to affirm that the Iraqi regime, by persisting in its failure to hand over the remaining prisoners, is contravening both the spirit and the letter of Security Council resolutions 686 (1991) and 687 (1991). In doing so, it is guilty of a flagrant breach of the provisions underlying the cease-fire declaration. All members of the Security Council and international humanitarian organizations are also urged to put pressure on the Iraqi regime with a view to ensuring its full and prompt implementation of the pertinent Security Council resolutions.

6/ See document A/45/1048-S/22893, dated 6 August 1991.

/...

0200

Annex VII

Letter dated 8 August 1991 from the Permanent Representative of Kuwait to the United Nations addressed to the Secretary-General 7/

On instructions from my Government, and with reference to my most recent letter, dated 5 August 1991 and issued as document S/22893, I have the honour to transmit to you herewith a detailed list, by nationality, of persons imprisoned or detained in Iraq; the total number of such persons is 2,479. A copy of this list has been sent to the International Committee of the Red Cross.

1.	Kuwaitis	1,839	
2.	Non-Kuwaitis	462	(of unknown nationality)
3.	Nationals of the United Arab Emirates	2	
4.	Saudis	66	
5.	Syrians	18	
6.	Egyptians	35	
7.	Omanis	2	
8.	Lebanese	14	
9.	Somali	1	
10.	Bahrainis	3	
11.	Filipinos	7	
12.	Indians	13	
13.	Pakistanis	4	
14.	Iranians	12	
15.	Sri Lankan	1	

We request that you do everthing within your power to exert pressure on the Iraqi authorities in order to secure the release of those prisoners and detainees and to put an end to their suffering and that of their families. We hope that all States and international organizations will express in no uncertain terms their resolute condemnation of the inhumane practices of the Iraqi authorities in detaining thousands of Kuwaiti nationals and persons of other countries who are residents of Kuwait.

7/ *See* document S/22921, dated 9 August 1991.

0201

/...

Annex VIII

Letter dated 29 August 1991 from the Minister for Foreign Affairs of Iraq to the United Nations addressed to the Secretary-General 8/

I wish to refer to the letter dated 17 July 1991 from the Permanent Representative of Kuwait to the United Nations, addressed to the President of the Security Council.

I have the honour to notify you of the following information concerning the situation of Kuwaiti nationals in Iraq since the end of the Gulf War.

1. The competent Iraqi authorities repatriated to Kuwait 6,328 Kuwaitis and 5 persons not of Kuwaiti nationality under the supervision of the delegation of the International Committee of the Red Cross (ICRC) during the period from 4 March to the present.

2. The ICRC delegation registered 3,400 Kuwaitis comprising 606 families who were in Iraq in addition to 159 individuals.

3. The Kuwaiti side agreed to the repatriation of 170 of the Kuwaitis referred to in paragraph 2 above. The Kuwaiti side is now attempting to delude Arab and international public opinion into believing that Iraq is concealing large numbers of Kuwaitis.

4. The Kuwaiti authorities are constantly endeavouring to impede the return of Kuwaitis to Kuwait on the pretext that verification procedures have not been completed. They have made a number of errors as testified by ICRC, the most recent of which was on 13 July when it had been decided to hand over a group of Kuwaitis but the Kuwaiti representative did not come to the Ar'ar area in Saudi Arabia to receive them. The handing over operation was postponed until 14 July, the ICRC delegation having confirmed that it had informed the Kuwaiti side of the time of the handing over.

We believe that the delay in the repatriation of the Kuwaitis who are still in Iraq, of which ICRC is aware, was directly caused by the Kuwaiti authorities who bear full responsibility for it.

Iraq is cooperating fully on this matter with ICRC and once again affirms its readiness to hand over all Kuwaitis who are in Iraq to the Kuwaiti side through ICRC. I should like the Secretary-General to exert pressure on the Kuwaiti side to receive them and not to exploit this matter for dishonourable publicity purposes.

8/ See document S/22992 (annex), dated 29 August 1991.

0202

원 본

외 무 부

종 별 :

번 호 : UNW-2853 일 시 : 91 0919 2130

수 신 : 장 관(연일,중동일,미일,기정)

발 신 : 주 유엔 대사

제 목 : 걸프 사태

표제관련 금 9.19 NYT 지 사설및 기사를 별첨송부함.끝

첨부(NYT):NYT 지 사설및 기사.끝

(대사 노창희-국장)

국기국 1차보 미주국 중아국 외정실 분석관 청와대 안기부

PAGE 1

91.09.20 11:40 WG

외신 1과 통제관

0203

UNW(F)-545 10919 2030

Measured Force on Iraq

President Bush has moved firmly but shrewdly to counter Saddam Hussein's persistent defiance of United Nations cease-fire resolutions. Yesterday he ordered American warplanes to prepare to escort U.N. helicopters should that be required to complete their arms inspection mission mandated by the Security Council.

The President has wisely resisted the temptation to bomb suspected weapons sites — an indiscriminate and probably futile approach. Instead, by backing up the U.N. mandate with an unmistakable threat of force, the President, in coordination with other Security Council members, reinforces respect for international law.

Mr. Hussein would be foolish to forget that Desert Storm was ended only on the basis of full compliance with U.N. resolutions requiring him to submit to full inspection and supervised destruction of his missiles along with any nuclear, biological or chemical weapons components.

The American planes are being made available to escort U.N. helicopters if Baghdad persists in obstructing their enforcement of these arms control provisions. The obstructions continue an Iraqi pattern of brazenly flouting cease-fire terms. These are not mere technical violations but a deliberate effort by Saddam Hussein to extract a psychological victory from the wreckage of military defeat.

Consider the record to date. Iraq has supplied inaccurate information about its missile stocks, enriched uranium supplies and chemical warheads. It refuses to acknowledge the existence of a biological warfare program that U.N. officials believe had reached at least the research stage. It has rewelded Scud missile launchers previously destroyed.

It has launched military incursions along the Kuwaiti border and fired weapons over the heads of U.N. inspectors seeking to visit a uranium enrichment facility. In the latest episode, it restricted helicopter inspections by imposing geographical, time and equipment limits on their flights.

Baghdad earlier this week began backpedaling on its helicopter restrictions, as it has done with other forms of non cooperation. Yesterday's deployment of U.S. warplanes is intended to add muscle to diplomatic pressures.

There remain two schools of thought at the U.N. on how to deal with Saddam Hussein. One would follow the old U.N. traditions of deference to sovereign leaders. Some diplomats even now look for ways for the Iraqi dictator to save face, by easing the Security Council's terms for oil sales, for example, or downplaying Iraqi cease-fire violations.

But world peace and security would be better served by the second approach — putting the needed muscle behind U.N. resolutions. Those resolutions, if carried out effectively, could form the basis for a new world order based on collective security and international law. President Bush does well to advance that no longer utopian cause.

첨부 UNW-2853

3-1

0204

U.S. WARNS IRAQIS IT MAY USE FORCE TO INSPECT ARMS

'PLENTY FED UP,' BUSH SAYS

He Authorizes American Planes to Provide Protection for U.N. Helicopter Flights

By ANDREW ROSENTHAL

Special to The New York Times

WASHINGTON, Sept. 18 — President Bush authorized American warplanes today to fly into Iraq to protect United Nations inspectors if President Saddam Hussein does not back down from [illegible] tions of his [illegible] helicopter inspec- [illegible] diplomatic [illegible] new threat of force, Mr. Bush said he was "plenty fed up" with Mr. Hussein's [illegible] of United Nations Security Council resolutions [illegible] Iraqi leader not to test American resolve once again.

But the President, perhaps mindful of the volatile political backdrop to his actions as the United States tries to arrange a Middle East peace conference, told reporters during a visit to the Grand Canyon today that he was confident there would be no outbreak of war.

Missiles to Saudi Arabia

Mr. Bush said he was also sending a new supply of Patriot air defense missiles [illegible] that the kingdom had given its assent to a new allied military operation, perhaps from its territory.

Mr. Bush said he was just doing some "prudent planning" on the strength of United Nations resolutions that he said permitted the further use of force to compel the destruction of Iraq's poison gases, Scud missiles and [illegible] lations. He said he [illegible] plans for military action against Mr. Hussein.

[illegible] better than to take on the United States of America," said Mr. Bush, whose words drew quick support from leading members of Congress.

Mr. Bush did not set a deadline for Iraqi compliance with the United Nations demand that its inspectors be allowed to fly into Iraq by helicopter. But it has been Mr. Bush's pattern in the last year to set deadlines and then follow with swift military action if they were not met, and officials said today that an ultimatum to Baghdad was under consideration.

Baghdad Eased Position

In the months since the war ended, the United States has implicitly threatened Iraq with the use of force as Baghdad balked at complying with a series of United Nations resolutions that established the cease-fire in the gulf and set the conditions for a permanent peace. Each time, Mr. Hussein backed down.

They said the United States had been on the verge of issuing an ultimatum when Iraq eased its stand on the helicopters somewhat over the weekend, saying it would agree to the inspection flights under conditions that were [illegible] ican-led West [illegible] by the Amer- [illegible] tions today [illegible] Mr. Bush's acmatic show of the West's determination to bend Baghdad to its will. Still, [illegible] renewed [illegible] raised the specter of a re- [illegible] after less than seven months of the uneasy peace that followed the Persian Gulf war.

U.S. Forces in Region

It also underscored the tenuous nature of the allied military victory over Iraq, which inflicted devastating damage on the Iraqi armed forces but left Mr. Hussein in power and set off armed conflict between Baghdad and ethnic and religious minorities in northern and southern Iraq.

A senior official traveling with Mr. [illegible] American forces would [illegible] additional [illegible] sent to Saudi Arabia within a day or two.

By tonight, there was no sign of any new deployment of American forces to the gulf region, where there are still about 36,000 American troops, along with about 60 warplanes in Saudi Arabia [illegible] more surface ships equipped with Tomahawk cruise missiles, which the United States used during the war against Iraq. American forces in Saudi Arabia were on a heightened state of alert today, Pentagon officials said.

'Plenty Fed Up'

Administration officials said the White House plan was to prepare American fighters, along with British and French warplanes, to fly air cover for allied helicopters carrying United Nations inspectors and, if necessary, move to stop any Iraqi attack on the aircraft and then retaliate with strikes against Iraqi positions.

Mr. Bush said he was confident that American warplanes would not have to go into action in Iraq once again to force Mr. Hussein to permit the United Nations inspections. A senior official said, "This is not Desert Storm II." [illegible]

But Mr. Bush said: "I'm plenty fed up. I think the man will see we are very serious about this."

Mr. Bush added: "There's no, you know, threats, there's just determination. That's all there is, firm determination that he will comply to the letter of the U.N. resolutions. And it's not just the United States, a lot of other countries feel this way too."

Asked if he could foresee a situation that would set off a new war, Mr. Bush said: "I don't think Saddam wants any of that. I don't think he does."

He paused and said, "I'm confident he doesn't. Absolutely confident."

[illegible] lican who is [illegible] the Foreign Relations [illegible] said Mr. Bush was taking "the appropriate precautions."

Referring to Mr. Hussein, the Sena- [illegible] anyone much hope that he will choose the sane and sensible course — voluntary compliance with an agreement to which, let us not forget, Iraq did agree."

In a formal statement issued by the White House today and in a letter to the leaders of Congress that was delivered on Monday, Mr. Bush said he was basing his planning on United Nations Security Council Resolutions 687 and 707.

Under those resolutions, the White House said, "Iraq is obligated to eliminate its weapons of mass destruction and its ballistic missile capabilities, [illegible] Special Commission and International Atomic Energy Agency inspection teams to verify Iraqi compliance."

The statement added that the inspectors must use helicopters to transport themselves around Iraq, but that Baghdad has refused to permit unfettered helicopter flights. At first, the Iraqis insisted that the United Nations teams [illegible] Iraqi helicopters manned [illegible] permit some outside helicopters [illegible] set strict conditions on their movements.

"This is a clear violation of U.N. Security Council Resolution 707, which permits the use of helicopters without condition."

3-2

0205

Bush Rattles Saber: Will Iraq Flinch?

By R. W. APPLE Jr.

Special to The New York Times

News Analysis

WASHINGTON, Sept. 18 — By threatening to send American war planes back over Iraq, President Bush is hoping to make President Saddam Hussein retreat and permit unfettered United Nations inspections, but if he fails, he will face few major diplomatic or political risks in taking direct military action.

Administration officials and other experts expressed doubt today that a new American initiative would disrupt the Administration's plans for a Mideast peace conference next month. In any event, these plans have been menaced by other developments, including the dispute over loan guarantees for Israel.

At first, the President and his senior advisers made clear, United States fighter-bombers would merely escort United Nations helicopters on inspection trips, but if that did not work, Mr. Bush would have to try other means to fulfill his pledge to prevent Iraq from amassing a nuclear arsenal.

The President's problem is whether military action would change much. During the Persian Gulf war air raids failed to destroy several of Mr. Hussein's nuclear and chemical weapons sites, and there is no reason to expect that they would do a lot better now. Punitive air strikes to "teach Saddam a lesson," as one official called them, are unlikely to break a man unbroken by the crushing defeat that the allies inflicted on Mr. Hussein earlier this year.

Coalition Remains Intact

The allied coalition remains more or less intact. The British, the French and the Soviet Union, the three key European allies during the gulf war, signaled that they were on board again in comments today, and Secretary General Javier Pérez de Cuéllar of the United Nations did likewise. Saudi Arabia has agreed to provide bases in return for Patriot missiles.

"I think the man will see we are very serious about this," the President said of Mr. Hussein. "He's not going to question our resolve on this."

Former Secretary of State Alexander M. Haig Jr. noted that Mr. Hussein had often backed down. On other occasions, however, he has shown that he is quite capable of taking a very dangerous line and walking straight into the lion's mouth," Mr. Haig said.

Mr. Hussein has clung to power despite his concession of defeat in the Persian Gulf war on Feb. 28. And since early this summer, he has put repeated roadblocks in the way of international teams sent to Baghdad to check whether he has carried out a United Nations resolution calling for the destruction of Iraqi installations for the making of chemical, biological and nuclear weapons.

The President is taking few risks in threatening military action.

Inspectors Are Obstructed

Just as he proclaimed his intention during the war of surviving to fight another day, whatever the allies threw at him, the Iraqi leader seems determined now to cling to as much of his weapons capacity as he can by outwitting the inspection teams.

Again and again, the Iraqis have withheld information or access, the United Nations has issued warnings, and Baghdad has yielded a bit of ground. But the inspectors charge that the Iraqis have continued to hide or destroy critical equipment and to take other steps to avoid full detection of their attempts to make weapons of mass destruction. One inspector has been shot at and others have been obstructed in attempts to stage surprise inspections.

"I have no indication that they are modifying their position so far," Mr. Pérez de Cuéllar said today.

A July 25 ultimatum issued by the United Nations produced no result. Washington talked about "military options" but did nothing when the deadline passed without action, and today's statements by Mr. Bush, six weeks later, constituted an attempt to restore credibility to his threats.

A Clear Field at Home

On the domestic political front, Mr. Bush appears to have a clear field. On the record, Democratic leaders said nothing critical of the President's saber rattling, and one of the party's leading foreign-affairs specialists commented privately, "It would be another low-risk, high-tech operation, and of course there's no longer any threat that these regional things will turn into superpower confrontations."

Those who have been critical of the President's decision to end the war when he did argue that the current difficulties demonstrate anew the costs of failing to break Mr. Hussein's power and drive him from office when the moment was ripe. But the Democrats are not prepared to make that a major theme.

Recent polls suggest that much of the American public wants to concentrate on domestic issues (and indeed Mr. Bush was doing so today on his Western trip when he paused at the Grand Canyon to warn Iraq once again). But few politicians of either party doubt that the President could quickly rally the country behind a new military effort to insure that Mr. Hussein does not equip himself with nuclear weapons.

The yellow ribbons are still on doorways around the country, suggesting that the surge of patriotism of nine months ago is not yet spent, and T-shirts inspred by the gulf war are still selling well. Mr. Bush has shown conclusively that he can quickly focus the country's attention on foreign affairs when he seeks to, and to change the terms of political discourse.

"Our problem," another prominent Democrat said, "is that we are in a period of instability abroad. We don't have any candidates with foreign-policy credentials, and every time something like this happens, you can almost see the voters running for shelter to the Republicans and George Bush."

3-3

0206

원 본

외 무 부

종 별 :

번 호 : UNW-2854 일 시 : 91 0919 2130

수 신 : 장 관(연일,중동일,기정)

발 신 : 주 유엔 대사

제 목 : 안보리 회의

1.안보리는 금 9.19 공식회의 (3008차)를 갖고, 안보리결의 706호 (이락민의 인도적 긴급소요 및 이락산 석유수출 일부허용)이행을 위한 연호 유엔사무총장안 (S/23006) 을 승인하는 결의안을 표결결과 찬 13, 반1 (쿠바), 기권1 (예멘)로 채택하였음 (안보리결의 712 호)

2.금일 회의시 예멘, 쿠바가 표결전 발언한바 양국공히 상기 결의안은 결의 706호의 연장임을 지적하면서 706 호 책택시 취한 입장을 재확인하였으며, 특히 쿠바는 본건 결의안의 주권 평등원칙 위바,안보리 월권문제를 제기하였음

3.표결후에는 미국 (이락정부의책임강조), 프랑스 (본건 이행안의 조기새행요망)가 발언 하였음

4.한편 이락도 표결에 앞서 발언한바, 결의 706호 및 금번 결의를 자국에 대한 경제적인 포위공격 (ECONOMIC SIEGE) 행위라고 비난하였으며, 특히 본건 결의안 본문 1, 2, 3, 6 항에 이의를 제기하였음.

첨부(FAX): 상기 결)(의안(S/23045) 끝

(대사 노창희-국장)

국기국 1차보 중아국 외정실 분석관 청와대 안기부

PAGE 1 91.09.20 11:45 WG

외신 1과 통제관

0207

SEP 19 '91 21:24 KOREAN MISSION P.1

UNITED NATIONS — UNW(F)-544 10919 2030 (총32)

Security Council

PROVISIONAL

S/23045
18 September 1991

ORIGINAL: ENGLISH

7/2호

Belgium, France, Romania, Union of Soviet Socialist Republics, United Kingdom of Great Britain and Northern Ireland and United States of America: draft resolution

The Security Council,

Recalling its previous relevant resolutions and in particular resolutions 661 (1990), 686 (1991), 687 (1991), 688 (1991), 692 (1991), 699 (1991), 705 (1991) and 706 (1991),

Expressing its appreciation for the report (S/23006) dated 4 September 1991 submitted by the Secretary-General pursuant to paragraph 5 of resolution 706 (1991),

Reaffirming its concern about the nutritional and health situation of the Iraqi civilian population, and the risk of a further deterioration of this situation, and underlining the need in this context for fully up-to-date assessments of the situation in all parts of Iraq as a basis for the equitable distribution of humanitarian relief to all segments of the Iraqi civilian population,

Recalling that the activities to be carried out by or on behalf of the Secretary-General to meet the purposes referred to in resolution 706 (1991) and the present resolution enjoy the privileges and immunities of the United Nations,

Acting under Chapter VII of the Charter of the United Nations,

1. Confirms the figure mentioned in paragraph 1 of resolution 706 (1991) as the sum authorized for the purpose of that paragraph, and reaffirms its intention to review this sum on the basis of its ongoing assessment of the needs and requirements, in accordance with paragraph 1 (d) of resolution 706 (1991);

3480E /...

첨부 UNW-2854

3-1

0208

2. Invites the Committee established by resolution 661 (1990) to authorize immediately, pursuant to paragraph 1 (d) of resolution 706 (1991), the release by the Secretary-General from the escrow account of the first one-third portion of the sum referred to in paragraph 1 above, such release to take place as required subject to the availability of funds in the account and, in the case of payments to finance the purchase of foodstuffs, medicines and materials and supplies for essential civilian needs which have been notified or approved in accordance with existing procedures, subject to compliance with the procedures laid down in the report of the Secretary-General as approved in paragraph 3 below;

3. Approves the recommendations in the Secretary-General's report as contained in its paragraphs 57 (d) and 58;

4. Encourages the Secretary-General and the Committee established by resolution 661 (1990) to cooperate, in close consultation with the Government of Iraq, on a continuing basis to ensure the most effective implementation of the scheme approved in this resolution;

5. Decides that petroleum and petroleum products subject to resolution 706 (1991) shall while under Iraqi title be immune from legal proceedings and not be subject to any form of attachment, garnishment or execution, and that all States shall take any steps that may be necessary under their respective domestic legal systems to assure this protection, and to ensure that the proceeds of sale are not diverted from the purposes laid down in resolution 706 (1991);

6. Reaffirms that the escrow account to be established by the United Nations and administered by the Secretary-General to meet the purposes of resolution 706 (1991) and the present resolution, like the Compensation Fund established by resolution 687 (1991), enjoys the privileges and immunities of the United Nations;

7. Reaffirms that the inspectors and other experts on mission for the United Nations, appointed for the purpose of this resolution, enjoy privileges and immunities in accordance with the Convention on the Privileges and Immunities of the United Nations, and demands that Iraq shall allow them full freedom of movement and all necessary facilities;

8. Confirms that funds contributed from other sources may if desired, in accordance with paragraph 1 (c) of resolution 706 (1991), be deposited into the escrow account as a sub-account and be immediately available to meet Iraq's humanitarian needs as referred to in paragraph 20 of resolution 687 (1991) without any of the obligatory deductions and administrative costs specified in paragraphs 2 and 3 of resolution 706 (1991);

/

3-2

0209

9. Urges that any provision to Iraq of foodstuffs, medicines or other items of a humanitarian character, in addition to those purchased with the funds referred to in paragraph 1 of this resolution, be undertaken through arrangements which assure their equitable distribution to meet humanitarian needs;

10. Requests the Secretary-General to take the actions necessary to implement the above decisions, and authorizes him to enter into any arrangements or agreements necessary to accomplish this;

11. Calls upon States to cooperate fully in the implementation of resolution 706 (1991) and the present resolution in particular with respect to any measures regarding the import of petroleum and petroleum products and the export of foodstuffs, medicines and materials and supplies for essential civilian needs as referred to in paragraph 20 of resolution 687 (1991), and also with respect to the privileges and immunities of the United Nations and its personnel implementing this resolution; and to ensure that there are no diversions from the purposes laid down in these resolutions;

12. Decides to remain seized of the matter.

0210

UNITED
NATIONS

Security Council

Distr.
GENERAL

S/RES/712 (1991)
19 September 1991

RESOLUTION 712 (1991)

Adopted by the Security Council at its 3008th meeting,
on 19 September 1991

The Security Council,

Recalling its previous relevant resolutions and in particular resolutions 661 (1990) of 6 August 1990, 686 (1991) of 2 March 1991, 687 (1991) of 3 April 1991, 688 (1991) of 5 April 1991, 692 (1991) of 20 May 1991, 699 (1991) of 17 June 1991, and 705 (1991) and 706 (1991) of 15 August 1991,

Expressing its appreciation for the report dated 4 September 1991 submitted by the Secretary-General pursuant to paragraph 5 of resolution 706 (1991), 1/

Reaffirming its concern about the nutritional and health situation of the Iraqi civilian population and the risk of a further deterioration of this situation, and underlining the need in this context for fully up-to-date assessments of the situation in all parts of Iraq as a basis for the equitable distribution of humanitarian relief to all segments of the Iraqi civilian population,

Recalling that the activities to be carried out by or on behalf of the Secretary-General to meet the purposes referred to in resolution 706 (1991) and the present resolution enjoy the privileges and immunities of the United Nations,

Acting under Chapter VII of the Charter of the United Nations,

1. Confirms the figure mentioned in paragraph 1 of resolution 706 (1991) as the sum authorized for the purpose of that paragraph, and reaffirms its intention to review this sum on the basis of its ongoing

---

1/ S/23006.

91-30826 3626Z (E) /...

0211

assessment of the needs and requirements, in accordance with paragraph 1 (d) of resolution 706 (1991);

2. Invites the Security Council Committee established by resolution 661 (1990) to authorize immediately, pursuant to paragraph 1 (d) of resolution 706 (1991), the release by the Secretary-General from the escrow account of the first one-third portion of the sum referred to in paragraph 1 above, such release to take place as required subject to the availability of funds in the account and, in the case of payments, to finance the purchase of foodstuffs, medicines and materials and supplies for essential civilian needs that have been notified or approved in accordance with existing procedures, subject to compliance with the procedures laid down in the report of the Secretary-General as approved in paragraph 3 below;

3. Approves the recommendations in the Secretary-General's report as contained in its paragraphs 57 (d) and 58;

4. Encourages the Secretary-General and the Security Council Committee established by resolution 661 (1990) to cooperate, in close consultation with the Government of Iraq, on a continuing basis to ensure the most effective implementation of the scheme approved in the present resolution;

5. Decides that petroleum and petroleum products subject to resolution 706 (1991) shall while under Iraqi title be immune from legal proceedings and not be subject to any form of attachment, garnishment or execution, and that all States shall take any steps that may be necessary under their respective domestic legal systems to assure this protection, and to ensure that the proceeds of sale are not diverted from the purposes laid down in resolution 706 (1991);

6. Reaffirms that the escrow account to be established by the United Nations and administered by the Secretary-General to meet the purposes of resolution 706 (1991) and the present resolution, like the Compensation Fund established by resolution 692 (1991), enjoys the privileges and immunities of the United Nations;

7. Reaffirms that the inspectors and other experts on mission for the United Nations, appointed for the purpose of the present resolution, enjoy privileges and immunities in accordance with the Convention on the Privileges and Immunities of the United Nations, and demands that Iraq allow them full freedom of movement and all necessary facilities;

8. Confirms that funds contributed from other sources may if desired, in accordance with paragraph 1 (c) of resolution 706 (1991), be deposited into the escrow account as a sub-account and be immediately available to meet Iraq's humanitarian needs as referred to in paragraph 20 of resolution 687 (1991) without any of the obligatory deductions and administrative costs specified in paragraphs 2 and 3 of resolution 706 (1991);

/...

0212

9. _Urges_ that any provision to Iraq of foodstuffs, medicines or other items of a humanitarian character, in addition to those purchased with the funds referred to in paragraph 1 of the present resolution, be undertaken through arrangements that assure their equitable distribution to meet humanitarian needs;

10. _Requests_ the Secretary-General to take the actions necessary to implement the above decisions, and authorizes him to enter into any arrangements or agreements necessary to accomplish this;

11. _Calls upon_ States to cooperate fully in the implementation of resolution 706 (1991) and the present resolution, in particular with respect to any measures regarding the import of petroleum and petroleum products and the export of foodstuffs, medicines and materials and supplies for essential civilian needs as referred to in paragraph 20 of resolution 687 (1991), and also with respect to the privileges and immunities of the United Nations and its personnel implementing the present resolution, and to ensure that there are no diversions from the purposes laid down in these resolutions;

12. _Decides_ to remain seized of the matter.

0213

UNITED
NATIONS

S

Security Council

Distr.
GENERAL

S/23108
24 September 1991

ORIGINAL: ENGLISH

LETTER DATED 19 SEPTEMBER 1991 FROM THE CHAIRMAN OF THE SECURITY COUNCIL COMMITTEE ESTABLISHED BY RESOLUTION 661 (1990) CONCERNING THE SITUATION BETWEEN IRAQ AND KUWAIT ADDRESSED TO THE SECRETARY-GENERAL

I have the honour to inform you that the Security Council Committee established by resolution 661 (1990) concerning the situation between Iraq and Kuwait at its 49th meeting, held on 19 September 1991, in accordance with paragraph 2 of resolution 712 (1991), decided to authorize, pursuant to paragraph 1 (d) of resolution 706 (1991), the release by the Secretary-General from the escrow account of the first one-third portion of the sum referred to in paragraph 1 of resolution 712 (1991), that is, of 1.6 billion United States dollars, such release to take place as required subject to the availability of funds in the account and, in the case of payments to finance the purchase of foodstuffs, medicines and materials and supplies for essential civilian needs which have been notified or approved in accordance with existing procedures, subject to compliance with the procedures laid down in the report of the Secretary-General contained in document S/23006 as approved by paragraph 3 of Security Council resolution 712 (1991).

(Signed) Peter HOHENFELLNER
Chairman
Security Council Committee established by resolution 661 (1990) concerning the situation between Iraq and Kuwait

-----

91-32467 2668h (E)

0214

UNITED
NATIONS

A S

General Assembly **Security Council**

Distr.
GENERAL

A/46/509
S/23088
30 September 1991

ORIGINAL: ENGLISH

GENERAL ASSEMBLY
Forty-sixth session
Agenda item 46
CONSEQUENCES OF THE IRAQI OCCUPATION OF AND AGGRESSION AGAINST KUWAIT

SECURITY COUNCIL
Forty-sixth year

Note by the Secretary-General

The Secretary-General has the honour to transmit to the members of the General Assembly and of the Security Council a letter dated 27 September 1991 addressed to him by the Director General of the International Atomic Energy Agency concerning the resolution adopted on 20 September 1991 by the General Conference of the Agency entitled "Iraq's non-compliance with its safeguards obligations" (see annex).

91-31883 2752d (E) /...

0215

ANNEX

Letter dated 27 September 1991 from the Director General of the International Atomic Energy Agency addressed to the Secretary-General

At its meeting on 12 September 1991 the Board of Governors of the International Atomic Energy Agency took note of the Government of Iraq's further non-compliance with its obligations under its safeguards agreement with the Agency, reaffirmed the requests and demands made in the resolution passed on 18 July 1991 (GOV/2532) and requested the Director General to report this as required by Article XII of the Statute.

Article XII.C of the Agency's Statute and Article III.2 of the Agreement Governing the Relationship between the United Nations and the International Atomic Energy Agency require the Board to report non-compliance with safeguards obligations to the Security Council and General Assembly of the United Nations. I would, therefore, appreciate it if you could bring this action by the Board to the urgent attention of the Security Council and of the General Assembly. A copy of the records of the Board's meeting will be sent to you as soon as they are available.

In accordance with Article VII of the Relationship Agreement, I am at the disposal of the Security Council should the Council so desire.

Further, the Agency's General Conference, at its 341st plenary meeting, on 20 September 1991, adopted resolution GC (XXV)/RES/568 - "Iraq's non-compliance with its safeguards obligations" - in which it, among other things, requested the Director General to report the views of the General Conference to the Secretary-General of the United Nations. A copy of that resolution, adopted by 71 votes to 1, with 7 abstentions, is attached. A copy of the records of the General Conference relating to this issue will be sent to you as soon as they are available.

(Signed) Hans BLIX
Director General

0216

/...

APPENDIX

Iraq's non-compliance with its safeguards obligations

Resolution adopted by the General Conference of the International Atomic Energy Agency at its 341st plenary meeting, on 20 September 1991

The General Conference,

(a) *Noting* United Nations Security Council resolution 687 (1991) and 707 (1991),

(b) *Deploring* Iraq's non-compliance with its safeguards obligations with the International Atomic Energy Agency and violation of its obligations under the Treaty on the Non-Proliferation of Nuclear Weapons and Security Council resolution 687 (1991),

(c) *Recalling* with approval the statements and actions of the Director General and the Board of Governors concerning Iraq's non-compliance with its nuclear non-proliferation obligations, including the Board resolution of 18 July 1991 and the report by the Board to the General Conference dated 13 September 1991,

(d) *Deeply concerned* by the continuing Iraqi efforts to obstruct implementation of Security Council resolution 687 (1991) and 707 (1991),

1. *Supports* the above-mentioned actions taken by the Board of Governors;

2. *Strongly condemns* Iraq's non-compliance with its nuclear non-proliferation obligations, including its safeguards agreements with the International Atomic Energy Agency;

3. *Demands* that Iraq immediately and fully comply with all of its nuclear non-proliferation obligations;

4. *Commends* the Director General and his staff for their strenuous efforts in the implementation of Security Council resolutions 687 (1991) and 707 (1991), in particular the detection and destruction or otherwise rendering inoffensive equipment and material which could be used for nuclear weapons;

5. *Requests* the Director General to report the views of the General Conference to the Secretary-General, and to report to the Board of Governors and to the thirty-sixth General Conference on his efforts to implement Security Council resolutions 687 (1991) and 707 (1991), and decides to remain seized of this issue.

0217

UNITED
NATIONS

S

Security Council

Distr.
GENERAL

S/23091
30 September 1991

ORIGINAL: ENGLISH

LETTER DATED 25 SEPTEMBER 1991 FROM THE PERMANENT REPRESENTATIVE OF THE UNITED STATES OF AMERICA TO THE UNITED NATIONS ADDRESSED TO THE SECRETARY-GENERAL

In accordance with paragraph 4 of Security Council resolution 700 (1991), I have the honour to provide you with the following report regarding the measures taken by the Government of the United States of America to give full effect to the provisions of paragraph 24 of Security Council resolution 687 (1991).

The United States Government has continued to apply the stringent legal and interdictory measures that it introduced shortly after Iraq's invasion of Kuwait on 2 August 1990.

On 2 August 1990, President Bush signed Executive Order 12722, blocking Iraqi government property and prohibiting transactions with Iraq. On 9 August 1990, the President signed Executive Order 12724, which expanded the restrictions mentioned in Executive Order 12722. Among other items, these executive orders prohibit exports and imports of goods and services between the United States and Iraq, forbid activities by persons in the United States that would promote the export or transshipment of goods to Iraq and blocked all property of the Government of Iraq. Use of American private transportation means and related facilities to trade with Iraq have been similarly prohibited by regulation. On 5 November 1990, the United States Congress enacted the Iraqi Sanctions Act of 1990, which affirmed the sanctions imposed by the President and provided for certain penalties with respect to violations.

Pursuant to these orders, the Department of the Treasury has frozen all bank accounts of the Iraqi Government and has promulgated regulations to restrict Iraqi access to its funds and to ensure that funds will not be made available to Iraq and those who would facilitate commodity trade with Iraq. Thus, the Government of the United States has taken the actions necessary to conform strictly to the prohibitions contained in all the relevant United Nations Security Council resolutions. These United States restrictions remain in effect today.

91-32020 3323a (E) /...

0218

In sum, the United States Government by law and by the vigorous administration of its implementing regulations, as well as by employment of American military resources, has done all within its power to achieve the goals set out in paragraph 3 of Security Council resolution 661 (1990) and paragraph 24 of resolution 687 (1991).

(Signed) Thomas R. PICKERING

0219

외고문서 비밀해제: 걸프 사태 21

걸프 사태 유엔안전보장이사회 동향 4

초판인쇄 2024년 03월 15일
초판발행 2024년 03월 15일

지은이 한국학술정보(주)
펴낸이 채종준
펴낸곳 한국학술정보(주)
주 소 경기도 파주시 회동길 230(문발동)
전 화 031-908-3181(대표)
팩 스 031-908-3189
홈페이지 http://ebook.kstudy.com
E-mail 출판사업부 publish@kstudy.com
등 록 제일산-115호(2000. 6. 19)

ISBN 979-11-6983-981-5 94340
979-11-6983-960-0 94340 (set)